HOLLYWOOD DYNASTIES

HOLLYWOOD DYNASTIES

STEPHEN FARBER and MARC GREEN

FAWCETT CREST • NEW YORK

Library of Congress Catalog Card Number: 83–46126

ISBN 0–449–20799–4

This edition published by arrangement with Delilah Communications, which is distributed by Putnam Publishing Group

Lyrics from "Sweet Sue–Just You" used on page 178 Copyright
1928 Renewed by Shapiro, Bernstein & Co., Inc. Used by
Permission

Special thanks to Marilyn Schatzberg and Jim Webb

Manufactured in the United States of America

First Ballantine Books Edition: August 1985

This book is dedicated to our families

TABLE OF CONTENTS

"And don't you go naming my grandson T.C. It's too big a bag for him to carry. He'll have too much to live up to 'cause there'll never be another like me."

—WALTER HUSTON'S DYING WORDS TO BARBARA STANWYCK IN *The Furies*

PREFACE

IT is hard to pinpoint the exact moment when an idea for a project such as this first takes hold. But one encounter we had a few years ago stands out in both our minds. We happened to meet with an aspiring film producer. Still in her twenties and without a movie credit to her name, this young woman was nonetheless ensconced in a comfortable suite on the Paramount lot. She had a desk piled high with scripts, a personal secretary to field her calls, a winning smile, and a lot of opinions. How, we wondered, had she managed to secure such a privileged position at Paramount when other, more seasoned producers were out hustling for a sinecure? Only after we learned that the young woman's father headed one of the three major television networks did the answer become clear.

If you are not on the lookout, the pervasive family ties of the entertainment business might easily go unnoticed. Once you have been alerted, however, Hollywood relatives seem to be as ubiquitous as flies at a picnic. After our meeting with the Paramount producer, we found ourselves constantly hearing or reading about the scion of yet another prominent clan: here an Arkoff, there an Axelrod, everywhere a Carradine. Television was awash in Reiners and Aldas, Van Pattens and Tinkers. The movies were rife with Pickers and Plummers, Hyamses and Loews.

We decided to compile a list of Academy Award winners since 1970, just to see how many of them we could link to another famous family member. There were, of course, the obvious second-generation names: Jane Fonda, best actress for *Klute* (1971) and *Coming Home* (1978); Liza Minelli, best actress for *Cabaret* (1972); Tatum O'Neal, best supporting actress for *Paper Moon* (1973); Richard Zanuck, executive producer of best picture winner *The Sting* (1973); Keith Carradine, writer of the best song for *Nashville* (1975); Michael Douglas, co-producer of best picture winner *One Flew Over the Cuckoo's Nest* (1975); Vanessa Redgrave, best supporting actress for *Julia* (1977). There were the famous parents whose sons or daughters have also plied the trade. Helen Hayes, best supporting actress for *Airport* (1970), is the mother of actor James MacArthur. John Mills, best supporting actor for *Ryan's Daughter* (1970), is the father of Hayley and Juliet Mills. Henry Fonda, best actor for *On Golden Pond* (1981), is the father of Peter and Jane. But there are many others whose family connections may be less well-known: Bert Schneider, producer of best feature documentary *Hearts and Minds* (1974), is the son of former Columbia Pictures chairman Abe Schneider; and the film's co-producer and director, Peter Davis, is the son-in-law of Herman Mankiewicz, who won an Oscar in 1941 for the script of *Citizen Kane*. Francis Coppola and his father Carmine both won Oscars for *The Godfather, Part II* (1974)—Francis for co-writing, directing, and producing, and Carmine for his work on the musical score. Stanley Jaffe, producer of best picture winner *Kramer vs. Kramer* (1979), is the son of Columbia board chairman, Leo Jaffe. Sally Field, best actress for *Norma Rae* (1979), grew up with her stepfather, onetime Tarzan Jock Mahoney. Sissy Spacek, best actress for *Coal Miner's Daughter* (1980), was introduced to the business under the auspices of her cousins, Geraldine Page and Rip Torn. Timothy Hutton, best supporting actor for *Ordinary People* (1980), is the son of actor Jim Hutton. Best picture winner *Chariots of Fire* (1981) was released by The Ladd Company, the mini-studio founded by the son of Alan Ladd. Warren Beatty, best director for *Reds* (1981), came to Hollywood when his sister, Shirley MacLaine, was already established as a major star; she in turn was named best actress for *Terms of Endearment* (1983). If such a compilation were expanded to include not just recent Oscar winners but prominent personalities in all phases of the industry, it might well consume this entire volume, for family networks have loomed large in craft guilds and unions as well as the more visible professions of acting, directing, and producing. The Westmores (make-up), the Butlers and Stradlings (cinematography), and the Steinkamps (editing) are just a few of the more notable examples.

In fact, as we pursued this project, it seemed to be growing like Topsy into an unwieldy book of lists. We soon realized that we were not seeing the forest for the family trees. Rather than merely enumerating relationships, we wanted to explore their dynamics. What are the real advantages of growing up inside the movie business? How are the sons and daughters of show business families affected by the in-fighting, the maneuvering, the high-stakes deal-making that they observe behind the scenes? And most important of all, how do they go about earning the name that is already theirs? For the second and third generations of a celebrated Hollywood dynasty, the legacy of fame can be a decidedly mixed blessing. In feudal societies, the idea of handing down power and position may be taken for granted. But in America, where each generation is expected to prove itself, inherited glory is always suspect. Living in the shadow of a famous performer or a legendary mogul, children may be overwhelmed by a reputation they cannot match; they may feel paralyzed by expectations they cannot fulfill.

We hoped to discover what it was that distinguished the survivors from the casualties among the heirs to Hollywood's family thrones. In addition, we wanted to paint a picture of family life in Hollywood—so different from domesticity in other American communities—and reveal the interweaving of personal and professional drives within the powerful dynasties.

In planning the book, we decided to concentrate on several major families whose histories and experiences we consider emblematic. Our focus has been on American filmmakers (thus eliminating people like the Kordas and the Redgraves), on movies rather than television. We wanted to study succession, so we omitted famous siblings such as Joan Fontaine and Olivia DeHavilland or Warren Beatty and Shirley MacLaine.

Even the longest chapters, it must be said, do not pretend to offer definitive histories of particular families. Lengthy biographies have already been written about many of the dominant members of these clans. Our intention is not to recapitulate those biographies but to zero in on family relationships and their impact on careers. We wanted to allow family members to express their own reflections on one another and their own views of the benefits and drawbacks of belonging to a show business dynasty.

We have used firsthand interviews to tell most of the story. Considering how much of their private lives they had to reveal, we were gratified that so many of the people we had decided to write about agreed to share their thoughts and impressions with us. Without their cooperation, this book could never have come to life. We have also benefited from observations offered by many of our subjects' personal and professional associates, some of whom requested that their anonymity be preserved or that their remarks not be for attribution; we have respected their wishes. Among those who spoke to us on the record, we are grateful to: Alan Alda, Gerald Ayres, A. Scott Berg, Dick Berg, Jeff Berg, Tony Berg, Tony Bill, David Brown, Carmine Coppola, Italia

Coppola, Robert Cohn, Bruce Cohn Curtis, Jamie Lee Curtis, Jack Cummings, Anne Douglas, Kirk Douglas, Michael Douglas, Peter Vincent Douglas, Jane Fonda, Peter Fonda, Edith Mayer Goetz, Samuel Goldwyn, Jr., William Hayward, S.E. Hinton, Alana Ladd Jackson, Michael Jackson, Andrea Jaffe, Leo Jaffe, Stanley Jaffe, Fay Kanin, William Katt, Philip Kaufman, Wendy Kout, Alan Ladd, Jr., David Ladd, Max Laemmle, Karl Malden, Christopher Mankiewicz, Don Mankiewicz, Joseph L. Mankiewicz, Tom Mankiewicz, David Manson, Ed Margulies, Stan Margulies, Paul Mazursky, Jack Nicholson, Anthony Perkins, Richard Pryor, Robert Radnitz, Jack Schwartzman, Daniel Selznick, Carole Serling, Judy Goetz Shepherd, Richard Shepherd, Talia Shire, Milton Sperling, Robert Stevenson, Venetia Stevenson, James Toback, Carol Lee Veitch, John Veitch, Jack Warner, Jr., the late Hannah Weinstein, Lisa Weinstein, Paula Weinstein, Arthur Whitelaw, Barbara Goetz Windom, and Richard Zanuck. Exclusive interviews which Stephen Farber conducted with Francis Ford Coppola, George Lucas, Liza Minnelli, and Bert Schneider prior to the writing of this book have also been utilized.

On a more personal note, we would like to thank our agent, Candace Lake, for her encouragement and wise counsel. We are very grateful to Jeannie Sakol of Delilah Books for her unstinting enthusiasm and her shrewd editorial judgment during every stage of this project. Her colleague Richard Amdur also provided many helpful suggestions. Charles Higham read the manuscript and assisted us in clarifying a number of important issues. Research on the book was aided immeasurably by the facilities of several special libraries, particularly the Margaret Herrick Library of the Academy of Motion Picture Arts and Sciences, whose staff is among the most knowledgeable and gracious we have encountered anywhere. We are also indebted to Gregory Blair for his careful transcription of interviews, and to Michael Dempsey for his meticulous typing of the manuscript. Not only did Michael put in many late hours in front of the word processor, he also gave us the benefit of his keen critical perceptions and his vast knowledge of film history and lore. Ellen Wilson Green deserves a word of special thanks for her patience and support during the two years that this project absorbed us.

Stephen Farber and Marc Green
Los Angeles, California
April 1984

WHAT PRICE HOLLYWOOD?

TO the outsider, Hollywood may seem like a gold rush town, where any enterprising prospector can stake his claim and strike it rich. It is an image of the movie capital that Hollywood itself has reinforced over the years. In motion pictures as various as *Merton of the Movies* (1924 and 1947), *The Skyrocket* (1926), *Once in a Lifetime* (1932), *Going Hollywood* (1933), *Singin' in the Rain* (1952), *Hearts of the West* (1975), and even *The Muppet Movie* (1979), filmmakers have promulgated the same hopeful homily: you may be an unknown today, but you can make it to the promised land of fame and fortune as long as you have enough luck, pluck, and God-given talent.

If any one fable crystallizes the myth, it is the familiar melodrama that first reached the screen under the title *What Price Hollywood?*, David O. Selznick's 1932 production in which Constance Bennett played a tender-hearted waitress who rises to stardom while her mentor, a top director, hits the bottle and then the skids. Five years later, Selznick had the scenario reworked into *A Star Is Born* and cast Janet Gaynor as the dreamy-eyed Esther Blodgett, whose career starts to soar just as that of her alcoholic husband, an established star named Norman Maine, has begun to sink. By 1954, it was Judy Garland's turn to smile through her tears in the now-classic musical remake, and in 1976 Esther Blodgett found herself reincarnated as a rock singer in the person of Barbra Streisand.

For the 1937 version of *A Star Is Born*, David Selznick had his writers create a telling prologue, in which Esther informs her provincial Midwestern family that she dreams of going to Hollywood and becoming a famous movie star. As she reveals her fervent hopes, Esther is mocked by most of her relatives, but not by her ninety-year-old grandmother, who provides the money Esther needs to make her journey west, along with a homespun sermon recalling her own youthful aspirations. "When I wanted something better," the old woman muses, "I came across these plains in a prairie schooner with your grandfather. People laughed at us just like they did at all the other pioneers—they said this country would always be a wilderness—but we didn't believe that! We had a new country to make—and besides, we wanted to make our dreams come true . . . There'll always be a wilderness to conquer, Esther. Maybe Hollywood's the wilderness now." Granny sees Esther off at the town's tiny railroad station and, as the westbound train pulls in, she shouts, "Here comes your prairie schooner!" Fade out—Fillmore, North Dakota. Fade in—Hollywood and Vine.

This equation of succeeding in Hollywood with vanquishing the wilderness may now seem like a quaint conceit, but to the founding fathers of the movie industry, it represented a credo earnestly held. For David Selznick, it was a legacy from his own father, one of the forgotten pioneers of silent picture days. Most of the originators of the movie business, including the senior Selznick, were poorly educated immigrants who could barely speak English when they arrived in the United States. But when they reached the "wilderness" of Southern California, it was as if they had discovered the land of milk and honey. Their personal rags-to-riches sagas were real-life enactments of the classic Horatio Alger success stories popularized in the late nineteenth century. At a time when economic hardship and industrial retrenchment were conspiring to cast doubt upon the validity of the success mythology elsewhere in the country, the brash young pioneers of the booming movie industry offered living proof that the American dream was alive and well. If the son of a junk dealer from Minsk, or a penniless glove peddler from the Warsaw ghetto, or a pool hustler from the Lower East Side could all rise to control major corporate empires, hobnob with royalty, and make more money than the entrenched aristocracy, perhaps America was still a land of limitless opportunity.

Though it may continue to fire the imaginations of moviegoers yearning for their own shot at glory, the value of the *Star Is Born* myth as a representation of reality has diminished considerably with the passage of time. Today the optimistic fable survives not so much in stories about Hollywood stardom as in fatuous odes to "little people" who make it big in some field other than the movies—in boxing (*Rocky*), in ballet (*Flashdance*), or on Broadway (*Staying Alive*). Indeed, filmmakers seem to recognize that a Horatio Alger tale of sudden success in Hollywood strains credulity. When the myth is seriously applied to contemporary Hollywood, it is more likely to be turned on its head—as in *Star 80*, Bob Fosse's grim warning about the perils of surrendering to the dream.

Even by 1937, when David Selznick produced his archetypal rendition of *A Star Is Born*, there were factors at work which were undermining the rosy picture of Hollywood as a last frontier; the homelier truth was that the movie industry was already an incestuous family business, and newcomers were finding it harder and harder to break in. What was once a wide-open field at every level had turned into the private preserve of a well-connected few. In many respects, Hollywood was being transformed into a looselyrun oligarchy, what the descendant of one prominent moviemaking clan has called a "miniature House of Hapsburg."

Because they were creating a brand new industry, perhaps because they were essentially a community of Jews in a larger Gentile society, the early moguls closed ranks, staffing the studios with their own relatives and cronies. Their shared backgrounds and values led them to associate with each other socially even as they warred in business. Their sons and daughters married into other film business families, consolidating influence and power. Denied admission to the clubs and schools of established Los Angeles society, the moguls formed an exclusive little enclave of their own, where a few patriarchs consciously set out to build dynasties. Universal's first chieftain was known as "Uncle" Carl Laemmle because of all the nephews and distant cousins he imported from Europe to work on the lot. Columbia was dubbed the Pine Tree Studio because of its numerous "Cohns." And the initials MGM were said to stand for "Mayer's-Ganz-Mishpochen" (Yiddish for "Mayer's whole family") because Louis B. Mayer loaded the payroll with so many of his relatives, including his brother, his nephew, and his son-in-law, David Selznick.

Before long, everyone began to hear stories of some idiot nephew assigned screenwriting credit for a movie whose title he couldn't pronounce, or of an ungainly daughter miraculously transformed into a glamorous starlet, or of a deadbeat brother-in-law hired to direct because his family got tired of lending him money. Nepotism was rampant—not just because of the moguls' solicitousness toward the poor relations among them, but because it was fairly easy to find work for a stray in-law or a ne'er-do-well cousin in the thriving, expanding movie business. Since it was such a new industry, the qualifications for filling most jobs were only vaguely defined. Of course, many businesses have traditionally been staffed by relatives of the boss; the movie industry is hardly unique in that regard. The difference is that some people may harbor the illusion that moviemaking, a creative art as well as an industry, should be freer of nepotism than automobile manufacturing or the funeral trade. It is an illusion that fables like *A Star Is Born* have helped to perpetuate.

THE tale of Esther Blodgett, the unknown who skyrockets to sudden fame, is only half of the story of *A Star Is Born*. The other half, the descent of Norman Maine from stardom to dissipation and suicide, represents a second archetypal myth of the Hollywood experience; it has spawned another series of Hollywood-on-Hollywood films, garish horror stories about the underside of the movie business such as *Sunset Boulevard*, *The Bad and the Beautiful*, *The Big Knife*, *The Goddess*, *Whatever Happened to Baby Jane?*, and *The Legend of Lylah Clare*. Those lurid Hollywood gothics have had their analogues in real life. Indeed, such dark tales have been acted out offscreen more frequently than have the nonfiction counterparts to Esther Blodgett's triumphant ascension. Like Norman Maine, many movie stars and moviemakers have succumbed to bizarre excesses and self-destructive impulses, and the pressures of the business have torn their families apart.

Christopher Mankiewicz, the son of Joseph L. Mankiewicz (writer-director of *All About Eve*), tells of a meeting he had with two old friends, Peter Fonda and Bill Hayward. (Fonda and Hayward shared a family connection; Peter's father, Henry Fonda, had once been married to Bill's mother, Margaret Sullavan.) Mankiewicz was then an executive with United Artists, and they were discussing a project that would become the ill-fated *Wanda Nevada*, starring and directed by Peter Fonda and produced by Hayward. In the midst of an argument, Fonda silenced the group by interjecting. "We shouldn't really argue. We should drink a toast."

"Why?" Mankiewicz asked, bewildered by this non-sequitur.

"Because we survived," Fonda replied. "Don't you realize that all three of our mothers committed suicide?"

It might be argued that the grotesque, often tragic dramas played out in these famous Hollywood families are typical of what goes on in most bastions of privilege and wealth. Certainly the combination of inherited wealth and family pride has placed a special burden on the children of other American dynasties—from Henry Adams to Edie Sedgwick. But in Hollywood, the dramas are more sensational, more ostentatious, somehow more spectacular. In a community where private life is lived so publicly, ordinary domestic intrigues, parental conflicts, and sibling rivalries can take on a heightened, histrionic quality, making them even harder to resolve.

Despite the disruptions in their own families, moviemakers frequently served up an idealized image of family life for public consumption. At MGM, Louis B. Mayer oversaw production of the most memorable of that studio's many paeans to family loyalty, the 1944 musical *Meet Me in St. Louis*, directed by Vincente Minelli and starring the woman who would soon become his wife, Judy Garland. The film is a series of achingly beautiful cameos drawn from a yellowing family album, evoking a lost world that we long to revisit. Scene after scene freezes a nostalgic dream of family devotion: the noisy but affectionate dinners where everyone helps to prepare homemade catsup; father and mother singing a duet at the piano as the children bring their dessert and gather round; Judy, left stranded by her date, accompanied by her dapper grandfather to the high school dance; Judy comforting her younger sister, Margaret O'Brien, as she faces the trauma of leaving their home town. Although it is meant to be glowing and ebullient, the film is steeped in sadness, for it forces us to contemplate the distance between our own discordant family lives and the warmth of this nurturing clan.

The gap between fantasy and reality was even greater for the makers of the movie—Louis B. Mayer, Vincente Minnelli, Judy Garland. Mayer was a moody, tyrannical husband who divorced his wife of more than forty years to wed a much younger woman; his two daughters have carried on a lifelong feud; and Mayer disinherited his older daughter Edie because he was warring with her husband. There was very little connection between life with father Mayer and the images he wept over in *Meet Me in St. Louis*. Similarly, the tender on-screen portrait of a blissful marriage could be strikingly contrasted with the stormy offscreen relationship of the Minnellis, a contest of two unbending egotists. In addition, Judy Garland's real-life relationship with her mother and sisters bore no resemblance to the familial allegiance celebrated in *Meet Me in St. Louis*. Judy fought savagely with her overbearing stage mother, Ethel Gumm. When Judy's second daughter, Lorna Luft, was born in 1952, Judy left orders at the hospital that Ethel was not to be permitted to see her newborn grandchild. Two months later, Ethel was stricken with a heart attack and died in the parking lot of Douglas Aircraft, where she was earning sixty-one dollars a week as a clerk. She and her famous daughter had not spoken for years.

At Twentieth Century-Fox, one of Darryl F. Zanuck's most popular and prestigious productions was the 1940 drama *The Grapes of Wrath*, directed by John Ford and starring Henry Fonda. It remains one of the screen's most heartfelt tributes to a close-knit, indestructible family unit. Yet the rancorous private lives of both the Zanuck and the Ford families stand in sharp opposition to the inspiring cohesiveness of the Joads. The same could be said of Henry Fonda, who throughout his long career frequently found himself playing the stalwart, dutiful son or the doting husband and father. Many of his films were sentimental stories about familial love: *Spencer's Mountain*, *On Golden Pond*, and *Yours, Mine, and Ours*. But Fonda himself was married five times; two of the women he married committed suicide; and his relationships with his children during much of his life were chilly and strained.

It would be easy to accuse Mayer, Garland, Minnelli, Zanuck, Ford, and Fonda of rank hypocrisy, promoting virtues which they themselves blithely disregarded. But the impulse to produce or participate in such idylls on film probably testifies to their yearning for the kind of family bonding that their own lives lacked. How much stronger was the melancholy that their children must have felt as they pondered the disparity between their own painful home lives and the poignant images of loving American families that their parents had conjured on the screen.

PIONEERS

1

FOUNDING FATHERS
AND JUNIOR PARTNERS

*"I have known the others: the drug victims, the perverts,
the well-meaning, misdirected, badly aimed projectiles of
their fathers' ruthless power drives.
I've seen the neurotic wrecks, overdriven like engines
unable to attain the high-speed ascendencies they thought
their fathers demanded of them—because the fault was
not always the father's, it was as often due to the son's
inability to accept his own mediocrity."*

—JESSE L. LASKY, JR.

AROUND the turn of the century, a young journalist by the name of Hutchins Hapgood wrote a series of articles about the immigrant Jews of New York's Lower East Side, later collected under the title *The Spirit of the Ghetto*. Observing the picturesque bustle of activity among the pushcart peddlers of Rutgers Square, Hapgood was struck by the many "strange types" he saw; but he was impressed, too, by how "strangely Americanized" they were all becoming. "When you notice that practically everybody is in business," he wrote, "you will understand why practically everybody is, to a greater or lesser degree, in spirit an American..." The dominant effect of the scene was that of "eager, militant business." As Hapgood noted, "The old man peddling from door to door, or tending his pushcart in the crowd, may be a poet or a scholar, with the spirit of universal brotherhood or an impassioned love of the Talmud in his soul. Some of the young women in the crowd may be fervent socialists, strike leaders and exhorters. Complex, indeed, is this mass of human beings, representing many civilizations and many conflicting tendencies, but united—and this is the point—in one great absorbing spirit—the spirit of business; the thing that is rapidly making them American citizens in fact as well as in name..."

Hutchins Hapgood optimistically believed that Immigrant Jew-

3

ish businessmen, "impelled by keen interest and ambition," would naturally "rise in the exciting world of America"; they would see "old barriers" disappear as they explored the broad range of commercial activities that this country had been built upon. As the refugees moved beyond the confines of the ghetto, however, and sought new outlets for their entrepreneurial aspirations, they soon discovered that a majority of businesses were closed to them, controlled by an entrenched plutocracy which looked upon them with suspicion and scorn. But the fledgling motion picture industry was still wide open; it was disreputable enough to provide fertile ground for wildcatters and speculators. Realizing the vast commercial possibilities of the new medium, immigrant Jews were among the first to invest in the new-fangled nickelodeons and "flickers." As their investments began to pay off handsomely, these enterprising young men did indeed "rise in the exciting world of America." But unlike the broad-minded observer Hapgood, they themselves saw no connection between their success as Americans and the spirit of the ghetto. In their own minds, the rise to financial prepotency and the road to cultural acceptance both seemed to demand a denial of their roots.

Budd Schulberg has written of the "Jewish days" before his father, B. P. Schulberg, and his father's one-time partner, Louis B. Mayer, had ascended to the ranks of full-fledged moguldom. The two families would gather at one another's modest, middle-class homes in Los Angeles to share Sunday brunch of lox and pickled herring and warm bagels, and L. B. would "reminisce about having courted [his wife] Margaret on his junk wagon." In due course, Schulberg and Mayer would rise to rule over separate empires, and joust like warring monarchs. The pattern they followed was a common one among the early moguls. The cordial alliances they had formed during years of struggle fell by the wayside, along with the trappings of their humble origins. The junk wagons gave way to chauffeur-driven limousines; the lox and herring to *pate de fois gras* and oysters on the half shell; the little stucco bungalows to spacious Beverly Hills *palazzi*; and the loyal Jewish wives to more glamorous *shiksas*. Not just Mayer, but Sam Goldwyn, Jack Warner, David O. Selznick, and Harry Cohn all divorced their Jewish wives and married much younger Gentile women. For these men, the surest sign of having reached their pinnacle of success was to have at their side the real-life equivalent of those beautiful "American" goddesses whom they had all enshrined on screen.

It was standing policy among the Jewish moguls not to cast Jewish actors or actresses in their movies if they "looked" Jewish or had Jewish-sounding names. When Danny Kaye (born David Daniel Kaminsky) balked at the idea of having his nose bobbed, Louis B. Mayer assured him that he could demonstrate the shape of things to come by having Kaye's brother undergo the rhinoplasty first. (Danny declined the offer.) Almost all the moguls had similar compunctions about anything that smacked of "Jewishness" on screen, and a few carried their discomfiture to the point of self-loathing. The most extreme case was Harry Cohn, who used to boast that the only Jewish actors he had under contract at Columbia played Indians. When asked to contribute to a fund for Jewish relief during World War II, Cohn replied, "Relief for the Jews? What we need is relief *from* the Jews."

Even though they tried to distance themselves from their Jewish backgrounds, the studio potentates retained a commitment to one traditional Jewish idea—that of family responsibility. Not only did they dispense jobs to their relatives, they brought their aging parents out to retire in the California sunshine. As Budd Schulberg had observed, Old Man Warner, Old Man Cohn, Old Man Mayer— as they were officially known—all seemed to be "mystified that from their loins had sprung such unlikely offspring as a loud, wisecracking, sports-jacketed Jack Warner; a profane, irreverent, mob-oriented strongman like Harry Cohn; or a crafty, ambitious powerbroker like Louis Mayer . . . Somehow the seed of the Old World had produced these brash, amoral, on-the-make Americans. The sons with their bankrolls and their girlfriends and their *fuck-you's* would tolerate and humor these old men as relics of the past."

According to Schulberg, the moguls' fathers underwent profound culture shock when they arrived in Los Angeles and found themselves without a true synagogue to worship in. The Wilshire Boulevard Temple—where their sons would occasionally show up to observe Yom Kippur (if schedules permitted) or to attend a bar mitzvah (if the boy's father was important enough) or to be counted among the mourners at a funeral (if, please God, it wasn't their own)—seemed more like a glitzy movie palace than a house of worship. The mellifluous Rabbi Edgar Magnin presided over his sanctuary with papal panache, and the bearded elders were repulsed by his monument to mammon. They demanded an Orthodox synagogue, and so their sons obligingly rented a little cottage on a Hollywood side street, sent over crews of studio carpenters

and set painters to refurbish the interior, and converted it into a
shul. A real rabbi, complete with *tallis* and *peis* and long black
beard, was imported from New York, and the patriarchs were
driven down in studio limousines to meet him at the train station.
"While the old beards worshipped in their Hollywood *shul*," Schulberg concluded, their sons, having fulfilled their filial obligation,
continued to worship "at the altar of the box office."

What little training the moguls' sons and daughters had in the
traditions of their ancestors would come from Rabbi Magnin's
"Sunday school," a far cry from the rigorous Talmudic instruction
to which most of *them* had been subjected in their youth. Many
of their children grew up with only the vaguest inkling that they
were Jewish at all. Barbara Goetz Windom, the daughter of producer William Goetz and Edith Mayer Goetz, and the granddaughter of Louis B. Mayer, recalls the elaborate Christmas parties
and Easter egg hunts her family used to host. When she married
her second husband, actor William Windom, she asked that the
ceremony be held at the famous Wayfarers' Chapel overlooking
the Pacific Ocean. "My mother was just horrified," Barbara reports.
"She said my father would be very upset if we had a Christian
service. It was the first I'd heard of any reference to being Jewish."

Constantly groping for respectability, the moguls and their families doggedly sought instruction in the ways of the Gentile leisure
class. For wives, the ritual of assimilation required that they emulate the activities of America's recognized *grandes dames*; they
would pore through the latest women's magazines trying to figure
out which pastimes were *au courant* among the New York society
set. "Ceramics, sculpture, mosaics—they went through it all,"
Dore Schary's daughter, Jill Schary, has remarked. "And after the
style passed, everything would go into the maid's room. Maids'
rooms were veritable museums of past decades of fashionable
ladies' no-longer-fashionable arts and crafts." The Saturday-night
ladies, as the moguls' wives came to be known, took up party-
giving with a vengeance, though they were always careful to
maintain the proper aura of exclusivity by barring mere suburban
matrons from their lists of invitees. "They wanted no part of the
nice Jewish upper-middle-class ladies of Beverly Hills, with whom
they probably had more in common than they did with Mrs. Norman Chandler," Schary acidulously notes. Though they frequently
had difficulty knowing just how to behave in front of their newly-
acquainted English butlers and French maids, the Saturday-night
ladies eventually mastered the superficial techniques of *hauteur*.

It took time and practice, screenwriter Frances Marion has said, but at last "the intrepid hostess no longer rushed to the door with a hearty 'Hello, kid!' or 'Howya, babe!' but waited discreetly in the drawing room and greeted her guests with a desultory 'Charmed you could come this evening, *cherie*.'"

While their wives rehearsed the rituals of WASP gentility, the moguls themselves might be found at their private horse-breeding farms or perhaps playing polo or shooting quail with the likes of William Randolph Hearst or Jock Whitney. Politically, their hankering for acceptance manifested itself in exaggerated patriotism. As grateful recipients of American's plenitude, they held unswervingly to the conviction that this country and its leaders were above reproach. They seemed always to be somewhat in awe of governmental authority, secretly fearful that the benign gods responsible for their abundant good fortune might suddenly turn on them and strip away their wealth and power. Lurking somewhere in their collective unconscious was probably the spectre of the plundering cossack, ready to swoop down and drive them out of this promised land. Characteristically, when Congressional witch-hunters sent their snoops to town in the late 1940s, the moguls cooperated cravenly, eager to assist in ferreting out any of their employees tarred with that most wretched of epithets, "un-American." "Don't make trouble" was their shared motto; after all, they reasoned, making trouble is what started the pogroms. "One of the reasons for their constant internecine warfare," Sam Goldwyn, Jr. suggests, "was that they felt they could only make trouble with each other."

Because most of Hollywood's founding fathers were men of enormous ego, they had a strong desire to see their power and glory endure. It was important for them that their progeny inherit not just their fortunes, but their renown as well. Jewish tradition forbids the naming of children after the living, but most of the Jewish moguls defied that convention and named their sons after themselves: Carl Laemmle, Jack Warner, Sam Goldwyn, Jesse Lasky, and Irving Thalberg all had firstborn sons named "Junior." Bearing the name of a Hollywood potentate proved to be a crushing burden for most of the heirs apparent. Some, like Paramount founder Adolph Zukor's son Eugene, managed to survive by simply lowering their sights. "Eugene is very sensible," the elder Zukor told an interviewer in 1952. "He avoids an inferiority complex by being himself completely." During most of his working years, Eugene Zukor served as head of Paramount's casting department, where he discharged his duties with drone-like discipline. When asked which Paramount stars he had discovered as the studio's man in charge of talent, Eugene took credit for none. "I don't kid myself I'm another Adolph Zukor," he confessed. "Father is a forger of dreams. I don't like danger, and I'm content not to dream, so I look straight ahead . . ."

Only a few of the moguls' sons were either wise enough or wary enough to avoid the family business altogether. Irving Thalberg and Norma Shearer took pains to give their children a "normal" upbringing; they even went so far as to recruit an ordinary little boy from Glendale to come live with them in their Santa Monica beachfront mansion so that Irving, Jr. could have the benefit of non-celebrity companionship. The ploy may have had some effect on young Thalberg. He is one of the few of the flock of "juniors" who eschewed a job in the movie industry, and he is now a respected professor of philosophy (whose field of specialization is "free will"). Unfortunately, the lad who was plucked from obscurity to play out the prince-and-pauper fantasy inside the Thalberg household did not fare so well; friends report that the experience left him so unsettled that he has spent most of his adult life trying to make sense of his unlikely childhood.

In contrast to Professor Thalberg, most of the other moguls' sons found the exercise of free will considerably more difficult when they had to decide on a career. (Perhaps his father's early death had something to do with freeing Irving, Jr. from the pressure to join the executive ranks.) In most cases, the law of succession was inescapable; it was only a matter of time before the movieland princes would be called to enter the privy councils of their fathers' studio kingdoms.

IF one were asked to name the day on which the Hollywood rite of primogeniture was first set in motion, the answer would probably be April 28, 1929—the twenty-first birthday of Carl Laemmle, Jr. His father took the occasion to give young Laemmle a present: the job of running Universal Studios.

It was the sort of move that people had come to expect from kindly old "Uncle Carl," Universal's founder and the most notorious practitioner of nepotism in the business. By the time Carl Laemmle, Sr. made his son production head of the studio, entire boatloads of poor relations from his native Bavaria were already roaming the back lot, many of them employed in jobs that had not even existed before the phalanxes of cousins and nephews appeared to fill them. When "Junior" Laemmle, as he would be called until the day of his death, was handed the reins of the company in 1929, it was almost as if he were taking command of a combination gypsy-camp-and-cousins-club, rather than a thriving commercial enterprise.

To the dismay of most other Universal executives, Junior promptly set about charting a new course for the studio. His father had established Universal in 1912 as a purveyor of one- and two-reelers. As it evolved, the company's policy was to churn out hundreds of cheap Westerns and light-hearted comedies aimed at the family audience; that was the sort of product that could be easily sold overseas, a market which the other studios tended to ignore. But Junior abandoned this tried-and-true formula and initiated his own schedule of big-budget productions. His first effort, Lewis Milestone's film of Erich Maria Remarque's powerful anti-war novel, *All Quiet on the Western Front*, was a huge box office success, and it won the Academy Award as best picture of 1930. The following year saw the release of another commercial and critical triumph for Universal, the faithful film version of Broadway's piquant lampoon of the movie business, *Once in a Lifetime*. Perhaps the only people in the movie industry who were not surprised by the success of these more sophisticated films were the Laemmles themselves. Junior and Uncle Carl saw to it that *Lifetime* contained a headnote, in which they lauded themselves on their courage in bringing this satire of Hollywood's own mores to the screen. In an even more extravagant display of self-congratulation, Uncle Carl commissioned the English author, John Drinkwater, to write his authorized biography. Published in 1931, the obsequious tome contained Uncle Carl's blatant bid for a Nobel Peace Prize—an honor to which he believed himself entitled for having presented *All Quiet on the Western Front* to the world's moviegoers. Drinkwater endorsed the Nobel notion with these words: "If such a consummation comes about, a dual purpose will be served, for not only will this pioneer of the motion picture industry be receiving a well-merited award, but recognition will be given to the idea of the cinema art as it relates to matters of world concern."

As the risks he was taking seemed to pay off, Junior Laemmle became bolder still. He played a major part in bringing the horror genre into the sound era, sponsoring *Dracula*, with Bela Lugosi, and *Frankenstein*, with Boris Karloff. Indeed, during the first few years of his tenure as Universal's production chief, Junior appeared to be a veritable *wunderkind*; evidently, his father's confidence in him had not been misplaced. But as swiftly as Junior's reputation had been made, just as swiftly was it destroyed. Because other studios had already cornered most of the top actors, writers, and directors in the business, it was difficult for Universal to compete on an even footing. Moreover, as the Depression dragged on and ticket sales began to taper off, it became harder and harder to turn a profit on the big-budget pictures that Junior had committed the company to making. Several of his costume pictures—including *Captain of the Guard*, *Sutter's Gold*, and an early sound version of Dickens's *Great Expectations*—were costly failures. When Junior refused to curtail his lavish productions, Uncle Carl reluctantly removed his son and replaced him with his son-in-law, an agent named Stanley Bergerman. Bergerman was married to Rosabelle Laemmle, who had been romantically linked to Irving Thalberg before the mercurial young producer left Universal in 1923 to become the favored protégé of Louis B. Mayer.

Stanley Bergerman failed to salvage Universal. In 1936, Uncle Carl decided to cut his losses and sell the company to an English consortium, Standard Capital. Cleaning out the lot, the new owners discovered dozens of names on the payroll belonging to dead or nonexistent employees. Uncle Carl's surviving relatives were purged, thinning the work force considerably. No longer the beneficiaries of his seemingly inexhaustible largesse, most of them were never heard from again.

One Laemmle relative did achieve distinction: his nephew, director William Wyler, whose many credits include *Mrs. Miniver*, *The Best Years of Our Lives*, *Detective Story*, *Friendly Persuasion*, *Roman Holiday*, *Ben-Hur*, and *Funny Girl*. But the fate of another of Uncle Carl's nephews, Richard Laemmle, was probably more typical. In 1979, Richard, who claimed to have worked at Universal as a screenwriter, producer, director, and film editor, was discovered living in a 1960 Ford station wagon. He had been roaming up and down the California coast in his car for years, supporting himself on his Social Security benefits. The Humane Society officers who picked him up did not deem his station wagon a suitable home for Richard's "family" of eleven dogs, and a jury convicted him of cruelty to animals. He paid his fine and resumed his nomadic travels.

As for Junior Laemmle, his career went steadily downhill after his father fired him. Junior's second cousin, Los Angeles theater owner Max Laemmle, describes Junior as a "weak personality" who was effective only "as long as he had the guidance of his father." Junior suffered from an almost pathological need to win his father's approval. When he told his father that he had asked actress Constance Cummings to marry him, Uncle Carl refused to sanction the match because Cummings was not Jewish. Incapable of defying his father, Junior broke his engagement and spent the rest of his life as a bachelor, furtively entertaining prostitutes at his baronial estate in Benedict Canyon, which visitors described as looking more and more like Frankenstein's castle as the years passed. A lifelong hypochondriac, Junior enlisted in the army during World War II, but he had his chauffeur drive him to answer roll call every morning at the Long Island base camp to which he had been assigned. When roll call was over, Junior was driven back to his hotel suite, where he would languish away the afternoons, placing regular phone calls to his West Coast doctor to describe his myriad ailments. He was given a medical discharge in 1944 and returned to Hollywood, where he made a feeble attempt to resume his producing career. His office would issue periodic announcements of forthcoming projects, but no productions ever reached the screen. In the 1960s he contracted multiple sclerosis, and on September 24, 1979—half a century after his father made him head of Universal Studios and forty years to the day after his father's death—Carl Laemmle, Jr. succombed to a stroke in his run-down Beverly Hills mansion.

ANOTHER Mogul's son recalls his last meeting with Carl Laemmle, Jr.: "He was dying of disappointment—because he had failed the expectations of his father and been put on the dust heap before he was twenty-five." The words were written by Jesse L. Lasky, Jr., for whom the tragic case of Junior Laemmle would serve as a haunting admonition. Like Carl Laemmle, Sr., Lasky's own father was one of the industry's true pioneers. Jesse Lasky, Sr. was a successful vaudeville producer at the time he decided to take a chance on motion pictures. He joined forces with a failed actor named Cecil B. De Mille (the brother of Lasky's friend, stage director William De Mille) and came to Hollywood in 1913, when it was still little more than an orange grove. They rented a barn and shot a Western called *The Squaw Man*, starring the Broadway actor Dustin Farnum. It was the first feature made entirely in Hollywood and became the infant industry's biggest moneymaker.

Merging with Adolph Zukor's Famous Players Company to form the studio that would eventually be called Paramount, Lasky and De Mille continued to prosper through the decade of the 1920s, Lasky as a producer, De Mille as a director. Lasky's special knack was for finding stars; he was responsible for introducing to the American screen performers as various as Carole Lombard, Douglas Fairbanks, Jr., Bing Crosby, Gilbert Roland, Cary Grant, Charles Laughton, and Maurice Chevalier.

With his gentle demeanor, quiet voice, and little pince-nez, Jesse Lasky always seemed a bit out of place in the boisterous, knockabout movie business. In 1932, a battle broke out between the sales and theatrical exhibition departments at Paramount. Lasky volunteered to a diminution of his own power within the organization in order to placate the warring parties. A reorganization of the company ensued, and Lasky was bought out of his contract. He became an independent producer at Fox, where he made *The Power and the Glory* with a little-known actor named Spencer Tracy. Lasky scored his most notable success in 1941 with *Sergeant York*, starring Gary Cooper. The movie earned a substantial profit, but Lasky was advised to record the earnings as a capital gain, a move which later cost him every penny the picture made, and more. His last days were spent fending off the Internal Revenue Service, standing by helplessly as his material possessions were auctioned away to satisfy the debt collectors. His relationship with his wife Bessie, a highly-regarded painter and occasional poet, had already deteriorated. Seeking refuge in the teachings of Christian Science, Theosophy, and other, more occult forms of spiritualism, he vainly tried to reach some understanding of this drastic reversal in his fortunes so late in life.

The senior Lasky's quest for religious solace was to be reenacted years later by his younger son, Bill. (When Sam Goldwyn was told that the second Lasky son would be named William—after Jesse Lasky's friend, William De Mille—Goldwyn snapped, "Why would you name him Bill? Every Tom, Dick, and Harry is named Bill.") Born in 1921, when his father was at the height of his glory as a silent film producer, Bill Lasky was a pampered child. An avid animal lover as a youngster, he pursued his interest in zoology into adulthood. Shortly after finishing work for his father as an assistant director on *Sergeant York*, Bill raised the money to make a short film about a polio-stricken boy who discovers a wounded eagle in the Malibu hills. Nursing the bird back to health, the crippled lad finds the inspiration to walk again. Bill

FOUNDING FATHERS AND JUNIOR PARTNERS **13**

wrote, directed, and shot the film on a shoestring budget, and it was nominated for an Academy Award as best short in 1941, the same year that Gary Cooper picked up his Oscar for *Sergeant York*.

The Boy and the Eagle was the high point of Bill Lasky's filmmaking career. He married Margery Lowe, the personal assistant to *Sergeant York*'s director, Howard Hawks. The marriage floundered because of Bill's admitted immaturity and his inability to stay gainfully employed. He landed a job at the reptile house of the Griffith Park Zoo but was eventually fired. He tried operating a pet business, which he called "Of Cabbages and Hummingbirds," but that, too, failed. He hit bottom when he finally found himself forced to sell off his prize hummingbird collection just to buy food. "Loss. Loss. Loss. That was the story of my life," he confessed. "I had lost my business, my Laurel Canyon house, my hummingbirds, and, now, even my dignity and pride." On more than one occasion, he attempted suicide.

Through his friend Tommy Rettig, the former child star of the *Lassie* TV series, Bill was introduced to Buddhism. He was forty-seven at the time of his conversion. For five years, he knelt before his *butsudan*, chanting solemnly and rubbing beads. But a nagging sense of despair persisted. It wasn't until he converted once again that Bill Lasky finally arrived at a spiritual stasis. Under the tutelage of the eupeptic television evangelist Kathryn Kuhlman, he became a born-again Christian and assumed the presidency of the Beverly Hills chapter of the Full-Gospel Business Men's Fellowship, a kind of right-wing Christian version of the Rotary. His 1976 book, *Tell It on the Mountain*, a curious amalgam of autobiography and religious testimony, acknowledges the influence of Billy Graham, Jimmy Swaggart, Rex Humbard, and Pat Boone in turning his life around. In it, Bill Lasky describes the success he feels he finally achieved after a lifetime of failure—not by following the trail blazed by his mogul father but by marching in step with Christ.

Unlike his younger brother Bill, Jesse L. Lasky, Jr. managed to collect a number of respectable film credits, primarily as a screenwriter for his father's former partner, Cecil B. De Mille. Jesse L. Lasky, Jr. went to work for De Mille after graduating from Princeton in 1932, and he wrote (or co-wrote) some of De Mille's most popular movies, including *Union Pacific*, *Reap the Wild Wind*, *Unconquered*, and his two Biblical flesh-and-flagellation epics, *Samson and Delilah* and *The Ten Commandments*. It was while working on the latter that De Mille ordered Lasky, in his capacity as the "unit Jew," to write a scene capturing the spirit of the Exodus from Egypt. Lasky was Jewish in name only, having received but a passing familiarity with his religious heritage. To satisfy the boss, however, he pored over Torah and Mishnah, searching for the spiritual essence of the first Passover. He proceeded to write what he thought would be an appropriately moving and reverent scene and proudly showed his handiwork to De Mille. The director read it, pronounced it cheap and meretricious, spat upon the pages, and called Lasky a traitor to his race.

(Though he was himself one-quarter Jewish, De Mille had a reputation as a closet anti-Semite. His haughty disdain was not reserved for Jews alone. When his adopted daughter Katherine announced that she intended to marry a young Mexican-American actor named Anthony Quinn, Cecil B. was predictably incensed. In time, he relented and went so far as to build the newlyweds a brand new home on De Mille Drive, perched just below his own sprawling mansion. "And every night," John Barrymore assured Quinn, "your father-in-law will step out on his balcony and urinate upon you—a golden stream in the moonlight.")

When the market for De Millean spectacle dried up, Jesse Lasky's, Jr.'s career as a screenwriter began to dry up with it. Like his father before him, he was forced to declare bankruptcy. In collaboration with his third wife, Pat Silver, he drifted into writing B-pictures and series television in the early 1960s. He moved to England and worked on episodes of *The Avengers* and *The Saint*. "The golden age of the Hollywood writer was heading into its winter," Lasky decided. He landed a couple of writing assignments at Twentieth Century-Fox, but his screenplays, which were conceived as lavish, big-budget productions, were reduced to cheap potboilers. (The title of one of them, *Seven Women from Hell*, was nearly changed to *Six Women* as a cost-cutting maneuver.)

Jesse Lasky, Jr. turned to other forms of writing—a novel, a verse play, a book about Laurence Olivier and Vivien Leigh, an affectionate memoir of his experiences in the bygone glory days. Its rueful title asks a question that vexes many other second-generation movie folk: *What Ever Happened to Hollywood?*

FOR Jesse Lasky, Sr., the foray into the entertainment business had begun when, after failing to strike it rich in the Alaska gold rush around the turn of the century, he moved on to Honolulu and parlayed his cornet-playing talent into a job as the only white man in the Royal Hawaiian Band. Later, his sister Blanche and he put together a vaudeville act called The Musical Laskys. The suggestion that Jesse try his hand at moviemaking had come from his brother-in-law, an indefatigable salesman named Sam Goldfish, who had once worked as a glove cutter in the factory owned by the uncle of Lasky's wife in upstate New York. Ironically, Blanche had married dapper Sam Goldfish to get out of show business. She had grown weary of the uncertainties and vicissitudes of life on the road. "She thought Sam would offer a stable businessman husband far removed from the hectic dream stuff of theater folk," Blanche's nephew, Jesse Lasky, Jr., has observed. "She could not have chosen a worse escape hatch in young Sam—who would later change his name to Goldwyn."

The film production company which Sam Goldfish convinced his brother-in-law to start with Cecil B. De Mille was Sam's own passport to Hollywood. As third partner in the enterprise, however, he quickly became the odd man out. Incapable of getting along with the equally temperamental De Mille, Goldwyn severed the alliance. "I was always an independent, even when I had partners," he said many years later.

A born loner, Goldwyn seems to have achieved an intimate rapport with only one individual in his lifetime. At the age of forty-three, fifteen years after he divorced Blanche Lasky, Goldwyn fell in love with a pretty twenty-one-year old actress named Frances Howard. They were soon married, and Frances gave up acting to devote herself to the far more demanding career of being Sam Goldwyn's wife. After their only child, Samuel, Jr., went off to college, Frances took an office next to her husband's and became his unofficial production assistant. Among other contributions, she discovered the source material for *The Best Years of Our Lives* while leafing through a magazine.

Upon graduating from the University of Virginia, Sam, Jr. returned to Hollywood and also joined his father in the family business. Though he credits his father with giving him enormous practical insight into the day-to-day operations of the movie business, Sammy—as he is still called—admits that it was not always easy to live up to the Goldwyn name. Nor was it always easy to communicate with the elder Goldwyn, whose garblings of the English language have become such a staple of Hollywood lore. Sam, Jr. tells of showing his father the rushes of a movie he was in the process of shooting, and asking for his professional opinion. "Jesus Christ, that's all wrong," said Sam, Sr. after viewing the footage. Sammy kept asking his father to be more explicit. *What* exactly was wrong? "I don't know what's wrong," came the reply, "but goddammit, fix it!" And with that, his father marched out of the screening room. The next morning, Sam, Sr. invited his son to join him for breakfast. "Keep the gun under the table," he said over juice and coffee. Since Sam, Jr. was not carrying a gun, he was befuddled. "In melodrama, keep the gun under the table," Sam, Sr. said. "You pull the gun out too fast."

Finally, what his father was trying to tell him became clear. "I had done something in the first reel that I should have saved for the fourth reel," Sammy says.

He made the necessary changes and invited his father to view the revised version.

Sam, Sr. was pleased. "See," he said, "I told you that in the first place."

According to Samuel Goldwyn, Jr., one of the most valuable lessons his father taught him was not just to produce movies but to hold onto them. "With every film he made," says Sam, Jr., "my father raised the money, paid back the bank, and kept control of the negative, rather than give it up to a studio. He said, 'You be careful with those films. Some people will tell you they're not worth anything, but don't you believe it.'" As it turned out, the elder Goldwyn was right. By retaining control of the prints of his movies, he was able to reap huge profits when new markets opened up for them in television and theatrical re-distribution.

For many years, Samuel Goldwyn, Jr. has tried to emulate his father as a maverick producer. Interestingly, several of his films— *Huckleberry Finn*, *The Proud Rebel*, *The Golden Seal*—have dealt with the theme of coming of age and the efforts of young boys to achieve a measure of independence from their fathers. Shying away from the more explosive conflicts between fathers and sons, most of these pictures have been somewhat muffled in their treatment of the subject. Sammy's most exuberant and successful film, *Cotton Comes to Harlem*, is perhaps the least typical. A no-holds-barred comedy about drugs, crime and urban corruption, it was one of the first movies of the early 1970s to give black actors and a black director (Ossie Davis) a chance to participate in a main-stream Hollywood movie. *Cotton Comes to Harlem* was a far cry from the stultifying, safely restrained material that has been Samuel Goldwyn, Jr.'s usual trademark.

In some sense, the conscientious adherence to "good taste" may be one of Samuel Goldwyn, Jr.'s more unfortunate legacies from his father. The classic Samuel Goldwyn product, epitomized by his rendition of *Wuthering Heights*, starring Laurence Olivier and Merle Oberon, is handsomely photographed but rather too stodgy to be compelling. Goldwyn's production of *The Little Foxes*, an all-too-faithful transcription of Lillian Hellman's well-made play, is brought to life only by Bette Davis's bravura performance as the most ravenous of the family of Southern vipers. When Goldwyn filmed Hellman's *The Children's Hour*, he changed the title to *These Three* and saw to it that the lesbian elements of the plot were expunged. *Porgy and Bess*, *Oklahoma!*, and *Guys and Dolls* were all dutifully filmed plays with music rather than vibrant movie musicals; if they succeeded at all, it was because of the engaging source material. Goldwyn's most entertaining movies— *Ball of Fire* and *Stella Dallas*, with Barbara Stanwyck, and *Come and Get It*, with Frances Farmer—were the least pretentious. Like the finely-tailored suits he was fond of wearing, or the self-created name he adopted, Goldwyn's penchant for high-toned, belletristic material was essentially a cover-up, testifying to his lifelong yearning for dignity and class. But the vulgarian that lay beneath those outward pretensions was considerably more vital, and probably more interesting as well. If he had let that aspect of himself show up more often in his work, the Goldwyn oeuvre might have been less tasteful, but more enduringly exciting.

Samuel Goldwyn's, Jr.'s first wife was the daughter of playwright Sidney Howard. Their son John has followed his father into production; he works as an executive with The Ladd Company. In 1969 Sammy married a television writer by the name of Peggy Elliott, with whom he has two children.

After a long period of inactivity during the 1970s, when both his parents suffered lingering illnesses and died, Samuel Goldwyn, Jr. announced plans to revitalize the company that bears his father's name. In 1983, he moved the Samuel Goldwyn Company into a lavish suite of offices in Century City, hired dozens of new employees, and set out to produce as well as distribute new films. By reissuing such Goldwyn favorites as *Oklahoma!*, he hopes to generate enough revenues to finance the production of several movies each year. In addition, he keeps on the lookout for marketable foreign films which his company can distribute on the art-house circuit. (He has already had success in this vein with *Gregory's Girl*, *Spetters*, *Stevie*, and *The Gift*.) "We're going to revive a dying empire," Sam, Jr. says resolutely. The cornerstone of that revival is the library of films that his father so carefully created and retained. As he charts his own future course, Sam Goldwyn, Jr. is almost literally building on the past.

"I didn't have the classic battles with my father that the sons of some of the other founders may have had," Sam Goldwyn, Jr. says, reflecting on his relatively tranquil childhood. If the Goldwyns had trouble communicating, the barrier between them was more linguistic than emotional. Such was not the case for Jack Warner and his son, Jack Warner, Jr. The name Warner Communications, as the family business would eventually come to be known, carried a heavy freight of irony for Jack Warner, Jr., who recalls asking his father, "Why is it that you and I are in the communication business, and yet we seem to have so much difficulty communicating with each other?"

Jack, Jr. says that even as a youngster he would write memos to his father rather than speak to him directly. The only time he remembers his father trying to sit down with him and have an earnest, heart-to-heart talk was after Jack, Sr. had seen a stage production of Eugene O'Neill's sentimental family drama, *Ah, Wilderness!* "He was not the easiest man to gain confidence with," says Jack Warner, Jr. "It really didn't matter whether you were his son, or a casual acquaintance, or an agent. He existed behind a self-made wall. Besides, a lot of him wasn't all that nice to know. At times he gloried in being a no-good sonofabitch." If he was brusque and brutal in face-to-face confrontation, Jack Warner, Sr. had a reputation for being even surlier when his victims were not around to defend themselves (or cower). "He had a rapier-like wit at the expense of the absent," says his son. "Nobody left the dining room until after he did—and not out of respect."

"Jack Warner is a man who would rather tell a bad joke than make a good movie," Jack Benny once quipped. To most of those who knew him, Jack Warner the jester was fundamentally insecure, a bilious megalomaniac forever retreating behind the defensive mask of the borscht-belt comedian. "As a little boy I started building up layers of insulation, and now I have the hide of an elephant," he candidly remarked in his generally less-than-candid autobiography, *My First Hundred Years in Hollywood*. No one, regardless of how esteemed or dignified, was spared his tasteless jokes. Introduced to Madame Chiang Kai-shek, he apologized for forgetting his laundry. When Albert Einstein paid a visit to the Warner studio in the early 1930s, Jack pumped the professor's hand and immediately informed him, "I have a theory of relatives, too. Don't hire 'em."

Jack Warner, Jr., who witnessed that improbable exchange, does not recall whether Einstein was amused, but he does point out a certain paradox in his father's jest. "If his brothers hadn't hired him," says Jack, Jr., "he'd have been out of work." Though Jack Warner was certainly the best-known of the moviemaking Warners, the fact is that he was the last to enter the business, and he did so only after his older brothers, Sam, Albert, and Harry, agreed to take him in.

They had built their studio in 1919. Sam, the most popular and genial of the brothers, was responsible for introducing the company to sound—over the strenuous objections of his skeptical siblings. When the Warner production of *The Jazz Singer* ushered in the sound era in 1927, Warner Bros. was on the track to becoming one of the industry's leading studios. After Sam died, his three surviving brothers each carved out a separate fiefdom within the studio empire. Parsimonious Albert, called "the major" because of the commission he carried from the Army Signal Corps, served as treasurer; he would periodically send out crews to comb the lot for stray nails to be retrieved and used in building future sets. Harry, the shrewdest businessman of the group, was in charge of the New York office and oversaw the financial and administrative end of the operation. Jack, the youngest of the brothers, was put in charge of production.

Like a mafia family, the Warners struck up alliances with other powerful clans whose interests they shared. The Greek immigrant Skouras brothers—Charley, George, and Spyros—held sway over the Warner theater division after their own chain of moviehouses was absorbed by the Warner empire. And the Warners even had their *consigliere*, an outsider who was taken into the business and performed so brilliantly that he became practically a member of the family. His name was Darryl F. Zanuck, and he served as their trusted aide-de-camp until he broke with them in 1933 and moved on to head his own studio, Twentieth Century-Fox. After Zanuck's departure, Jack Warner became the undisputed lord and master of the Warner lot, presiding with an iron fist.

Jack was the showman, Harry the educator—and together they somehow managed to meld their different instincts into a special brand of moviemaking. They signed a unique group of stars—Humphrey Bogart, James Cagney, Errol Flynn, Bette Davis, Joan Blondell, Lauren Bacall—tough guys and brassy broads. If Warner Bros. was a dream factory, the dreams it traded on were usually grounded in hard reality. From the company's first big success, *My Four Years in Germany in 1917*, through *I Am a Fugitive from a Chain Gang* (1932) and *Confessions of a Nazi Spy* (1939), Warner Bros. was known for producing hard-hitting, topical entertainments. It helped to created the gangster genre with Jack's pet projects, *Little Casesar* in 1930 and *The Public Enemy* in 1931; in addition, chiefly as a result of Harry's influence, the studio lent new respectability to the movie medium among aficionados of the legitimate theater by presenting Max Reinhardt's imaginative rendering of Shakespeare's *A Midsummer Night's Dream* in 1935 and the screen biographies starring the famous stage actor Paul Muni— *The Life of Emile Zola* and *The Life of Louis Pasteur*. Later, Warners defined the hardboiled romantic melodrama in such films as *The Maltese Falcon*, *High Sierra*, *Casablanca*, and *Mildred Pierce*.

Though the differences in their tastes and values seem to have generated beneficial results for Jack and Harry Warner professionally, those same differences led the two brothers to despise each other personally. Harry, in his role as self-appointed patriarch, despaired of his younger brother's profligate behavior. Jack, his parents' favorite, resented his older brother's moralizing interference in his life. The rift widened in 1932, when Jack divorced his wife Irma to marry a petite, dark-eyed actress named Ann Page. (Her first husband, Joseph Page, was a Valentino-style contract player with Warner Bros. and a pal of Jack's; it was Jack who had given Joseph the marquee-worthy moniker, Don Alvarado, inspired by the name of a downtown Los Angeles street.) Harry was outraged by Jack's desertion of his first wife for the *shiksa* Ann, and he considered it a stain upon the family honor. Bad feelings simmered between them for almost thirty years and reached the boiling point in the late 1950s, when the brothers agreed to sell their interest in the company to a group of outside investors. Harry unloaded his stock at $25 a share, but at the last minute Jack reneged on his end of the deal and refused to sell. (When he finally did sell a decade later, the value of his stock had risen to more than $80 a share.) Harry believed that Jack had betrayed him, and he never forgave his younger brother. During the year before Harry died in 1958, the two men did not speak.

Jack's own last years were not without bitterness. He reaped some $25 million from the sale of his Warner Bros. stock in 1967 and retired to Palm Springs, but he found it impossible to enjoy a leisurely retirement. His phone stopped ringing, the steady stream of important visitors slowed to a trickle, and Jack Warner felt like a fish out of water in his desert hideaway. "You're nothing if you don't have a studio," Warner sadly told a friend. "Now I'm just another millionaire, and there are a lot of them around." He made inquiries about returning to Warners, but the new management team headed by ex-agent Ted Ashley felt it was doing just fine without him. Jack produced two films on his own—a slavishly literal-minded transcription of the jingoistic Broadway musical *1776* and a revisionist Western about Billy the Kid called *Dirty Little Billy*, both of which flopped at the box office.

Harry Warner pinned his hopes for continuation of the Warner dynasty on his only son, Lewis. In 1932, however, at the age of twenty-two, Lewis developed blood poisoning while vacationing in Cuba. His gums became infected and before his father could bring him back to New York, pneumonia set in. Lewis died within a matter of weeks.

Harry's daughter Doris was married for a time to director Mervyn LeRoy, whose credits for his father-in-law's company included *Little Caesar* and *I Am a Fugitive from a Chain Gang*. Doris became one of the social lionesses of Hollywood during her marriage to LeRoy, and continued to be a celebrated hostess during her subsequent marriages to director Charles Vidor and impresario Billy Rose. Her son, Warner Leroy, carries on the tradition as the proprietor of New York's posh eatery, Maxwell's Plum. Doris Warner's younger sister, Betty, married writer-producer Milton Sperling, who produced such films as *Murder, Inc.*, *Sun Valley Serenade*, *The Court Martial of Billy Mitchell*, and *Marjorie Morningstar*. Sperling left Warner Bros. in the 1930s to join Darryl Zanuck at Twentieth Century-Fox. When his father-in-law insisted that Sperling return to the fold after the war, he agreed to sign on with Warners. Harry Warner rewarded him with a lucrative production deal, guaranteeing Sperling's company 50 percent of the profits from any films it produced under the Warner banner. The arrangement led a group of Warner stockholders to sue, charging that Sperling's company was being unfairly enriched by Warner Bros. The case was carried all the way to the Supreme Court, and the stockholders lost. "After Warner bookkeeping," Sperling says, "the profits amounted to very little anyway."

Jack Warner's only son, Jack, Jr., may not have been temperamentally equipped for the wheeling and dealing of the movie business, but he entered it as inexorably as a wolf cub joins the pack. Though he was a talented pianist and had some thought of pursuing a career in music, his father vetoed the notion. Jack, Jr. was a Warner, and Warners made pictures.

Father and son had never spent much time together, and their strained relations were aggravated even further when the boy was eighteen and Jack, Sr. divorced his wife Irma and married Ann Page. Jack, Jr. had always been closer to his mother than to his father, and when his parents separated, he naturally took her side. (Or, as one family member has said, "he lacked the cunning to stay neutral.") Nonetheless, he wanted to indicate some respect and affection for his father. Though he was technically not a Junior because his father and he had different middle names, he decided to call himself Jack Warner, Jr. The effort at reconciliation failed. Jack's second wife had a daughter by her previous marriage, Joy Page (who married William Orr, the head of Warner Bros. Television). Jack and Ann also had a daughter, Barbara Warner, who was married at various times to Paris restaurateur Claude Terrail, French composer Raymond Le Senschal, and comedy writer Cy Howard. These two girls became Jack's favorites, and Jack, Jr. was reduced to second-class status within the family.

After graduating from the University of Southern California, Jack, Jr. moved through a succession of mid-level jobs at Warner Bros.—producing industrial films, working in distribution and marketing. Whether it was because his father refused to give him sufficient authority or because of something lacking within himself, Jack Warner, Jr. never became a potent force inside the Warner organization.

In 1958, Jack Warner, Sr. was involved in a near-fatal automobile accident in the south of France. His son immediately flew over to be at his side. Upon his arrival in France, Jack, Jr. issued a statement to the French press which became so garbled in translation that it appeared to indicate that Jack, Sr. was already dead. According to one version of events, Jack, Sr. claimed to have won $50,000 at the gaming tables just before his accident, and he had asked a croupier to hold the money for him. But when the croupier read the news of Warner's "death," he disappeared with the money. Not only was Jack, Sr. infuriated by having lost the cash, he was incensed that his son had even mentioned death in his statement. After that incident, he fired off instructions to Warner Bros. headquarters that Jack, Jr. be canned from the company. When Jack, Jr. returned to work after coming back from France, Milton Sperling recalls, "he found his desk on the sidewalk." Thereafter, father and son were permanently estranged. When Jack Warner, Sr. died at age eighty-six in 1978, it was reported that he had shrewdly written his will in such a way as to preclude the possibility of a legal challenge by his son. He left Jack, Jr. $200,000—just enough to prevent a will contest.

(Ironically, the will was challenged, not by Jack Warner's son, but by his niece Lita, the daughter of his older brother Sam. She claimed that Albert, Harry, and Jack had used $100,000 bequeathed to her by her father to finance their company after her father's death in 1927. In return, each of them had made a deathbed promise to Sam that they would repay the debt to Lita. Both Albert and Harry had left her $1.5 million in their wills, but Jack left her nothing.)

Looking back now on his turbulent relations with his father, Jack Warner, Jr. appears to have made his peace with the past. "My relationship with my father was corroded," he admits, but he adds that the rift was probably inescapable. "To become the dynamic, driving, forceful head of a great enterprise, something is going to give in the home," Jack Warner, Jr. says. "He was a self-centered man, and his family came second. For me, it's the opposite." Jack, Jr. feels that the example of his father's egomania and the unhappy home life that arose as a result impelled him to set very different priorities for himself. A thoughtful, rather gentle man, he made up his mind to be the kind of devoted husband and father that his own father never was, even if certain career goals had to be sacrificed. Married to his wife Barbara for thirty-five years, doting on his daughters and young grandchildren, Jack Warner, Jr. has no regrets about the choice he made. "The front office types, the ulcer-prone, are not to be terribly envied," he says. "They may make a lot of money, but they're going to spend most of it at Cedars-Sinai, or in analysis, or on a wonderful mausoleum."

After being barred from the Warner lot by his father, Jack, Jr. worked briefly in independent production with unspectacular results. He produced a couple of small features in the 1950s: *Brushfire*, starring John Ireland, and *The Man Who Cheated Himself*, with Lee J. Cobb and Jane Wyatt. He tried his hand at other business ventures—an unsuccessful attempt to import cameras from Japan, a Century City gourmet cheese store opened up in partnership with his wife. He calls the gourmet shop a "fascinating" enterprise, though he eventually gave it up. "The retail business was too hard on our feet," he explains.

An extension course in creative writing at the University of California, Los Angeles, led Jack Warner, Jr. to realize his secret ambition of putting together a novel. In 1982, at the age of sixty-six, he brought out *Bijou Dream*, a long, flaccid narrative about the adventures of a driven movie tycoon who wars with his two brothers, abandons his first wife for a slut, and betrays the trust of his only son. The book received little critical support and promptly found its way to the remainder tables. Though Jack Warner, Jr. denies that *Bijou Dream* was a *roman a clef*, insisting that he drew on his observations of many movieland clans for his fictional rendering of events, certain analogies to the history of the Warner family are unmistakable. Harry Warner's former son-in-law, Milton Sperling, describes it as "a very accurate book—probably the most comprehensive history of the Warner tribe written. Why he didn't use the proper names I can only explain by his fear of his father rising from the grave and seizing him by the throat."

Jack Warner, Jr. has explained his own reasons for not writing a true-life history of the Warners. "It's been done, it's being done, it'll be done by others. And mine would probably turn out to be self-serving. Whoever does it should be a non-participant and less involved. Besides, the fiction writer is God on a typewriter. He can move lives around the way he wants to." According to Jack, Jr., he painted his portrait of movie mogul Ham Robbins, the rapacious anti-hero of *Bijou Dream*, with "real colors." Feeling like "God on a typewriter," Jack Warner, Jr. seems to have fulfilled a lifelong goal. After spending his youth and most of his adult life in the shadow of one of Hollywood's most despotic power brokers, it is finally *his* turn to move lives around.

FORTY years before Jack Warner, Jr. set down his vision of the Hollywood rat race in *Bijou Dream*, the scion of another prominent movieland dynasty etched a far more caustic and unsparing picture of backstabbing in Babylon. Budd Schulberg's *What Makes Sammy Run?*, published in 1941, remains one of the most penetrating glimpses of the Hollywood scene ever written by one of Hollywood's own. Narrated by the author's alter-ego, a screenwriter named Al Manheim, the book is Manheim/Schulberg's hard-edged portrait of the quintessential huckster, Sammy Glick—a shamelessly self-promoting louse who claws, cajoles, and connives his way into the upper echelons of the movie business. In a sense,

the book is a lament for the visionary architects of Hollywood—
Griffith, Chaplin, and Budd's father, B. P. Schulberg—whom the
author saw being eaten alive by this new breed of vermin. Chronicling Sammy Glick's swift ascent up the ladder of success, Manheim records a paradigm of the American experience: "all the
glory and the opportunity, the push and the speed, the grinding
of gears and the crap."

In creating *What Makes Sammy Run?*, as well as his subsequent
Hollywood novel, *The Disenchanted*, Budd Schulberg did not just
draw on his experiences as a bright young screenwriter laboring
in the dream factory; he was drawing on his firsthand observations
as a privileged "Hollywood prince." Budd's father, Benjamin Per-
cival Schulberg, was Irving Thalberg's principal rival for the title
of resident intellectual among the early studio chieftains. According to Budd, his father was "a man of literary taste and knowledge,
who read Conrad, Melville, and Galsworthy out loud to us when
we were children, who had a great sense in his best years of the
creativity of other people. This was one of his strong points. One
of his weak ones was not being able to see through the opportunists
who would woo him, flatter him, and eventually undermine him."

B. P. had worked as a publicist and scenarist in New York for
Adolph Zukor and his Famous Players Company. Following Zukor's
dictum that movie actors must be turned into movie stars, B. P.
discovered the value of a clever sobriquet in selling his actors to
the public. It was he who dubbed Mary Pickford "America's
Sweetheart," and he promoted his personal discovery, Clara Bow,
as the "It Girl" (though the term was actually coined by the novelist
Elinor Glyn). In addition to the kewpie doll Clara, B. P. made
stars out of Gary Cooper, Claudette Colbert, Fredric March, and
George Raft. His production of *Underworld* in 1927 broke new
ground in cinematic realism and gave rise to the gangster cycle.
The next year, he produced *Wings*, the last of the silent spectaculars
and the first movie to win an Academy Award. He was promoted
to head of production at Paramount, an enormously powerful position since the studio was then the largest feature production company in America. By 1931, while the nation was in the throes of
the Depression, B. P. Schulberg was earning more than half a
million dollars a year and living like a king.

When Paramount reorganized in 1932, however, Schulberg was
bumped from his job, a victim of the executive reshuffling that
has been a common practice in Hollywood for sixty years. B. P.
had fallen prey to a similar power play a dozen years earlier, when

a man named Hiram Abrams usurped his position at United Artists, the production alliance which Schulberg had conceived to enable major stars like Douglas Fairbanks, Mary Pickford, William S. Hart, and Charlie Chaplin to make pictures as independents. "He sort of lost faith in people at the time," Schulberg's wife later commented. "I remember saying to him that he had nothing on paper to protect himself. But he was very trusting and very naive and only twenty-six. He sued and lost the case." When he was betrayed a second time, Schulberg made up his mind to exit the executive suites and concentrate on producing his own films. But the man who once had the reputation as "the best factory foreman in the business" was losing his touch. His wife and son have suggested that B. P. suffered from a thin skin and was constitutionally incapable of slugging it out in the same ring with such unscrupulous Philistines as L. B. Mayer or Harry Cohn. But screenwriter John Bright, who worked for Schulberg on his production of *John Meade's Woman*, believed that Schulberg's decline "was due mainly to his clutching marriage to cliché—perhaps his only fidelity." In Bright's words, "Schulberg was a lunatic—about dames and booze, with excess of both, but particularly about gambling. Managing a production company was his avocation between benders, and his responsible hours shrank from early afternoon to early cocktails." Like his protégée Clara Bow, Schulberg was one of the tragic casualties of the industry's transition from silent films to talkies, seemingly unable to make the adjustment to the new form. He moved from one studio to another, shunned by the Hollywood muftis. Stubborn, opinionated, used to the exercise of power, B. P. was never one to suffer fools gladly. Now he had many fools to contend with, and most of them were above him in the studio pecking order.

By 1949, Schulberg found himself unemployed and flat broke. In desperation, he placed a full-page ad in *Variety*, begging for work. "This is the only industry I know. I am able to work as hard as anyone in it," he wrote. "I believe the many creative artists I have discovered will agree with me that industry loyalty is a two-way street. Surely I have made some mistakes—as who hasn't? What is the juridical code of the industry? Life imprisonment for a misdemeanor and execution for violating a parking law?" Recalling the inglorious demise of the great silent era director, D. W. Griffith, he went on to ask, "Must we always wait until a productive pioneer is found dead in some 'obscure Hollywood hotel room' before reflecting upon an 'indifferent and forgetful' industry?"

B. P.'s humiliating plea went unanswered. In 1950, he died of a stroke at the Bucks County farm of his son Budd. His final request to Budd was that his ashes be placed in a box and delivered by messenger to the office of his one-time partner and arch-enemy, Louis B. Mayer (with whom he had been feuding ever since the two men shared rented studio space in the 1920s). "Then when the messenger gets to Louis's desk," B. P. instructed his son, "I want him to open the box and blow the ashes in the bastard's face."

B. P. Schulberg had followed the familiar pattern of abandoning his Jewish wife in favor of a younger woman. In his case, however, there were a couple of twists. For one thing, Sylvia Sidney, the young New York actress for whom B. P. left his wife, was herself Jewish. For another, B. P.'s wife was hardly a stereotypical, long-suffering helpmate, bound to hearth and home. Adeline Jaffe Schulberg was the sister of agent-producer Sam Jaffe, who once worked for B. P. at Preferred Pictures. As her husband's fortunes rose, Ad set out to become the doyenne of Hollywood's most sophisticated set. She was a social and political trend-setter, with a quartet of culture heroes consisting of Leon Trotsky, Sigmund Freud, John Dewey, and an obscure domestic relations judge named Ben Lindsey whose theory of "companionate marriage" (a highfalutin term for "try before you buy") she was instrumental in popularizing. Ad also helped to organize the first birth control clinics in the western United States. After her divorce from B. P. in 1933, she moved to London and ran an underground railroad for European intellectuals and performers fleeing the Nazi occupation.

Ad always prided herself on her keen eye for spotting talent. In fact, it was she who discovered the woman who would become B. P.'s paramour, Sylvia Sidney, in a Broadway play called *Bad Girl*. Although B. P. himself was lukewarm about Sylvia's talent at first, Ad convinced him to sign the dark-haired beauty to a Paramount contract. Ad set up her own talent agency and, while her ex-husband's career was sliding downhill, hers flourished. For almost forty years, she reigned as one of the most influential agents in the fields of literature and entertainment, with a roster of clients that included Marlene Dietrich, Fredric March, Fanny Hurst, Rex Reed, and her son Budd.

As the first issue of Ad and B. P. Schulberg's highly-charged union, young Budd Schulberg had a remarkable childhood, which he deftly chronicled in his 1981 memoir, *Moving Pictures: Memories of a Hollywood Prince*. According to Budd, Ad was so ambitious for his intellectual progress that she started him off in the right direction while still carrying him in the womb, spending "as much time as she could in libraries, taking poetry courses at Columbia and reading Tennyson, Milton, and Shelley." Clearly, it was Budd's destiny to become a writer. Upon graduating from Dartmouth, Budd returned to Hollywood in 1936 and was hired by David O. Selznick as a junior writer on *A Star Is Born*. In 1941, the publication of *What Makes Sammy Run?* earned him the fury of Hollywood titans like L. B. Mayer, who saw themselves mercilessly skewered in the novel and who retaliated by trying to have young Schulberg blackballed from future screenwriting assignments. Despite the opposition, he did find work; his screenplays for the hard-hitting melodrama about labor union conflict, *On the Waterfront*, and the incisive satire of television hype, *A Face in the Crowd*, were two of the best examples of film writing to appear in the 1950s. With his brother Stuart, Budd produced the film of his screenplay for *Wind Across the Everglades* in 1958, a taut tale of the battle between an idealistic ecologist (Christopher Plummer) and the leader of a strange swamp-dwelling band, played by Burl Ives. (Stuart Schulberg became a television news executive in the 1960s and was for eight years producer of the NBC *Today* show. He died in 1979.)

Most of Budd Schulberg's writings have centered on men of talent or principle overwhelmed by the forces of crass opportunism, or else destroyed by their own appetite for wealth and fame. In *A Face in the Crowd*, for example, the hayseed-philosopher played by Andy Griffith turns into an egotistical monster as he achieves television stardom. *The Disenchanted*, based on Schulberg's experience collaborating with F. Scott Fitzgerald on a lightweight college caper called *Winter Carnival* for United Artists in 1939, captures the sorry spectacle of one of America's most gifted novelists sinking into dissolution as he squanders his talent on a Hollywood trifle. In 1972 Schulberg published a collection of six essays on twentieth century American writers—Sinclair Lewis, Willliam Saroyan, F. Scott Fitzgerald, Nathanael West, Thomas Heggen, and John Steinbeck—called *The Four Seasons of Success*. In each of his six case studies, Schulberg noted the writer's hunger for success, and the destructive effects of early celebrity or public indifference. The theme is carried through in *Moving*

Pictures, in which Schulberg chronicles the meteoric rise of his own father and shows how the seeds were sown for his subsequent decline.

Certainly the example of B. P. Schulberg's fickle relationship with the movie industry had a seminal impact on his son's literary vision, as well as on the direction of his career as a writer. More than most sons of Hollywood, Budd Schulberg possessed a clear creative talent. But he became increasingly leery of abandoning himself to the same unforgiving business and the same specious definition of "success" that ruined his father. As a result, his screenwriting output waned in the 1960s, and he devoted himself instead to playwriting, fiction, reportage, and teaching, including a stint as director of the Watts Writers Workshop in California. Had he continued to write for the screen, Budd Schulberg might have qualified as one of the movies' brightest talents. Despite a few impressive credits, however, his main contribution to the movies has been as astute observer rather than active participant.

ONE of Budd Schulberg's most stinging essays appeared in 1967. Reviewing Bob Thomas's biography of Columbia Pictures boss Harry Cohn in *Life* magazine, he took the occasion to recount how the barbarous "King Cohn" had personally abused his father B. P., his mother Ad, and his wife, actress Geraldine Brooks. After losing his job at Paramount, B. P. Schulberg suffered the indignity of having to go to work for Cohn. If B. P. was one of Hollywood's more cultivated gentlemen, Cohn was its consummate boor. "You dumb sonofabitch," he taunted B. P., "if you had any brains, you'd still be running Paramount, instead of working for me." At the same time that B. P. was a Columbia producer, his ex-wife Ad was serving as Cohn's East Coast story editor and talent scout. One day Ad came out to visit B. P. on the Columbia back lot. As Ad walked onto the set, Harry Cohn's rasping voice was heard booming over the loudspeakers: "Hey, B. P., how does it feel to have a wife who knows more about pictures than you do?"

Geraldine Brooks's father, James Stroock, head of the Brooks Costume Company in New York, was a friend of Cohn's. As an aspiring actress, Geraldine went to Cohn's office for an interview. She was a teenager at the time, and Cohn scolded the girl for wearing an off-the-shoulder blouse; he then proceeded to yank at the blouse. As Geraldine ran out the door, Cohn shouted after her, "You'll never work in this town again."

While most of the other moguls sought to rise above their

humble origins and acquire the accoutrements of refinement and culture, Harry Cohn remained shamelessly coarse to his dying day. In the words of Elia Kazan, "He liked to be the biggest bug in the manure pile." Cohn had been a pool hustler and song plugger in his youth, and he never lost the swagger of the bold, street-wise manipulator. He was, in Budd Schulberg's words, "The Horatio Alger of the four-letter word who made the Sammy Glicks of Hollywood's Poverty Row in the twenties look like Boy Scout leaders, who rose to something like respectability in the thirties as production chief of a company whose name (Columbia) he could never learn to spell, but whose ironic trademark (Blind Justice holding the torch) was superimposed on some of the great celluloid of the Golden Age—*It Happened One Night*, *Mr. Deeds Goes to Town*, *Mr. Smith Goes to Washington*."

Harry Cohn fought with everyone, but most violently with his brother Jack, who ran Columbia's financial operations out of New York. Their bitter family feud paralleled that of the Warners. So rancorous was the war between the Cohns that for much of the time they headed Columbia Pictures, the brothers could only communicate with one another through intermediaries. Jack once tried to depose Harry as production chief. The coup backfired and only intensified the brothers' mutual suspicion and hatred.

When his first wife could not give him an heir, Harry Cohn divorced her, and he offered to pay a starlet $175,000 if she would bear him a son. The deal was nixed, and he later married an actress named Joan Perry, who did bear him two sons. They also adopted a daughter. After Harry Cohn's death, his widow married actor Laurence Harvey.

Harry Cohn's three children were very young when he died in 1958, and none of them has followed their father into the movie business. Harry, Jr. (who was actually born Harrison Perry Cohn but later asked his father's permission to change his name and become a junior) owns a ranch in the California desert town of Twenty-nine Palms.

Unlike Harry's children, Jack Cohn's three sons all had ambitions to enter the family business. The oldest, Ralph, had little luck when he tried to produce movies but found his niche as the head of Screen Gems, a small television unit that Columbia was forming on the q.t. so as not to outrage exhibitors. Ralph turned Screen Gems into a large and highly profitable operation before his death in 1959.

Jack's second son, Joseph, changed his last name to Curtis and became an advertising executive. But he was soon drawn back to movies. In 1949, Joseph purchased Malcolm Johnson's Pulitzer Prize-winning exposé of union corruption among longshoremen and hired Budd Schulberg to fashion a screenplay on the subject. When Curtis submitted the script to his uncle, Harry Cohn turned it down, and eventually the rights reverted to Schulberg. According to Joseph's son, Bruce, his father's lawyer was also Sam Spiegel's lawyer, and when Curtis's option expired, Spiegel became interested in the property. Thanks to Spiegel's relentlessness, Elia Kazan and Marlon Brando were signed for the film. With those added enticements, Columbia—which had rejected the project initially—agreed to distribute *On the Waterfront*.

When the movie finally reached the screen and was greeted with universal acclaim, Joseph Curtis was devastated. "The picture opened on a rainy Wednesday night at the Astor Theater in New York," his son Bruce reports. "My father stood there watching the crowds go in, and he said, 'If this picture wins the Oscar, I'll die.' He was dead that Saturday. He was only thirty-six."

After his fatal heart attack, Joseph's company, Monticello Film Corporation, now under the direction of his widow, filed suit against Schulberg, Kazan, Spiegel, and Columbia Pictures—the Cohn family's studio—for "unlawful appropriation," demanding all profits and revenues from *On the Waterfront*. The film did indeed win the Academy Award as best picture of 1954, and Monticello asked the Academy to take back Schulberg's Oscar, contending that Monticello was "the true owner of the story." But with the primary witness dead, the lawsuit was settled out of court and the Oscar flap dismissed. Bruce Cohn Curtis reports, "My grandfather, Jack Cohn, took my mother to the Oscars that year, and he said to everybody, 'That's my son's movie.' Jack died two years later. He never got over it."

Jack's surviving son, Robert Cohn, was a contract producer at Columbia for twenty years. His credits were mostly undistinguished: *Rusty Leads the Way*, *The Killer That Stalked New York*, *The Barefoot Mailman*, *Mission Over Korea*, and his most profitable picture, *The Interns*. In 1967, he produced a semi-documentary, *The Young Americans*, celebrating a wholesome teenage singing group. It played in a few cities and promptly bombed, but Cohn entered it in the Academy Awards competition of 1968. The picture won the Oscar as best documentary, and Cohn proudly presented the statuette to his mother shortly before she died—a recompense for the trophy which the family felt it had been denied for *On the Waterfront*. When the Academy learned that *The Young Americans* had actually been in theatrical release the previous year, Robert Cohn became the only person in history forced to return an Oscar; the Academy Award that had sat briefly on the mantelpiece of Jack Cohn's widow was ignominiously removed. "Producing that picture was my last activity at Columbia," Robert Cohn says.

Of the third generation Cohns, one still works in Hollywood. Joseph Curtis's son Bruce has been an active producer for over a decade. When he entered the business, he decided to retrieve the name of Cohn, dubbing himself Bruce Cohn Curtis. "I had this sense of dynasty," Bruce explains. "I felt the Cohn name should continue. It didn't hurt the Kennedys or the Rockefellers to carry on the family name. I look at those people as role models."

Bruce Cohn Curtis's first production, *Otley*, starring Tom Courtenay, received a few nice reviews but died at the box office. Later, Bruce became better known for producing exploitation movies. "I have been called the low-budget Ross Hunter," he once said of himself, though even that appellation may be a bit exalted for the perpetrator of *Joyride*, *Roller Boogie*, *Hell Night*, and *The Seduction*. The high point of Bruce's career has been the TV movie *Born Innocent*, best remembered as the opus in which Linda Blair is violated by a broomstick. The low point was unquestionably a comedy called *Chatterbox*, about the travails of a woman with a talking and singing vagina. "I had to live that down for a long time," Bruce Cohn Curtis confesses. "It's not one I want to put on my tombstone. And yet the people who saw the picture liked it very much."

Tombstones seem to be on his mind lately. "Our side of the family had a big mausoleum out in Brooklyn," Bruce reports. "And then everybody sort of moved to California—my grandmother, my mother, my uncle. So we decided to buy a new family plot out here at Hollywood Memorial Park. We bought the last piece of lake frontage. We didn't know it, but it turned out to be right next to Harry Cohn's place. Isn't that incredible? So we brought Grandpa and Uncle Ralph and my father out, and they're all here in this big esophagus."

If the legend of the Cohn family lives on, it is less for the quality of their movie-making than for their occasional malapropisms and for their enduring, sometimes endearing, vulgarity. As Bruce Cohn Curtis contemplates the family "esophagus," he offers an unwittingly pessimistic speculation on the probable future of this once potent clan: "Uncle Harry's there in Hollywood Memorial Park. Joan Cohn will be there. And we're right next to him. One day all the Cohns of Columbia Pictures will be there."

ALTHOUGH rumor had it that the remains of another founding father, Walt Disney, were cryogenically preserved and awaiting a twenty-first century thaw, the truth is that he too rests in a family crypt. Some of his longtime associates felt that Walt would have turned over in his Forest Lawn grave had he known that his company's biggest hit since his death would turn out to be *Splash*, about a sex-hungry mermaid parading through Manhattan in the buff. But Walt's genius was his ability to apprehend the mood of the times, and chances are he would have endorsed the aquatic romp.

The puritanical influence at the Disney studio was not so much Walt as his older brother Roy. Like the brothers Cohn and Warner, Walt and Roy carried on a lifelong tug-of-war. The Disney company always stood apart from the rest of Hollywood, largely because of the specialized product it purveyed, but also because of the special background of the men who ran it. Right from the start, however, there were intriguing similarities between this middle-American WASP clan and the powerful Jewish families who dominated the industry.

After serving in the Army during World War I, Roy Oliver Disney had taken a job working as a teller at the First National Bank in Kansas City. When he contracted tuberculosis, he was sent to recuperate at a Veterans Hospital in West Los Angeles. Walt, who had dreams of breaking into the movie business, sensed an opportunity and followed his brother to Southern California in 1923. He had tried his hand at making animated cartoons the year before in Kansas City, but his Laugh-O-Grams Film Corporation quickly went bankrupt. Determined to make a go of it this time, Walt borrowed $200 from Roy, $500 from an uncle, and kicked in $40 of his own to hire a small crew of animators, painters, and inkers. In 1926, the Disney Brothers Studio set up shop in the Silver Lake district, just north of downtown Los Angeles. Walt convinced Roy that a single name would be more easily remembered by the public, and so the company was re-dubbed the Walt Disney Studio. Hoping to enlist a larger studio to distribute their cartoons featuring Mickey Mouse, the Disneys approached MGM chief Louis B. Mayer, who turned them down flat. Mayer scoffed at the notion that the little rodent would ever make it in pictures since, as L. B. informed the Disneys condescendingly, it was common knowledge that "every woman is frightened of a mouse." From then on, the Disney brothers determined to go it alone.

While Walt drew the "cels" for their animated menagerie, Roy acted as sometime cameraman and full-time bookkeeper. His stolid, frugal temperament complemented Walt's more extravagant, free-wheeling manner. Without Roy's watchful eye on the company accounts, Walt's second business venture might well have met the same ignominious fate as the first. But as the Disney product began to find its market and the studio started expanding, Roy's penny-pinching and skepticism proved more and more nettlesome to Walt.

By 1932, the Disneys' "Silly Symphony" series had revolutionized the animation industry and the Mickey Mouse fan club had enrolled more than a million members. Walt was fascinated by the new color techniques that the Technicolor Corporation was just beginning to introduce. He was working on a cartoon called "Flowers and Trees" and he wanted to add color to the picture. But, as Walt later confessed, he was already laying out more money for production than Roy saw coming in, and Roy was growing nervous; the idea of squandering more dollars to experiment with the new color process "stuck in his craw," Walt told his daughter Diane. "Roy has always lived with figures," Walt explained. "People who do that are apt to add up the cost of the thing they've already produced instead of adding up how much it may earn for them." In the end, Walt won the battle, and the first "Silly Symphony" in Technicolor brought the Disneys a new rush of bookings as well as the first Academy Award ever given to a cartoon.

The conflict between Walt's innnovative instincts and Roy's closefisted management followed the brothers throughout the four decades of their partnership. Their fiercest quarrels came in the mid-1940s, when Walt wanted to commit the company to making full-length cartoon features. Roy contended that neither of the two projects Walt proposed, *Peter Pan* and *Alice in Wonderland*, would ever find an audience. When Walt later revealed his ambitious plans to create a vast amusement complex in a stretch of Orange County farmland, Roy shook his head in disbelief. To him, the plans for Disneyland looked like little more than the blueprint for a fool's paradise.

Yet it would be wrong to imply that Roy Disney's nay-saying did nothing more than inhibit or infuriate his younger brother. In some sense, Walt craved his brother's penurious presence; it liberated him from the need to fret about finances himself. Walt was always notoriously nonchalant about money; as late as 1956, he had only $6000 in his personal bank account. With Roy around to play the role of cautious grown-up, Walt could give his own child-like imagination free rein.

Stan Margulies, the top television producer (*Roots*, *The Thorn Birds*) who once worked as a publicist for the Disney Studio in the 1950s, remembers a screening-room incident that illustrates the point. Walt had gathered all his top executives to view footage of the climactic episode in *20,000 Leagues Under the Sea*, containing an elaborate underwater battle with a giant squid. "They had built a tank," Margulies recalls, "and we had special effects men coming out of our eyeballs. But when we looked at the squid fight cut together, it really wasn't good. The lights went on and Walt said, 'We're going to have to do it again.' He didn't hesitate for a minute. That was like a $300,000 decision at a time when $300,000 was the equivalent of $3 million today. A lot of producers would have considered the price tag and said, 'It's good enough.' I always remembered that as one of the most courageous producing decisions I ever saw. Apart from Walt's genius, the great thing he had going for him was that when he said, 'It's not good enough, let's do it again,' he knew that Roy was the one who would go out and find the $300,000. That wasn't Walt's concern. Roy's job was to find the money." For his part, Roy Disney had no illusions about his function in the organization. "My job is to help Walt do the things he wants to do," he once declared.

In the mid-1960s, Walt was diagnosed as having lung cancer, but he worked to complete his most far-reaching plans; he was drawing sketches for his proposed city of the future, Epcot Center, as he lay dying in the hospital. After Walt's death in 1966, it fell to Roy Disney to carry on the policies and programs of the company that bore his brother's name. For the five years that Roy was in charge of the Disney Studio, the company managed to hold its own. But the Magic Kingdom was never quite the same. "Everything was less happy after Walt died," says Robert Stevenson, the favored Disney director who made the studio's top-grossing picture, *Mary Poppins*, in 1964. "The family feeling was gone."

Roy Disney's decision to run the company as a team operation—depending on the advice and consent of a loyal set of executive cronies Walt and he had assembled over the years—was always viewed as a stopgap measure. "I know a committee form is a lousy form in this business," Roy admitted, "but it's the best we've got until someone in the younger crowd shows he's got the stature to take over leadership." Roy himself understood that he was both too old and probably too unimaginative to fill that role.

As Roy looked to the "younger crowd" for his successor, two obvious candidates emerged. Roy's son, Roy Edward Disney, came to work at the studio in the early 1950s, producing some of the True-Life Adventure features and Disney TV programs of the period. He moved steadily up the ranks and was named to the board of directors in 1967. His chief rival for the top post was Walt's son-in-law, a former pro football player named Ron Miller who joined the company three years after marrying Diane Disney in 1954. (Diane's sister Sharon was married to an architect named Robert Borgfeldt—later changed to Brown—who worked with Walt in developing Disney World; he died in 1967.) Like Roy Edward Disney, Ron Miller was elected to the Disney board of directors in 1967 and he, too, was given increasingly responsible management positions with the company.

Roy Disney died in 1971; five years later, an internal battle developed over which of the two rival heirs apparent, Ron Miller or Roy Edward Disney, would be named production head of the Disney Studio. Miller won out, and Roy Edward left the company, announcing plans to "strike out on my own and do things that were difficult to do within the Disney organization." Most of the movies he talked about making never reached the screen. One that did was a low-budget documentary about yacht racing entitled *Pacific High*, which included a few interviews with some tough-talking sailors. The seamen's raunchy language turned *Pacific High* into the first film bearing the Disney name to receive an "R" rating.

Despite the fact that he lost his power struggle with Ron Miller, Roy Edward Disney is hardly suffering financially. He owns a broadcasting company, and his family holds almost half a million shares of Disney stock. When he resigned from the Disney board in 1984, amid speculation that he would lead a proxy battle to take over the company, he was its largest single stockholder. According to *Forbes* magazine, which includes his name regularly in its annual listing of the 400 richest men in America, his minimum net worth stands at $180 million.

Having bested Roy Edward Disney for the job of executive vice president in charge of production in 1976, Ron Miller was easily catapulted to the very top rungs of the Disney hierarchy. In 1980, he was named president and chief operating officer of the company, and, in 1983, was appointed chief executive officer. "With the successful opening of Epcot Center and preparations nearly complete for both the start of Tokyo Disneyland and the Disney Channel this April," announced Disney board chairman Carl Walker in 1983, "it is a logical time for Ron to assume leadership of the company." Conspicuously absent from Walker's statement was any mention of the Disney record in the area of operations which had first propelled the company to prominence—filmmaking. Although its television and amusement park enterprises had continued to generate profits in the years since the founding Disney brothers died, the feature film division had become something of a loss leader for the corporation. Trying to broaden its audience by modifying its squeaky-clean image, Disney embarked on a slate of PG-rated films, most of which were box-office duds. Hugely expensive productions such as *The Black Hole*, *Something Wicked This Way Comes*, and *Tron* disappointed expectations. Other more modest pictures, such as *Tex* with Matt Dillon and *Night Crossing* with John Hurt, did even worse. For the most part, the Disney division has depended on reissues of such classics as *Fantasia*, *Cinderella*, and *Snow White* to generate revenues for the company.

In 1983, Miller brought in a new production chief, Richard Berger, formerly a vice-president at Twentieth Century Fox, to set Disney on a brand new course. Berger tried to woo new filmmakers to the Disney lot, and he assured the industry that Disney, under its new Touchstone division, was now prepared to back the same movies that any other studio would make. As one of Berger's associates put it, "We'll consider anything—short of out-and-out raunch and slasher films."

But what is the price of such a policy? For years, Disney had the distinction of being the last surviving studio operated like a family business, and it was the last to give its own unmistakable imprint to all its products. As film critic Richard Schickel has pointed out, even into the 1970s—long after the absolute power of the other studios had evaporated—Disney stood firm. It refused to join the bidding for overpriced properties; maintained its own staff of contract writers, producers, and directors; and safely assumed that the Disney imprimatur above a title meant more to the moviegoing public than the name of any star. But while the American families who were the bulwark of Disney's market continued to watch the Disney TV shows and patronize the Disney amusement parks, they seemed to lose interest in its G-rated picture shows. In attempting to move beyond its traditional audience, the Disney studio is caught in a bind. It must compromise its biggest selling point—the purity of the Disney image—in order to meet the vagaries of the marketplace.

To some that may have seemed like a no-win situation, but Disney's maiden effort under the new Touchstone label, the boy-meets-mermaid comedy *Splash* starring Tom Hanks and Darryl Hannah, suggested that the new policy may succeed quite nicely. The film garnered the best opening box office returns of any picture in Disney history. In marketing the film, Touchstone did an effective job of blurring its link to the studio that once produced *Mary Poppins* and *Cinderella*, and the teenage audience which might otherwise have sneered at a whimsical Disney fairy tale enthusiastically embraced the picture. Other Touchstone films made less of a splash, and in late 1984, Ron Miller was finally ousted from the studio, along with Richard Berger. Paramount's successful president, Michael Eisner, took over the job of running Disney. Roy Edward Disney returned to the board, where he sits alongside Walt's widow, Lillian.

Walter Elias Disney was certainly the most visionary of the early Hollywood moguls. He was the first to recognize the need to diversify his company, the first to exploit the vast production possibilities of television, and the first to create an entertainment empire that extended beyond the movie screen and would eventually reach around the world. The profits from those enterprises have kept his company moving ahead even when its film production has faltered, and they have kept it strong enough to prevent its being swallowed up by the conglomerates which have already absorbed Paramount, Columbia, Universal, and Warner Bros. With its extensive land holdings, its low debt, and its sometimes undervalued stock, Disney has long been a potential target for takeover by some larger corporate entity. Without the farsightedness and ingenuity of the Magic Kingdom's founding father, the last of the great family-run studios could be headed into the same impersonal void that has consumed all the others.

2

BLOOD FEUDS:
The Mayer-Selznick-Goetz Clan

"Blood is thicker than 'The Hollywood Reporter,' but not much..."

—WILLIAM GOETZ

THE moviemakers of Hollywood's heyday were often described as America's royalty, but when they died, the splendor of their lifestyle died with them. Today, only a few vestiges of that imperial grandeur remain. A visitor to Edith Mayer Goetz's Holmby Hills mansion may feel that he is stepping back in time, re-entering that lost realm. The butler who opens the door carries impeccable credentials, having served the Queen Mother at Buckingham Palace before taking up residence at this lesser palace in Southern California. He shares the servants' quarters with a small platoon— Edith's personal maid, downstairs maid, kitchen maid, chauffeur, cook, private secretary, and gardener. (There is also a separate orchid tender for the greenhouse.) Inside the Goetz home, the pale green walls are lined with Monets, Cezannes, Renoirs, and Van Goghs. The Louis XV end tables are covered with framed photographs of modern potentates: in some of these pictures, Edith's father, Louis B. Mayer, stands alongside Winston Churchill or William Randolph Hearst; in others, Edith and her late husband, producer William Goetz, are seen chatting with Harry Truman or Pablo Picasso.

These days the house is usually silent. Except for her retinue of servants, Edith Goetz lives alone, as she has since her husband's death in 1969. Occasionally, she holds a small dinner party that is a pale echo of more glorious affairs in the past. Billy Wilder once said, "The highest accolade for someone coming into this town was to be invited, not to Pickfair, but to the Goetzes. The Goetzes had the best food, the best people, and the best things on the walls!"

Edith maintains meticulous records of all her dinner parties, a complete book of menus and guest lists, and she still leafs through them from time to time. The menus and invitations were always cross-referenced, so that no guest was ever served the same food twice. "You can read the whole history of Hollywood just from my book of menus," Edith says. "You'll see Miss Rosalind Russell and Mr. Freddie Brisson at one party. Then Miss Russell and some other man. Then Miss Russell and Mr. Brisson quite often. And all of a sudden it's Mr. and Mrs. Brisson. Or you'll see Alexander Korda and Merle Oberon a couple of times, then Mr. and Mrs. Korda, then Sir Alex and Lady Korda. The other day I was looking at the guest list for the party we had when J. Arthur Rank bought International Pictures. The people who were there! Cary Grant, Ronald Colman, Gary Cooper, Sam Goldwyn, Judy Garland and Vincente Minnelli, Henry Fonda, Greer Garson, Joan Crawford, and on and on."

Today the Goetz home no longer welcomes such a star-studded assemblage. The mansion is a repository of mementos. And with its abundant works of art, all perfectly positioned and carefully lit, it almost literally has the look of a museum. An air of melancholy hovers over the house, for the resplendent world that it evokes has disappeared. "It's mind-boggling to me that Edie still lives in that huge house all by herself," says her former son-in-law, Richard Shepherd. "I don't know how anybody lives that way or even thinks that such a world exists any more."

SEVERAL miles across town, in a more modest home perched beneath the famous H-O-L-L-Y-W-O-O-D sign, Edith Goetz's nephew, Daniel Selznick, also spends much of his time reflecting on the family heritage. Born in 1936, Danny is the son of Irene Mayer Selznick (Edith's younger sister) and David O. Selznick, and the favorite grandson of Louis B. Mayer. Danny prefers to live unpretentiously, rather than in the opulent style to which his lineage might seem to entitle him. A soft-spoken, intelligent man, he drives an old convertible with a rip in the canvas roof, not the obligatory Rolls Royce or Mercedes-Benz. But then, Daniel Selznick has not really "made it" in Hollywood. He wants desperately to produce films, but has so far made little headway. "I wish Danny could get that first picture made," his aunt, Edith Goetz, says with a sad shake of her head.

BOTH Edith Goetz and Daniel Selznick received a measure of attention with the publication of Irene Selznick's best-selling autobiography, *A Private View*, in 1983. Over the years Danny has vainly tried to mend the rift between his mother and his aunt, a rift that has been building for half a century. Irene's book, with its sarcastic, sometimes gratuitous digs at Edith, has driven a final wedge between the two sisters. In her memoirs Irene portrays Edith as a snob, an opportunist, and a selfish social butterfly more concerned about her dinner parties than about their father's fatal illness. As Christopher Lehmann-Haupt noted in his sensibly lukewarm review of the book in the *New York Times*, Irene lavishes bouquets on her friends and hurls "rotten tomatoes" at her foes, most of which "land directly in the face of the author's sister, Edith Goetz, who comes out sounding difficult, if not impossible, though that may just be because Mrs. Selznick has her way with their history." Edith calls the book "a pack of lies." She claims that she has only read scattered parts of it. "Why should I read anything negative?" she asks. "If jealousy is the reason for her comments, then it only breeds hatred."

This bitter feud between two women in their late seventies may seem somewhat pathetic in its vitriol, but it epitomizes the strife that has continually surfaced within this most legendary moviemaking clan. Of all Hollywood families, the Mayer-Selznick-Goetz dynasty is the most seminal and perhaps the most illustrious. Their successes were spectacular, their failures catastrophic, and when they fought, their conflicts were almost Shakespearean in magnitude. Film writer Molly Haskell has noted the "Lear-like overtones" in the story of the embattled Mayer daughters vying for their father's favor. These characters may not war in iambic pentameter, but their family dramas have been played on a grand scale.

THE fates of the Mayers and the Selznicks were intertwined over a period of six decades. Both Lewis J. Selznick and Louis B. Mayer, the family patriarchs, were immigrant Jews born in Russia. Lewis J. Zeleznick, born on May 2, 1870, came from Kiev to Pittsburgh, where he began work as a jeweler. He decided to enter the movie business after a meeting with a boyhood chum, a herring salesman turned film producer. Lewis told his family, "Today I met my old friend Mark Dintenfass. He is the dumbest man I ever knew. If he can make money in pictures, anybody can."

In 1912, with his name Americanized to Selznick, Lewis followed Dintenfass into the Universal Film Manufacturing Company in New York. Selznick got his first job with a bold ploy. Arriving at the Universal studio to peddle jewelry, he found an empty desk and sat down, announcing that he was a new employee; before long he promoted himself to general manager. (That kind of moxie has not entirely disappeared. It is amusing to note that, some sixty years later, Steven Spielberg claims that he utilized a similar maneuver to situate himself on the Universal lot and thus launch his own spectacular career. Legend has it that he slipped away from the Universal tour, found a vacant office, and settled in. These stories may be apocryphal, but both Selznick and Spielberg were shrewd enough to perceive the publicity value of such engaging myths.)

In 1915 Lewis Selznick joined with Arthur Spiegel in the World Sales Corporation and produced his first silent film, *The Common Law*. He signed many rising stars—Clara Kimball Young, Norma Talmadge, the Russian actress Nazimova—and bought popular Broadway plays for filming; some of his early adaptations included *Trilby*, with Clara Kimball Young, and *Wildfire*, with Lillian Russell and Lionel Barrymore. Later Selznick and Adolph Zukor formed the Select Film Corporation. Perhaps Selznick's major contribution to the film industry was his recommendation of Will Hays, President Warren Harding's Postmaster General, to be head of the newly formed Motion Picture Producers and Distributors of America. It was Hays who, in 1930, introduced the Motion Picture Production Code, the industry's infamous censorship charter which sanitized—and emasculated—American movies for almost four decades.

Mayer was born fifteen years after Selznick, in Minsk. His exact birthday is unknown, though he later settled on July 4, as an expression of his patriotic zeal. Actually, Mayer emigrated first to New Brunswick, Canada, where he joined his father in the junk business. But when he moved to Boston, he bought and operated a small movie house; from theater ownership he moved into distribution, and later into production as well.

Like Selznick, Mayer helped to set the moral tone for the new medium, though in his case it was a far more conscious plan. Puritanism was a deep-seated part of his personality. He was devastated by the death of his mother in 1913, when he was still a young man living in Boston. His reverence for her was at the root of all his moral values. When he first met screenwriter Frances Marion, Mayer told her, "I worship good women, honorable men, and saintly mothers." Mayer's first film production, in 1918, was called *Virtuous Wives*; its title summed up his credo. "I will make only pictures that I won't be ashamed to have my children see," he proudly declared. "I'm determined that my little Edie and my little Irene will never be embarrassed. And they won't, if all my pictures are moral and clean."

Mayer and Lewis Selznick had crossed paths a few years earlier, when Mayer was the New England distributor for Selznick's Select Film Corporation. The methodical and cold-blooded Mayer and the hedonistic, mercurial Selznick took an instant dislike to each other. Their personalities were utterly antithetical. A born showman and gambler, Lewis was known as "Selznick the Jester," and he gave his lavish movie premieres a raucous circus atmosphere. When called before a Senate investigating committee looking into charges of financial misdealings in the infant film industry, Selznick testified that he had invested $1,000 in one movie company and cleared $105,000 ten weeks later. Echoing his slander of his old pal Dintenfass, Selznick gleefully told Congress, "Less brains are necessary in the motion picture industry than in any other." After the Russian Revolution Lewis cabled Czar Nicholas: "When I was a boy in Russia your police treated my people very badly. However no hard feelings. Hear you are now out of work. If you come to New York can give you fine position acting in pictures." Unfortunately, Nicholas had a previous engagement—with a Bolshevik firing squad.

Selznick brought his two older sons, Myron and David, into the business at an early age. The two participated in story conferences at their father's studio while still in their teens. (The youngest son, Howard, had little interest in movies, and little of the drive possessed by his father and two brothers. David and Myron would one day set Howard up as a florist, but the "Forget-Me-Not Flower Shop," in an unhappy travesty of its name, faded quickly into oblivion.) Even in public school, the boys were given allowances of several hundred dollars a week and told, "Spend it all. Give it away. Throw it away." Their father encouraged them to live beyond their means, so that they would be impelled to work that much harder.

Lewis Selznick's extravagance eventually proved his own

undoing. In 1923 he overextended himself and was forced to declare bankruptcy. The stars he had under contract left the fold, and he searched in vain for a benefactor to rescue him. A few years earlier, when he broke away from the Select Pictures Corporation to form his own company, Lewis had taken most of Select's stars with him. His ex-partner Adolph Zukor was furious and vowed revenge. After Selznick's bankruptcy, Zukor refused to come to Lewis's aid. Louis B. Mayer also turned a deaf ear to Selznick's pleas for help. Because of his high-handedness during better times, Lewis Selznick now found himself without allies in the business.

The reversal in the fortunes of the Selznick family was staggering. From a seventeen-room, $18,000-a-year apartment on Park Avenue, Lewis moved his family into a tiny three-room flat. His wife sold her jewelry, fired the chef, and learned to cook all over again. During the next several years Selznick kept trying to regain a foothold in the film business, but all his efforts were futile. When he died in 1933, he had been out of work for a decade, and his name had been forgotten by the new generation.

The trauma of Selznick's sudden descent from wealth to poverty plagued his sons all their lives. In the case of Myron Selznick, the pain of his father's failure created an obsessive desire for revenge. Myron became an agent, and by the mid-1930s he had succeeded in assembling the most dazzling roster of clients in Hollywood—including such stars as Katharine Hepburn, Carole Lombard, Myrna Loy, Helen Hayes, Ginger Rogers, Fred Astaire, Gary Cooper, Henry Fonda, and Laurence Olivier, as well as directors Frank Capra, Ernst Lubitsch, and Leo McCarey. Myron forced the studio executives—his father's foes—to pay dearly for all this talent. He even broke an unspoken rule of the industry when he stole Paramount's three biggest stars—Kay Francis, William Powell, and Ruth Chatterton—and spirited them over to Warner Bros. The head of Paramount was his father's nemesis, Adolph Zukor, and while Zukor fumed, Myron Selznick felt that he had scored a victory for Lewis. Top screenwriter Ben Hecht said of Myron, "His work of vengeance changed the Hollywood climate. It doubled, tripled, and quadrupled the salaries of writers, actors, and directors, myself among them."

Like his father, Myron was an extravagant gambler; he was also an inveterate womanizer and a heavy drinker. Some of those close to him speculated that he secretly detested being an agent and longed to do more creative work. In any case he destroyed himself quickly and effectively; he died of a heart attack in 1944, at the age of forty-five.

Although David Selznick would eventually fall victim to some of the same reversals as his father and his brother, no one would have guessed it early in his career, when he swiftly established himself as one of the most brilliant young producers in the business. In 1926, at the age of twenty-five, David applied for a job at Metro-Goldwyn-Mayer, but Louis B. Mayer remembered his conflicts with David's father years before, and he resolved that no Selznick would ever work for him. Undeterred, David went directly to Mayer's superior, Nicholas Schenck, president of Loew's, the company that owned MGM. Schenck had met and liked David Selznick several years earlier; he bypassed Mayer and arranged a job for David as assistant to Harry Rapf, the man in charge of all B-pictures at MGM. Selznick immediately demonstrated his intelligence and ingenuity in making low-budget Westerns, and within a matter of months, his salary rose from $100 to $3,000 a week. He won the grudging respect of his father's old enemy, L. B. Mayer, but he clashed with Mayer's head of production, young Irving Thalberg, and left the studio soon afterwards.

WHEN David Selznick came to work at MGM in 1926, it was already on its way to becoming the top studio in town. In 1924 Mayer's own production company had merged with the Goldwyn company and the Loews' Metro company to form Metro-Goldwyn-Mayer. In planning the merger, Mayer remembered that Lewis Selznick's name had been lost when he created the Select Pictures Corporation with Adolph Zukor. Mayer regarded that as the beginning of Selznick's downfall, and he resolved that his own name would never be forgotten now that he was in a position to insure its survival. Written into his MGM contract was the provision that "in all advertising and paid publicity the name of Louis B. Mayer shall be prominently mentioned as the producer of said motion picture photoplays."

If Mayer's approach to business differed from that of Lewis Selznick, he was also Selznick's antithesis in his attitude toward raising his children. To be sure, he had daughters rather than sons, and he demonstrated the Jewish father's fiercely protective stance toward his two princesses, Edith (born in 1905) and Irene (born in 1907). As they grew older, both sisters chafed under their father's strictures. "We weren't allowed to go to dances at school,"

Edie recalls. "In fact, we rarely left our house without our parents. If I had a beau, Dad would take the phone calls."

Mayer controlled his daughters' lives in other ways as well. He was adamantly opposed to their seeking either higher education or gainful employment. "A daughter of *mine* go to college?" he once asked scornfully. "Become an *intellectual*?"

Edie studied ballet and voice and harbored dreams of becoming an actress, but her father squelched these ambitions. She recalls her disappointment: "When I was eighteen, I had an opportunity to audition in New York. I remember going to see Dad and telling him I wanted to go. I'll never forget his answer. He said to me, 'You're the best goddamn actress of 'em all. But you need it for living.'"

Ironically, although Mayer's attitude toward his daughters may seem crudely paternalistic and sexist, in his professional life he demonstrated less prejudice toward women than almost any other early studio head. He constantly depended on the advice of strong, maternal figures. While still in Boston, his first business partner was a woman named Fanny Mittenthal. The first film he produced was directed by a woman, Lois Weber. He gave screenwriter Frances Marion a privileged position at MGM, where her credits included several Garbo films, such as *Anna Christie* and *Camille*. Mayer's assistant, Ida Koverman, former secretary to Herbert Hoover, was known to be a trusted confidante; anyone who wanted to get to Mayer had to be cleared by her. And in his later years, he put his own life in the hands of a female physician, Dr. Jessie Marmorston. Like Mayer, Dr. Marmorston was a Russian-Jewish immigrant who had grown up in poverty; she had put herself through medical school at a time when women doctors were a rarity. Mayer was impressed by her perseverance, and he sought her counsel in many personal and professional matters.

When it came to his own daughters, however, Mayer wanted them sheltered from the working world. Edith claims that she does not regret giving up the idea of a career. Her life's course was set when she met William Goetz, an up-and-coming producer and the youngest brother in another prominent movie clan. Goetz's brother Harry was treasurer at Paramount; another brother, Jack, had started an important film laboratory; a third brother, Ben, was a founder of Republic Pictures. Ben later became the head of MGM's offices in London, while still another brother, Charles, worked for United Artists in New York.

William Goetz had a reputation as a quipster and wit. When

Edith Mayer was introduced to him at the Ambassador Hotel in Los Angeles, she had already heard about his irreverent sense of humor. "I had never laughed so much in my whole life," she says of their first date. "I think I fell in love with him right then."

After checking into Goetz's background, Louis B. Mayer asked that the new suitor come to dinner so that he could pass inspection. "Bill was as relaxed as he could be," Edie recalls. "He was so funny. But Dad didn't laugh once. Afterwards Dad said to me, 'He's a very nice young man. But what's with the jokes?' It wasn't jokes. Bill never told jokes. It was just quick wit. But Dad didn't appreciate it. Later, when we got married, Dad would laugh if Bill said, 'That's a green book on the table.' He had very little sense of humor himself, but he knew that Bill was a wit, so he figured that anything Bill said must be funny."

When Edith married Bill Goetz in March of 1930, their wedding was the social event of the season. "When we got engaged," Edie reports, "I said, 'I don't want a large wedding, Dad.' And he said, 'The wedding isn't for you. It's for *me*.' Adrian designed my dress and my veil. I think there were about 700 or 750 people at the wedding, all movie people. Most of them I didn't even know. I hadn't met Mary Pickford yet, but she was there. There were gifts from the President and the governor. I even remember a man with a gun over his shoulder patrolling the house to guard all the presents."

Just six weeks after Edith's marriage to Bill Goetz, there was another wedding in the Mayer household. At a New Year's Eve party in 1926, Irene had met David Selznick, who was then working for Harry Rapf at MGM. "Harry felt that Dad was holding us on too tight a leash," Edith recalls, "and he arranged for both Irene and me to meet David Selznick. I got one look at this zebra, and I said to Irene, 'You can have him.'" Irene was not especially impressed with the brash young producer either, but their paths continued to cross, and eventually a romance developed.

Mayer disapproved at first, chiefly because of his disdain for Lewis Selznick and his extravagant ways. Mayer gradually came to accept the match, but he was furious when Irene and David told him that they wanted to be married in just a few weeks' time. What's more, they would not allow him to plan the kind of extravaganza he had thrown for Edie. And when L. B's father died unexpectedly, Irene and David still refused to postpone their wedding. A test of wills ensued, and tempers had not cooled by the time the ceremony took place in April of 1930. Mayer did not speak to either Irene or David at the wedding.

The conflict over the wedding seems to have created a strong measure of ill will between Edith and Irene. In her autobiography, Irene says that she expected Edie to take her side against her father, but was let down by Edie's refusal to plunge into the fray. Edith claims to have no recollection of these backstage intrigues. "Why should I have come to Irene's defense?" she asks innocently. "The whole thing had nothing to do with me."

In any case, Mayer could not delay the marriage of Irene and David, which actor/producer John Houseman has called "Hollywood's most glamorous dynastic union." And whatever Mayer's initial reservations about David Selznick as a son-in-law, once the marriage was a *fait accompli*, family loyalty took precedence over any feelings of displeasure or anger. Mayer had always believed in making his business a family business. He had already appointed his younger brother Jerry as the studio's general manager, even though they quarreled constantly. In addition, his nephew Jack Cummings (the son of his sister Ida) was a favored producer at MGM.

Now Mayer intended to see to it that his sons-in-law would take their places under his command. When David Selznick married Irene, he was employed by Paramount, but he soon left his job there, frustrated by his subservient position. He wanted to set up his own independent production company, but he knew that he could do it only if the major studios would agree in advance to distribute his films. His father-in-law called a meeting of all the studio heads and warned them that if they agreed to Selznick's proposal, a dangerous precedent would be established, and the absolute power of the studios would be broken. The other studio chiefs heeded Mayer's advice, and Selznick's dream of an independent company collapsed. He reluctantly went to work at RKO, where he oversaw the production of *King Kong*, the ingenious fantasy that set the standard for monster movies in the years to come. He also cast Katharine Hepburn in her very first movie, *A Bill of Divorcement*.

David Selznick's track record at RKO was impressive, but when Merlin Hall Aylesworth succeeded Hiram Brown as president of the studio, Aylesworth changed Selznick's contract, reducing David's autonomy. This was exactly the situation that Louis B. Mayer had anticipated, and he felt the time was right to lure his son-in-law back to MGM. Mayer offered Selznick a choice contract—a $4,000-a-week salary and a free hand in choosing properties and stars. Irving Thalberg, in frail health, suspected that his influence at the studio was being usurped. A trade paper, *The Hollywood Spectator*, sympathized with Thalberg and announced the appointment of Selznick with the line that has become the classic apothegm on Hollywood nepotism: "The son-in-law also rises."

But before long, David Selznick had silenced the cynics and even earned the respect and friendship of Thalberg. Selznick's first triumph for MGM came in 1933 with his all-star production of *Dinner at Eight*, a stylish comedy featuring Jean Harlow, John Barrymore, Marie Dressler, and Wallace Beery. Always a fan of the "classics," Selznick then put Dickens's *David Copperfield* and *A Tale of Two Cities* before the cameras and turned out creamy-smooth, craftsmanlike adaptations of both. Perfect casting again enhanced both movies. *Copperfield* boasted a dazzling ensemble of character actors headed by W. C. Fields as Micawber, Basil Rathbone as Murdstone, Edna May Oliver as Aunt Betsy, and Roland Young as Uriah Heep; while Ronald Colman made an ideally dashing and dissolute Sydney Carton in *A Tale of Two Cities*.

Once again, however, Selznick bridled at his secondary position. Although he had been frustrated in the attempt to strike out on his own a few years earlier, this time he was determined to succeed. In 1935, he defied his father-in-law and left MGM to form Selznick International Studios. Financier John Hay Whitney invested in the new company, along with Myron Selznick, Dr. A. H. Giannini of the Bank of America, and Irving and Norma Shearer Thalberg. (Thalberg, who had become a kind of surrogate son to Mayer, was probably pleased to see a rival depart from MGM.) Selznick bought the old Thomas Ince Studios in Culver City, just a few blocks from his father-in-law's empire, and announced that he would "put my family's name on a trademark and restore it to its former importance in the movie world." He signed a releasing deal with United Artists, the company formed several years earlier by Charlie Chaplin, Mary Pickford, Douglas Fairbanks, and D. W. Griffith.

Selznick's first production at Selznick International was an adaptation of another of the novels he had adored as a child, *Little Lord Fauntleroy*. Ben Hecht sent him a wry telegram. "The trouble with you, David, is that you did all your reading before you were twelve." But Selznick's passion for strong narrative, instilled in him by the books he read as a boy, was his greatest strength as a producer. He followed *Fauntleroy* with *The Garden of Allah*, a casbah romance starring Marlene Dietrich and Charles Boyer. It epitomized Selznick's second strong preference—for florid romantic melodramas, particularly tales of thwarted or unrequited love. Selznick combined both tastes in the crowning work of his career, *Gone With the Wind*. He bought the novel before it was published, in 1936, but filming was held up while Selznick negotiated with his father-in-law.

Everyone agreed that only one actor could play Mitchell's roguish hero, Rhett Butler. Polls and fan letters overwhelmingly pointed to the one inevitable choice: Clark Gable. But Gable had an iron-clad contract with MGM, and in order to get him, Selznick had to go hat in hand to Louis B. Mayer. At first Mayer postponed the deal, insisting that "the King" was so booked up with MGM movies that he would be unavailable for another two years. Then Mayer made a stipulation: in return for lending Gable, MGM would become a partner in the production, acquiring exclusive distribution rights to the picture as well as a 50 percent interest for the first seven years. In the end, Selznick's share of the profits from *Gone With the Wind* was cut by at least $25 million as a result of his father-in-law's hard bargain.

According to legend, virtually every actress in the world sought the role of Scarlett O'Hara, and filming had already begun when Myron Selznick came to the sound stage where the burning of Atlanta was being recreated. In the midst of the conflagration, Myron approached his brother David and introduced him to Vivien Leigh, a young actress who was visiting Hollywood with her lover, Laurence Olivier, one of Myron's clients. Myron exclaimed, "David, I want you to meet your Scarlett O'Hara!" David Selznick was reportedly thunderstruck by Leigh's resemblance to the green-eyed vixen described by Margaret Mitchell.

That is a charming bit of Hollywood lore, but the truth may be more convuluted. Contrary to myth, Vivien Leigh was hardly an obscure actress at the time. She had appeared in many acclaimed stage productions in England as well as in two films—*Fire Over England* and *A Yank at Oxford*—that David Selznick had certainly seen. According to Olivier, Vivien "had an almost demonic determination to play Scarlett" before she came to Hollywood. There was one major obstacle, however. Her affair with Olivier had provoked a well-publicized scandal in England, since both of them were married at the time that they began seeing each other. This suggests a possible reason for manufacturing the Cinderella story of Leigh's magical appearance at the eleventh hour. If it had been reported that David Selznick was actively seeking this notorious woman to play the most coveted role of the century, he might have been publicly pilloried for selecting not just a foreign actress but an immoral home-wrecker as well. If instead it could be reported that he happened upon his Scarlett by accident, and at the last possible moment, this charming fairy tale could help to defuse the scandal that might otherwise have surrounded the selection. That is only speculation, but the legend of Leigh's discovery has never quite rung true. In *Memo from David O. Selznick*, Rudy Behlmer notes that "correspondence regarding Selznick's initial meeting with Vivien Leigh, her testing for the role of Scarlett, the reactions to the tests, the unofficial selection of her for the role . . . is all conspicuous by its absence in the Selznick files." Selznick was well known for putting everything in writing. Why he never wrote anything about the casting of Vivien Leigh is a matter for future historians to ponder.

The movie, of course, went on to win eight Academy Awards and established Selznick as the most-celebrated producer in Hollywood. Even in the present era of blockbusters, *Gone With the Wind* has still been seen by more people than any other movie in history—even more than have seen *E.T.*, *Star Wars*, or *Jaws*. Before *Gone With the Wind* was released, Selznick had already rushed into production with an adaptation of Daphne Du Maurier's best-selling Gothic romance, *Rebecca*. Selznick cast Laurence Olivier as the enigmatic Maxim De Winter, brooding about his dead wife; Olivier wanted Leigh as his co-star. But Selznick felt that another neophyte actress, Joan Fontaine, would be more appropriate casting as the mousy young woman who becomes the second Mrs. De Winter. Selznick's instinct was once again right on the mark, and *Rebecca* established Fontaine as a major star just as *Gone With the Wind* had catapulted Vivien Leigh to international prominence. In addition, thanks in large part to Alfred Hitchcock's stylish direction (in his first American effort) the film captured the novel's overripe romanticism and the elegant sense of dread that it evoked. *Rebecca* became the Academy Award-winner as best picture of 1940, as *Gone With the Wind* had been in 1939.

GRATIFIED as he was by the enormous profits MGM made on *Gone With the Wind*, Mayer was still irritated that Selznick would not come back to work for him. He also tried to hire his other son-in-law, without success. William Goetz had worked for the Fox studio in the early 1930s. Then when Darryl F. Zanuck was forming Twentieth Century Pictures, which would eventually merge with Fox, L. B. Mayer paved the way for Goetz to join the new company. Mayer offered to invest $375,000 in Zanuck's company if Bill Goetz could come on as a partner. Mayer's boss, Nicholas Schenck also put in $375,000 to make his brother Joseph a third partner. Mayer even loaned out some of his players—Wallace Beery for *The Bowery*, Clark Gable for *Call of the Wild*—to help the company get started. Of course Mayer's assistance was not entirely altruistic. He had substantial stock in the new company, purchased in the name of the Mayer Family Fund. He kept half the shares himself and divided the rest among Edith and Bill Goetz, and Irene as well. (David Selznick refused his father-in-law's gift.) All of them got very rich on their Twentieth Century-Fox stock; they sold their shares years later at a monumental profit.

In addition to making his fortune, Bill Goetz became a vice president at Twentieth, and while Darryl Zanuck was serving in World War II, Goetz ran the company. It was Goetz who discovered Betty Grable and Alice Faye and oversaw such films as *Guadalcanal Diary*, *The Song of Bernadette*, and *Hello, Frisco, Hello*. But in the early 1940s, when Goetz tried to wrest control of the company from Zanuck, Joseph Schenck threw his shares to Zanuck, and Goetz was ousted.

L. B. Mayer saw an opportunity to solidify the family business by hiring Goetz at MGM. He offered Goetz a weekly salary of $10,000. Goetz refused, preferring, like Selznick, to retain his independence. Mayer was angered by the rejection, but he said nothing until he and the Goetzes went out one evening to the Players restaurant, the fashionable Sunset Strip watering-hole owned by writer-director Preston Sturges. "Dad seemed very uptight all through dinner," Edie recalls. "Afterwards, he asked me to dance with him. While we were out on the floor, he put his hands on his hips and said, 'So you don't want your husband to work for me?' I said, 'I don't know what you're talking about.'"

Mayer informed Edie of his generous offer to Goetz. "I was in a state," Edie admits. "On the way home, the minute I got in the car, I said to Bill, 'Darling, is it true that you turned down that kind of money?' He said, 'Yes. If I took the job, the first thing I would do is fire your father!'"

Although he was disappointed, Mayer assisted Goetz in another venture. He gave Goetz $1 million to capitalize his new International Pictures Corporation. (David and Irene Selznick were furious that Goetz chose the name "International" for the new company, feeling that he had stolen it from Selznick International.) Goetz was a top executive with the company, and when it merged with Universal to become Universal-International, Goetz became head of that studio. During his reign Universal produced such diverse films as the popular comedy *The Egg and I*, the Ronald Colman Academy Award-winner *A Double Life*, and the Ma and Pa Kettle series.

While at Universal, Goetz did something which would permanently alter the nature of the industry; he became the first executive ever to give an actor a percentage of a movie's profits. In order to lure James Stewart into accepting the lead in a Western called *Winchester 73*, Goetz signed a contract allotting Stewart 50 percent of the picture's profits. (Ironically, the agent who negotiated the deal for Stewart was Lew Wasserman, who would later become head of Universal himself.) Mayer objected violently to this percentage deal and berated his son-in-law for surrendering to Stewart's demand; he rightly perceived it as a lethal challenge to the absolute financial power of the studios. Nonetheless the deal went through.

Tiring of the executive ranks, Goetz left Universal in 1953 and became an independent producer, making such films as *Autumn Leaves* with Joan Crawford, *They Came to Cordura* with Gary Cooper, *Me and the Colonel* with Danny Kaye, and his most acclaimed production, *Sayonara*, which won four Academy Awards in 1957. (That film, like most of Goetz's productions, seems lumbering and creaky today. Goetz was a solid commercial producer, but most of his films have not worn well; he did not have his brother-in-law's knack for engineering lasting popular entertainments.)

It was during this period that the Goetz home became the hub of the Hollywood social circuit. Edith points out that Cole Porter was a special devotee of her soirees. "He was a hedonist," she says, "and he loved the way I entertained." Edie's chief rival in the hostessing derby was Harry Warner's daughter Doris, who was at various times Mrs. Mervyn LeRoy, Mrs. Charles Vidor, and Mrs. Billy Rose. The two women vied for the most illustrious guests. "If you got an invitation from Edie and Doris for the same evening, it was a major crisis," recalls Milton Sperling, who was married to Doris's sister Betty. "Those two women carried on their fathers' rivalry with a vengeance."

The Goetz dinner parties were known for their special flourishes, such as the handwritten menus that Edie placed in front of every plate on the table. "I'm not sure I would regard that as essential," says Edie's former son-in-law, Richard Shepherd, "but it certainly is the top of the line in accoutrements to good living." In 1958 Shepherd was trying to cajole the Goetzes' neighbor, Gary Cooper, into accepting the lead in *The Hanging Tree*, Shepherd's first project as an independent producer. Shepherd flew up to Cooper's cattle ranch in Montana for a script conference. "It was freezing cold," Shepherd recalls, "and all I wanted Gary to do was say 'Yup' about the script. At the end of the day he took us into a bunkhouse like the ones you see in old Westerns, and a bunch of cowhands were sitting around the table getting ready for dinner. And there in the center of the table was a blackboard with the dinner menu written in chalk. Gary turned to me and said in his laconic style, 'You see, your mother-in-law's got nothing on us.'"

FOR more than a decade, the Mayers, the Selznicks, the Goetzes and their children held forth as the major ruling family of Hollywood. They were at the peak of their power and influence from the 1930s until the mid-1940s. For nine straight years Louis B. Mayer earned the highest salary of anyone in the United States— $1.3 million a year plus bonuses. Selznick's success with *Gone With the Wind* and *Rebecca* made him the most admired producer in the industry, and as long as he could stay away from a poker game, one of the richest. And through his art collection and other investments, Goetz was quietly accumulating a fortune that would ultimately leave him a wealthier man than either his father-in-law or his brother-in-law.

Even in the period when they lived like royalty, there were foreshadowings of the discord and disintegration to come. Like his father, David Selznick was a compulsive gambler. One night at the Clover Club, a popular Hollywood gambling spot, Selznick lost $50,000. He wanted to write a check to cover his losses, but the management demanded cash. Frantically, Selznick phoned his wife, who in turn called her father. L. B. Mayer immediately contacted the managers of all the theaters in the neighborhood that were showing MGM pictures and ordered them to bring their night's receipts to the Clover Club. They complied, and the $50,000 was raised. By the time the booty was counted, however, Selznick had dropped another $10,000 at the tables.

Gambling was not David's only vice. Movie people liked to think of themselves as the avant garde and often experimented with any new drugs boasting magical powers. For their part, Hollywood doctors were eager to gain entrée to the social set inhabited by moviemakers and movie stars. Their supply of drugs provided the necessary ticket of admission. In the 1930s one such social-climbing physician prescribed Benzedrine for David Selznick when the impact of the stimulant was still under investigation. Selznick grew increasingly addicted to the amphetamines he gobbled. "These pills gave David what amounted to a couple of days extra a week," Irene has noted. "They also took years off his life, he later agreed. Much later."

By the mid-1940s this most potent Hollywood dynasty had begun to crumble. Ironically, it was in the 1940s, just as their own families were coming apart, that Mayer and Selznick both created their most glowing screen testaments to the family. Mayer produced the sentimental *Andy Hardy* series with Mickey Rooney, *The Human Comedy* (written by William Saroyan and again starring Mickey Rooney as the epitome of the small-town American boy), and the 1942 Academy Award-winner, *Mrs. Miniver*, a tribute to an English family whose solidarity is meant to stand for the strength of the Allies during World War II.

Selznick went in direct competition against his father-in-law by producing his own home-front family drama, *Since You Went Away*, a cloying three-hour epic that he wrote as well as produced. An American version of *Mrs. Miniver*, it suggested that we would win the war because of the love and endurance contained within the American family, which nurtured its departing soldiers and embodied the highest values for which they were fighting. *Since You Went Away* starred Claudette Colbert as the family matriarch; her two daughters were played by the teenage Shirley Temple and, as her older sister, Jennifer Jones, Selznick's newest discovery. Jones's lover in the movie, a soldier going off to war, was played by her real-life husband, Robert Walker. But when they appeared together—for the only time—in *Since You Went Away*, Jennifer Jones and Robert Walker were already estranged, and the reason was David O. Selznick.

Jennifer Jones, the daughter of a Texas film exhibitor, was born Phyllis Isley on March 2, 1919, in Tulsa, Oklahoma. She had come to New York in 1937 to study acting, where she met and married Walker, also a struggling young actor. A few years later they decided to seek their fortunes in Hollywood. Walker began working steadily, while Phyllis tested for David Selznick, who changed her name to Jennifer Jones and signed her to a long-term contract with his studio.

It was Selznick's brother-in-law, William Goetz, who gave Jennifer her biggest break. Goetz was running Twentieth Century-Fox at the time and was searching for a young actress to play the lead in *The Song of Bernadette*, a film adapted from Franz Werfel's book about the French peasant girl who created the shrine at Lourdes. Goetz wanted an unknown actress for the role, and he asked Selznick to recommend one of his contract players. After viewing some footage of Jennifer, Goetz selected her, attracted by the innocence and purity of her face. It proved to be a stunning debut, and earned Jennifer the Academy Award as best actress of 1943. The morning after she picked up her Oscar, Jennifer Jones announced that she was suing Robert Walker for divorce.

By that point Jennifer's affair with Selznick was no secret. Shortly after he began his romance with Jennifer, Selznick ran into his sister-in-law, Edie Goetz, at a party given by Claudette Colbert. "He was more than a little drunk," Edie recalls, "and he grabbed my arm. I said, 'You're hurting me, David. Let go!' He said, 'I want to tell you something. I'm going to prove to the world that I can have my cake and eat it, too.' He was talking about Jennifer."

Irene Selznick's account of the breakup of her marriage is among the least candid sections of her book. She implies that Selznick's affair with Jennifer had little to do with their separation, but those who knew him realized that David's romance with Jennifer Jones was very different from his rumored extra-marital flings with Constance Bennett, Joan Crawford, and other actresses. Some say his obsession with Jennifer grew out of her youth and malleability. He was seventeen years her senior, and he reveled in his power as he imagined creating a goddess for the world to worship.

The final separation between Irene and David occurred in 1945, during the production of *Duel in the Sun*, Selznick's epic Western starring Jennifer Jones. Irene claims that she could never understand his interest in the project, but its appeal to him was certainly clear enough to others. The film's director, King Vidor, once commented that in the scenes of passion between Jennifer and Gregory Peck, he could actually hear Selznick's heavy breathing on the preliminary soundtrack of the film. On its initial release the movie was jokingly referred to as "Lust in the Dust." The film was uncharacteristic of Selznick in its forsaking of the moodily romantic for the bluntly carnal. The scenes that portray Jones's half-breed Pearl Chavez as a sex-crazed animal seem ludicrous today, but they reflect Selznick's own surrender to an all-consuming sexual obsession at this particular moment in his life.

In other respects as well, the film was a deeply personal project, with intriguing psychological underpinnings for those who know the Selznick saga. (Selznick himself contributed to the screenplay.) One could see Pearl's father, played by Herbert Marshall, as Selznick's vision of his own father—a shady gambler but loving parent who dies in disgrace. Pearl's adoptive father—the cantankerous, reactionary tycoon played by Lionel Barrymore—resembles Louis B. Mayer. Barrymore's neglected, unhappy spouse, Lillian Gish, might be Mayer's mistreated wife Margaret. And Selznick himself identifies with Pearl, the woman torn between the good, responsible rancher (Joseph Cotten) and the sexy outlaw (Gregory Peck). Her divided nature reflects Selznick's uncertainty about whether to stay with his respectable wife, Irene, or abandon himself to illicit passion with Jennifer. The movie is as mixed up as its heroine—hypnotized by unbridled sensuality while it condemns this sensuality as immoral. More than any other, this movie suggests the crucial difference between Selznick and his father-in-law. Unlike Mayer, Selznick had a streak of defiant hedonism in him; he dared to make a more blatantly erotic film than Mayer would ever have sanctioned. And yet he shared Mayer's taste for moral homilies. He wanted to celebrate sex, but could not help associating it with destructiveness and violence. *Duel in the Sun* is far too overblown and schizoid to be taken seriously as a work of art, but it is certainly a more revealing document than Irene Selznick, or most film historians, for that matter, have recognized.

At the climax of the movie, Jones and Peck, each mortally wounded by the other, crawl desperately across the sagebrush for one final, torrid embrace. A friend of Selznick's, writer Andrew Solt, suggested that this operatic finale was excessive and had to be cut. But Selznick refused. "You should have seen Jennifer's belly after that scene was made," he said. "It was scratched and bruised, livid with the marks of that beautiful and terrible trial. I don't see how that scene could be cut. She put so much into it."

Selznick and Jennifer were married in 1949, when he was forty-seven and she was thirty. Irene had already taken her two sons, Jeffrey Lewis and Daniel Mayer, and moved with them to New York, where she embarked on a career as a theatrical producer. Her first production—Arthur Laurents's *Heartsong*—was a flop, but Audrey Wood, Tennessee Williams's agent, showed her the manuscript of *A Streetcar Named Desire*, and Irene took it on as her next project. The play's director, Elia Kazan, initially regarded her as a dilettante, and they had numerous conflicts as the production was being prepared. Nevertheless, with the ideal cast of Jessica Tandy, Marlon Brando, Kim Hunter, and Karl Malden, *Streetcar* triumphed on Broadway. Malden recalls one minor squabble over the scene in which Stanley pulls Blanche's clothes out of her trunk: "Irene was never satisfied with the stuff that came out of the trunk," Malden reports. "The prop department put some clothes in there, and Irene said, 'It doesn't look right.' Kazan disagreed. He said, 'It's good enough.' She said, 'No, it's not.' Finally Irene went out and got the clothes herself, and they looked right. She was a damn good producer." Even Louis B. Mayer, who had been extremely skeptical of Irene's decision to become a producer, was impressed when he came to an out-of-town preview. "In his way I think Dad was proud of Irene," Edie notes.

After the overwhelming success of *Streetcar*, Irene produced other plays on Broadway—*The Chalk Garden*, *Bell, Book and Candle*, and *The Complaisant Lover*—and became a highly respected figure in the theatrical world. Years before writing her autobiography, she commented on how she emerged from the shadow of her husband and father: "Where there are men like that around, a woman either withdraws completely into her own shell and thickens it as fast as she can, or she sticks her neck out and develops muscle she never knew she had before."

It can be argued that Irene Selznick came into her own as a consequence of her husband's romance with Jennifer Jones. The fourth party to the affair was not so lucky. Robert Walker began drinking heavily after his divorce from Jones. Though he continued to work in such films as *The Clock*, *Till the Clouds Roll By*, *Strangers on a Train*, and *My Son John*, he deteriorated physically and emotionally. In 1946 Walker received a suspended sentence for hit-and-run driving. After a second arrest on a drunk driving charge, he spent six months at the Menninger Clinic trying to dry out. He was married briefly to director John Ford's daughter Barbara, but they separated after just five weeks, with Barbara declaring that Walker had no intention of consummating the marriage. In 1951, while Walker was drinking, he took a sedative, sodium amytol, that had been prescribed by his physician. The combination of the drug and the alcohol proved lethal.

During the same period that David Selznick's marriage to Irene was disintegrating, Louis B. Mayer was in the process of ending his own forty-year marriage to his wife, Margaret. The daughter of a part-time cantor and kosher butcher, Margaret Shenberg Mayer never quite adjusted to the rapid change in her lifestyle when her husband conquered Hollywood. She continued dressing in a rather dowdy fashion, and Mayer often asked his friends Hedda Hopper and Ad Schulberg to take Margaret shopping with them in hopes of improving her wardrobe. But if she was persuaded to buy a stylish new dress, she would wear it only once, then send it back east to a poor friend or relation. In the 1930s Margaret underwent a hysterectomy; the depression that followed the operation led to a nervous breakdown and confinement in a sanitarium.

In 1944, the year that MGM's *Meet Me in St. Louis* created an indelible valentine to domestic bliss, Mayer moved out of the family home in Santa Monica. In 1947 the divorce was finalized. Mayer gave Margaret a generous settlement, but she never quite recovered from the pain of the separation, and she remained in frail health throughout the rest of her life. Shortly before her death in 1955, she destroyed all the scrapbooks she had kept chronicling the rise of Louis B. Mayer.

Even before his divorce, Mayer had begun courting younger women to affirm his virility. The spectacle was comic at times. Mayer's biographer Bosley Crowther described his philandering this way: "He'd waste so much time talking about the magnificence of virtue and motherhood that he'd argue or bore his willing companion into a state of complete frigidity. The lady, ready to be obliging, would find herself confronted with a middle-aged satyr who was also a full-time moralist."

In 1948, at the age of sixty-three, Mayer married Lorena Danker, formerly a bit player at Warner Bros. Lorena was a pretty Gentile woman, the widow of an advertising executive, and some twenty years younger than Mayer. Though Mayer believed his second marriage would give him a new lease on life, his last years were not much happier than his abandoned wife Margaret's. But his troubles were professional rather than personal. Mayer had always had a tense, uneasy relationship with his boss, Nicholas Schenck, the owner of Loew's, which controlled MGM. But the two kept the peace until an ambitious fellow named Dore Schary came to work at MGM. A conflict between Schary and Mayer soon developed, and Schenck unexpectedly backed the upstart Schary; Schenck gave Schary the credit for improving the studio's fortunes in the early 1950s. Mayer was forced to resign in 1952, and he left the kingdom he had helped to found. He expected his court to accompany him into exile and was disappointed when there were no mass defections. As he told one friend bitterly, "I was fool enough to believe that when I left here half the studio would follow me wherever I went. But not one of them—not a single one of them . . ."

Mayer's grandson, Daniel Selznick, recalls the outcast mogul's desperate last years: "I saw my grandfather both at the peak of his power, and at the end without any of his power. He couldn't talk about his feelings, but I'd hear about what was going on from my mother and Lorena. I would hear about how he was trying behind the scenes to buy up Metro stock. You could see what was going on in his mind. He was determined to get back the job, whatever it took. He was exposed when he had a very considerable and growing proportion of stock, and that was really humiliating. Everyone assumed that L. B. Mayer could live quite peaceably. Nobody dreamed that he was so tied to MGM that he couldn't give it up. It was a ghastly, traumatic experience for him."

Another trauma poisoned Mayer's last years—a rift with his daughter Edie and her husband Bill Goetz that proved to be irreparable. Mayer and Goetz were very dissimilar. While Mayer owned a dozen paintings by Grandma Moses, Goetz had an unrivalled collection of French Impressionist art that Mayer scorned. Their different tastes in art were indicative of a more profound divergence on the subject of politics. While Mayer was a staunchly right-wing Republican, Goetz was a liberal Democrat. Mayer tolerated his son-in-law's political apostasy for a time, but the conflict erupted during the 1952 presidential campaign.

Mayer of course was supporting Dwight Eisenhower, while the Goetzes backed Adlai Stevenson. Goetz was also a friend of Dore Schary, who asked if he could hold a Stevenson fundraising benefit at the Goetzes' home. Goetz knew that his father-in-law would be offended, so he declined. Schary had the party at his own house, but the invitations read "William Goetz and I invite you." Mayer was furious, partly because Goetz allowed his name to be used to endorse Stevenson, but even more because Goetz had allied himself with Mayer's enemy, Schary. Mayer broke with the Goetzes, did not speak to them for the rest of his life, and cut them out of his will. In his autobiography, Schary reports that Goetz told him ruefully of the Stevenson benefit, "Mine was the biggest contribution anyone made to the Stevenson campaign."

Edie Goetz still does not believe that the disagreement over politics was the real reason for the schism. "You can pin it on politics," she says. "It's easy to say that. But it wasn't true. The fight happened a week after Bill had turned Dad down for the second time. Dad had lost his job at MGM, and he wanted to start his own production company. He wanted Bill to come in with him as a partner, and Bill said no. Dad couldn't take rejection."

Edie's daughter, Judy Shepherd, agrees that the real basis of the feud "was that my father was so independent. Maybe my grandfather felt he wouldn't have lost the studio if my father had been there with him." Whatever the reason for the blowup, Mayer denounced his son-in-law, calling him a "Communist" and a Judas. Edith remembers her last phone conversation with her father. It developed into a heated argument in which L. B. continued to castigate Goetz. "What do you want me to do, divorce Bill?" Edie asked incredulously. "I've lived with him longer than I've lived with you, and get it through your head, I love him!"

Mayer was unbending. He said he would continue to see his daughter but would not acknowledge his son-in-law. "When I see Bill, I'll turn my head away," Mayer declared.

Edie said that this was out of the question.

"All right, when you both come in the room, I'll turn my head away," L. B. shot back.

"That's fine, Dad. Good-bye," Edie snapped as she hung up the phone.

Probably neither of them realized at that moment that those would be the last words they would ever speak to each other. They were both proud people, and neither would apologize to the other. Mayer's nephew Jack Cummings, producer of such MGM films as *The Stratton Story* and *Seven Brides for Seven Brothers*, says of the rift, "Mr. Mayer expected unchallenged obedience from his daughters, unchallenged obedience from everyone in his family. Looking at it from his point of view, he felt that Bill and Edie owed him something. I think he lost sight of the fact that she was Bill's wife. She had to stand by her husband. What kind of woman would she be if she had not? The thing that makes it tragic to me is that she loved her father, and he loved her. He was anguished about it afterwards, but he had taken a stand. And he was a stubborn man."

Edie remembers the aftermath of the fight this way: "Lorena would call me and say, 'He was up all night crying his heart out.' I said to her, 'It's very simple. He has to go to the phone, pick up the receiver, dial my number and apologize to Billy. But you

see, Lorena, that takes humility, and that's the one thing he lacks.'
Sometimes I wonder, should I have gone over there? But I couldn't
do that to my husband."

Mayer's rage even extended to his granddaughters, Judy and
Barbara Goetz, who had both been very close to him. They shared
his love of horses and had spent a good deal of time at Mayer's
breeding farm. After 1952 he refused to speak to them. "I wrote
to him when I was going to get married in 1954," says Judy Goetz
Shepherd, "and he never answered."

When Judy and Richard Shepherd had their first child in 1956,
they were living in New York. A month after the baby was born,
Judy and Richard were walking with the infant outside the Plaza
Hotel. As they approached the hotel entrance, they were startled
to see Louis B. Mayer emerge from the Plaza. Judy rolled the
baby carriage toward him eagerly. "Hi, Grandpa," she called out.

Mayer turned to see who had addressed him, gave Judy an icy
stare, marched past her, and got into his waiting limousine without
so much as glancing down at the baby, his first great-grandson.
"That was my only contact with L. B. Mayer," recalls Richard
Shepherd. "He walked right by Judy, who had nothing to do with
the fight, and right by this poor thirty-two-day-old baby who had
nothing to do with it, either. That's some insight into the nature
of the gentleman."

In 1957 Mayer was dying of leukemia. For a while he refused
to believe how gravely ill he was, and he continued to carry on
like a monarch in exile. His friend Clarence Brown, a contract
director at MGM, said, "He was a dying man, but there he was
still trying to run things, still bossing people around. Only now
the only people he could boss were a bunch of twitty nurses."

Toward the end Mayer seemed to know the truth. His doctor,
Jessie Marmorston, told Bosley Crowther that he kept crying out
for his estranged daughter: "Is she here yet? Is she outside?" But
Edith was not called to his bedside. Dr. Marmorston later told
Edie, "I didn't let you know because he would have been dead
within a few days anyway, and it's a scene you never could have
forgotten."

In her book, Irene also reports that the dying Mayer cried out,
"Is she here yet? Is she outside?" But she insists that he was calling
for *her* rather than for Edith. The pronoun makes it ambiguous,
and probably no one will ever know for certain which daughter
he craved to see. Like the characters in *Rashomon*, each sister is
convinced of her own version of the events. Even now, more than

twenty-five years after Mayer's death, the two women continue to battle over which of them was really her father's favorite.

Edie did attend her father's funeral—a star-studded gathering at the Wilshire Boulevard Temple with a eulogy delivered by Spencer Tracy. Edie's husband, William Goetz, stayed home. Afterwards, Edie had nightmares. "I kept seeing my father in his open casket," she says. "He looked so shriveled and tiny. But I have no regrets. I did what I had to do."

When Mayer's will was read, it turned out that he had a smaller fortune than most people believed. He left an estate of $7.5 million, most of it to set up a foundation to perpetuate his memory. "As Bill prophesied, he took his money with him," Edie comments bitterly. He bequeathed modest sums to his widow Lorena, and to his daughter Irene and her two sons. But he specifically excluded his daughter Edith "or any other member of the Goetz family" on the grounds that "I have given them extremely substantial assistance during my lifetime." Almost petulantly, he referred to how he had aided William Goetz's career and noted that Goetz's attitude was to be "distinguished from that of my former son-in-law, David Selznick, who never requested or accepted assistance from me in the motion picture industry."

Edie says that her lawyer suggested she sue her dead father for libel. "I wouldn't have kept the money," Edie insists. "I would have given it to charity. I had a very rich husband; I didn't need it. But I would have broken the will, and there would be more money for Lorena and his grandchildren and Irene as well. But Bill wouldn't let me do it."

No doubt the will exacerbated the tensions between Mayer's daughters. Irene claims that the bitter estrangement began even before the will was read, when she called Edie to tell her that Mayer had died. Edie retorted huffily that she already knew, and Irene found her tone callous and unfeeling. "That was all," Irene writes, "and it was the last straw. It was also the last word spoken between us for many years." She would not permit Edie to ride with the immediate family to Mayer's funeral. "However cruel," Irene has written, "the fact was that Edie had made it impossible for me to ride with her on that occasion. Anything but that."

Edie recalls the incident somewhat differently. As she tells it Irene's refusal to ride with her had more to do with Irene's dislike for Edie's daughter Judy. Two years earlier, when Margaret Mayer died, she had bequeathed $100,000 apiece to three of her four grandchildren but had given Judy Goetz—her first grandchild—

the choice of $100,000 or her diamond ring. Judy chose the ring, and this incensed Irene. "She wrote me a horrible letter insulting Judy," Edie says. "She refused to have anything to do with Judy after that. And when I told her Judy was coming with me to Dad's funeral, that's why she wouldn't let us ride with her."

After Mayer's death, relations between Edith and Irene were chilly for many years. But the sisters had come to a makeshift truce by 1969, when Bill Goetz died and Irene came to stay with her sister during the mourning period. "Irene moved in here and was very sweet to me," Edie recalls. "After that we stayed friendly, sent gifts to each other, talked on the phone. A couple of years later she came out to California for the summer, and Judy said to me, 'Please don't have her stay at the house.' So I had the chauffeur drive me to the airport to meet her, and we dropped her off at Sara Mankiewicz's. I invited Irene for dinner that night. So help me God, I could only get nine people to come. The list of people Irene doesn't like! But I didn't invite her to stay with me, and from that day on, there's been a strain. She *cannot* take rejection. I've always said my sister was the most rejected woman I've ever known—rejected by Dad, rejected by her husband. If you were to ask her who she'd invited for dinner, she wouldn't tell you, for fear someone she invited wouldn't show up. That's fear of rejection."

In explaining her alienation from her sister, Irene emphasizes fundamental differences in their personalities. In contrast to her own seriousness of purpose, Irene characterizes Edith as a frivolous socialite who "believed expenditure should be conspicuous." This characterization would no doubt find many supporters. Edie's lifelong career as the premier hostess of Hollywood hardly qualifies her as an intellectual heavyweight. Despite the fact that Edith may have been cut out of her father's will as a result of a conflict over Adlai Stevenson, she admits that she has no real interest in politics. When Gore Vidal called her to donate money to his 1982 Senate campaign, Edie said she would be happy to contribute so long as her name was not used. "But do you want Jerry Brown to be senator?" Vidal asked her.

"I don't give a damn," Edie replied. "I'm apolitical. But I want you to be happy, Gore."

If Edie is blithely unconcerned about social responsibility and political issues, at least she does not pretend to be other than what she is. Irene portrays herself as a far more humane and enlightened soul. Others have painted a somewhat different picture. Tennessee

Williams, for one, wrote in his memoirs of Irene's less-than-generous attitude toward his longtime lover, Frank Merlo: "I remember how Irene Mayer Selznick, daughter of that awful old Louis B., used to invite me to socially prestigious dinners at the Pierre and say, 'Ask Frankie to drop in afterward.' 'Tell her to go fuck herself,' was his invariable and proper remark when I relayed these insulting invitations."

Another incident suggests that Irene is not wholly free of hypocrisy. Irene berates Edith for her insensitivity when their father was dying. Yet in *A Private View* Irene does not write a word about her mother's funeral. Her cousin Jack Cummings sheds light on this omission. He and his uncle, L. B. Mayer, happened to be in New York at the same time in 1955. Mayer called Cummings at eight one morning and asked him to come right over to the Hampshire House, where Mayer and his wife Lorena were staying. "I went over," Cummings recalls, "and he was so agitated that he was shaking. He said to me, 'Your aunt is dying, and I called Irene in Europe and told her. She's not coming to see her mother.' She was working on *The Chalk Garden* with Enid Bagnold at the time. My uncle was dreadfully disturbed with Irene. She not only did not come to see her mother, she never appeared at the funeral which she conveniently left out of the book."

No doubt, the intense sibling rivalry between Edith and Irene was aggravated by the fact that each of them possessed precisely what the other lacked. Disappointed at having given up her dream of a career, Edie must have envied Irene's professional accomplishments as she imagined the triumphs as her own. Her former son-in-law, Richard Shepherd, notes, "Edie talks about what she could have done and might have done and would have done and didn't. Whether that's accurate or not, I have no way of knowing. Irene *did* do those things."

For her part, Irene could not help recognizing that Edie's marriage to Bill Goetz was radically different from her own marriage to Selznick. By all accounts the Goetzes had an extraordinary relationship. Edie adored Bill, and he more than adored her. He spoiled her shamelessly, inspiring the oft-repeated line about them: "Whatever Edie wants, Edie Goetz." The simple fact is that Edie had a bright and popular husband who doted on her for forty years, a fact that must have provoked Irene's envy when she suffered through David Selznick's self-absorption and infidelity.

Despite all the apparent differences between Edith and Irene, one suspects that on some fundamental level, the two sisters are more alike than either of them would care to admit. "I wouldn't want to go one-on-one with either of them," comments Dick Shepherd, "because they're very willful, purposeful women. Outwardly they may be different, inwardly they both come from that Mayer mettle."

In writing her memoirs, Irene made her feelings about Edith part of the public record. It may be worth mentioning that whatever her private feelings about Irene, Edith did not publicize them until asked to respond to Irene's version of events as recorded in *A Private View*. What impels an elderly woman to vilify her own sister in print? None of the alleged injuries visited upon Irene by her sister would seem to justify or explain this public ridicule. "How can Irene *hate* me this much?" Edie asks sadly.

But perhaps she unwittingly answers the question when she says simply, "I never felt that involved with my sister. I didn't know she was so involved with me. When I look back, I can't seem to remember her at all. She didn't seem to be part of my life." That disregard may be what galled Irene most of all.

The feuds within this family are so scalding because of the high stakes involved and the formidable nature of the combatants. Other families fight, but rarely so fiercely or unforgivingly. "Underneath all the anger, I think there was a lot of hurt," says Richard Shepherd of the Mayer family warfare. "I think most of us tend to rail out to cover pain."

AFTER he separated from Irene, David Selznick's career began to go into a downward spiral. In some sense he was paralyzed by the unprecedented success of *Gone With the Wind*, hesitant to make any decision out of fear that it might be the wrong one. After that movie opened, he did not start another film for three years. Instead he made his money by demanding huge loan-out fees for the services of stars—such as Ingrid Bergman and Joan Fontaine—whom he had under contract. Fontaine resisted when David proposed lending her out to Fox to star in *This Above All* opposite Tyrone Power; she noted in outrage that her salary was to be $6,000 while Selznick raked in $75,000. Eventually, they reached a more equitable arrangement, but Fontaine commented angrily that Selznick had become a "peddler in horseflesh rather than a creative moviemaker."

Finally Selznick began to produce films again, though with only intermittent success. *Spellbound* and *Duel in the Sun* were box office hits, but those were to be the last. *The Paradine Case* and *Portrait of Jennie* were costly failures. By 1948 he was $12 million in debt, but he refused to declare bankruptcy, lest he repeat his father's humiliating defeat. He produced *Terminal Station*, a well-intended but disastrous romantic drama directed by Vittorio De Sica, then once again ceased filmmaking altogether for several years. Selznick talked about adapting *War and Peace*, but Dino De Laurentiis beat him to it. He then planned to film the entire Bible for television—a typically grandiose Selznick project that never materialized.

Instead of sending his fabled memos to the creative personnel on his films, Selznick would pen them to the president of an airline after a bad flight or to the owner of a restaurant after a bad meal. When he did write memos on the subject of moviemaking, it would often be to the director of one of Jennifer's films, not his own. He tried to supervise every detail of her appearance, even when he was not officially involved with her films. Vincente Minnelli reports that when he was directing Jennifer in *Madame Bovary*, Selznick even expressed firm opinions on his wife's eyebrows: "It would be sheer folly to tamper with them to the slightest extent," Selznick declared in a memo. "I will appreciate it if you will leave them strictly alone, and will assume this to be so unless I hear from you further."

Finally, in 1957, Selznick did fulfill a lifelong dream and brought Ernest Hemingway's World War I romance, *A Farewell to Arms*, to the screen, with Jennifer as nurse Catherine Barkley and Rock Hudson as Frederic Henry, the injured ambulance driver who falls in love with her. But things went badly from the start. The original director, John Huston, left the film, frustrated by Selznick's obsessive need to control matters himself. As Selznick admitted, "In Huston I asked for a first violinist and instead got a soloist." Huston was replaced by the more docile Charles Vidor. Still, the conflicts between producer and director continued as filming dragged on in Italy. "This picture is going to kill me," Vidor complained. In fact, he died two years later. His widow, Doris Warner Vidor, described the nightmare of the production: "Every time a scene was shot, David would send Charles a memo dissatisfied over something involving Jennifer. No matter how small—such as there's a line under her chin, or those beautiful apple cheeks are not shown to full advantage."

Despite all these painstaking efforts, the film turned out to be a stillborn epic. Most critics panned it and were especially harsh on Jennifer Jones. Speaking for the majority, the *Saturday Review*'s

Hollis Alpert wrote, "Miss Jones has a good deal of skill as an actress, but she's a fairly mature woman now, the mother of children, and that big movie screen has a gruesome way of revealing the disparity between what might be termed screen age and actual age."

Undaunted, Selznick set in motion a film of another of his favorite novels, F. Scott Fitzgerald's *Tender Is the Night*, again with Jennifer playing a much younger woman. But this time Selznick had to bow out as producer before Twentieth Century-Fox would agree to finance the film. David, who was always desperate for money, had sold several of his films to British television, and the outraged British exhibitors signed a resolution to boycott all subsequent Selznick movies from their theaters. This threat made Fox president Spyros Skouras jittery, and he demanded that Selznick sell *Tender Is the Night* outright to Fox if he wanted it made. Selznick tried to retain script approval, but the studio ignored his voluminous memos. "By that time," his son Danny says, "he was considered such a megalomaniac, such a bundle of headaches and so responsible for pushing pictures above their cost that nobody wanted to deal with him."

Disheartened by what he regarded as the mutilation of *Tender Is the Night*, Selznick wrote a valedictory of sorts to Spyros Skouras: "I regret this new evidence of the complete passing of showmanship from the industry, as well as the new attitude of indifference to promises. I can only look back nostalgically on different days that produced different results. I think this is where the bus stops."

After that, Selznick continued to play the role of Hollywood tycoon, but his efforts were increasingly pathetic. He spent almost as much time planning the tenth birthday party of his daughter, Mary Jennifer, as he had once spent planning his film projects. For a time he became absorbed by a scheme to turn *Gone With the Wind* into a Broadway musical, but that project fizzled. And the films he announced never went before the cameras. He complained constantly that his tombstone would read, "Here lies the man who made *Gone With the Wind*." His prediction was not far from the mark. Selznick died of a heart attack in 1965, at the age of sixty-three. At the time of his death, David O. Selznick had been forgotten by many in the industry. After all, he had not had a hit in twenty years. As Dore Shary commented, "In shallow waters the dragon becomes the joke of the shrimp."

Danny Selznick offers some poignantly vivid memories of his father's last years. "When I'd come out to visit him," Danny says, "it was always, 'Next year we're going to do something...' It was never, '*Now* we are shooting...' I now believe that what he needed was a studio behind him. He was trying to do too much himself.

"The single most painful experience of his life has to have been the making of *A Farewell to Arms*. It was a book he had admired for so many years. It was a part for which on so many levels Jennifer seemed suitable, but of course she was younger when he first considered it for her. While he was making it, I'd get letters from him from Europe which were painful and heartbreaking. When I saw him, I saw what toll the film had taken on him. The worst moment actually was at the Roxy Theater when the film was opening. He wanted to sit there with me. I hoped to Christ that it would be wonderful. And I sat there in shock. Beginning with the degree of hysteria in Jennifer's performance, everything was wrong. There was my father sitting with me waiting for me to tell him what I thought of it. I don't even know what I said. But the reviews were so harsh that whatever I had said would have been mild in comparison. There had been such a publicity fanfare: 'In the tradition of *Gone With the Wind*...' He was hoping for Academy Awards across the board, and I don't even know if there were any nominations. I'm sure that experience had an effect on my decision not to go into the film industry when I got out of college. I said to myself, 'Look at what the film industry does to you. It eats you up and spits you out finally. Here's a man who was a genius and a giant in the industry, and he's lost it somehow.' Watching him in those last years and admiring him as I did was terrible, just terrible."

AT first, Jennifer Jones did not fare well after David Selznick's death. She kept acting, but her only jobs in the late 1960s were in B-pictures like *The Idol* and *Angel, Angel, Down We Go*. In 1967, reportedly despondent over the death of her friend, actor Charles Bickford, she checked into a Malibu motel under the name of Phyllis Walker. She took some Seconals, then called her physician and told him she wanted to die. After swallowing more pills, she drove out to a deserted cliff overlooking Point Dume. She climbed down to the beach, where she was later discovered lying unconscious in the shallow surf. Her stomach was pumped, and she recovered. Later Jones admitted that this had not been her only suicide attempt. "I have attempted suicide three times," she acknowledged, "when I was at points of deep despair. It was a cry for help."

In 1971 Jones married multimillionaire tycoon and art collector Norton Simon. She and her husband established the Jennifer Jones Simon Foundation for Mental Health and Education. The Simons frequently turn up on the society pages, a fixture at parties and museum openings. Although Simon has bought potential film properties for Jennifer, none of them reached the screen. Jennifer once owned the rights to *Terms of Endearment* but was unable to get the film made as a vehicle for herself. Jennifer's last film role was as Fred Astaire's charred love interest in *The Towering Inferno* (1974).

Jones's two sons by Robert Walker were just ten and eleven when their father died. They had a hard adjustment. After Jennifer married Selznick, the boys' stepfather built them their own cottage in back of the mansion where he lived with Jennifer. His way of dealing with the Walker boys was to write a check for anything they wanted. The two brothers were very different. Robert Walker, Jr. was prone to trouble, while Michael was class president and a fine student. Both Walker boys took up acting for a while, though Michael's career was very short-lived. Bobby Jr. played the lead in *Ensign Pulver*, a follow-up to *Mr. Roberts*, and a supporting part in *Easy Rider*. In 1974 *Parade* magazine reported that he had given up his film career to become a limousine chauffeur at a salary of $200 a week. More recently, however, he returned to acting, appearing occasionally on television and in feature films.

Jones's daughter by Selznick, Mary Jennifer, also tried to become an actress, but her half-brother, Danny Selznick, tells of the problems she had carving out her own identity. "I had a chance to see the attention Mary Jennifer received as Jennifer Jones's daughter," Selznick says. "And because Mary Jennifer was an intuitively gifted child, but not the brightest person in the world, I saw the real problem she had. She asked herself, 'Why am I receiving this attention? And, more important, how can I continue to receive it? I'm used to it.' So she said she wanted to be an actress. It turned out she actually had a natural acting talent, which I encouraged her very specifically to develop through technical training. I helped arrange for her to go to study with Uta Hagen in New York. But it was hard for her to differentiate between seeing acting as a craft to learn and seeing it as attention to one's self."

In 1976, at the age of twenty-one, Mary Jennifer plunged to her death from the top of an office building in Los Angeles. "I was devastated when Mary died," her mother commented. "She had gone through treatment and, I thought, was at peace with herself. You never know—about the mind."

MOST of the other members of the Mayer and Selznick clan have attempted to find a place for themselves in the industry at one time or another. One of the most prominent Selznicks was a cousin of David's, Joyce Selznick, an adopted daughter of Lewis's brother Phil. Joyce was known as the most powerful casting agent in the business from the late 1940s until the time of her death in 1981. Her "discoveries" included Tony Curtis, Candice Bergen, Faye Dunaway, and Cicely Tyson.

Edie Goetz's two daughters have both had at least peripheral connections to the movie business. Judy Goetz married Richard Shepherd, who began as an agent and eventually ran the motion picture division at Creative Management Associates. He also produced films, and Judy claims that her father aided her husband's career when he was starting out. "My father was responsible for setting Dick and Martin Jurow up in a partnership," Judy says. "He lent them the money they needed to get started." Shepherd, on the other hand, downplays any hints of nepotism. He feels that what his father-in-law gave him was the example of his unpretentious, informal way of doing business—a style that he has tried to emulate as a producer and executive. "Today's corporate executives take themselves so damn seriously," Shepherd notes. "That wasn't Bill's style, and I've tried to be like him." Shepherd climbed steadily through the ranks. During the 1970s he worked as head of production at Warners and later at MGM, the studio that Judy's grandfather had built.

Judy and Dick Shepherd were divorced in 1978, after twenty-four years of marriage. Their younger son Tony is head of talent for producer Aaron Spelling. Scott Shepherd—the baby whom Louis B. Mayer snubbed in 1956—has worked as a screenwriter and story editor on *Matt Houston*, a TV series produced by his brother's boss, Aaron Spelling.

Edie's other daughter Barbara is one child of Hollywood who recoiled from the world in which she was raised. "I really wanted to be like everybody else," Barbara says, describing her childhood with a certain revulsion. "I wanted to wear tennis shoes and be able to do all the things that I wasn't allowed to do. We had all those wonderful paintings on the wall, but that didn't impress me. I thought everybody else had the same paintings. I didn't know at the time that theirs were reproductions. My friends all walked to school or rode their bicycles, and we were never allowed to go out in the street or walk anywhere. It was embarrassing for me to have a limousine. If I invited people over, there were so many knives and forks, and nobody knew what to use. The door was so big and grand; the whole house was so big and grand. I just wanted to be a regular kid."

It was not just the formality that distressed Barbara, but the lack of family closeness. "We had very little family life together," she reports. "We went off to school early, and my mother was always asleep. When we came home, there was nobody there except the governess. The family never had meals together. We had dinner with the governess, and if the governess had a day off, we had a relief governess."

While she was attending Mills College in Oakland, Barbara eloped with a nineteen-year-old Stanford student named Todd Clare and moved to the East Coast for a number of years. After divorcing Clare, she returned to Los Angeles and married actor William Windom. That marriage also ended in divorce six years later. In the last decade Barbara has established herself as a successful interior decorator. She has furnished the Bistro Gardens restaurant in Beverly Hills, a fur salon on Rodeo Drive, as well as the homes of Carroll O'Connor, Linda Evans, and other stars.

Barbara and her mother rarely see each other, but Barbara maintains a close relationship with her aunt Irene, whom she sees as being very much like herself. Both stuttered as children, both moved away from their families to establish their independence, and both have achieved success as single career women.

David and Irene Selznick's older son Jeffrey worked for his father as production manager during the making of *A Farewell to Arms*. He stayed on in Europe, produced a film in England and a couple more in France, none of which was very well received. At last, he abandoned the movie business and opened a string of boutiques on the island of Jamaica. He suffers from lupus, a debilitating arthritic condition.

His younger brother Daniel says that the failures of his brother and his father discouraged him from entering the film business for a long time. But Danny finally decided to take the plunge himself. It was, in effect, his destiny to make movies. There had always been great expectations of Danny, for he was treated from childhood like the crown prince of Hollywood. Louis B. Mayer adored the boy and would proudly predict that his grandson was going to be President of the United States. Danny recalls his own relationship with his grandfather. "He was so attached to me, so encouraging, supportive, warm and involved that part of the time it's as if it all happened a few years ago. He was a very important part of my growth as a child. If a grandparent is that adoring of you, it does wonderful things to you in terms of your own belief in yourself.

"One of the things I loved doing with him was going to the previews of the new MGM movies, especially the musicals. It was harder once I went back east to school, but I'd go to California in the summers and over Christmas vacations. That period of the late forties is a very rich period. It's when all the Arthur Freed musicals were produced. And at the previews we'd show up in the custom-made Chrysler that K. T. Keller made available to him, with a neon reclining lion on the hood. When he rolled up to the theater, there was no doubt who was inside the car. I'd sit in the back with the entourage that always accompanied him. He'd always say, 'Do you know my grandson?' Most of them did, but they'd say, 'Yes, Mr. Mayer. Hello, Danny.' And then he'd ask my opinion afterwards, which was a kind of intoxicating thing to have happen to you as a child. It's no wonder I was so opinionated by the time I got to be twenty-one. And I'd tell him if I thought this section was slow or that section didn't work. He did not, I have to say, take any negative comments well. He probably took them better from me than from most people, but he never took them well. As far as he was concerned, all those pictures were perfect. But he listened, and he cross-examined me."

During those years Danny justified his grandfather's pride. He attended prep school in Pennsylvania and then went on to Harvard, where he had a distinguished academic record. He looks back fondly to the glory days of his youth: "I was feature editor of the George School News, where I am happy to say we won a medalist award for feature writing in a competition with 1,100 other school newspapers. That made me very proud. Then at Harvard I worked successfully in theater. A play that I wrote was produced and received quite a bit of good critical notice."

After leaving Harvard, Danny sought a career in the theater; he worked for a time as an assistant stage manager. He also did some free-lance writing for newspapers and magazines. During this period his father alternated between encouraging and discouraging words about the film business, depending on his own fluctuating fortunes. "My father sent me many letters," Danny recalls, "about what a great life I could have as a lawyer or a diplomat or a doctor."

It was after David Selznick's death in 1965 that Danny came to California for an extended period of time to deal with his father's estate. There he renewed a friendship with director Peter Bogdanovich, who enlisted him as assistant on the latter's first feature, *Targets*. "All I needed," Danny comments, "was to go through the experience of one film to know that it was going to be hard to keep me away from it."

Then, in what is probably the high point of his career to date, Danny Selznick went to work at Universal. Danny had written a letter to Jules Stein, the head of the Music Corporation of America (MCA) "saluting him for the way something he'd done publicly had been managed. I had been trained to write either thank-you notes or letters of appreciative commendation when I saw good work done. It was part of the old upbringing. And he called me and said, 'That's one of the most intelligent letters I've seen in some time. Come and have lunch with me.'"

That lunch eventually led to a job for Danny as executive assistant to the studio's rising vice president, Ned Tanen. Selznick worked at Universal for four years and was instrumental in developing a series of low-budget films, including Dennis Hopper's *The Last Movie*, Peter Fonda's *The Hired Hand*, and George Lucas's *American Graffiti*. Since leaving Universal, Selznick has tried to produce films independently. Several projects were announced and then fell through. "I didn't play the game the way it's supposed to be played," he says now. "I didn't hire an agent. I was incredibly cocky about believing that because my opinion had been taken seriously when I was in the Universal Tower suite, it would also be taken seriously when I was a producer. It wasn't. I thought I'd established some credibility in the industry, and that when I optioned something, there were a few people out there who cared. Nobody gave a damn. I kept doing what I'd done at Universal, which was going after gifted directors who hadn't yet proven themselves. I wasn't running after the hot people that everybody else was running after. I wanted to be more innovative."

Danny has made only a few films in recent years. He directed a couple of documentaries for French television—one on Ronald Reagan, another on Hollywood musicals. Meanwhile, his wife, Joan Keller, won an Academy Award for producing the best short of 1970, *The Magic Machines*.

After years of postponements, Danny finally did sell a four-hour television miniseries, *Blood Feud*—about the war between Bobby Kennedy and Jimmy Hoffa—to Operation Prime Time; it was syndicated and shown on most local stations in 1983. Aside from high praise for Robert Blake's performance as Hoffa, it drew only a lukewarm reception. Nevertheless, Danny believes that things are looking up. "I am beginning to find that I am almost undiscouragable," he says. "I intend to get these pictures produced for the big and small screen that will prove to myself and to others that I have something to offer. It's taken me a long time to get to this point."

Selznick's main visibility during the last decade has not been as a producer in his own right but as keeper of the flame for his father and grandfather. As literary executor for David Selznick's estate, he was responsible for initiating two books—*Memo from David O. Selznick* and *David O. Selznick's Hollywood*—that have helped to maintain and even enhance his father's reputation. "The flame doesn't need a lot of guarding," Danny says. "And I don't find it in any way a distraction from my own life or an intrusion on developing my own talents. I find it part of a proper way of paying respect to my father."

Selznick is also director and president of the Louis B. Mayer Foundation, which had been established by his grandfather's will. Selznick says, "My grandfather left behind a body of money that he wished spent in part to perpetuate his memory. So I have the position of keeping that flame alive prominently, significantly, intelligently. In trying to make the selections of where to spend our money, I am consciously aware that my grandfather is not always held with the respect he deserves." The Foundation is trying to change that. It recently gave the American Film Institute a $1 million grant—in exchange for which the AFI has named a building on its Los Angeles campus the Louis B. Mayer Library. Selznick admits that his role with the Foundation is quite unique, "an unusual variation on how children are dealing with their forbears. It's part of my job to do just that."

Danny speculates on his own position in the industry relative to the preeminence enjoyed by his father and grandfather: "Some people often ask me, 'Aren't you sorry that your father and your grandfather aren't around to open doors for you the way Darryl Zanuck opened doors for Dick?' From what I have read and heard about the control that Darryl Zanuck exerted on his son's career, I can only say that no, I'm not sorry that my family was not around to be of help. While my father was a far kinder and, I think, more deeply gifted man than Zanuck, nevertheless he did like to control things in his own charming way. He wouldn't have let me alone to do what I wanted to do. He would have second-guessed, third-guessed, pulled strings, moved things around, made a lot of opportunities possible, but in the end the credit wouldn't have been mine. I never would have known what I had done and what he had done. It wouldn't have been any good for me.

"I had an absolutely ideal relationship with my father because, while I was back east, I would only see him for three weeks at a time and they would be a wonderful three weeks. Fifty-two weeks of David Selznick would have probably been hard to take. Had I had him around all the time, I can only multiply the intense interest and involvement he took in my personal life, what summer theaters I was going to, what classes I was taking, what analyst I was seeing, what diets I was on, etc. Had we lived in the same city, I wouldn't have known how to say no to him. He was a very hard man to say no to. My mother's emotional makeup was not unlike my father's. I have often been told that I had the two most opinionated parents that anybody ever knew. It's a mixed blessing. On the one level, there's no privacy and no peace, and on another level, you do have the benefit of cumulative years of wisdom."

Nevertheless, a melancholy tone comes into Danny Selznick's voice when he talks about his own achievements in relation to those of his father and grandfather. "It's taken me a long time," Selznick muses, "longer than I would have liked ideally, for me to come into my own creatively and have my name known as its own entity. Even now I consider myself so little known that when people say to me, 'Are you *the* Daniel Selznick?' I know they *must* mean David O. Selznick. And I say, 'Do you mean me?' If they do, I'm delighted. But usually that's not the case. They will say, 'Did you produce *Gone With the Wind*?' I'll say, 'Look at me. Do I look old enough to have produced *Gone With the Wind*?' And then reality sets in. There's something very sweet in a way about people feeling that my father is still alive."

Why is it that Danny's impressive pedigree has not enabled him to make more of a mark for himself in Hollywood? Perhaps he faces more than his share of jealousy or hostility from others who regard him as an overprivileged Hollywood prince. Or perhaps the problem, as Danny himself suggests, is that "I am simply not aggressive. I never had the ability to push myself forward. I don't think I have any problems with living up to the name of Selznick. It sounds simplistic, but I have to reach my own goals.

I have to succeed at what I'm trying to do, and ten years from now I can look back and say, 'I sure didn't do as well as my father.' Or 'It looks as if I've done almost as well.' I'm not haunted by or inhibited by the family standard. It's just there, and I'm proud of it."

One acquaintance of his suggests, "Danny Selznick is the type of person who probably would have succeeded spectacularly in almost any other field. It's a shame that he entered the movie business." There simply are so few films made today, and so few risks taken, that someone with Danny's high standards and offbeat tastes is inevitably going to be spending most of his time inactive and frustrated. His lack of aggressiveness only compounds the problem. In another field his natural abilities might have enabled him to accomplish far more by age forty-five or fifty.

"THERE is no hatred on the earth," Arthur Miller has written, "no resentment as coruscating as that between related people, as all civil wars display." Hollywood has had its own civil wars, none more ferocious than that within the Mayer-Selznick-Goetz clan. The most majestic Hollywood dynasty is in disarray, divided by cruel and petty skirmishes, feeding off its own past glory. The most newsworthy event within the family in recent years has not been a hit film or an Oscar victory but the publication of Irene's memoir, a wistful invocation of days past. Her sister Edith still lives grandly, but she is practically entombed in a time warp, surrounded and insulated by her memorabilia.

Danny Selznick's steadiest job is with the Louis B. Mayer Foundation, where he is employed to keep his grandfather's name alive. Because of the opulent world that he saw his parents and his grandparents inhabit, it was probably inevitable that Danny chose to pursue a career in films; the glamorous empire that his forbears conquered drew him like a magnet. Danny shared their love of movies, but he lacked their remorseless drive and their sharp showman's instinct for predicting popular tastes. Perhaps his gentleness is a reaction against the more ruthless side of the Hollywood panjandrums he has known since childhood. Perhaps the wealth Danny enjoyed while growing up robbed him of the fierce ambition instilled in his father and grandfather by the poverty *they* experienced as boys. And it is also possible that even if he possessed their drive and vulgar appetite for business, he would have faced a rougher passage in an industry that had become far less receptive to audacity and innovation than the one his family helped to create. But his career to this point has seen him expending energies and talents that might have flowered more completely if he had not been mesmerized by the movies. Despite his intelligence—or perhaps because of it—Daniel Selznick stands as one of the most affecting examples of the child of Hollywood still struggling to measure up to his heritage.

3

DFZ AND THE DAUPHIN:
The Zanucks

"Dick is his own man. But the stamp is on him."

—DAVID BROWN

ON a sunny May afternoon in 1967, Darryl F. Zanuck, trailed by his customary retinue of studio lackeys, marched into the Starlight Roof ballroom of Manhattan's Waldorf Astoria Hotel. On this rather special occasion, the annual stockholders' meeting of the Twentieth Century-Fox Film Corporation, the train of attendants was headed by a rather special fellow. "Leading the convoy," reported John Gregory Dunne, "but a half step behind his father, the dauphin to the king, was Zanuck's only son, Richard Darryl Zanuck . . ."

It was a triumphant moment for the Zanucks, father and son. Together, they had rescued Fox from the brink of extinction. Five years had passed since the company's disastrous "Greek interlude," during which the studio had fallen under the sway of Spyros Skouras and his hand-picked lieutenant, Peter Levathes. Exercising his clout as the company's biggest stockholder, Darryl Zanuck had succeeded in toppling the Skouras regime and had taken over as president of the company. To replace Levathes as head of production, he had chosen someone whom he felt supremely confident was "the best guy for the job," his twenty-seven-year-old son, Richard.

Now, after half a decade at the helm, the Zanucks could point to an impressive string of hits for Fox, led by *The Sound of Music*, fast on its way to becoming the biggest blockbuster since *Gone With the Wind*, and Darryl Zanuck's personal production of *The Longest Day*, already the top-grossing black-and-white movie in history. Under the leadership of the two Zanucks, Twentieth Century-Fox had been propelled from a period of near bankruptcy into an era of enormous corporate prosperity. As the Zanucks took their bows before the grateful stockholders, the applause was long and loud. For Darryl F. Zanuck and his son, a seemingly unbeatable team, the Starlight Roof was the top of the world.

THREE-and-a-half years later, on a bleak December day in 1970, Richard D. Zanuck marched into another synod of the Twentieth Century-Fox Film Corporation, not trailing after his father this time, but prepared to confront him. The company's board of directors was convening amid rumors of a major executive shake-up. Things had not gone well for Fox in the time since the Zanucks' shared ovation at the Waldorf. Buoyed by the sensational profits of *The Sound of Music*, the studio tried unavailingly to duplicate the formula with more big-budget musical extravaganzas—*Dr. Dolittle*, *Star!*, and *Hello, Dolly!* Intent on repeating the commercial success of *The Longest Day*, millions were being poured into a second World War II epic, the catastrophic *Tora! Tora! Tora!* Behaving as if its motto were "Nothing succeeds like excess," the company was drowning in red ink.

As he prepared to face the board of directors that day, Richard Zanuck mulled over the origins of this unlikely confrontation. With the help of another studio vice-president, David Brown, he had drawn up a master plan for the future direction of Twentieth Century-Fox. Among its provisions was the recommendation that Darryl F. Zanuck be named chairman of the board, so that Richard could succeed him as president. Darryl smelled a palace coup. Richard Zanuck and David Brown argued privately that the change in titles was part of a larger strategy for insuring the Zanuck family's continued hegemony. But DFZ (as everyone, including his son, called him) thought otherwise. He accused Richard of perpetrating "the con job of the century." And he made up his mind that his son and heir would have to go.

When it came time to consider the resolution demanding Richard Zanuck's resignation, a majority of the board voted aye. Most of them had been appointed by DFZ himself, and if he wanted Richard axed, so be it. The king prevailed; the dauphin was banished. The board of directors of Twentieth Century-Fox was not about to commit the ultimate act of lese-majesty, at least not yet . . .

IF Richard Zanuck is an example *par excellence* of the Hollywood crown prince groomed from childhood to occupy a position of power inside the movie industry, his father was something else entirely. Darryl Zanuck was an anomaly among the early moguls. While most of them were immigrant Jews from the ghettos of Middle Europe, Zanuck was a second-generation WASP from the American Middle West; he had no *landsmen* to pave his way or give him favors. As his wife Virginia was always quick to remind people, "He was a self-made little boy without relatives in the business."

Darryl Francis Zanuck was born on September 5, 1902, in the dusty little farming community of Wahoo, Nebraska. His father was the night clerk at the local hotel, inaptly named Le Grande. Frank Zanuck liked working the evening shift, since it gave him time to indulge his passion for poker. He was an incurable gambler, more likely to be found playing cards with the other night owls who hung out in the hotel lobby than tending his desk. Frank got away with that sort of thing because his wife would beg the owner to go easy on him. His wife was the owner's daughter.

It was common knowledge in Wahoo that Louise Torpin Zanuck had married beneath her station. In addition to Le Grande Hotel, her father owned practically everything else in town. Louise contracted tuberculosis when her son Darryl was six, and she moved to Southern California in search of a more comfortable climate. There she secured a divorce from Frank Zanuck and married a Bible-toting accountant named Norton—to whom young Darryl took an instant dislike. In contrast to the boy's flamboyant father, Norton was a penny-pinching martinet who physically abused his wife and stepson. If Darryl Zanuck's appetite for risk-taking and high-living was a legacy from Frank, his lifelong revulsion toward "money-men" and hypocrites was probably rooted in the disdain he felt for his stepfather.

The move to Southern California was fortuitous for young Darryl. Silent pictures were being shot in the neighborhood of his mother's Glendale home, and he would frequently play hooky from school to observe the goings-on. On one such outing, the crew needed an extra to play the part of an Indian child. Darryl donned a costume and wig—and made his motion picture debut as a Chippewa maiden.

After a stint in the army during World War I, Zanuck returned to Los Angeles and tried his hand at writing pulp fiction. His first sale, a story called "Mad Desire," was to Bernarr Macfadden's *Physical Culture* magazine. In florid detail, the author narrated the descent of a weak young soul who, after surrendering to the evils of drink, drugs, and sex, finds redemption in true love and body building. ("Yes, Loma dear, it was happiness and you—or grief and the dope. I chose the first.") His growing reputation as a pulp writer won Zanuck a meeting with Sol Wurtzel of the Fox Film Company, who bought one of his ideas as a vehicle for the studio's leading star, William Russell.

When Zanuck discovered that the man who adapted his story for the screen was paid more money than he was for writing the original, he decided to become a screenwriter himself. He landed a few assignments but soon realized that his asking price would go up if he had the added cachet of being a book author. *Habit and other Stories* by Darryl Zanuck, published by a vanity press in 1923, promptly found its way into every production office in Hollywood. It was a strange miscellany, consisting of one new yarn, a couple of rejected scenarios, and a long testimonial the author had once been commissioned to write for a product called Yuccatone Hair Restorer. Zanuck sold the four sections of the book to different producers, earning himself the handsome total of $11,000. Three of its four chapters, including the hair tonic testimonial, were turned into silent pictures.

As a writer, DFZ was fast, slick, and incredibly prolific. Luckily, those virtues were more highly prized in the movie business than narrative logic or scintillating wit, both of which he lacked. Through a director pal named Mal St. Clair, he received an assignment from Warner Bros. to write scripts about the adventures of an intrepid German shepherd. Rin Tin Tin woofed his way into the hearts of the nation, and Darryl F. Zanuck was on his way to becoming one of the highest-paid screenwriters in town.

He soon moved into production, supervising *The Jazz Singer* in 1927. When the first "talking picture" clicked with the public, ushering in a new cinematic era, Warner Bros. was saved from another of its periodic declines, and Darryl Zanuck was dubbed The Boy Wonder of Hollywood. He continued to prosper as production chief at Warners, overseeing such landmark films as *Little Caesar*, *The Public Enemy*, *42nd Street*, and *I Am a Fugitive from a Chain Gang*. Among the contract directors he was overseeing were Ernst Lubitsch and Mervyn LeRoy; his stable of players included Edward G. Robinson, Paul Muni, James Cagney, Barbara Stanwyck, Bette Davis, and Ruby Keeler. In 1933, the thirty-one-year-old Zanuck was earning more than a quarter-million dollars a year and presiding over the most thoroughly revitalized studio in Hollywood.

Producer Milton Sperling, who was Harry Warner's son-in-law and who worked for Zanuck at Warner Bros., recalls the first time he saw DFZ on the Warner lot: "He was carrying his polo mallet and was followed by his retinue of stooges. Suddenly, he stopped, walked over to the stage wall, and peed on it, all the while talking over his shoulder to the people he was with." Already the Zanuck legend was taking shape. Crude, impetuous, dynamic—DFZ delighted in creating an outrageous image of himself, one that would magnify his stature in the eyes of his underlings. Physically, he stood a mere five-foot-five, but in the minds of his co-workers, and eventually the public, he would become larger than life. Chomping on his big cigar, peering out from behind his dark glasses, this Napoleonic figure was to become everyone's idea of the movie mogul *sans pareil*.

Despite the $5,000-a-week salary he was being paid to run Warners, and despite the fact that he had been given (in his words) "*practically* a free hand" to make decisions there, DFZ knew that as long as Jack and Harry Warner were around, ultimate authority would rest with them. The heads of rival studios, including MGM and Columbia, tried to lure him over, but he resisted their tempting offers. If he was going to walk out on his Warner Bros. contract, it would not be to play the role of hireling—regardless of how well-paid he might be. He wanted to set up a studio of his own.

In April of 1933, he seized the opportunity to do just that. Suffering a somewhat delayed reaction to the Great Depression, the Hollywood studios had jointly agreed to cut costs by reducing salaries for all personnel by 30 percent. Price Waterhouse and the Motion Picture Academy, the arbiters responsible for reinstating the cut salaries at each studio, locked horns with Harry Warner over the timing of the reinstatement at Warner Bros. Zanuck sided with the employees, arguing that he had agreed to let the Academy and Price Waterhouse decide when full salaries should be restored. Zanuck and Harry Warner became embroiled in a bitter argument over the issue, which Jack Warner tried in vain to mediate. In the end, Zanuck resigned, in his words, "as a matter of principle."

It was also a matter of expediency. The studio labor dispute gave Zanuck the pretext he needed to breach his Warner contract.

Joining forces with Joseph Schenck (whose venture capital came from his brother, MGM president Nicholas Schenck) and William Goetz (who was being bankrolled by his father-in-law, Louis B. Mayer), DFZ founded the new company that was to become Twentieth Century-Fox. Except for a brief interval during the war when Goetz took over the studio (leading to his own swift severance when DFZ returned), Zanuck was the undisputed king of Fox.

If he ruled with an iron hand, he was also an inspiring force. He moved like a small hurricane, overseeing every corner of the huge lot. His enthusiasm for moviemaking was contagious, and even his most ardent enemies conceded that Zanuck was the most energetic of the Hollywood rajahs. He seized on *ideas* and transformed them into movies. "He always pounded into me the need to examine the basic idea," says his son Richard. "No matter how many stars you put in the damn thing or how well it's directed, if you're wrong about the basic notion, there's very little you can do to salvage it." From the time he was at Warner Bros., Zanuck had a particular passion for melodramas torn from the headlines. At Fox, his pet projects were topical stories on subjects ranging from the plight of the dispossessed (*The Grapes of Wrath*), to anti-semitism (*Gentlemen's Agreement*), racial prejudice (*Pinky* and *No Way Out*), and mental illness (*The Snake Pit*). Some of these films may now seem dated and flat-footed in their handling of complex themes, but when they were released, they had an urgency that held audiences in thrall.

In a 1937 *New Yorker* profile of Darryl Zanuck, Alva Johnston noted that Zanuck's talent as a filmmaker was essentially journalistic. He did not create the gangster cycle or the "social consciousness" genre, Johnston pointed out. He did, however, know when the moment was right to start making such films and when it was right to *stop* making them. Zanuck, Johnston said, possessed "the sovereign journalistic gift of getting bored in time and dropping a theme before it becomes a public nuisance."

In contrast to Louis B. Mayer or Jack Warner, Zanuck's strength as an executive was never in his eye for acting talent. The Fox stable contained few thoroughbred talents: performers such as Don Ameche, John Payne, Alice Faye, Betty Grable, Cornel Wilde, Carmen Miranda, Dana Andrews, Jeanne Crain, and Vincent Price were the Fox "stars." Even the company's best players—Tyrone Power, Gene Tierney, Linda Darnell—might have been considered borderline compared to MGM's Garbo, Tracy, and Hepburn or Warners' Davis, Cagney, and Bogart.

On the other hand, Zanuck had a keener sense of storytelling than any other mogul. Though his own efforts at writing were usually quite dreadful, he had an editor's instinct for spotting the gift in others. He understood the importance of a solid script. "Usually, the writer is the first person that everyone pisses on," notes his son Richard. "But DFZ really had a great deal of respect for writers." Among the first-rate screenwriters whom DFZ had under long-term contract at Fox were Nunnally Johnson (*The Grapes of Wrath*), Philip Dunne (*How Green Was My Valley*), and Joseph L. Mankiewicz (*All About Eve*).

Zanuck always prided himself on being in the forefront of the latest trends. After the Second World War, Fox became the first American studio to follow the example of the Italian neo-realists and produce a series of documentary-like movies filmed on actual locations. Such films as *The House on 92nd Street*, *Boomerang!*, *Call Northside 777*, and *Kiss of Death* won praise for their gritty realism and set a whole new direction for Hollywood movies. By 1950, Zanuck's face was on the cover of *Time*, crowned in celluloid. "Producer Zanuck is richly endowed with tough-mindedness, talent, an outsized ego, and a glutton's craving for hard work," the *Time* story declared. "These qualities, indulged with endless enthusiasm for a quarter century, have not only sped him to the top, but have somehow left him free of ulcers and in the pink of health."

Back in the days when DFZ was an up-and-coming writer for silent pictures, Mal St. Clair, the same man who had introduced him to Rin Tin Tin, also introduced him to a pretty young actress named Virginia Fox. As a performer, Virginia's main virtue was her ability to take direction. "If I was hanging from an elk's head and they said, 'Hold it,' I held it," she later said. "I did whatever I was told." That was an attribute that would serve her well when, after a whirlwind courtship, she married Darryl F. Zanuck in 1922. She became the model "studio widow," patiently indulging her husband's absenteeism, his megalomania, even his well-known philandering. As with so many other moguls, extramarital encounters were practically a daily ritual with DFZ. "Headquarters would close down every afternoon between 4:00 and 4:30," recalls Milton Sperling. "That was Zanuck's playtime. He had a constant stream of women eager to award their favors because he had so many favors to give in return." Actress Corinne Calvet provides a rather graphic account of one such late-afternoon encounter with DFZ. "Dramatically, he turned on his heels and stood a few feet away

from me with his erect penis standing out of his unzipped pants,"
Calvet reports in her autobiography, *Has Corinne Been A Good
Girl?* Deciding that she would indeed be a good girl, she declined
his invitation to "come to Palm Springs for a weekend of sunny
sex play" and left the office, convinced that "Zanuck, the big
movie mogul, just enjoyed being a flasher."

Whatever attention or affection Virginia Zanuck was preempted
from giving her husband, she bestowed instead on her children
and friends. She loved to entertain, though her style was more
relaxed and casual than that of the "Saturday night ladies" like
Edith Goetz and Doris Warner. Instead of elegant soirees and
formal dinners, Virginia preferred presiding over weekend-long
festivities at the family's Santa Monica beach house filled with
leisurely breakfasts, afternoon croquet, and the endless pranks
foisted upon unwitting guests by her husband·and his chums. After
Virginia died in 1982, her daughter Darrylin took out an ad in
Variety to thank her mother's many friends for their condolences.
She referred to Virginia Fox Zanuck as she thought she should be
remembered—"the hostess of Hollywood."

In the summer of 1951, Darryl and Virginia were in Paris,
where they were introduced to a green-eyed Polish playgirl and
sometime model named Bella Wegier. Bella had recently been
divorced from a wealthy industrialist. She was vivacious and exotic,
if not conventionally beautiful. Both Zanucks were instantly
charmed, and they started seeing the girl frequently. Virginia took
her shopping and to lunch. Darryl took her to bed. According to
Bella, it was Mrs. Zanuck who proffered the invitation to "come
to America and be our guest." When Bella turned up in Los
Angeles a year later, Darryl and the "hostess of Hollywood" invited
her to move into the Santa Monica beach house. There Virginia
and Bella laughed and shared pleasantries during the day, and
Darryl and Bella resumed the affair at night.

Bella Wegier soon became so enamored of her newfound bene-
factors that she wanted to honor them somehow. Taking her cue
from the Zanuck's well-known fondness for acronyms (as reflected
in the name of their family mansion, dubbed Ric-Su-Dar in tribute
to their three children, Richard, Susan, and Darrylin), she borrowed the first letters from their respective names and christened
herself Bella Darvi. Darryl embarked on a feverish campaign to
make Bella into an American star, working the Fox publicity
machine overtime on her behalf. He first cast her as an atomic
scientist setting sail on a fateful submarine voyage in Sam Fuller's

Hell and High Water. Undeterred by her limp performance in this low-budget programmer, DFZ awarded her a featured role in the lavish 1954 Cinemascope production of *The Egyptian*, to be directed by Michael Curtiz, with Marlon Brando starring. Just before shooting was to begin, Brando's agent called Zanuck to inform him that his client was pulling out of the project. "He doesn't like Mike Curtiz," the agent explained. "He doesn't like the role. And he can't stand Bella Darvi." The Brando part went to Edmond Purdom, who was almost as stiff as his mummified co-star. *The Egyptian* was an unmitigated clinker. In his *New York Times* review, Bosley Crowther described the film as "a dull one to sit through," and assigned much of the blame to the "ponderous parading of boudoir pretense and the monotony of Miss Darvi's smirk."

Meanwhile, the relationship between DFZ and "La Bella Darvi" was becoming more intimate and less discreet. The Fox publicity department still took care to send out press releases suggesting that Bella was being squired about town by eligible young bachelors. An excerpt from some studio-prepared "Notes" for gossip columnist Dorothy Manners is typical of the claptrap flackery: "Bella seems not to be lonely in Hollywood. She has been glimpsed dining and dancing with such a variety of swains as John Carroll, Nicky Hilton, Bob Calhoun, Frank McCarthy, Gary Steffan, and others." The B-movie star Brad Dexter was her most frequently named beau. But almost all of Bella's "swains" were in fact casual acquaintances or beards for DFZ. Susan Zanuck, who shared the annex of the Santa Monica beach house with Bella while her father was carrying on the affair, finally had a heart-to-heart talk with Virginia (who, incredible as it may seem, apparently never knew— or let on that she knew—the true nature of Darryl's interest in Bella). Alerted at last to the fact that her husband's attachment to their young friend was something more than professional or avuncular, Virginia threw them both out of the house. For Darryl F. Zanuck, more than a marriage had ended.

"MY separation and break-up from Mrs. Zanuck came at the same time as my divorce or breakup with Hollywood," DFZ would later remark. "Both came to a head together. My mood was to escape, to get away from the scene, the social scene, and everything connected with it."

"He felt he had been doing the same thing for twenty years," says Richard Zanuck, looking back on that turning point in his father's life. "He was bored. Though he would sometimes take off for four weeks to ski or go hunting in Alaska or Africa, he really felt he was a slave to his position and to the studio. He needed a change." Darryl Zanuck dealt with his sudden mid-life crisis as he dealt with everything else in his life—decisively and flamboyantly.

DFZ recognized that his personal life was crumbling in much the same way that the studio system he had helped to create was collapsing around him. Stars had begun forming their own production companies in the early 1950s, and the contract system was disintegrating. Television was keeping ticket-buyers at home, and movie revenues were declining. Hollywood, as a vibrant, innovative center of feature film production, was being supplanted by Paris, London, and Rome. In 1956, DFZ made up his mind to resign his post as head of Fox and move to Europe. He demanded—and received—from the Fox board a multi-picture deal to finance his independent company, DFZ Productions. According to the terms of his contract, he would be given free rein to make whatever pictures he wanted; the only condition was that any film with a budget in excess of five million dollars would require the approval of the Fox board.

DFZ arranged a generous property settlement for Virginia and set off with Bella for Europe. But instead of devoting himself to film production, he spent most of his time following Bella across the continent as she indulged her insatiable appetite for gambling, drifting from casino to casino until they both ran out of money. Bella gambled away almost every *sou* Zanuck could muster. She would pawn her jewelry, then call DFZ to get her out of hock. On one occasion, he had to impose on his pal, Howard Hughes, to bail her out of a $50,000 gambling debt. One longtime aide recalls seeing the two of them at a French gambling house: "She was sitting at the high stakes roulette table, and Zanuck was standing behind her. She was losing badly, and she kept saying, 'Give me chips!' He dug in his pocket and stacked the chips in a neat little pile in front of her. Then she said, 'Get more!' Ten years before, any woman who talked to him that way would have been pulled up by the hair. But now he just trotted off and got the chips. There was a theory that he had suddenly become impotent and she had found the way to turn him on. Who knows? Why else would someone have given up his whole life to chase this silly woman around Europe?"

DFZ's inaugural project as an independent producer, *Island in the Sun*, won some notoriety as the first American movie in which a white woman (Joan Fontaine) was kissed on screen by a black man (Harry Belafonte). It stirred considerable controversy, especially in the American South, and turned a handsome profit. But the productions that followed *Island in the Sun* were expensive failures. So was the affair with Bella Darvi. After one particularly bitter row in 1957, they parted company for good. Bella tried vainly to revive her acting career—in between suicide attempts. In September of 1971, she turned on the gas in her small Monte Carlo apartment and killed herself.

When Bella disappeared from his life, Darryl found another protégée in the person of Juliette Greco, the svelte, sultry-voiced chanteuse who was being touted as the successor to the legendary Edith Piaf. Unlike Bella Darvi, Juliette Greco was already a European celebrity when she met Darryl Zanuck. She was not yet a movie star, however, and he was determined to mold her into one. Because he believed she needed "important" pictures to showcase her talents, DFZ secured two major literary properties, Ernest Hemingway's *The Sun Also Rises* and Romain Gary's *The Roots of Heaven*, for her. Juliette co-starred with Tyrone Power, Ava Gardner, Errol Flynn, and a newcomer named Robert Evans, in *The Sun Also Rises*, but under Henry King's leaden direction, the movie was a box office flop. With John Huston signed to direct *The Roots of Heaven*, DFZ was convinced that this impassioned plea for wildlife preservation would become the critical and commercial success that he so desperately needed to re-establish his tarnished reputation. He poured everything into the abortive project, transporting his entire staff to French Equatorial Africa so that he could personally supervise the production and—more importantly—be with Juliette.

Before DFZ went off to Africa, his company acquired the rights to Meyer Levin's bestselling novel, *Compulsion*. A fictionalized account of the notorious Leopold-Loeb "thrill murder" trial, the book had already been turned into a successful Broadway play. Off in the jungle with the crew of his magnum opus, DFZ needed someone else to oversee filming of the more modest courtroom melodrama, *Compulsion*. In the past, it was not unusual for him to delegate such responsibilities to his cronies. Georgie Jessel, for example, who served as unofficial court jester in the Zanuck palace, received most of his producing assignments at Fox (such as *I Wonder Who's Kissing Her Now* with June Haver, and *I Don't Care* with Mitzi Gaynor) because he was the monarch's boon companion. Once, DFZ even gave his ski instructor, Otto Lang, a shot at producing; he was so pleased with the results that he rewarded Lang with a multi-picture contract. Unlike Mayer or Laemmle, DFZ did not have a flock of relatives to whom he doled out jobs. His son-in-law, Robert Jacks (married at the time to Zanuck's daughter, Darrylin), was a contract producer with Fox, but Jacks was busy with DFZ in Africa. Fortunately, by the time *Compulsion* was ready to be made, DFZ's only son, Richard, had graduated from Stanford and entered the family business. DFZ was eager to emulate the other moguls and bring his heir into the fold. At the age of twenty-three, Richard Zanuck was named to produce *Compulsion*.

There were those who thought that a beach party movie would have been a more appropriate initiation into the ranks of production for young Zanuck. The story of two brilliant, bookish college students who set out to commit the perfect crime, *Compulsion* depicted a world that seemed utterly remote from the experience of former surfing bum "Dickie" Zanuck. But like Artie Strauss and Judd Steiner, the Leopold and Loeb characters in Meyer Levin's story, Richard at least knew what it was to be rich, spoiled, and a thrill-seeker. By his own account, he had been "the wildest kid in the West—rough, rowdy, an all-American brat. My parents tried to hide me from guests because I might punch somebody in the stomach or butt him with my head." For his sixteenth birthday, he was given a brand new car, even though he had not yet learned how to drive. Three days later, careening down a steep canyon road at eighty miles an hour, he smashed into another vehicle, nearly killing the occupants. Once he was picked up by the police in Palm Springs when a knife fight broke out during a wild party. Though he was bright and well-schooled by his father's coterie of private tutors, young Richard generally preferred riding a motorcycle or surfboard to hitting the books.

On the set of *Compulsion*, however, Richard demonstrated the same sort of purposeful approach to work that characterized his father. He was, to quote a *New York Times* article on the making of the film, "a chip off the old block in more ways than one." The *Times* reporter was particularly struck by the physical resemblance between the novice producer and his legendary father, noting that Richard had even grown a small mustache—"thin and slick, as though applied with a make-up brush"—that accentuated the likeness. Richard brought *Compulsion* in ahead of schedule and under budget. As it turned out, the movie was a considerable *succes d'estime*, and a money-maker to boot. It was, in fact, the only profitable production of DFZ's company during the late 1950s. It was also the only one that DFZ was not personally involved in making. With the plaudits he earned for *Compulsion*, Richard Zanuck had come a long way toward proving himself, at the same time that his father's multi-million dollar spectacle—*The Roots of Heaven*—was dying at the box office.

Two years after the release of *Compulsion*, DFZ tried to duplicate its success by personally producing another courtroom melodrama, *Crack in the Mirror*. That project reunited two of the stars of *Compulsion*, Orson Welles and Bradford Dillman, with the film's director, Richard Fleischer. A couple of new elements were introduced: the female lead was Darryl Zanuck's lady friend, Juliette Greco, and the screenwriter was Mark Canfield, an alias for none other than Darryl F. Zanuck. *Crack in the Mirror* opened to terrible reviews and promptly vanished. It was around this time that Richard Zanuck shaved off the mustache.

After a series of well-publicized quarrels, Juliette Greco walked out on Darryl Zanuck and commenced writing her decidedly unflattering memoir of their affair, *Je Suis Comme Je Suis (I Am What I Am)*. "I have always loved lost causes," Juliette mused. "He [Zanuck] was like an orphan to me. I was attracted to that poor little rich man who was in some ways blind, deaf, and dumb." Comments like that, together with her denigrating descriptions of his hot temper, his jealousies, and his "baby doll pyjamas," so enraged DFZ that he slapped her with a $20,000 defamation of character suit. Serialization of the book in European magazines was cancelled as a result. As a parting gift, Juliette had presented Zanuck with a miniature schnauzer, who became his constant companion in her absence. Milton Sperling recalls seeing DFZ in Paris, sitting at his customary table for two, holding the little dog on his lap: "He looked forlorn. Here was this great man, looking as if he was waiting for some girl to come, some girl who was cheating on him. You could almost imagine her saying to him, 'Here, you hold the dog!'" DFZ was nearing sixty. Alone with his schnauzer, he became a familiar, if pathetic, sight on the streets of Paris.

While DFZ licked his wounds and dined with the dog, Richard Zanuck was busy preparing his second production at his father's company offices on the Fox lot. The movie was *The Chapman Report*, based on Irving Wallace's best-selling novel about a Kinsey-style sex survey. Although an elegant and respected director, George Cukor, had been signed to direct the film, the controversial subject matter was causing jitters among the studio flacks. DFZ's spats with Juliette Greco had recently filled the gossip columns. How would it now look if the production company headed by this well-known libertine were to make a salacious picture under the Fox banner? Reacting to the charges that he was involved in producing "a dirty picture," Richard Zanuck carefully dissociated himself from his father's public image. "Being a family man," he told the press, "I'm not going to put anything on the screen to make me blush in front of my children." But Spyros Skouras, the bluenose Greek tycoon who had assumed the helm at Fox during Zanuck's exile, was not convinced. He instructed his production chief and fellow Greek, Peter Levathes, to cancel the production just as it was about to go into rehearsal.* Richard Zanuck was livid. He called his father in Paris and told him the news.

"They'll never know what hit them," said Darryl Zanuck.

From his Parisian outpost, DFZ had observed the decline of Twentieth Century-Fox with dismay and simmering anger. Though he knew that his own productions had done nothing to enhance the studio's standing, he blamed most of what had gone wrong on Skouras's ineptitude and bad taste. From the golden years of Zanuck, the studio had descended into the dark ages of the "Greek interlude." Its production schedule was clogged with such threadbare testaments to Skouras's and Levathes's common ancestry as *It Happened in Athens* and *The 300 Spartans*, or else with lifeless programmers starring the likes of Jayne Mansfield, Fabian, and Gary Crosby. It was a steady menu of Greek treats and sweet confections—baklava for the masses.

Skouras had been an exhibitor, Levathes an ad man, and DFZ considered both to be ignoramuses on the subject of production. Zanuck's departure from Fox in 1956 had opened the door for Skouras, as the company's second largest stockholder, to assume control of the company. Now DFZ was ready to retrieve the fortress he had abandoned half a decade earlier. Personally and professionally, he was finally pulling himself together, as he supervised the filming of *The Longest Day* in 1961, which he felt confident would restore his lost prestige. Recreating the invasion of Normandy with his mammoth international cast, he was once again doing what he did best: making decisions, barking orders, taking charge. (His libido, too, had been rejuvenated; he had a new consort at his side, a young red-haired model named Irina Demick,

*A few months later, *The Chapman Report* was reactivated at Warner Bros.

who was given a plum role in the movie as a French Resistance fighter.) DFZ saw *The Longest Day* as his personal masterwork, and he had no intention of permitting Skouras and the rest of the Fox management to bungle its release. It was time to take matters into his own hands.

"I own with my family about 280,000 shares of stock and the voting control of it all," Zanuck wrote to the board of directors of Twentieth Century-Fox on June 6, 1962. "I have a personal interest in the survival of the Corporation as well as a certain amount of pride in what was once described as 'the best operating Studio in the industry'. . ." A bitter power struggle ensued.

Zanuck confessed that his record as an independent producer since *Island in the Sun* had been dismal. "I cannot defend my position," he said, "nor can I blame it on bad luck . . . I believe that I have now profited by errors in judgment, and I am no longer confronted with private or personal problems which obsessed me prior to commencing *The Longest Day*. I will continue to make mistakes in this highly speculative business, but the 'know-how' I have acquired as a result of my failures and the lessons I have learned have been of enormous value." On June 11, 1962, Zanuck conferred in New York with Judge Samuel Rosenman, chairman of the Fox board of directors, and Robert Lehman, another prominent member of the board. They went over the list of nominees which the board had prepared to put forth as Skouras's successor as president of Twentieth Century-Fox. James Aubrey, Mike Frankovich, and Otto Preminger were among the candidates. Zanuck later described the candidates as capable men but "utterly idiotic recommendations" for the presidency. "I frankly wanted to vomit," he said.

Zanuck returned to Paris and mulled over his strategy. He sent a cable to the Fox board, saying, among other things, "I have not been offered the presidency of Twentieth Century-Fox. Whether or not I would accept it depends on certain vital circumstances." He went on to suggest that *if* the position were offered, he would expect not to be "second-guessed" by inexperienced "committees." The text of Zanuck's cable was picked up by the press, and the Fox board found itself with a public contest for control of the company. Skouras tried to marshal support for his increasingly tenuous position, but the tide had already turned against him. Zanuck simply had too much influence—based on his family's stock interest in the corporation, his personal reputation as a filmmaker, and his undisputed "know-how." DFZ made a personal appearance before the board and allowed himself to be grilled on subjects ranging from his extravagances as a producer to his peccadilloes as a ladies' man. He survived the inquisition, and when it was all over, the two Greeks were out, the two Zanucks were in, and Twentieth Century-Fox was back under the command of the man who had first shaped its destiny.

The first order of business was to shut down the studio. With the exception of the TV series, *Dobie Gillis*, shooting on the Fox lot was immediately suspended. An unofficial head of his father's purge squad, Richard Zanuck was in charge of handing out the pink slips. "Things were so tight," he said, "we were trying to figure out ways to get another janitor off the payroll." When the dust finally settled, it was generally recognized that the corporate housecleaning, however difficult and unpleasant, had been an essential first step in straightening out the mess left by the Skouras regime.

The biggest headache of all remained out of reach—*Cleopatra*. So much money had already been poured into the behemoth production by the time the Zanucks inherited it that they, like the company accounts, were completely at a loss. As a parable of wretched excess, the story of *Cleopatra*, from its beginnings as a small Joan Collins vehicle to its butchered final cut at the hands of DFZ, remains one of the most outlandish real-life dramas in the history of Hollywood. Zanuck's public feuds with the film's director, Joseph L. Mankiewicz, and its stars, Elizabeth Taylor and Richard Burton, made headlines for months. DFZ was determined to save Fox from financial ruin by pulling in the reins, but Mankiewicz, Taylor, and Burton fought him at every turn. On one occasion, Richard Zanuck was dispatched to Paris to try and dissuade Burton and Taylor from filing a $50 million breach-of-contract suit against the studio. As it happened, Elizabeth Taylor had been a childhood playmate of Darrylin Zanuck, Richard's sister; and Burton had dated Susan Zanuck, his other sister. If Burton and Taylor had been excessive in their demands, they knew from personal observation that the Zanucks were not exactly avatars of thrift. Elizabeth opened the meeting by telling Richard Zanuck, "You're a brat, and you always were a brat." She proceeded to remind him of the day he and young Irving Thalberg, Jr. tied her to a beam in the Thalberg basement while she screamed her lungs out for help. Richard Zanuck realized that this was hardly a time to reactivate old grudges, and the whole matter of the lawsuit was put on hold indefinitely.

Since it was too late to abandon *Cleopatra*, the Zanucks were determined to economize on other projects. In this period of extreme budget-cutting, one property posed a special problem. Fox owned the rights to the Rodgers and Hammerstein musical, *The Sound of Music*, based on the story of the singing Trapp family's escape from Nazi persecution. It would be an expensive movie to make, but one with obvious box office potential. Irving "Swifty" Lazar, the agent who had engineered the original sale to Fox, now had a buyer willing to take it off the Zanucks' hands. The proposed deal would yield Fox a $2 million profit. That was a tempting sum for a company teetering on the edge of bankruptcy. Nonetheless, the Zanucks turned it down. Two of DFZ's biggest hits had been stories of family survival—*The Grapes of Wrath* and *How Green Was My Valley*. He believed that *The Sound of Music* contained the same primal human theme, and he was determined to see it reach the screen. The gamble paid off richly—to the tune of about $200 million in profits. Together with *The Longest Day*, *The Sound of Music* pulled the studio out of the red. DFZ and the Twentieth Century-Fox Film Corporation were back in business.

Looking back on the dark days before his father and he assumed control, Richard Zanuck felt he understood what it was that had once brought the studio to the edge of ruin. "As the largest stockholders, my family stood to lose most if the company went under," he told John Gregory Dunne in 1967. "What nearly killed the company was the politics, the antagonism between the money people in the East and the picture people out here. With DZ in New York and me out here, that antagonism is gone now." In that halcyon time, Richard naively assumed that the family garrison was somehow immune to "politics." His father made no such assumption.

GONE were the days when a studio's earnings were fairly constant from year to year. As the number of productions shrank and individual budgets soared, a studio could post a $300 million profit one year and a $300 million loss the next. Following this roller coaster pattern, Fox's earnings took an unexpected nose dive in the late 1960s. By the summer of 1970, the studio was once again in terrible financial straits. Fox had its share of hits—*M*A*S*H*, *Butch Cassidy and the Sundance Kid*, *Patton*—but the post-*Sound of Music* extravaganzas like *Dr. Dolittle* and *Star!* were draining the company coffers. In addition, the gargantuan World War II epic, *Tora! Tora! Tora!*, was fast on its way to becoming *Cleopatra* redivivus. As the summer meeting of the board of directors drew near, a crisis was brewing.

Richard Zanuck recalls, "It became clear that we were going to have to tell the board some awful, shocking financial news about the corporation, including cutting off the dividend completely. DZ was so shocked and stunned—he had just flown in from Paris. David [Brown] and I met with him and decided that we'd better do some pretty big thinking before his marching into the board meeting the next day. We decided to call off the meeting altogether and hold it the following month. So DZ had his secretary get on the phone and call the whole board to tell them not to come to New York. And he left David and me to figure out a way to get out of this mess."

David Brown recounts what happened next. "We wrote a memorandum telling the board that we had a radical new direction for the company which we had hoped to present at that very board meeting, but owing to the difficulty of getting all the information together in time, we were obliged to postpone the meeting. The board of directors received the memorandum announcing this very radical and far-reaching plan for the corporation that would take us well into the twenty-first century. Everybody accepted that. Then DFZ turned to us and said, 'Now what the fuck will the plan be?'"

That evening, Richard Zanuck and David Brown dropped DFZ off at the airport and proceeded down to Richard's house in Newport Beach. There they brainstormed for several days, composing the revolutionary white paper that would, they hoped, divert the board's attention from the shocking financial news and direct it toward the rosy future. "Many of the things that were in that plan were matters that Dick and I wanted the company to adopt all along, and this gave us an opportunity to define them," David Brown says. Among its two dozen provisions, the white paper urged that the Stanford Research Institute be engaged to make a comprehensive study of distribution, marketing, and production; that the corporate headquarters be moved to the West Coast; and that a chief financial officer be hired for the company. There was also a recommendation for changing the corporate name to Twenty-first Century-Fox. (After all, the millennium was only thirty years away.) A final suggestion was more ticklish: Darryl F. Zanuck would move up to become chairman of the board, and Richard Zanuck would take over as president.

When he read the white paper, DFZ was infuriated. "What the

hell does a chairman *do*?" he seethed. After all, that was the same position to which Skouras had been relegated when DFZ himself took over as president in 1962. Though his son and David Brown tried to assure him that they would still function as the same old triumvirate, DFZ was not convinced. He had always been suspicious of the man directly below him in the studio hierarchy. "He had a history of eliminating number-two guys," Richard Zanuck points out. "Going way back to Bill Goetz, who tried to take over during World War II, and then Arnold Grant, who was instrumental in bringing him back into the corporation [in 1962]. Number Two Man was a revolving door department." And now it was Richard's turn to go out the revolving door.

"It's easy for me to understand what went on in DFZ's mind," Richard Zanuck said a few years afterwards. "He was too big . . . too powerful. He had survived hundreds of corporate struggles and bleaker days than this, and he couldn't get it into his head that times had changed. So he thought I was trying to put him out to pasture. Which was wrong, because I always thought our only hope for survival was staying together. He never bought that I didn't want to take control away from him. And if you don't buy that, then everything I did from that point on is suspicious.

"He took it as a direct challenge to the throne," Richard observed. "And when there's a direct challenge to the throne, it has to be dealt with. Even if it's by one's only son . . ."

David Brown's wife, *Cosmopolitan* editor Helen Gurly Brown, identifies another party to the conflict—DFZ's newest paramour, a French-born fashion model and aspiring actress named Genevieve Gilles (nee Gillaizeau) who was forty-four years DFZ's junior. "David and Dick fell out with Darryl over the issue of placing Genevieve in a movie," Mrs. Brown has revealed. "The stockholders were restless over some recent flops, and Dick and David thought it was bad timing to risk casting an inexperienced girl in an expensive film. Darryl was furious. He thought Dick and David were plotting to wrest control of the company from him and that David, in particular, was the Svengali, as he put it. That was the beginning of the forcing out of my husband and— since he would not abandon 'Svengali'—of Dick Zanuck."

Richard Zanuck agrees that his own antipathy toward Gilles probably aggravated the tensions with his father. "I had a very large loathing for this girl," he says. "I had weathered, rather pleasantly in most cases, many of my father's other girls, so it wasn't that there was any rivalry or jealousy between son and girlfriend. It was just that this particular one was really bad news and caused him, myself, and the company a lot of trouble. When she knew that she had a real enemy in me, she did a lot of unfair and unfortunate pillow talk, which didn't help my father's and my relationship."

DFZ's deteriorating health was another contributing factor, according to Richard. "He went through a very bad period at that time, physically and emotionally," Richard says. "He was showing some very early signs of senility. He became paranoid, partly, I think, because he felt his power with women and in life generally emanated from that position at the studio. He felt that any removal of that power would de-ball him, not only in the business world but in his social life. He was scared things would crumble for him if he was moved aside."

As the day of reckoning drew near, it became increasingly clear that both Richard Zanuck and David Brown had their heads on the chopping block. In a last-ditch effort to save themselves, they tried to enlist the aid of the man whom they had personally recruited to take over the job of chief financial officer of the company, a position that had been created as a direct consequence of their white paper recommendation. The man was Dennis C. Stanfill, an Annapolis graduate, Rhodes scholar, and former Wall Street analyst.

David Brown recalls an encounter he had with Stanfill shortly before Richard Zanuck and he were fired: "He took me aside in the empty boardroom, which was to be our execution chamber at a later time, and he said, in an uncommon conspiratorial tone for Dennis, 'Do you think we can get Dick to fly to Paris and get this terrible thing patched up?' I said it would be wonderful if it *could* be, but I didn't know whether Darryl Zanuck should be flying to New York or *who* should be doing the patching up."

On the eve of their final day as members of the Fox board, Richard Zanuck and David Brown placed a late-night call to Stanfill at the St. Regis Hotel and asked him to join them at "21" for a drink. "We said that we knew that on the agenda of the board there would be a resolution asking for our resignations," Brown says. "And we asked Dennis where his hand would be when that resolution came up. He said, 'Look, I'm a new boy here. I'm very appreciative of what you've done. But how long do you think I would last if my hand doesn't go up?'"

"I asked him to do something much more simple," Richard Zanuck adds. "There was just a bare quorum by one person. Many directors had stayed away—conveniently went to the Caribbean or wherever—didn't want to be involved in this. I said, 'Dennis, why don't you get a cold, get the flu, and don't show up? The meeting will have to be called off. Because if they don't have a quorum, they can't *fire* us.' But he didn't do it. Of course, that would have only prolonged things for a month, but perhaps during the month things could have been patched up."

Darryl Zanuck had always played for keeps, even with his son. When he was a boy, Richard would play badminton with his father, who never permitted him to score a single point that wasn't earned. DFZ wanted to *win*, no matter what the match, no matter who the opponent. In this most crucial battle of his career, he would emerge victorious again. Although the board of directors was the official governing body of the corporation, DFZ controlled its agenda and its operations. Theoretically, the board had the authority to approve or nullify any decision made by the president. But to do so would have required a majority of the board, and the members were too fearful of incurring the wrath of DFZ to attempt a mutiny, at least on this issue at this time. When the crucial vote was taken, a majority voted to give DFZ exactly what he wanted. On December 31, 1970, Richard Zanuck and David Brown were both given the ax.

The task of closing them off the lot fell to Dennis Stanfill. "I'll never forget his words," comments David Brown. "He said, 'You know, there's a ritual to severance.' I'd never heard that expression before, which meant, 'Get your ass out of here before sunset, because the longer you hang around, the more difficult it becomes.'"

"My car was parked at the curb with my name along the side in front of the building," recalls Richard Zanuck. "I couldn't get into the car because the painter was down on his knees in front of the thing painting my name out. I couldn't open the door without asking him to stand up so I could drive off. And, of course, our secretaries were practically frisked when they left. We were treated badly in terms of this ritual of Dennis's."

For Richard Zanuck, the humiliation was painful. "Being barred from the lot which had been my backyard playground. Being unceremoniously thrown out after working my balls off and delivering some very prominent and significant pictures. At that time, I thought it was the end of everything, and I doubted that I would ever recover. After all, how often is one head of a major film corporation? And thrown out by one's own father?"

In a *Variety* article which appeared shortly after Richard Zanuck was fired, a couple of other Fox executives were quoted as saying that Brown and he had been let go "because their modern pictures were not in tune with modern times." Richard Zanuck did not take the charge lightly. He fired off an angry letter to the editor, suggesting that since they were all part of the management team together, his accusers should at least share responsibility for such fiascoes as *Hello-Goodbye* and *Che!* He did not mention his father by name, but he didn't have to. Anyone who read *Variety* knew that those two bombs had been DFZ's own pet projects—*Hello-Goodbye* a disastrous vehicle for Genevieve Gilles, and *Che!* a stillborn biography of Che Guevara which Zanuck hoped would replicate the spirit of *Wilson*, his 1944 film about the rise and fall of an American president which he had always considered his neglected masterpiece.

Looking back on the rupture in their relations, David Brown suggests that DFZ's suspicions derived from an almost childlike envy. "I always enjoyed DZ's confidence," he says, "and that became a very dangerous thing later on, as my relationship with Dick progressed, I'll never forget DZ saying, 'I always thought you were basically loyal to me.' And I said, 'I didn't know I'd ever have to make the choice.' He was suspicious of Dick's and my relationship, and perhaps even jealous. He wanted the relationship for himself."

In addition, Brown describes a curious kind of role reversal which he believes took place between Darryl and Richard Zanuck during the period that DFZ was off making pictures in Paris and Dick was minding the store at Fox: "I've always thought that at a certain point, Dick became the father, and Darryl in a strange way became the impetuous son. Darryl had the capacity to make every picture, even the most modest, minor little thing, into the Second Coming. And Dick would have the difficult job of bringing him back to earth. He was dealing in the real world of the studio, fretting for the absent DFZ. I always detected in the relationship between DFZ and Richard something resembling sibling rivalry, between a young man and a man who never wanted to grow old."

A few months after being canned from Fox, Richard Zanuck and David Brown accepted an invitation to join the new management troop at Warner Bros., the same studio Richard's father had left thirty-eight years earlier when he founded Twentieth Century-Fox. Unfortunately, working for Warner chief Ted Ashley proved far more constricting than working for Dad. Zanuck and Brown left Warner Bros. after eighteen months to form an independent production company; they turned out a series of undistinguished flops—*Sssss, The Girl From Petrovka, Willie Dynamite, The Black Windmill*. But this brief period of unsatisfying filmmaking was not a total loss, for it was during this time that the seeds were sown for the duo's remarkable future.

During their stint as executives at Warners, Zanuck and Brown had worked with producers Julia and Michael Phillips and Tony Bill and screenwriter David Ward on a picture called *Steelyard Blues*, starring Jane Fonda and Donald Sutherland. Though the movie failed commercially, Richard Zanuck had supported the project, and he established a good rapport with the producers. Now Bill and the Phillipses had another script by Ward called *The Sting*. The cleverly constructed screenplay about a pair of Chicago con artists was a hot property, and all the studios were bidding high. Richard Zanuck called in his chit. In return for coming on as executive producers, Brown and he delivered Paul Newman, Robert Redford, and director George Roy Hill, who had made *Butch Cassidy and the Sundance Kid* at Fox when Richard Zanuck was head of production there. The deal was sealed—and with it, the stature of Richard Zanuck as a pivotal force in the New Hollywood.

The movie copped the Oscar as best picture in 1973 and proved pure gold at the box office. In 1975, Zanuck and Brown topped even this stunning success. They hired a young director named Steven Spielberg, with whom they had worked on an early Goldie Hawn vehicle called *The Sugarland Express*, to direct the film version of Peter Benchley's bestselling novel, *Jaws*. The picture turned Spielberg into the most sought-after new director in Hollywood and made Zanuck and Brown two of the richest movie-makers in history. With the profits he garnered from his percentages of *Jaws* and *The Sting*—to date, the films have grossed more than $300 million and $200 million, respectively—Richard Zanuck earned more money than his father had in an entire career.

THE Fox board's removal of Richard Zanuck in December of 1970 proved a pyrrhic victory for his father. Even before that fateful confrontation, DFZ had been losing touch with the company; he was spending most of his time in Paris overseeing *Hello-Goodbye*, the insipid love story starring Genevieve Gilles which he had ordered into production over the strenuous objections of Richard Zanuck and David Brown. An acquaintance recalls visiting DFZ on the set. A simple scene was being shot in which

Gilles was to walk down three steps, pick up a phone, and say, "Hello." During the first take, she stumbled on the steps. During the second, she dropped the phone. During the third, she made it down the stairs, picked up the phone, and said, "Yes," instead of "Hello." The comedy of errors proceeded all morning long, until the director, Jean Negulesco, finally gave up and called for a lunch break.

"How long is this going to go on?" the visitor asked Negulesco.

"Forever, I hope," replied the director. "I'm getting $5,000 a week."

Even after DFZ's careful supervision of the final cut, there was no concealing the truth. The critics were scathing in their assessments of Genevieve's thespian abilities. The *Saturday Review*'s Hollis Alpert confessed to being "sickened" by "the non-talent of the breast-baring Miss Gilles." The *Hollywood Reporter* conceded that Gilles "possesses a lovely mouth" but concluded that she "needs experience or tutoring in acting." The *Los Angeles Times* summed up the case for the prosecution: "The entire film is a showcase for the non-acting and frequently unintelligible Miss Gilles, a former Paris model and now a gorgeous starlet in the hallowed Fox tradition of Irina Demick, Juliette Greco, and Bella Darvi."

With the release of *Hello-Goodbye*, DFZ's reputation was in tatters. "It was really a dreadful goddamn thing," Richard Zanuck says. "During the whole course of the picture, my father stayed in Europe, where it was being made. He kept stringing everyone along, saying what a great, great picture this was going to be. But then when it was released, everyone's worst fears were confirmed. That was the crowning blow. He lost all credibility."

A group of dissident shareholders was formed to challenge DFZ directly. Calling themselves the Twentieth Century-Fox Stockholders' Protective Committee, they distributed a broadside with the headline, "WE HOLD DARRYL F. ZANUCK AND THE MANAGEMENT OF TWENTIETH CENTURY-FOX RESPONSIBLE FOR THE MOST DRA-MATIC LOSSES IN THE COMPANY'S HISTORY." The insurgents found a willing ally in Richard Zanuck, still smarting from the humiliation of his recent firing. His mother jumped into the fray on the side of her son. "You'd think those fellows, Dick and David, were criminals, the way they've been treated," Virginia Zanuck declared. She announced that she, too, would support the Stockholders' tective Committee against her estranged husband. "Dick has his battles, and I have mine," she told columnist Joyce Haber. "I have

100,000 shares and I take care of a lot of my grandchildren. It would kill me if everything goes down the drain. I don't know what Darryl wants. He's built up this dynasty, and now he's destroying it."

DFZ's power as the biggest individual stockholder was effectively nullified by his family's opposition. It soon became clear that the Stockholders' Protective Committee would have the votes it needed to win the proxy fight. The king had no choice but to abdicate; in September of 1971 Darryl F. Zanuck finally stepped down as head of Twentieth Century-Fox. Asked by a reporter how he felt, DFZ replied, "You want to know how I feel? I feel tired." He was succeeded as studio boss by Dennis Stanfill, the chief financial officer whom Richard Zanuck and David Brown had originally recruited to help them implement their ill-fated plan for reorganizing the studio. DFZ was given the empty title of "chairman emeritus" together with a meaningless production deal. He was, indeed, being put out to pasture.

Darryl Zanuck never quite recovered. At first, he would fire off angry memos to the new ruling junta at Fox, complaining of slights, real and imagined. But nobody was paying much attention to the old dog, whose bark now was more ferocious than his bite. In the words of his son, DFZ eventually "tuned out" of Hollywood. "It was a very sour period," Richard recalls. "He never fully recovered from the blow of being eased into oblivion by the company he founded. There was a rapid deterioration physically and mentally."

A defeated old man, DFZ left Hollywood for good. He took up residence in Palm Springs, with the bedridden wife whom he had abandoned some twenty years earlier, when he had wandered off to Europe and into the series of affairs with his various starlet-protégées.

Having been consigned to the uncomfortable role of elder statesman for almost a decade, Darryl Zanuck died in Palm Springs in 1979 at the age of seventy-seven. Though he had already given most of his money to his wife in a property settlement when he left for Europe in 1956, he still left a sizable estate of his own, including his 200,000 shares in the Twentieth Century-Fox Film Corporation. The bulk went to his wife, his son and two daughters, and his twelve grandchildren. There was also a small bequest to Genevieve Gilles, the last of his European mistresses.

Gilles's Hollywood career had faded quickly after 1971, by which time her mentor had been kicked upstairs at Twentieth

Century-Fox and her own Fox contract was cancelled by the new command, lest it prove "embarrassing" to the company. (A similar fate befell Richard Zanuck's second wife, Linda Harrison, a.k.a. Augusta Summerland. She appeared in *Planet of the Apes* for Fox while her husband was production head, and she had a featured role in the *Bracken's World* TV series—about the behind-the-scenes intrigue at a motion picture studio—which was also made at Fox. Her contract was terminated around the same time as Gilles's, and the same reason was cited.)

Gilles's acting jobs evaporated after she and the senior Zanuck went their separate ways. She started her own production company in 1975 and bought the rights to a Newberry Award-winning children's book, *Julie of the Wolves*, about an Eskimo girl lost in the tundra who finds herself adopted by a wolf pack. "This book will become a family picture with a lot of taste, a touch of class," she told Earl Wilson. Conveniently ignoring her several nude scenes in *Hello-Goodbye*, she added, "I don't want to be involved in any sex, blood, or violence films for my first production." Gilles's producing efforts proved no more successful than her attempts at acting, however, and by 1980 she was toiling as the merchandising "symbol" for a Japanese cosmetics firm. That year, she filed suit against the Zanuck family, alleging that Richard Zanuck had exerted "undue influence" over his father and cheated her out of her rightful share of the Zanuck fortune. According to Gilles, she had been promised 45 percent of DFZ's property in six separate wills. Her attorney, Marvin Mitchelson, described the action as "the first palimony suit against a dead man's estate."

It was no secret that the Zanuck children had barely tolerated their father's succession of mistresses. Although they, like their mother, made allowances for DFZ's licentiousness, they never quite accepted it. No doubt their reservations were as much monetary as moral. Bella Darvi, Juliette Greco, Irina Demick, and Genevieve Gilles had become almost as expensive for DFZ to keep as his most lavish movies were to make. When the family fortune is at stake, there are bound to be fears that some outsider will try to move in and usurp it. The Gilles lawsuit lent credence to those suspicions. Not surprisingly, perhaps, the decision to sue for a "rightful share" infected the family unit, too. In 1982, after Virginia Zanuck died in Palm Springs, David Brown, acting as guardian *ad litem* for Richard Zanuck's young sons, filed suit on their behalf against Darrylin Zanuck de Pineda, Richard's elder sister. (His other sister, Susan, had died in 1980 at the age of forty-six.) The suit alleged that Darrylin had exerted "undue influence" over her mother to undercut the share of Virginia Zanuck's estate that Richard's sons were to have received.

In December of 1981, Virginia Zanuck had drawn up a will leaving her estate to Darrylin and Darrylin's children and Richard and his children. But in April of 1982, she rewrote the will, bequeathing most of her estate to Darrylin. Richard's sons, who were to have received $2 million each under the terms of the first will, were given $5,000 each in the second. "I didn't think my mother could have been in her right mind to do that," Richard says. Richard Zanuck conferred with his attorneys and with David Brown, who is the boys' godfather. After reviewing the evidence, they decided to file suit. "I certainly didn't want another will contest," Richard says. "The secretaries don't even know where to file things any more. I say, 'File this in the will contest,' and they say, 'Which one?'"

Richard believes that the rift between his sister and himself was brought on by fundamental differences in their attitudes toward money and work. "I was the only working member of the family," he says. "My two sisters lived off the residue of the family fortune. I, being a workaholic for many years, was apart from their whole philosophy." When his own fortunes as a producer outstripped his father's, relations with the rest of the family grew strained. "What was disturbing to my two sisters, and even, strangely enough— and I'll never quite understand this—to my mother, was that I was becoming more successful than my father," he says. "There was a basic, almost unrealistic resentment when the receipts from *The Sting* and *Jaws* came in and they realized that I had amassed more money with one or two pictures than my father had in a lifetime of work. They never were able to understand it. I didn't change. My bank account changed, but I didn't. But their attitude toward me changed. It went beyond envy. A *dislike* set in. They looked upon me differently, as if they were dealing with a different person."

Though Darrylin herself has not spoken publicly on the subject, her attorney, Malcolm Ellis, told the press that Virginia Zanuck made a videotape prior to her death in which she discloses her intention to disinherit her son. Ellis has said that the recording reveals why Mrs. Zanuck was cutting Richard out of the will and why she was giving his sons only token sums. Allegedly, Virginia Zanuck revised her will because Richard was so wealthy and Darrylin was not; because, while Darrylin had waited on her "hand

and foot," Richard had rarely come to visit her; and because Richard had been harsh with his two grown daughters by an earlier marriage, Virginia and Janet, each of whom was bequeathed $100,000 in their grandmother's will.

"It's sister against brother," Ellis said. "They have these family feuds on television, on *Dallas* and *Dynasty*, but I'll tell you, these real life cases, with real life families, can have a lot more drama than soap operas."

The legal skirmishing over the elder Zanucks' wills spread to other fronts as well. In her suit to have Darryl Zanuck's 1973 will set aside, Genevieve Gilles submitted a statement signed by Thomas L. Shirley, a friend of the Zanuck family, stating that Darrylin Zanuck de Pineda had once admitted to him that, after conferring with her mother, she forged her father's signature on his last will, in order to make sure that DFZ's fortune did not go to Gilles. Shirley claimed that, after he stated publicly that Darrylin and Virginia "conspired to forge the will of Darryl F. Zanuck," they falsely accused him of stealing money from the family so as to discredit his testimony. He sued the estate of Virginia Zanuck for $20 million in damages for slander and invasion of privacy. In 1983, Shirley appeared on the syndicated television series *Lie Detector* and told his version of events. Darrylin immediately filed a $60 million slander suit against Shirley, the producers of the show, and the show's host, attorney F. Lee Bailey, who allegedly said that handwriting experts had determined the signature on Darryl F. Zanuck's will was a forgery. In all these cases, the ligitation drags on.

LAWSUITS and wills aside, the Zanuck family legacy cannot be measured solely in terms of shares of stock or millions of dollars. Richard Zanuck inherited from his father the true insider's knowledge of how movies are made, as well as the passion for making them. From the time he was eight years old and peddling *The Saturday Evening Post* on the Fox lot until he took over as head of production there at the age of twenty-seven, Richard Zanuck was continually trained in the craft of moviemaking. "I was *groomed* for that job," he says. "I knew the lot, I knew the people. I had a wealth of background and experience just by being with and working with one of the great teachers. I was doing what I was supposed to do.

"My father was demanding," Richard admits, "but he also filled me with a sense of heritage, of knowing who I was. He made me

feel special, that I had special opportunity to take advantage of."
The self-confidence which his father instilled in him freed Richard
Zanuck from the psychic impediments to which so many other
children of rich and powerful parents have been subject. There is
no doubt in his mind that it *was* an advantage to be Darryl Zanuck's
son. "When I was ready to step up, the door was open for me,"
he says. "This can be a very unforgiving and cruel business if you
are *not* trained or prepared, or if you don't have a lot of confidence
in yourself. There's not a lot of mercy. If the arched eyebrows get
to you, you can be pushed back down very easily."

Observes David Brown, "In powerful families such as the
Zanucks, generally speaking, the children fail to emulate, much
less surpass, the achievements of the parents. Only in certain
carefully regulated families, like the Zanucks or the Kennedys,
has it been possible." But there was at least one crucial difference
between Darryl Zanuck and Joseph Kennedy. Although DFZ had
groomed his son to be his successor, when the time actually came
to abdicate, DFZ was not willing to turn things over. "Dick cut
that cord himself, because he had to," Brown maintains. "He had
the option to leave it in, but he didn't."

In his partnership with David Brown, Richard Zanuck has
achieved the combination of freedom and power which he never
quite had with his father. With Brown acting as the East Coast
contact, Richard Zanuck is free to be one of the "picture people"—
the only role he relishes. He finally enjoys the benefit of a genuine
collaboration without being under anyone's thumb.

"Either one of us could do it on our own," David Brown
suggests, "but it wouldn't be as much fun." Both Richard Zanuck
and he believe that the example of DFZ's megalomania contributed
to their own determination to keep the partnership a viable one.
"I've seen what happens to solo players," Brown says. "Darryl
Zanuck, like many innovators, had to go it alone. But if you look
at the history of this industry, you find that most of the great men
who founded it wound up alone, without the support systems that
made them great."

For his part, Richard Zanuck is intent on making his working
relationship with Brown an alliance of coequals in every respect.
"I never again wanted to get into the situation where I was looking
over my shoulder," he remarks. "I wanted to have a partnership,
without any sign or possibility of the kind of internecine warfare
and jealousies and antagonisms that did unfortunately work their
way into the relationship between my father and myself."

The partnership with David Brown works for other reasons as well. Brown was a seasoned journalist and respected New York editor when Darryl Zanuck brought him out to Hollywood in 1951 to head the story department at Fox. Suave, erudite, immensely shrewd, he knows the New York literary scene, has numerous contacts in it, and enjoys a reputation for keeping one step ahead of all the manifold contemporary trends that his wife's magazine so assiduously chronicles. In some sense, he functions as Richard Zanuck's pipeline to the outside world, a function DFZ never needed to have performed for him. Zanuck senior was an adventurer, a restless globe-trotter whose curiosity took him from the plains of Nebraska to the African veldt—and all points between. Zanuck junior, by contrast, has led a fairly insular life. He is a creature of Hollywood, swaddled in moving pictures, with little of the broad experience and almost none of the wanderlust his father possessed. Richard is most comfortable poring over scripts and making deals at his studio office, or else relaxing at his Santa Monica home. (It is, in fact, the same beachfront house his parents owned when Richard was a youngster.) Growing up on the Fox lot, Richard Zanuck had the benefit of practical, firsthand training in virtually every aspect of the movie business, but it seems to have left him with little interest in, or time for, other pursuits. When asked whether he ever considered another career, Richard simply answers no: "I don't know anything else, really."

The insularity of his upbringing is reflected in his work. Most of his productions, and certainly the two most successful ones— *The Sting* and *Jaws*—have been movie-inspired movies, skillful but synthetic concoctions reeking of the backlot. Richard Zanuck has rarely attempted to move beyond mainstream commercial entertainment and deal with subtler, more demanding subject matter. His choice of material generally reflects the masculine conditioning he received from his father. Darryl Zanuck always prided himself on being a "man's man"; he lived his life as if he were auditioning to be a Hemingway hero. While Richard Zanuck does not emulate his father's aggressive machismo in his day-to-day business dealings, it is notable that most of his productions, beginning with *Compulsion*, have been movies about male bonding. *Butch Cassidy and the Sundance Kid*, *M*A*S*H*, *The Sting*, *Jaws*, *The Island* and *Neighbors* are among the films with which he has been most closely associated. In all of them, the relationship between male friends is central; women are relegated to colorless supporting roles. Even in *The Verdict*, the most penetrating study of human

ABOVE: "Uncle" Carl Laemmle, 1931. RIGHT: Carl with his son, "Junior," 1931. For his twenty-first birthday, Junior received a unique gift from his father: the job of running Universal Studios.

Aʙᴏᴠᴇ: *Samuel Goldwyn, 1930.*
ʙᴇʟᴏᴡ: *Walt Disney, 1945.*

ABOVE: *Jack Warner breaking ground for the Warner Brothers Studios, Hollywood, 1919.*

MIDDLE: *Goldwyn with Ingrid Bergman and husband Roberto Rossellini upon her return to America after a seven-year absence, 1956.*

RIGHT: *Nearly half a century later, Warner with Audrey Hepburn at a reception celebrating the release of "My Fair Lady," London, 1965.*

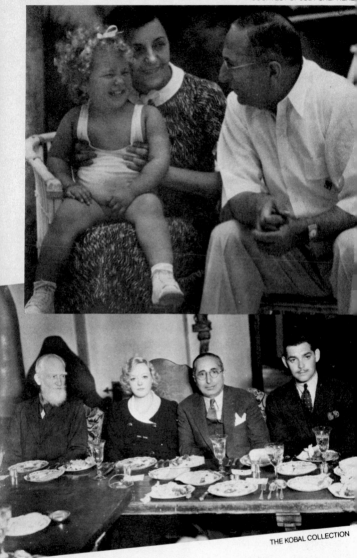

BELOW FROM LEFT: George Bernard Shaw, Marion Davies, Louis B. Mayer, and Clark Gable at an M-G-M luncheon honoring Shaw's arrival in Hollywood, 1933.
ABOVE: Louis B. Mayer with wife Margaret and granddaughter Judy (Edith's daughter), 1935.

ABOVE: *Edith and Irene Mayer at their father's beach estate, Santa Monica, 1928.*
BELOW, FROM LEFT: *Barbara Goetz, Edith Mayer Goetz, Judy Goetz, Margaret Mayer, Danny Selznick, Irene Mayer Selznick, Jeffrey Selznick, 1940.*

L*EFT: David O. Selznick,
age eleven, 1913.*

*MIDDLE: Clark Gable and
Vivien Leigh in Selznick's
classic, "Gone With the
Wind," 1939.*

*BELOW: Jennifer Jones and
then-husband Robert
Walker in the Selznick production, "Since You Went
Away," 1944.*

*OPPOSITE PAGE: William and
Edith Goetz, early 1960s.*

LEFT: *David O. Selznick with first wife, Irene Mayer...*
RIGHT: *...and with second wife, Jennifer Jones.*

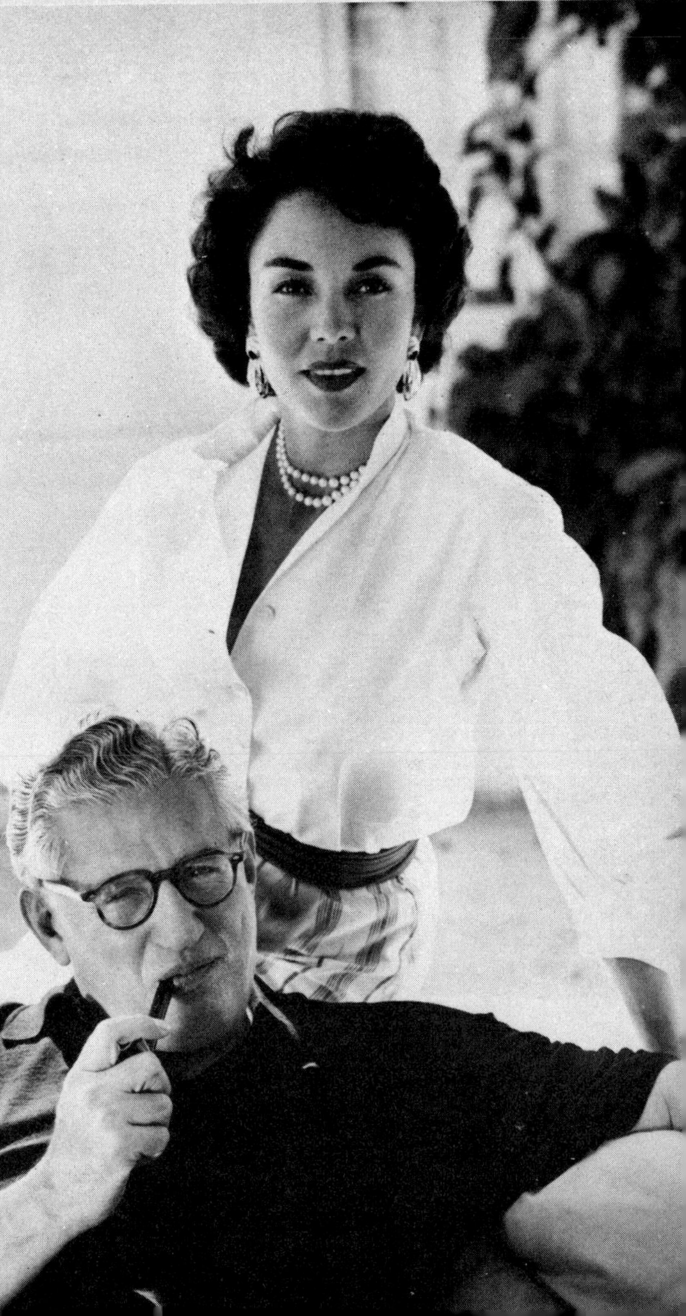

LARRY EDMUNDS COLLECTION

BELOW: *Darryl F. Zanuck on safari, early 1940s.* OPPOSITE, BOTTOM: *David Brown and Richard Zanuck on location during the filming of "Jaws," 1974.*
OPPOSITE, ABOVE: *Paul Newman and Robert Redford in the Zanuck/Brown production, "The Sting," 1973.*

BELOW: *Darryl Zanuck with wife Virginia, Hollywood, 1941.*

LEFT: *The first of DFZ's "protégées," Bella Darvi as she appeared in "The Egyptian," 1954.*

PICTORIAL PARADE

LEFT: *Brad Dexter escorting Bella to the premiere of "The Egyptian" at Grauman's Chinese Theatre, Hollywood, 1954.*

MOVIE STAR NEWS (2)

RIGHT: *DFZ with Juliette Greco before departing for Paris to film "Crack in the Mirror," 1960.*

PHOTO TRENDS

ABOVE: *With Irina Demick, 1962.* RIGHT: *With Genevieve Gilles, 1968.*

BELOW LEFT: *Tony Curtis, 1959.*
BOTTOM RIGHT: *With wife Janet Leigh and Jamie Lee, age two, 1961.*
RIGHT: *Janet with Jamie Lee (hands over her ears) and Kelly, Disneyland, 1963.*
BELOW: *Jamie Lee with Eddie Murphy and Dan Aykroyd in "Trading Places," 1983.*

MEMORY SHOP

CINEMABILIA

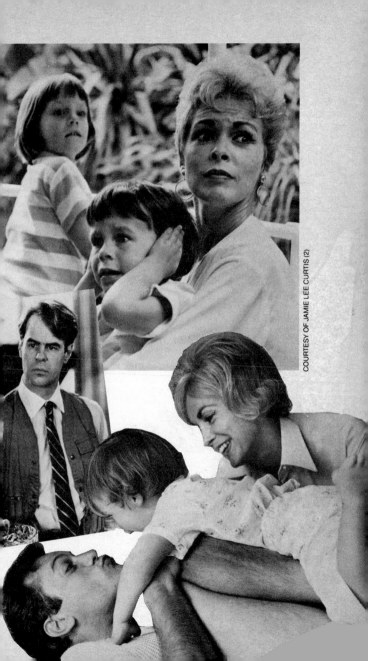

Liza Minnelli being directed by her father Vincente in "A Matter of Time," 1976.

relationships produced by Zanuck and Brown, the deepest affection is between the two male lawyers, played by Paul Newman and Jack Warden. Newman's romantic interest, played by Charlotte Rampling, turns out to be a treacherous opportunist. It is a one-dimensional, unconvincing characterization, and the movie's major flaw. This same sexual prejudice has infected most of Zanuck and Brown's productions, preoccupied as they are with the mystique of male camaraderie.

AFTER a long association with Universal, where they made *The Sting* and *Jaws*, Zanuck and Brown entered into a lucrative production deal in 1979 with Twentieth Century-Fox, the studio from which they had both been booted ten years before. When they moved into their new suite on the Fox lot, the massive desk once occupied by Darryl Zanuck was taken out of storage and placed in Richard's spacious new office. Fox chairman Dennis Stanfill, the man who had cast the decisive vote in the resolution to fire Zanuck and Brown a decade earlier, saw to it that they were welcomed back with the appropriate pomp and circumstance. "He had my office measured to the inch so that it would match the one I had when I was in charge of the studio," Richard says. "He was meticulous about everything when we came back."

But things did not go well for Zanuck and Brown at Fox. They had returned to work with Dick Zanuck's friend, Alan Ladd, Jr., who was then Fox's production head. But shortly after they signed with Fox, Ladd left the studio in a dispute with Stanfill and set up his own company. The new Fox command, under Alan Hirschfield and Sherry Lansing, approved only one Zanuck/Brown project in the entire three-and-a-half years they were there, *The Verdict*. Zanuck publicly described Hirschfield as "wishy-washy and two-faced," a characterization which reportedly infuriated Hirschfield and hastened the departure of Zanuck and Brown when their contract expired in 1983. "We were brought there by Laddie to make two or three pictures a year," says Richard Zanuck. "Instead, almost every movie we submitted was rejected. Fortunately, *The Verdict* was well received critically and commercially. But if it had been a flop, our careers would have been damaged immeasurably. We didn't go there to sit in big fat nice offices drawing down a very healthy producer's fee. We came to make it on the back end, off profits. Well, if you don't make any pictures, there aren't going to be any profits."

Richard Zanuck's frustration with the vacillation of the

Hirschfield-Lansing regime was shared by other producers at Fox. But in his case, the dissatisfaction was compounded by memories of how things used to be at the same studio when his father was in charge. "It's very tough," Richard says, "having watched and then worked under a person who was filled with so much authority and knowledge, to deal with the types we deal with today, who are basically not creative, not *lovers* of motion pictures. Harry Cohn, Jack Warner, Darryl Zanuck—say what you will about them, those guys were showmen, and they moved movies. It's very frustrating for creative people to work in an atmosphere where there isn't leadership, where there are just a lot of maybes. You prefer hearing 'No' to having things dragged out."

In his 1937 *New Yorker* profile of Darryl Zanuck, Alva Johnston remarked that Zanuck, like so many other half-educated moguls, possessed a "vehemence, decisiveness, and single-mindedness which are commonly educated out of college men." The advantage of the semi-literates, Johnston argued, is that they are forced at an early age "to accept responsibility, to make decisions." Comparing his father to General George Patton, the subject of one of their most successful movies during the years they ran Fox together, Richard Zanuck makes an observation about DFZ that recalls the evaluation Alva Johnston made almost half a century before. "He had guts—the sort of thing that's lacking today," Richard says. "He was more than willing to take the responsibility; he was willing to take the blame. He would say yes or no. Right or wrong, that was it. Today, things have to go before committees, and a lot of people will stick their noses in. In those days, he and the other studio heads made decisions on the spot, and that was that. They would ask, 'Is it any good?' and if they thought it was, that was enough to put a picture into production.

"He had a big ego," Richard goes on, "but God knows he also had an overabundance of talent and enthusiasm, and the latter quality is the thing most lacking in today's motion picture business. Nobody at the top has any enthusiasm. If he saw the seed of something in a script, he made you feel you had the greatest motion picture project imaginable, and that enthusiasm was passed down."

A certain enthusiasm for moviemaking is only one of the legacies he passed down to Richard. Other scions of pioneer families have tried and failed to make the move into contemporary Hollywood. Richard Zanuck has somehow managed to blend his insider's knowledge of the business with a canny sense of the current marketplace. Alone among the descendants of the legendary moguls, he has bridged the gap between the old Hollywood and the new. The Zanuck name is perhaps the only one that has continued to be in the front ranks of film production from the very beginning of the sound era down to the present day.

IN 1975, when Zanuck/Brown Productions was flush with success from two of the biggest blockbusters of the decade, *The Sting* and *Jaws*, a flattering profile of Richard Zanuck and David Brown appeared in *New York* magazine. The thrust of the article was that, of all the so-called independents in Hollywood, Zanuck and Brown were the most spectacular: "No longer are they the son of Darryl Zanuck and the husband of Helen Gurley Brown," the article proclaimed. "They are the hottest of the hot."

The writer asked Richard Zanuck whether he would want his own sons to go into the business.

"Sure. If they want to," Richard Darryl Zanuck replied. "As a matter of fact, they'll probably knock me off."

THE AGE OF
CELEBRITY

4

STARCHILDREN

"Expectations to live up to
Comparisons to live down
Limelight is their legacy
These heirs to the celluloid crown."

—FROM A POEM BY CARRIE FISHER

OVER the years nepotism has worked its way into every facet of the industry. Beginning in the era of silent pictures, movie moguls routinely eased their children and other relatives into the business. It was rare, however, for the stars of silent movies to recruit their children to follow in their footsteps. Charlie Chaplin's son Sydney and daughter Geraldine became actors years later, but in the early decades of Hollywood, one did not see the heirs of Keaton or Swanson or Barthelmess or Bow being groomed for stardom. The explanation is simple enough. For the most part, movie actors in those days were powerless employees; they were in no position to hire their relatives even if they wanted to. And recognizing the uncertainty of the actor's lot, the stars offered little encouragement to their children.

There was one notable exception: Douglas Fairbanks, Jr. was the first person turned into a movie star largely because of the mystique surrounding his father's name. He became an actor not because his father wanted him to follow his lead, but because producer Jesse Lasky recognized that the Fairbanks name could enhance the commercial possibilities of some of his company's films. Douglas, Jr. began acting when he was just thirteen. At the time, his mother was broke, having invested her divorce settlement from Douglas, Sr. in failed ventures. Her gallant teenage son felt impelled to come to her rescue, and so he accepted Lasky's offer to star in *Stephen Steps Out* in 1923. Before long there were two swashbuckling Fairbankses in the movies.

In 1919, Douglas Fairbanks, Sr., his second wife Mary Pickford, and Charlie Chaplin became the first major stars to form their own production company, United Artists. Their initiative influenced a later generation of stars, just as the success of Douglas Fairbanks, Jr. set the precedent for the next wave of movie nepotism. During the 1940s and 1950s the studio contract system collapsed, and movie stars broke away to form independent production companies. Gradually, they arrogated the power of the early moguls. As they accumulated greater influence and prestige, the stars formed dynasties of their own. Doting on celebrities and their offspring, the media abetted this empire-building. The studios, recognizing the box office draw of a famous name, capitalized on the trend even if it meant losing their own hold on the big-name talent which had once been their prize possession.

By now, families of famous stars have solidified their positions in the industry. Consider the case of Jamie Lee Curtis. By the time she was twenty, she was queen of the Bs—fending off rapists, killers, and disfigured maniacs in a medley of stalk-and-slash thrillers. But Jamie, the fiesty heroine of *Halloween*, *The Fog*, *Prom Night*, and *Terror Train*, wasn't exactly plucked from obscurity to become the movies' latest imperiled virgin. She is the daughter of two of the top stars in the 1950s, Tony Curtis and Janet Leigh. Although Jamie claims that, like any other aspiring actress, she auditioned for her first starring role in *Halloween*, the producers surely must have recognized the promotable value of the Curtis name on a movie house marquee. Publicists delighted in comparing Jamie's role as a modern-day damsel in distress with her mother's most memorable part—that of the young woman screaming her lungs out while being stabbed to death in the bloody shower scene of Alfred Hitchcock's *Psycho*. In the opening scene of *Psycho*, Janet Leigh had a chance to display her voluptuous body in a bra and skimpy half-slip. Jamie bared much more of *her* body as the easygoing prostitute in *Trading Places* and as the free-spirited radio deejay in *Love Letters*. Her stunning figure may be her most visible legacy from her mother, but she also has some of her father's wisecracking humor and bravado. The mix gives her a distinctive screen presence—that of a sensual tomboy—and it may also give her an edge over other starchildren who seem like little more than watered-down facsimiles of a single famous parent.

Although most of her peers do not show comparable promise, Jamie belongs to a legion of highly visible show business progeny. It is revealing that three of the four top-grossing films of 1983 featured children of well-known actors: *Return of the Jedi* with Carrie Fisher, *Trading Places* with Jamie Lee Curtis, and *WarGames* with Matthew Broderick (the son of actor James Broderick, best-remembered for the TV series, *Family*.) This is just one indication of the rise of the modern acting dynasties.

SUCH a development may have been a long time coming, but it was probably inevitable. Before the Hollywood princes and princesses gave any thought to an acting career, they were public figures. Even in their cribs, they were on display, and the fan magazines issued detailed bulletins on the growing pains of little Liza and Jamie and Carrie and Desi, Jr.

In a classic *Esquire* essay called "The Beautiful People," published in 1957, Helen Lawrenson caught the comic spectacle of bringing up baby Hollywood-style:

> Children have become so fashionable in Hollywood that any-body who is anybody has at least three or four (if for one reason or another they have none of their own, they adopt them in clusters), and they all have impeccable manners. They shake hands with each guest, remembering the name; they pass the caviar without spilling a single egg; they answer politely when spoken to; and, eventually, duly admired and appreciated, they file gracefully out again. Conscious of the rowdy awkwardness of your own and your friends' kids, you have a wild, fleeting conviction that these poised and charming moppets must be really well-trained midgets in disguise, rented for the occasion. But no, they are bona fide children, and although many of them go to boarding schools both winter and summer, from an early age, and at home are cared for by nurses and maids, nevertheless, they exist: living, visible, well-publicized proof that movie stars are, as they themselves so often tell you, just normal homebodies, leading quietly sumptuous lives surrounded with family devotion.

As Lawrenson suggests, children of Hollywood were often treated as little more than an extension of their parents' preoccupation with interior decorating; they were symbols and ornaments, placed for effect. Everything was designed for its publicity value, and it was sometimes impossible to distinguish spontaneous behavior from calculated poses.

In the household of Tony Curtis and Janet Leigh, as in so many Hollywood homes, prosaic domesticity was subsumed by a glamorous fantasy. The stars worked to uphold their image, even when they played. During the eleven years in which her parents were married (they divorced in 1962), Jamie Lee Curtis recalls, "My mom and dad had a thing called Camp Curtis. They had this huge house and pool, and they used to have all these people over during the summertime for big bashes. They have pictures of Bogie and Bacall and the Lawfords and Kirk Douglas and Sammy Davis, Jr. sitting around the pool in Camp Curtis T-shirts."

Curtis and Leigh carried on as if the studio photographers were always hiding behind the bushes. And much of the time the photographers really were there, intruding on the children's lives as much as on the parents'. "No matter what we did," Jamie Lee Curtis says, "there would always be someone saying, 'Stop, Janet, let's take a picture of you and your two beautiful daughters.' Any event turned into a photographic thing. It was very different then. When Farrah Fawcett was in Cannes a few years ago and there was this uproar about the paparazzi following her, she was upset because she had to make her way through 200 people. I have a photograph of my parents in Argentina—three *thousand* people with these two little heads in the middle of this throng."

The omnipresent photographers could transform simple outings into formidable expeditions. "We did Disneyland with a VIP tour," Jamie says. "When we went skiing, we always had a private instructor to get us to the front of the line so we wouldn't stand there and get mobbed. To this day I have a terrible fear of crowds. I can't go to rock 'n' roll concerts because I just freak out."

This feverish view of fans and crowds is one of the common nightmares of a Hollywood childhood. The terror was heightened because the stars' tots were so sheltered from the outside world; when they did catch a glimpse of the plebeians, it was often during a scene of mass hysteria that might have been drawn from *The Day of the Locust*. One of Christina Crawford's most vivid memories is of the time her brother, her mother and she were mobbed as they left the restaurant "21": "The moment those big heavy doors opened, I could feel a rush of cold air and hear the angry shouts of the huge crowd. The strange, angry people were everywhere! . . . It couldn't have been more than fifteen or twenty feet from the front door of the restaurant to the door of our limousine, but we couldn't get there! Literally hundreds of people were shoving pens, pencils, and autograph books at my mother . . . Chris and I were sobbing as we tried desperately to keep from being trampled underfoot by the big people . . ."

For some starchildren, the encounter with crowds was less traumatic, but it was invariably disorienting for them to see their parents worshipped by total strangers. "What is hard," suggests Kirk Douglas's son, Michael Douglas, "is to try to understand the amount of public loving and praise that a personality gets and measure that against some of the deprivation that you feel. Here's this public saying, 'You're wonderful, I love you, I want to kiss you,' and you're the son or daughter sitting over on the side. You may not even see much of your parent because he's so busy, working so hard. That in itself is difficult to accept, but it's more difficult when you're also watching this public display of adoration."

If Hollywood youngsters experienced a certain sense of unreality in their dealings with the outside world, the goings-on inside their own homes were no less bizarre. While every child knows a birthday party as something slightly more exotic than everyday life, the birthday celebrations of Hollywood children were baroque extravaganzas as disconnected from the everyday as a scene from one of their parents' most fantastical movies. Their already lavish yards were turned into miniature amusement parks where clowns, aerialists, and magicians would perform for the children, who were usually too formally dressed and too rigidly disciplined to enjoy the carnival. "The little girls wore itchy, starched, organdy dresses," Jill Schary has keenly observed. "Their hair, looking unlike hair, was tortured into long corkscrew curls dating back to Mary Pickford. The little boys wore proper Eton suits and had their hair slicked down with water, or greasy hair tonic, which made them look like snappy drowned rats."

Parents vied for the largest number of other starchildren who could be induced to put in an appearance at these galas, and if their famous mommies and daddies also stopped by for ice cream and cake, that was a major coup. The birthday boy or girl rarely knew more than a few of his or her guests. The only commoners invited to these affairs were the children of the servants who worked for the host parents. Needless to say, those interlopers did not exactly feel at home. Jill Schary has described the phenomenon: "The employer-parents of the birthday child would make too many raving compliments about the invited child's dress, which often was quite too frilly and not of the best material. Or, worse, the child would be dressed quite well, and the parents would say to each other, always within earshot of the child, 'Isn't that cute how Hilda (or Lula Mae or Rosita) spent her whole week's pay just to buy a nice party dress for my Susie's party.'"

The image of domestic tranquility that movie stars wanted to present to the public was always too antiseptic to be trusted—a series of tableaux posed for an official family album. Sometimes the picture turned grotesquely distorted as soon as the company went home. The stories of child abuse reported in Christina Crawford's *Mommie Dearest* and in *Going My Own Way*, Gary Crosby's memoir of life with Bing, represent the most extreme disparity between pretense and reality. Joan Crawford was so desperate to become a mother that she adopted four children, but her own emotional insecurities led her to turn against them in outbursts of savage cruelty. Bing Crosby was more remote with his four sons, a strict disciplinarian who meted out punishment like an unfeeling headmaster. According to Gary, his father had a "belt dotted with metal studs" that he used to whip his sons. The ritual was always the same: he made them lower their pants, and then, "Quite dispassionately, without the least display of emotion or loss of self-control, he whacked away until he drew the first drop of blood, and then he stopped."

Even in less deeply troubled Hollywood households, there was a sizable gap between the tintype created for the fanzines and family life as it was actually lived. The fact that so many movie star marriages were engineered for their publicity value did not contribute to family stability. As Jamie Lee Curtis points out, her parents' first date was something of a press agent's gimmick. "Their publicists put them together," Jamie says. "That's how they met. Nowadays a publicist would never put one star together with another one. They may secretly be *shtupping*, but you don't see two stars going out on an arranged date, which they used to do all the time." Almost in the manner of arranged marriages in royal families, stars were wedded and bedded because studio heads found the match commercially advantageous. Unlike the official marriages of the Hapsburgs or Tudors, however, there were no reasons of state compelling the star couples to stay together. Indeed, most of them separated after just a few years. If the weddings of Janet Leigh and Tony Curtis, Debbie Reynolds and Eddie Fisher, Sandra Dee and Bobby Darin, Suzanne Pleshette and Troy Donahue helped keep the fan magazines in business, so did news of the couples' marital spats and eventual divorces. As long as the unions lasted, of course, the studio publicists painted an umblemished portrait of conjugal contentment. The stars cooperated in the mythmaking—according to Carrie Fisher, she was actually conceived while her parents were filming *Bundle of Joy* in 1956.

That coy cinematic tribute to domestic bliss had little to do with the tempestuous relationship of Debbie and Eddie, the picture's young stars—or of other Hollywood celebrities, for that matter. In a less fluid, more stable milieu, a married couple's destiny may be more predictable. But in a business where phenomenal success and vast wealth can be accrued in very short periods of time, marriage has always been subject to special tensions.

The most obvious of these problems was professional rivalry, as exemplified by the marriage of Judy Garland and Vincente Minnelli. Garland and Minnelli were not actually competing in the same arena—Judy was an actress and Vincente a director—but the fact that they worked together did create conflicts between them. At first the collaboration was a rich and beneficial one for both of them. Judy lent her talents to three of Vincente's best films—*Meet Me in St. Louis*, *The Clock*, and *The Pirate* (and also to one section of *Ziegfeld Follies*); he in turn helped to transform her from gawky teenager to radiant young woman. Yet before long, competitiveness and jealousy infected their working relationships. Judy's psychiatrist asked for Vincente to be replaced as director of *Easter Parade*; the analyst explained to MGM executives that Judy's insecurities were aggravated when her husband directed her, for she felt it placed her in a subordinate position in her marriage as well as in her work. Since Judy was a more valuable commodity to the studio than Minnelli, her wishes—or those of her psychiatrist—were honored. Vincente was replaced by director Charles Walters. Although he never discussed the incident with Judy, Minnelli later admitted that he was deeply wounded by this snub.

Several months later Vincente was directing Jennifer Jones in an adaptation of one his favorite novels, *Madame Bovary*. At the same time, Judy was starring in a frivolous musical called *In the Good Old Summertime*. When Vincente told her about his rewarding experiences making *Bovary*, Judy was filled with envy. "Here you're working with these great talents," she exploded. "And what am I doing? Still playing the shopgirl on the corner." She could take no pleasure in her husband's good fortune; she could only compare his professional status to her own.

Not long afterwards, Garland and Minnelli separated. In their subsequent marriages both of them chose partners who represented less direct competition. Judy, increasingly insecure about her physical appearance, grew maniacally jealous and possessive, terrified of letting her husbands and lovers out of her sight. Judy usually provided the jobs for the men in her life. Her third husband, Sid Luft, managed her concert act and produced the 1954 version of *A Star is Born* for her. Her fourth husband, Mark Herron, directed her show at the London Palladium. But these working relationships, though less contentious than the one with Minnelli, spawned other problems. Most of these men recognized, to their chagrin, that Judy was top banana, and they chafed under this unequal arrangement. (Judy's daughter Liza Minnelli acted out a similar pattern in her first two marriages—to singer Peter Allen and producer-director Jack Haley, Jr. In both cases the marriage dissolved in part because the men resented being overshadowed by their famous wife. Allen's career blossomed only after his divorce from Liza.)

SINCE each of their parents may marry three or four times, Hollywood children often have more step-brothers and step-sisters, half-brothers and half-sisters than any of them can keep track of. The size of the family is constantly expanding or contracting, leaving a trail of siblings who may share a wing of the mansion for a couple of years and then never see one another again.

A consequence of these rapidly shifting alliances, as well as of the demanding work schedules of many stars, was that the children would spend more time with their maids and governesses than they did with their parents. "My mother was sort of a fairy tale figure to me," says Venetia Stevenson, the daughter of actress Anna Lee (one of the stars of *How Green Was My Valley* and many other John Ford movies) and director Robert Stevenson (*Jane Eyre*, *Mary Poppins*). "I remember going to visit her on the set and thinking how beautiful she was, but I was never close to her. Our nanny was the one who dressed me and bathed me. She was called Nanny Stevenson, and to this day I don't even know her real name. I think she was the one who told me that my parents were getting a divorce."

Liza Minnelli has commented on her surrealistic memories of playtime with Nanny Minnelli: "I can remember playing in the

Beverly Hills park with Mia Farrow and Candy Bergen and Tish Sterling, and while we sat in the sandbox we could hear our English nannies talking about picture deals and costume direction and whose employer was going to win the Academy Award."

Once the children grew too old to be attended by maids and nannies, they were shipped off to boarding schools, where they spent most of the year; they checked in with their parents on holidays and during summer vacations. "What kind of parents would send a kid away at six to make his own bed?" Peter Fonda once asked rhetorically, sarcastically commenting on the neglect he felt as a child.

Wherever they went to school, these star progeny faced suspicion and hostility from their classmates. "The day I walked into boarding school back east," Jamie Lee Curtis recalls, "there was this tough broad sitting there smoking a Marlboro. She looked up at me and said, 'You're Tony Curtis's daughter? I heard you were coming.' It's something that prefaced my life. I used to say I had the longest middle name in the world. My name was Jamie-Janet Leigh and Tony Curtis's daughter-Curtis. That was the way I was introduced. It went with me everywhere. I can't forget the poem they used to say to me at school after my father got busted for smoking dope. 'Your father's Tony Curtis/And your mother's Janet Leigh/Your father just got busted/But your mommy is free.' I had to deal with a lot of hostility because of an assumed arrogance and snobbiness and snottiness that we were all supposed to have. You had to fight doubly hard to prove that you weren't that way. And then you never knew if the kids who liked you liked you for you, or because you had money, or because it was fun hanging around with a famous kid."

Assailed by resentment at school, struggling to cope with marital breakups and malaise at home, these children often felt isolated and disoriented. To alleviate their emotional crises, Hollywood families turned to psychiatry with a zeal unmatched anywhere else in the country. Psychoanalysis was a favorite pastime among show people from the 1940s on, and Hollywood helped to popularize psychiatry for the rest of the country in the movies it produced. The psychiatrist was often portrayed on screen as a messianic figure who lays to rest the wrenching problems that family members cannot resolve among themselves. It is an image which has persisted from *Now, Voyager*—in which the suave, benevolent analyst, Claude Rains, liberates the timorous Bette Davis from her mother's domination—right up to *Ordinary People*, where a more dishevelled but equally omniscient Judd Hirsch rescues the troubled Timothy Hutton from the self-destructive tendencies engendered by his rigidly repressed parents. In creating such dramas, moviemakers were often reiterating the catechism that they observed in their own lives. In many movieland families, everyone—including the youngest toddlers—routinely took communion with the local shrink.

Sometimes children were not merely treated in the plush offices of a Beverly Hills analyst; a weekly or even daily headshrinking session was deemed insufficient to treat the more recalcitrant youngsters. When he was a teenager, Bill Hayward was committed to Menninger's sanitarium in Topeka, Kansas, by his father, agent and producer Leland Hayward. "From my point of view, I was incarcerated," Hayward says today. "I can look on it with some understanding because psychiatry was thought of very differently then. Everybody was very tuned into psychiatry. What I cannot understand is how people acted later. During the sixties a famous director was having some problems with his son. The kid got in trouble in prep school, and his father came to me and said, 'How do you feel about Leland sending you off to Menninger's?' I said, 'I have incredible resentment toward him. It seemed like a bad way to handle it. It's a terrible thing to lock someone up. When you're a kid and under age, you have no rights.' The director listened to me, and he turned around and locked his kid up. He took him to the same doctor who locked me up. Same as with me—one meeting in the doctor's office, and bang, off to the courthouse. This doctor obviously was a quick hand with a key. I later told my father I was still angry about what happened to me. I said to him, 'I know I was an asshole kid, but I still don't accept it.'"

There were even more harrowing stories. The prototypical Hollywood Gothic tale of growing up famous was written by Diana Barrymore, John Barrymore's only daughter. Her autobiography, *Too Much, Too Soon*, published in 1957, set the pattern for starchild confessions, and was an early precursor of Brooke Hayward's *Haywire* (1977) and Christina Crawford's *Mommie Dearest* (1978).

The Barrymores were the greatest American acting family. Maurice Barrymore (also known as Herbert Blythe) and Georgiana Drew were distinguished nineteenth century stage actors, and their three children, Lionel, Ethel, and John, all enjoyed illustrious careers, though John's alcoholic excesses brought on his early demise. His daughter Diana imitated him rather than her more stable aunt and uncle. Diana's mother was Blanche Oelrichs, who wrote poetry under the name of Michael Strange; her parents separated when she was an infant, and she had no recollection of meeting her father before she was nine years old. Diana's mother, a fixture of New York high society, spent little time with her child, and Diana was raised by governesses in Paris. Her father tried to reenter her life when she was older, but he had no conception of how to carry on a normal father-daughter relationship; he took her barhopping with him when she was just thirteen.

Diana showed promise as an actress, but she could not deal with the inevitable comparisons drawn between her and her renowned forbears. When she made her first movie (*Eagle Squadron*) for Universal in 1942, she recalled, "the makeup men groaned about my face . . . why, the Great Profile's daughter has no profile!" She had a few more movie roles, and then her career collapsed. Before long, alcohol brought her to the same shabby end that her father had met. Repeatedly arrested for drunkenness, she squandered the family fortune and was reduced to stealing food from supermarkets in order to survive. In 1960, at the age of thirty-eight—but looking at least twenty years older—Diana Barrymore was found dead in her apartment, three empty liquor bottles next to her bed. According to the autopsy report, she had succumbed to a deadly combination of alcohol and sleeping pills. (The Barrymore family is now enjoying something of a resurgence, thanks to the prominence of John's granddaughter, Drew Barrymore, the child of sometime actor John Barrymore, Jr.—John, Sr.'s son by actress Dolores Costello. Little Drew, who has appeared in *E.T.*, *Firestarter* and *Irreconcilable Differences*, has become the most sought-after child actress of the early 1980s.)

Shortly after *Too Much, Too Soon* hit the best-seller lists, Edward G. Robinson, Jr. wrote a similar memoir recounting his own dissolute youth, *My Father—My Son*. An alcoholic at eighteen, young Robinson was arrested more than once for drunk driving, writing bad checks, robbery, and assault and battery. His feuds with his parents and his drunken binges made headlines all through the 1950s. Reporters ghoulishly drew parallels between young Robinson's delinquency and his father's most famous screen role, as the underworld kingpin, Little Caesar. "Film Badman Sees Son Held in Real Crime" trumpeted a Los Angeles newspaper after one of Edward, Jr.'s arrests.

A decade later Robinson, Jr. made news again when he contested his mother's will. Citing his "unforgivable" conduct toward her, Gladys Lloyd Robinson had cut her son out of her $756,000 estate, leaving him nothing but a tea set, a baby chair, and a painting of himself as an infant—the only period of his life that his mother remembered with pleasure. Edward G. Robinson, Jr. made a bid to become an actor like his father, but was only able to secure a few bit parts. He died in 1974—one year after his father—reportedly of "natural causes," although his health had certainly been impaired by his drinking. He was forty years old.

During the 1950s and 1960s sensational stories about other starchildren also filled the tabloids. Gary Crosby was plagued by alcoholism from the time he attended college at Stanford. His brother Lindsay was arrested for drunk driving and disturbing the peace. The public devoured these tales of "Hollywood children run amuck." The idea that these tragically mixed-up kids could ever build respectable careers on their own was virtually unthinkable before 1960. The only press attention most of them received was when their names turned up on a police blotter or when they were involved in some notorious escapade. Frank Sinatra, Jr. got far more media coverage for his 1963 kidnapping than he ever did for a concert appearance. It was even suggested that he had arranged his own abduction as a publicity stunt, though that charge was never proved.

Whatever difficulties they faced growing up, the Crosby and Sinatra children were lucky enough to survive. Other starchildren succumbed before they could ever become functioning adults. Charles Boyer, Jr. was a struggling young actor who had just lost his job as a production assistant on one of his father's television shows when he walked into the bedroom of his West Los Angeles home and shot himself through the head. Paul Newman's son Scott was another aspiring young actor, afflicted with drug and alcohol problems throughout his teenage years. His father felt Scott was finally on the road to recovery, but in 1978, he was discovered dead in his apartment, the victim of an accidental overdose of valium and liquor. Children of Louis Jourdan, Jennifer Jones and Art Linkletter have been among the other youthful casualties. Jane Fonda speaks for many Hollywood children when she refers to her legacy as a "poison" passed on from one generation to the next.

DESPITE the grim, painful dramas played out inside their homes, when they grew older, most starchildren chose to enter the entertainment business; they usually sought acting careers like their parents, and some of them eventually had better luck than Diana Barrymore, Edward G. Robinson, Jr., Charles Boyer, Jr., or Scott Newman. In all cases, however, there were radical differences between their pursuit of their careers and the way in which their parents had approached the business.

Many movie stars of the 1940s and 1950s, like the early moguls, were motivated by a burning desire to escape poverty. For their pampered children, raised in the lap of luxury, the motivation could hardly have been the same. What drew the second generation to acting was partly the perception that their parents were special people. No matter how ambivalent they may have felt about where that special status left *them* in their parents' lives, they were irresistibly attracted to the attention that their parents received. If they enjoyed an early whiff of that adulation themselves, it only intensified the eagerness to perform. Alan Alda, the son of actor Robert Alda, remembers appearing on stage with his father when he was a boy. "He would take me to benefits at the Hollywood Canteen," Alan recalls. "We would do Abbott and Costello routines for servicemen. It's very seductive to be on the stage and hear that wave of laughter come back at you. Also, it was a way to be with my father, actually do his work with him. That's very appealing to a child, and I think that had a lot to do with my decision to become an actor."

Other Hollywood children felt the same rush of excitement when they had a chance to participate in their parents' world. "Whenever I went on the set," says William Katt, the actor son of Bill Williams (TV's Kit Carson) and Barbara Hale (Della Street on *Perry Mason*), "I would see so many people fussing over the actors. I rode in parades with my parents, and I saw all these people waving at them as if they were gods."

When asked why he became an actor, Lloyd Bridges's son Jeff once responded, "I guess it was because I really remember how much Dad got off on the success of *Sea Hunt*." Both Jeff and his brother Beau appeared on the show when they were children. Even if an acting career did not always seem terribly exciting or glamorous, it was still the only frame of reference these children had; many of them felt ill-equipped to cope with what they contemptuously refer to as "civilian life."

Most of the movie stars actively discouraged their children from performing. They recognized the phenomenal odds against success and wanted to shield their offspring from the constant rejection that is endemic to the profession. "My father knew what a hard life it is," Alan Alda says. "I think anybody who's gone through it would wish that their kids could find happiness doing something else. My father wanted me to be a doctor, so I tried taking a pre-med course in chemistry which I really was not interested in taking. I slept through most of the classes, and I think I got a score of ten on the final exam. I didn't want to get trapped into being a doctor. I got very depressed at the idea that I wouldn't be able to act."

Of course, it is also possible that some of the older generation felt a secret panic that their children might outstrip them if they did enter show business. When Keenan Wynn—whose main talent as a young man had been motorcycle racing—told his father, comedian and vaudeville star Ed Wynn, that he wanted to be an actor, the elder Wynn snapped, "What are you going to do? Ride a motorcycle up and down the aisles? You couldn't even get a job as a chorus boy in one of my shows—you can't do a simple dance step." Later, when Keenan began to get substantial supporting roles in films such as *The Clock* and *Neptune's Daughter*, Ed Wynn was asked about the kinds of parts his son played. With bilious wit Ed replied, "Keenan Wynn is the fellow who, when Esther Williams jumps into a pool, he gets splashed."

A few stars, by contrast, *did* want their children to follow in their footsteps and perpetuate the family name. Debbie Reynolds put Carrie Fisher in her Las Vegas nightclub when Carrie was only thirteen. Eventually Carrie left the act; as she explained later, "I got tired of being the oldest living child at the Tropicana belting out 'Wendy.'"

Judy Garland is probably the preeminent example of a movie star who chose—or attempted to choose—her children's career for them. She had Liza Minnelli play her infant daughter in the last scene of her MGM musical, *In the Good Old Summertime*. Later, in her variety shows, Garland brought all three of her kids on stage with her; Liza and Lorna Luft sang, while Joey Luft played the drums. Beyond that Judy tried to control every aspect of their professional and personal lives. She even selected Liza's first husband; it was Judy who discovered Peter Allen while touring the Far East, and encouraged both his musical career and his role as Liza's suitor. In steering her children toward show business, perhaps Judy was unconsciously repeating the cycle started by her own mother, Ethel Gumm, who put her three daughters on the vaudeville circuit. But while Ethel was a classic stage mother who lived vicariously through her children, Judy had a glittering career of her own. Arthur Whitelaw, a family friend and Broadway producer, points out that Judy Garland was completely "unlike Rose, Gypsy's mother, who was a frustrated performer and pushed her kids to do what she couldn't do herself. Judy didn't push her kids, but because they were around it from the time they were born, the kids decided they liked the life and wanted to be part of it. Judy was in the old showbiz tradition of the Seven Little Foys. Whenever she was on stage, she'd drag the kids on to perform. I never saw anybody like Judy in that respect."

To Judy Garland, practically "born in a trunk," it was simply inconceivable that her children could choose any career other than performing. Yet there is evidence that her attitude toward her oldest daughter was competitive as well as nurturing. Even though she had set Liza's course for her, when Judy actually saw Liza's career begin to soar, she could not suppress her envy. At times she dismissed Liza's talents, insisting that her daughter Lorna was a far more gifted singer. When Judy and Liza performed together at the London Palladium in 1964, Liza won over an initially skeptical audience and overshadowed her mother, who was in poor voice that night. But throughout Liza's performance, Judy reached over obtrusively to jab Liza's arm and adjust her microphone, as if to let the audience know who was in charge. Liza later said of that night, "I'll never be afraid to perform with anyone ever again after that terrifying experience. She became very competitive with me. I wasn't Liza. I was another woman in the same spotlight."

That kind of mother-daughter rivalry might have suffocated any other child, especially if her mother was as legendary a figure as Judy Garland. Yet Liza Minnelli managed to carve out a solid career of her own, and she helped to break the jinx that had affected most second-generation performers up to that time. She was one of the first starchildren to follow her parents into show business and make a go of it. What distinguished her from the likes of Diana Barrymore or Edward G. Robinson, Jr? Talent may be the most obvious answer, but in addition Liza possessed a strength which they did not, and she acquired her strength at a very early age. Adela Rogers St. John has reported an extraordinary interview she conducted with Judy Garland when Liza was only three years old. Little Liza sauntered into the room carrying a bright red umbrella, despite the fact that it was a sunny day. According to St. John,

> Judy said, 'But my angel pie, you don't want an umbrella—'
> Liza looked her young mother firmly in the eye. She said, 'How do you know I don't?' and she walked over to the balcony iron railing, with her umbrella still held high, and stood blandly contemplating the scenery.

Although she was always iron-willed, Liza was also self-protective enough to try to distinguish herself from her mother as she grew older. At first she chose to concentrate on dancing rather than singing so as not to compete with Judy directly.

Performing was always Liza's obsession. Her high school classmates resented her because of who her mother was, and Liza only compounded her problems by boasting to them of her friendship with Marilyn Monroe and her romance with George Hamilton. At the age of sixteen Liza decided to quit school and work in the theater. When she heard about an off-Broadway revival of *Best Foot Forward*, she went to audition. The producer, Arthur Whitelaw, claims that he did not know who she was at the audition but was simply bowled over by her talent. When he learned her identity, he and his partners recognized that the publicity surrounding the first stage appearance of Judy Garland's daughter could aid their show immeasurably. "From the day I first saw her," Whitelaw says, "there was never a doubt in my mind that she would become a star because she had the talent and she had the drive. Liza is like a horse with blinders on, and she always has been."

In 1964, when Liza was hospitalized with a kidney ailment, Judy wanted her to drop out of a stock company production of *Carnival* in which she was set to star. Liza disobeyed her mother and went on with the show. Judy later told her, "You know, that was the first time you defied me, and it infuriated me—but God, how I admired you for doing it!" In 1965, before her twentieth birthday, Liza won a Tony Award for her star turn in *Flora, the Red Menace* on Broadway. During the next years her career continued to flourish while Judy's floundered; the two of them played out a mother-daughter variation on *A Star Is Born*. By the late 1960s Judy was borrowing money from Liza, who grew more and more impatient with her mother's financial instability and her irrational moods. In 1969 Liza refused to allow her mother to visit the set of her second movie, *The Sterile Cuckoo*. Mother and daughter were somewhat estranged when Judy died later in 1969, but her mother's death seems to have freed Liza from any last remaining inhibitions. Not long afterwards she chose to star in her first movie musical, *Cabaret*, so that, as she said, "the public could make that final comparison and say, 'There she is in a musical movie. And that's what her mom did. *And* she's holding her own.'" She more than held her own. The hedonistic Sally Bowles was the kind of daring adult role that Judy had always wanted to play but rarely did. And the *Cabaret* performance won Liza an Academy Award, an honor her mother had never received.

Cabaret marked the high point of Liza Minnelli's movie career. Years later she made a film under her father's direction, *A Matter of Time*, co-starring Ingrid Bergman. The stodgy period piece about a chambermaid who imagines herself as a grande dame turned out to be an utter fiasco. It was heavily re-edited by its distributors, American International Pictures, mocked by most critics, and received very little exposure. Liza then made two big-budget productions: *Lucky Lady*, a clumsy romantic adventure film about rumrunners during Prohibition, and *New York, New York*, an audacious musical drama in which she looked startlingly like her mother. Both films flopped, and her Broadway musical *The Act* was roasted by the critics.

After several years away from movies, Liza had a supporting part as the object of Dudley Moore's inebriated attention in the 1981 comedy hit, *Arthur*, but she has not made another film since then. As a concert singer she remains one of the world's most popular entertainers, and in the last few years, she has begun to perform songs associated with both of her parents—songs like "The Man That Got Away" from *A Star Is Born* and "The Trolley Song" from *Meet Me in St. Louis*. She explained, "On the concert stage I have come out and said, 'These were my parents. This is who I am.' That freed me, it was a release." Her willingness both to stand up to her parents and acknowledge their influence has helped Liza to become one of the longstanding survivors among the starchildren. But she is no longer a major movie star. Director Ken Russell wanted her to play the lead in the film version of *Evita*, but producer Robert Stigwood vetoed the idea, and sought Elaine Page to recreate her stage role. Such rejection represents quite a comedown from the early 1970s, when Liza and Barbra Streisand were the only two young female stars considered for virtually every role. Liza's career has followed a somewhat similar pattern to her mother's. Both of them achieved movie stardom early in their careers, but then as their screen appearances grew more infrequent, they retained their superstar status only as a result of concert and nightclub performances.

Ironically, Liza's half-sister Lorna Luft has secured a more active—though far less distinguished—film career in recent years. Lorna's biggest break came when she filled in for Liza on the Golden Globe Telecast of 1978, singing the nominated song, "New York, New York." Since then Lorna has appeared in stage musicals and had juicy roles in two Allan Carr schlockfests—*Grease 2* and a remake of *Where The Boys Are*.

NOT many starchildren have had the kind of success Liza Minnelli enjoys, but more and more of them have followed in their parents' footsteps. And in the last two decades, several have managed to find rewarding careers as actors and entertainers. No longer are they seen as talentless clones of their parents, as were most of the starchildren who came of age in the 1950s. The Carradine brothers, Jeff and Beau Bridges, Candice Bergen, Lucie Arnaz, Carrie Fisher, and Jamie Lee Curtis are not superstars but they are all steadily working actors.

Some of these second-generation performers pursued their careers haphazardly when starting out. After all, they could afford to drift aimlessly for a few years, drop out and then impulsively decide to audition for a choice part. Things came easily to them. When Jeff Bridges decided that he wanted to act, he did not have to look hard or long for an effective agent. His father simply called his own agent and announced, "You will represent my son."

Because they leapfrogged over the competition, these second-generation performers frequently felt guilty about their success and were tormented by self-doubts. According to Jeff Bridges, "For a long time, I wondered whether my career had come to me because of my own talents or because of some kind of genteel nepotism. I went through years of thinking that I should be a musician, a painter, something that was clearly my own. The guilt caused big problems for me."

As adults, second-generation performers have faced subtle resentment not unlike the kind they had confronted as children; the suspicion that they owed their success to their famous parents bred jealousy among their colleagues. People in a position to hire them often had a "show me" attitude that unknown actors did not have to contend with. Lorenzo Lamas, who became a heartthrob playing Jane Wyman's amoral grandson on the prime-time soap opera, *Falcon Crest*, is the son of the late Fernando Lamas and

Arlene Dahl and the stepson of Esther Williams. He has talked about the pressures he felt: "When I went in on interviews I used to say I not only represented my myself but three other people . . . it was a double-edged sword because my parents and Esther got me through the door. It was almost like casting people and directors and producers were looking at me through a microscope, looking for any fault, because I came from such a background."

Hollywood kids frequently complain that they have to apologize for their family connections. Although Jamie Lee Curtis's godfather is Universal chairman Lew Wasserman (once her parents' agent), and although her first professional job was as a contract player at Universal, Jamie insists that one had nothing to do with the other. "I've never used my parents," she sighs. "But people have always thought it anyway. They will continue to think it, and it's something I will have to live with for the rest of my life."

Still, most of these starchildren would probably admit that the benefits of their lineage outweigh the drawbacks. For one thing, they are knowledgeable about the industry, able to see it in a more realistic way than children who grew up in Sheboygan, poring over movie magazines and idly dreaming of fame and fortune. "There's a certain savvy that you pick up," says Jamie Lee Curtis. "You have a matter-of-factness about the business. It's less of a dreamscape area because you know how movies are made. From an early age I could tell you the function of every single person on a crew. I'm a realist, a pessimist-realist, not a dreamer."

Venetia Stevenson makes a similar observation. "It's a really unstable business, especially if you're an actor or actress. But even if you work behind the scenes, it's still very unstable, and you're dealing with emotional people all the time. Growing up in it gives you a good start in understanding all that. Outsiders never quite catch on."

Stevenson, once the Chadwick School roommate of Christina Crawford, worked as an actress in the late 1950s and early 1960s; she played Ricky Nelson's love interest on *Ozzie and Harriet* and appeared in a string of B-movies. She was married briefly to actor Russ Tamblyn and later to Don Everly of the Everly Brothers. Today, in her mid-forties, Venetia Stevenson is an executive with Cinema Group, an independent producing and financing company.

Like Stevenson, many of the children of stars toyed with performing careers, then found that they lacked the talent to make it to the top. Often they entered another area of the movie business. Some became producers or executives, some writers or directors.

Jack Haley, Jr., David Niven, Jr., John Wayne's son Michael, and Paul Newman's daughter Susan have all had respectable producing credits. Groucho Marx's son Arthur became a well-regarded writer, as did Burt Lancaster's son Bill and Keenan Wynn's son Tracy.

The most eminent of this lot is John Huston, the son of a distinguished actor, who became a fine writer, a superb director, and late in life a colorful character actor as well. In one of the most remarkable family victories in movie history, John directed Walter Huston in the crowning role of the elder Huston's career, *The Treasure of the Sierra Madre*; both father and son won Academy Awards for their work on the film.

Stars have spawned a wide variety of filmmakers, and there are some droll variations on Hollywood's true-life dramas of succession, including the saga of producer Ray Stark, who owes much of his prominence to his mother-in-law. Stark is married to Fran Arnstein, the daughter of comedienne Fanny Brice and her first husband Nicky Arnstein. Stark began in the business as an agent but made his move to production in the early 1960s. One of his first projects was co-producing the Broadway musical *Funny Girl*, based on the life of Fanny Brice. He also produced the smash hit film version of *Funny Girl*, which was Barbra Streisand's first movie. Stark immediately signed Streisand to a five-picture contract, and most of her early films—*The Owl and the Pussycat*, *The Way We Were*, *For Pete's Sake*, and *Funny Lady* (the sequel to *Funny Girl*)—were made under Stark's banner. These Streisand vehicles were what launched Rastar Productions, later responsible for such hits as *Murder by Death*, *The Goodbye Girl*, *Smokey and the Bandit*, and *The Electric Horseman*. Rastar is one of the most successful independent production companies in Hollywood, but without the mother-in-law connection, it might not have moved past the starting gate.

MANY of the starchildren went through a period of rebellion against their background. "I used to dream of being normal," Jamie Lee Curtis says. "For me, if Sammy Davis or Kirk Douglas walked into the house, that was normal. So the outside world seemed exotic to me. And when I first moved out of our home in Benedict Canyon, I moved to a little house in the San Fernando Valley. That was my dream—a home in suburbia."

Jamie's stay in the suburbs was a brief one. She quickly returned to Hollywood, though she is still determined to have you see her as the girl next door rather than as a spoiled movie brat. Friendly and unaffected, she dresses casually and talks dirty. Now that she has gone through her own minor rebellion, she admits that she looks back nostalgically on that baronial world in which she was raised. "Everything had style then," she says. "We don't have clubs any more, the ones where it used to be cool to wear a nice dress and saunter down the aisle with your escort and wave to everybody. Nowadays actors hide; they ride the subway. Nobody sends thank-you notes any more. I send a thank-you note after everything. It's part of the old standard. When I read *Mommie Dearest*, I related to a lot of it. I got to keep all my Christmas presents, whereas Christina had to give hers away. But I did have to write thank-you notes just like her. I'm not saying it was 'No wire hangers!' in my house, but there *was* a time when we certainly kept all our clothes on plastic hangers. To this day I buy plastic hangers. Monogrammed towels and printed stationery are uncool now. But all that stuff was great. I still curtsy. If I meet someone really famous, I can bow and dip."

Jamie seems most fully at home in an unpretentious habitat, though she keeps at least one toe in the genteel milieu in which she was reared. For her parents the disappearance of that regal past must be more painful. According to Jamie, they have responded to the changes in Hollywood in different ways. "My mom is Pollyanna," Jamie says. "When Pollyanna died, my mom was born; she took her soul. It does get obnoxious at times. You'll say, 'But Janet, the big black man just beat you up and stole your purse.' And she'll say, 'Yes, but he needed it more than me . . .' My father, on the other hand, has anger and bitterness—a lot very well-founded, a lot not so well-founded. He really is angry about how the business has changed. He was pretty underrated. Nobody gave him the credit when it was important for him to get it."

Jamie seems to have a healthy sense of humor about the fluctuations in her own career. Now that she has sworn off horror movies, she is still searching for her place in the mainstream. Her impersonation of murdered Playmate Dorothy Stratten in the TV movie *Death of a Centerfold* was flat and unconvincing. On the other hand, her striking appearance as the hooker-with-a-heart in *Trading Places* established her as a rising young star, helping her to land a leading role in Warner Bros.' *Grandview U.S.A.*, as the owner of a small-town demolition derby. After that she won a co-starring role opposite John Travolta in *Perfect*, a Nautilus-pumping romance set in a California health club. Jamie notes a certain irony in her growing respectability as an actress: "When I made the horror films, all the women's rights groups were after me because I was supposedly promoting violence against women. But I never took off my clothes, I never swore, I never smoked dope. I was the all-American girl who stood up for her values and fought back. Now I've graduated from those films. I'm legitimate, and in most of the films I've done since then, I've played prostitutes and Playmates. I swear and I take off my clothes. It's been fun, and the pay is definitely better. But now the same women's rights groups that attacked me are calling me and asking me to join their organizations. And all I can say is, 'Fuck you!'"

Jamie's own no-nonsense, sardonic attitude toward fame is a positive side effect of her second-generation status. Success neither dazzles nor disorients her as much as it might a less experienced hand. Yet she secretly regrets the passing of her parents' world, when stars were treated like kings and queens. For a time she was engaged to production designer J. Michael Riva, who also happens to be Marlene Dietrich's grandson. Jamie stayed at Dietrich's apartment in New York while she was making *Trading Places*. "I can't tell you how great all the stuff in her apartment was," Jamie says. "Little things like jewelry boxes with her initials. You don't see that kind of thing any more. Now everybody uses Sportsac. Those little things are not essential. People will live without them. But they were nice, they were special."

Even for the most cynical of Hollywood's progeny, the trappings of Dietrich's era retain their allure. Yet those glamorous accoutrements count for little in today's unstable movie business. A famous name may count for more, but the most valuable legacy is probably the toughness that helped the starchildren withstand the pressures of their upbringing, and now enables them to secure their own foothold in a business radically different from the one their parents knew.

5

CITIZENS THREE: The Fondas

"Oh, they're not scared of you. They're scared of what you represent... What you represent to them is freedom... Oh, yeah—they're gonna talk to you, and talk to you, and talk to you about individual freedom—but they see a free individual, it's gonna scare 'em."

—JACK NICHOLSON TO PETER FONDA IN *EASY RIDER*

SUMMER of 1969, the sunset of a turbulent decade, saw the mood of the country turning bitter and apocalyptic. The antiwar movement was growing more militant in response to Richard Nixon's intransigence. The gap between the President's silent majority and the children of the counterculture widened to a dangerous chasm. And the savage "Manson Family" murders sounded a grim requiem for the Age of Aquarius.

Political and social upheaval usually stimulates invigorating artistic ferment, and that summer of 1969 was one of the most exciting periods in the history of American movies. Half a dozen low-budget pictures made by filmmakers outside the Hollywood mainstream suddenly seemed to augur an American New Wave: *Midnight Cowboy*, *Alice's Restaurant*, *Medium Cool*, *Last Summer*, and *Putney Swope* were cast with largely unknown actors and tackled controversial, contemporary subject matter. Audacious new writers and directors experimented with a raw, urgent, non-linear style, and optimists predicted a revolution in the very method of American film. *Newsweek* hailed the trend: "A personal cinema is being born, and in its films can be read the search for a better way of life."

Although that prediction proved overly sanguine and the American New Wave quickly ebbed, the events of that summer did have a lasting impact on American filmmaking. The abolition of the Production Code—the industry's self-censorship unit— meant that movies were freer to tackle bold topical themes. Many new young talents were introduced into the industry, and they helped to liberate movies from old restraints. Perhaps most importantly, Hollywood's obsession with the youth market, which did not really exist before that summer, has continued to dominate studio decision-making ever since.

At the center of this cinematic revolution was *Easy Rider*, a low-budget sleeper that turned into the most popular movie of the summer and was the first important American film to capture the idealism as well as the anger and paranoia of the under-thirty generation. The film followed the cross-country odyssey of two drug-dealing motorcycle bums traversing the rugged Southwestern landscape, encountering a gallery of native American eccentrics, until they meet a violent death at the hands of Southern bigots. *Easy Rider* caught the increasingly divisive tensions between young and old, hippies and red-necks, that were wracking the country; it had a profound effect on young audiences because it gave expression to their vague sense of themselves as innocent lambs, ripe for slaughter.

The movie also had a profound effect on its makers, many of them second-generation Hollywood personalities. *Easy Rider* was the first successful film for BBS Productions, an innovative new company founded by Bert Schneider, the son of Columbia Pictures chairman Abe Schneider. The film's director-co-star was Dennis Hopper, best known for his early performances with his friend James Dean in *Rebel Without a Cause* and *Giant*; Hopper was recently divorced from Brooke Hayward, the daughter of agent-producer Leland Hayward and actress Margaret Sullavan. Hopper's former brother-in-law, Bill Hayward, was associate producer of *Easy Rider*. The Haywards' childhood pal, Robert Walker Jr. (the son of Robert Walker and Jennifer Jones), had a featured part in the film. *Easy Rider* also marked the first major screen role for Jack Nicholson, who won an Academy Award nomination for his bravura performance as the drunken Southern lawyer accompanying the boys on their ill-fated journey.

Producing and co-starring was twenty-eight-year-old Peter Fonda. His father, Henry Fonda, was appearing in his sixty-eighth movie that summer, *Once Upon a Time in the West*. His sister Jane was already a movie star, known primarily for her roles in light comedies like *Cat Ballou* and *Barefoot in the Park*, and for her nude scenes in the campy comic strip *Barbarella*, directed by her then-husband, Roger Vadim. Peter had been the least prominent of the acting Fondas; that summer he suddenly outstripped Jane in popularity and influence.

Peter's role in *Easy Rider* as the existential dropout, Captain America, elicited a passionate audience identification. "As we enter the seventies," *Playboy* announced, "the decade's first authentic cult hero has already emerged: Peter Fonda, who personifies—on screen and off—the radical lifestyle that has gained increasing currency among young Americans. Not since James Dean's *Rebel Without a Cause* and Marlon Brando's *The Wild One* has a movie actor so captured the imagination and admiration of a generation."

Peter himself looks back nostalgically to that summer of 1969, and he vividly recalls the impact of *Easy Rider* on the throngs of young audiences who came to see it. "People were screaming in theaters at the end of the movie," he says. "The night it opened in Westwood, a girl fainted when she saw Dennis alive in the lobby after the movie; it had become that real to her. There was a great feeling we all had of being part of a moment in history. I don't know whether that will happen again for me in my lifetime. *Easy Rider* may have had more international influence than any other film. None of the Fonda films are remembered with such fervor—none of my father's films and none of my sister's films."

PETER and Jane Fonda began their professional acting careers at roughly the same time. Jane's first movie, *Tall Story*, was released in 1960; Peter made his stage debut on Broadway in 1961, in *Blood, Sweat and Stanley Poole*, and starred in his first film a year later. Up to that point few children of major stars had come close to matching the achievements of their parents. Diana Barrymore, Edward G. Robinson, Jr., and Gary Crosby were the butts of jokes or the objects of pity. The situation has changed so dramatically in the last two decades that it is easy to forget how precarious a future the younger Fondas faced when they were starting out. The example of their success is what lent credibility to the notion that second-generation performers could be something more than novelties of casting. In that sense, they paved the way for the hordes of other celebrities' children who would follow them into the profession.

In launching their careers, neither Peter nor Jane received much guidance from their father. Peter observes, "I used to lie and tell people that my father only encouraged me to do my best. In fact, Dad never said anything to me. I once asked John Huston's daughter, Anjelica, 'Did John ever say anything to you? She said, 'No. We lived in a gate house. He lived in a castle.' I thought, being the son of another actor, he would have some advice as to what to expect. But Anjelica was just as much out in the cold as I was."

Jane confirms that her father had difficulty offering the support that she and her brother needed. "I don't think he was able to understand the particular pressures on the child of a famous person," she says.

Not surprisingly, one of the main reasons Henry Fonda chose an acting career in the first place was to vent the intense feelings that he could not express in real life. It is hard to locate the roots of his emotional reticence. Henry never spoke in any depth about his childhood or his early family relationships, except to hint that his father, the owner of a print shop in Omaha, Nebraska, was himself a rather stern and taciturn man. Henry inherited those qualities, though they seemed to be magnified in him. He once recalled his relationship with his college girlfriend and his total inability to tell her that he loved her. "I couldn't say it to her face," Henry revealed. "So, that's me. And that's one of the reasons that the theater is such therapy. On the stage or in the movies, I can act it and I can say and do it all, but in real life . . . When I act I put on a mask and when I do that I'm not self-conscious or shy at all, because I know that when I'm on the stage I'm going to be funny or bright or brilliant—I'm going to be another person who isn't me at all. You see, I'm no good on my own."

On stage and on screen Henry Fonda embodied the ideal American hero for over four decades: he played presidents, legendary cowboys, brave soldiers, understanding fathers and unlettered sages. But his family saw him in a very different light—as an emotionally strangled man, terse and uncommunicative, frequently abrasive. As Jane once said of her childhood, "My father was not a demonstrative person, and never said, 'I love you,' and didn't hold you on his knees. In those days his major emotion was rage." Peter told *Playboy* in 1971, "I guess the first big shock my sister, Jane, and I experienced about my father was discovering that Henry Fonda wasn't perfect. My father was *presented* as perfect, but the man who played Abe Lincoln and Mr. Roberts and Tom Joad, the man who carried everybody's honesty and integrity on his shoulders, turned out to be a hollow man to us."

If Henry's remoteness and repression created problems for both children, they faced even more severe problems in relating to their mother. Henry Fonda's first marriage, to actress Margaret Sullavan, lasted only a few months. When he married Frances Brokaw, the attractive, wealthy young widow of financier George Brokaw, he seemed to have made a more fitting match. Jane was born in 1937, Peter in 1940, and the early family albums were filled with seemingly idyllic pictures.

Frances Brokaw Fonda had beauty, intelligence, wit, and wealth. But she had no career, and her tragedy was that she could not find a professional outlet for her abundant energies. Joshua Logan, a family friend and the man who directed Henry in *Mr. Roberts*, has described Frances as "very organized, very aggressive, very determined." Her aggressiveness was clearly frustrated in her role as Hollywood wife and mother. Desperate to assert herself, she turned into a martinet in rearing her children and made an occupation out of managing the family finances, becoming, in Henry's words, "obsessed with dollar signs and decimal points."

Henry's former wife, Margaret Sullavan Hayward, and her new family lived just down the block from the Fondas in Brentwood, and the Fonda and Hayward children became close friends. Bill Hayward gives his impressions of Frances Fonda: "She was only vaguely there. I always remember she was in another room, and a typewriter was always working and nobody ever knew what she was typing."

As she approached middle age, and her inchoate desire to express herself remained stifled, Frances became increasingly distraught. She suffered severe bouts of depression and was repeatedly confined to a sanitarium. No doubt Henry's constrained nature only made things harder for Frances. During one of his last interviews, given in 1981, Henry offered a telling insight into the part his own self-absorption may have played in causing her breakdown. Asked about Frances's mental problems, he responded in these words: "I never dreamed that it would be anything permanent. It was just a bore to have a wife who wasn't always well."

Reflecting on her mother's fate, Jane Fonda comments, "I think some people are born fragile, and they're just not equipped with the wherewithal to survive certain kinds of meanness and cruelty in the world. That might have been partly true of my mother." Today Jane has something of a feminist perspective on her mother's unhappy life: "Had she been part on this generation, with a different kind of support network among women, another kind of awareness and consciousness of the kinds of things that are done to women and how women can respond, that might have saved her. It's difficult to know. All I know is some of it had to do with the fact that she was middle-aged, and she'd never been taught to have anything but youth and beauty."

On April 14, 1950, the morning of her forty-second birthday, Frances Fonda went into the bathroom of the Craig Sanatorium in Beacon, New York and cut her throat from ear to ear with a small safety razor that she had used for shaving her body hair. That evening, after being informed of his wife's suicide, Henry Fonda went on stage and performed his part in the Broadway smash, *Mr. Roberts*.

Jane, age twelve, and Peter, age ten, were told that their mother had died of a heart attack. Eight months later, Henry married Susan Blanchard, the stepdaughter of Oscar Hammerstein II, a woman half his age, whom he had been seeing even before Frances died. (Henry and Susan had met through her step-brother Bill Hammerstein, the stage manager of *Mr. Roberts*.) Henry never told his children the truth about their mother's suicide, but they found out in other ways. A couple of months after her mother's suicide, Jane was at boarding school in Connecticut. She and her friend Brooke Hayward were reading a movie magazine that mentioned her mother's suicide in passing. "Is it true?" Jane asked Brooke, who was too flabbergasted to answer.

Jane later told Henry's biographer, Howard Teichmann, how she reacted to the discovery: "I was just stunned. It was dramatic ... I'm being perfectly honest; it was a combination of horror and fascination. How much more interesting than a heart attack." Jane asked her grandmother's nurse whether the story was true, and the nurse confirmed that it was. Jane never discussed the matter with her father.

Although Jane tried to maintain a stoical facade, she could not entirely suppress her grief. That summer, while she was at camp in New Hampshire, Jane had nightmares about her mother's suicide. Brooke Hayward wrote that when Jane awoke from these nightmares, she was "screaming so that the entire staff had to appear to calm her down." Henry Fonda was not informed, and it was not until years later that he learned she knew the truth about her mother's death.

For Peter the discovery of that truth was equally traumatic. Neither his father nor his sister told him that Frances had killed herself. Several years after his mother died, he was sitting in a barber chair in Rome when he picked up a magazine and happened to read about her suicide. Even today Peter is bitter about having been kept in the dark for so long. "Every time I'd come upon a new bit of family life which I should have known about and didn't," he says, "I'd have to deal with it right there with no help and no explanation."

Frances's life and death had a profound, enduring impact on both her children. Jane internalized many of the conflicts that troubled her mother. For one thing, she inherited her mother's obsessive concern about her physical appearance. As Jane writes in her best-seller *Jane Fonda's Workout Book*, "My mother . . . who was a rather slender, beautiful woman, was terrified of getting fat. She once said that if she ever gained weight she'd have the excess flesh cut off!" Jane herself was a chubby child and even when she lost weight, she was determined to lose more. "I was so conditioned to thinking of myself as fat that later, when I was really thin, I could never convince myself that I was thin enough," she writes. During her teenage years she fell victim to bulimia— eating binges followed by self-enforced vomiting—and also became dependent on Dexedrine and diuretics to help keep her weight down.

Jane also inherited her mother's disciplined, compulsive nature, but with one crucial difference. "I'm a survivor," Jane says simply. "Absolute survivor." And that core of strength undoubtedly helped her to overcome the trauma of her mother's suicide. Peter, who was younger at the time of his mother's death, had a far harder time absorbing the shock. For the next several years he engaged in wildly self-destructive behavior. "Peter took everything harder," Jane admits. "I don't know whether he felt things more deeply, but certainly the acting out was more visibly complicated than mine."

As Peter says, "One of the biggest fears I ever had was that craziness might be inherited, and that because my mother was bat-shit, I was going to be bat-shit, too. I was terrified that they'd put me in that little building and would never let me out."

In early January of 1951, while Henry Fonda was honeymooning with his third wife, Susan Blanchard, in the Virgin Islands, he received word that Peter had shot himself in the stomach and was close to death. Peter was staying with his maternal grandmother at the time, and he had cajoled her into letting him play with a twenty-two-caliber rifle locked in her closet. Whether the shooting was accidental or a ten-year-old's half-conscious attempt at suicide has never been conclusively established. Today Peter has blocked the incident from his memory and cannot recall exactly what happened. Henry Fonda was quietly furious with Peter, since he cut short his honeymoon to see to Peter's care. No doubt his anger was commingled with a profound sense of guilt.

That was not the last of Peter's problems. He was on the psychiatrist's couch at the age of eleven, and he later described himself as an alcoholic at fifteen. At prep school he began taking phenobarbitals to calm himself down. Once he got into a fistfight with a teacher who would not allow him to participate in the school's theater club. "I actually knocked him out with a punch," Peter says. "He refused to let me into the group because he was very angry about Henry. He saw Henry as being an evil person, having been married so many times."

Henry's marriage to Susan Blanchard lasted just five years. They adopted a daughter, Amy, in 1954, but their marriage broke up a year later. Susan said at the time, "I had mistaken Hank's silent shyness when I met him. Perhaps I thought of him as an American Gothic. It was part of his attractiveness. Later, I understood it reflected a rigidity. His was a personality completely different from my own." Susan took Amy with her and returned to live in New York.

In 1957, shortly after Henry married his fourth wife, an Italian baroness named Afdera Franchetti, Peter once again got into trouble, this time with drugs. Jane rushed down from Vassar to be with her brother and found Peter in a drug-induced daze, hiding in some bushes near his prep school. She called her father, and for the second time Henry had to interrupt a wedding trip to tend to Peter. The boy was pulled out of school and was sent to stay with Henry's sister in Omaha.

Peter looks back on his adolescent years as unrelievedly painful. "When I was growing up," he recalls, "I didn't understand why everyone would start acting different when I came into a room, why my date would sit over on the other side of the car. My friends finally told me, 'They don't know how to talk to you because you're Henry Fonda's son. You know so much more than they do.' I said, 'I know nothing, absolutely nothing. I want help. Give me a bare tit, goddammit.' I didn't need the pre-identity. I used to fight that; that was the biggest rebellion on my part. And that's one of the areas that I've really talked to my children about. I've been at it since they were real squeakers."

Henry Fonda could not help Jane and Peter through their adolescent crises. As Jane put it, "I was brought up where people didn't express what they really felt. You hid everything. You hid your fears and your sorrows and your pains and your joys and your physical desires. Consequently I was a zombie, living somebody else's image, and I didn't know who I was."

Bill Hayward contrasts his own troubled family to the Fondas: "Peter, I think, was always very aware that he came from a fucked-up family, a really fucked-up family. When I was a kid, I didn't have that feeling, I may have subconsciously known it, but Peter was always conscious of it. Henry was a very shy man, but very stern and very quick-tempered. I don't think my father ever could be as stern as Henry could. Leland wasn't quite as self-involved as Henry could be. Henry was real tough. At least that was the way he behaved with Peter."

Hollywood family annals are rife with tales of strained relationships, but the aborted communication among the Fondas seems especially poignant. For this was clearly a family in which father and children did have strong feelings for one another. It was not a household like Joan Crawford's, where the children were objects to be displayed. The Fondas cared for each other far more deeply, but they could not express those feelings openly. They seem to be a real-life counterpart to the WASP family in *Ordinary People*, inhabiting a realm where all emotion is suppressed.

Incapable of communicating with one another directly, the Fondas used the media to voice their personal feelings. There has probably never been another Hollywood clan that talked so freely to the press about other family members. They insulted each other, praised each other, baited each other, courted each other—almost as if the only way they could make contact was by this public plea for one another's attention.

When she first began working as an actress, Jane gave numerous interviews criticizing her father's marital record and recommending psychoanalysis. "Any man who is fifty-seven years old and has gone through four wives must be very, very unhappy," Jane declared. Henry responded in kind. He once remarked, "I'm between planes somewhere, and before long there's a reporter to interview me, and he has a clipping that says Jane Fonda thinks her parents led a phony life. Or that she thinks her father should have been psychoanalyzed thirty-five years ago. Now it's all right for her to think it, but I don't think it's all right for her to say so in interviews. After all, I *am* her father." On other occasions Henry criticized Jane's politics and made scathing comments about her various friends and lovers. He berated Jane for living openly with Roger Vadim before marrying him. Peter gave an interview in which he mocked Henry for his moralizing. "The only difference was that he'd send his chicks home every night. His duplicity blew our minds." Henry could be just as harsh in discussing Peter. As late as 1981, when asked about Peter's statement that he had once been crucified by some hoods in New York, Henry excoriated his son: "He's got the goddamndest imagination and he's a compulsive liar."

Although Henry Fonda may have been cantankerous and emotionally constricted, the integrity that he projected in the movies was not a total lie. Speaking about her upbringing and the scars that it left, Jane says, "The problem with wealthy and famous people very often is that even when they are home, they're not home. So much can get filtered through governesses and servants; the actual job of raising and nurturing the child is given over to hired hands. Peter and I were raised by governesses essentially. I think the saving grace was this unspoken but very much transmittable integrity and humility that my father had. He had very high standards, and that sort of filters through."

Or as Peter puts it, "My father was a real *citizen*. I think it was one of the things that made him such a tremendous folk star. I grew up with a true citizen. I didn't even learn about racism or prejudice until I was ten. I had never heard the words 'nigger' or 'kike' until I moved to Greenwich, Connecticut. I heard the words at school and asked my father what those words meant. He blew up. He said, 'Where'd you hear those words?' I was so damn naive. Well, I wouldn't mind being that naive for the rest of my life."

HENRY Fonda's career was substantially different from that of his children. His approach was, in Jane's words, "lovingly passive." That is to say, he was under contract to studios, took the films that were offered to him and rarely initiated his own projects. He produced only one film in his lifetime—*Twelve Angry Men*—and found producing so uncomfortable that he vowed never to do it again. He did not take charge of his film career in the way that his children eventually took charge of theirs, and consequently he never earned the huge salaries and percentages that they were able to command a generation later. As Peter points out, "My father was not the kind of star who got $5 million for a picture. The most he ever got was $250,000. He was embarrassed to ask for more."

Yet if he never had the power and autonomy that his children would achieve, in another sense Henry Fonda compiled one of the most remarkable track records in the history of American acting. And his children know that they will be very fortunate if they are able to continue working as long as he did. Henry Fonda's career remained in high gear for most of the fifty years that he worked at his craft. His career had peaks and valleys, but there were never any disastrously long, dry stretches.

A native of Nebraska, Henry had no burning desire to become an actor while he was growing up. At the age of twenty he was still pondering his future when a friend of his mother's, the founder of the Omaha Community Playhouse, inquired whether young Henry might be interested in joining the company. That family friend was Dorothy Brando; she had a newborn baby named Marlon, but Do—as all her friends called her—was too restless and creative to stay at home knitting baby clothes. Inspired by her enthusiasm, Henry Fonda decided to try his luck in the theater; he felt he had nothing to lose.

In 1928 he traveled east to Cape Cod and joined the University Players, a theatrical troupe made up of young actors from Ivy League colleges. In the company he met Joshua Logan, a Princeton graduate, and through Logan, he met another Princeton student, James Stewart, who became his roommate and lifelong friend. In the early 1930s both actors decided to try their luck in New York. A rising young agent named Leland Hayward (who would shortly marry Henry's ex-wife, Margaret Sullavan) took on Fonda as a client and helped him to land his first starring role on Broadway, in *The Farmer Takes a Wife*. That play about life along the Erie Canal in the mid-nineteenth century was a hit, and the *New York Times*'s Brooks Atkinson praised Fonda's work: "A manly, modest performance in a style of captivating simplicity." That phrase summed up Fonda's appeal at this early stage of his career. He was typecast as an American innocent, a virtuous man of the soil.

Twentieth Century-Fox bought the film rights to the play as a vehicle for Janet Gaynor. For the male lead Fox wanted an established movie star—either Gary Cooper or Joel McCrea. Fortunately for Fonda, neither of them was available, and so Henry won the chance to repeat his Broadway role for the movie version in 1936. He worked steadily during the next few years and hit his stride with a trio of films made for director John Ford in 1939 and 1940: *Drums Along the Mohawk*, *Young Mr. Lincoln*, and *The Grapes of Wrath*. His performance as Tom Joad, the angry, embittered farmer in *The Grapes of Wrath*, inspired the book's author, John Steinbeck, to write, "A lean, stringy, dark-faced piece of electricity walked out on the screen and he had me. I believed my own story again."

When Fonda returned from service in the Navy during World War II, he continued to work with Ford; he played Wyatt Earp in the classic Western, *My Darling Clementine*, and also starred in *The Fugitive* and *Fort Apache*. But Henry found himself increasingly frustrated by the contract he had signed at Twentieth Century-Fox. He despised Darryl F. Zanuck for casting him in what he called "some of the worst shit that I've had to do in films." Such pictures as *Rings on Her Fingers* with Gene Tierney and *The Magnificent Dope* with Don Ameche have been mercifully forgotten. In response to the poor roles he was being offered, Henry Fonda did something that was unheard-of at the time: although he was a top movie star, he returned to Broadway and stayed in the theater for several years.

Jane feels that particular turning-point in his career had something to do with the political shift in the country. "My father had a progressive tendency as a human being," Jane says, "and he began his career at a time when progressive films were being made. All of his best films, like *The Grapes of Wrath*, were liberal films. After the war he came back to a world of conservatism, of Eisenhower and McCarthyism, and his career was floundering. He then made a deliberate decision to leave Hollywood and go to Broadway."

Between 1949 and 1955 Henry Fonda did not make a single movie. Instead he starred on Broadway in the hit play *Mr. Roberts*; he also had long runs in *Point of No Return* and *The Caine Mutiny Court Martial*. When the movie version of *Mr. Roberts* was being planned in 1955, Henry almost missed getting the part. His friend Leland Hayward, who was producing the film, felt Fonda had been forgotten by moviegoers during his long absence from the screen. Hayward offered the part of Doug Roberts to William Holden and Marlon Brando, but John Ford—who was already signed to direct—refused to make the film without Fonda. The film of *Mr. Roberts* re-established Henry Fonda as a major Hollywood star. The following year he played Pierre to Audrey Hepburn's Natasha in *War and Peace*, then produced and starred in the taut courtroom drama, *Twelve Angry Men*. When his film career hit another slow period in the late 1950s, Henry again returned to his first love, the theater, starring in such Broadway hits as *Two for the Seesaw* and *Critic's Choice*. Fonda made his share of bad movies in the 1960s and 1970s out of a compulsion to keep working; no doubt he might have preferred to erase such titles as *The Dirty Game*, *Ash Wednesday*, *The Swarm*, and *Meteor* from his filmography. Again he returned to the theater for revitalization; in the last decade of his life he scored stage triumphs in *Darrow, The Oldest Living Graduate*, and *First Monday in October*. Fonda is one of the only American stars comparable to the great British actors who travel back and forth between theater and films all their lives. And that may be why Fonda's career had the span of Olivier's or Gielgud's, while so many of his contemporaries struggled to retain a foothold.

THERE is no doubt that Henry Fonda's example influenced his children to become actors, even if he did not encourage them directly. Peter speaks of what he learned about acting from observing his father prepare for a role. "I watched him work his parts up," Peter recalls. "He'd pay me $2.50 an hour to run lines for him. The man thought he had a tough time with lines. After about the fourth or fifth session, I realized he could memorize the phone book, but obviously I wasn't going to knock myself out of a job, so I ran lines with him. Sometimes he'd grope for the line, and I'd feed it to him, and he'd snap at me, 'I know the line.' What I saw him doing was not trying to learn the lines but learn the character, learn little definitions. He didn't realize this. He thought he was having trouble with lines, but what he was really doing was putting his character together. He'd watch the pieces develop in the way a line was read, and change from one pattern to a whole new pattern. And I saw what he was doing with his craft. That was wonderful for me."

Nonetheless, in launching their own acting careers, both Jane and Peter were conscious that Henry's reputation could be an inhibiting force. In order to establish her own identity, Jane decided to study acting at Lee Strasberg's Actors Studio. "I did not want to be in a position where people would say I was only getting a job because of my father," she explains. "Although I don't believe that anyone can teach talent, the fact that *I* knew I had gone about it seriously and thoroughly made a difference. I think I probably studied harder because of who my father was. If other people went to classes twice a week, I would go four times a week. Other people would do one scene every few months; I'd do two scenes. Even though I'm fairly driven anyway, I think it had to do with my need to be overqualified. Minorities know that feeling well, as do a lot of women, as well as children of famous parents. If they're conscientious and don't want to rest on the laurels of their parents, they tend to want to overqualify. My father was not happy that I went and studied acting. He had not done that. He had gotten his training as a lot of people did in those days, by working. But it wasn't so competitive then. There weren't as many people competing for a smaller and smaller number of jobs. He must have done three hundred jobs in summer stock and road shows before he ever came to Broadway, whereas my first job was starring in a movie, and I had to have a technique and at least appear experienced and professional. I don't think that he was sensitive to that change in reality. Also, I don't think he was able to understand the particular pressures on the child of a famous person and the psychological need to feel qualified."

Henry was dubious about his children's desire to pursue a career in acting. Jane recalls, "My father always talked about the number of friends he had who had been, as he said, 'bitten by the bug of acting' and didn't have enough talent to make it. So they'd work intermittently and do automobile shows and things like that. He didn't want that for us."

Jane always had difficulty eliciting praise from her father. She remembered a time, for example, when she had done a very exciting scene in Strasberg's class and wanted to share her exhilaration with her father. "I was panting with excitement," Jane reported. "I wanted to tell him about it. And I could see his curtain come down. He smiled, but I just didn't get through." Later, when Henry Fonda was asked about that particular incident, he said that he was deeply moved by Jane's enthusiasm but couldn't let her see what he was feeling. "It may be that I'm trying to hide my own emotions, and to her it's a curtain coming down," he conceded. "I can get emotional right now remembering Jane tell it, and probably the curtain came down to hide that emotion . . . I wasn't going to let her see me go on like this."

Despite Henry's apparent coolness, Jane did act with her father in small parts in a couple of stock company productions—*The Country Girl* in Omaha and *The Male Animal* on Cape Cod— after she graduated from high school. She also owed her start in movies to her father. It was Henry's friend Joshua Logan who originally signed Jane to a long-term contract and cast her in her first picture, *Tall Story*, when she was twenty-one and had no significant acting experience. Logan had liked Jane's work in summer stock, and he also recognized the publicity value of having a second-generation Fonda star in his movie. The film itself, a bubble-brained comedy about the romance between a college basketball player and a cheerleader, was not a happy experience for Jane, but it did turn her into a hot new starlet.

Jane plunged into her movie career with gusto. Her *Tall Story* co-star, Anthony Perkins, notes that she "was very determined even then, in her pre-political days." Her friend Brooke Hayward said, "I've never seen ambition as naked as Jane's." Jane's first movies were mostly forgettable products. Besides *Tall Story*, they included *Walk on the Wild Side*, a bastardized version of Nelson Algren's risqué novel about life in a brothel; *The Chapman Report*, based on Irving Wallace's luridly-detailed best-seller about a Kinsey-style sexual research experiment; and *Period of Adjustment*, based on a minor Tennessee Williams comedy. All three went belly up at the box office. In those early days Jane was dismissed by the press as a feather-weight talent capitalizing on her famous name. The first major reviewer to take a contrary view was *The New Republic*'s Stanley Kauffmann, who shocked his critical confreres when he declared in 1962, "A new talent is rising—Jane Fonda. Her light is hardly under a bushel, but as far as adequate appreciation is concerned, she might as well be another Sandra Dee. I have now seen Miss Fonda in three films. In all of them she gives performances that are not only fundamentally different from one another but are conceived without acting cliché and executed with skill. Through them all can be heard, figuratively, the hum of that magnetism without which acting intelligence and technique are admirable but not compelling."

Since *The New Republic* is hardly obligatory reading on the Bel-Air circuit, Jane's agent made copies of Kauffmann's review and had them sent to every producer in town, as well as to the *Harvard Lampoon*, which had named Jane worst actress of the year for her performance as the frigid young woman thawed by Efram Zimbalist, Jr. in *The Chapman Report*. Jane felt somewhat vindicated by Kauffmann's encomium, but she still believed she was struggling to compete with her father's reputation.

In 1963, Jane went to make her first film in Europe—a picture called *Joy House*, in which she co-starred with Alain Delon. She spent a good deal of time in Paris during the next seven years, and her European sojourn seems to have allayed some of her competitive feelings toward her father. "It was then that I became my own person," she said. "Maybe that's even why I went. Maybe going had to do with trying not to be Henry Fonda's daughter any more. Go to another culture. Prove myself on my own. The world I entered into there was so far removed from his background and his upbringing and his world views. I got over him as a problem-figure in my life."

That last statement is certainly arguable. For at the same time that she was declaring her independence from her father, Jane moved in and out of a series of romantic relationships with older, paternal men. During the early 1960s she had relied on Andreas Voutsinas, a director she had met at the Actors Studio whom many described as a Svengali treating Jane like his puppet Trilby. Then in Paris, she fell under the spell of Roger Vadim, who directed her in four films and eventually married her. Jane followed in the footsteps of Brigitte Bardot, Annette Stroyberg, and Catherine Deneuve—young actresses with whom Vadim carried on romantic liaisons while he molded them into sex goddesses for the world to adore. Jane became his first American odalisque.

UNLIKE Jane, Peter Fonda never had a burning desire to become a successful actor. As he says, "I was never bitten by the bug." But he drifted into the profession because it seemed like the logical thing for a Fonda to do. When his father praised his performance in a college play, Peter's remaining doubts were erased.

The problems that Jane had faced in establishing her professional identity were magnified for Peter. "I think it was far more difficult for Peter than for me," Jane says. "First of all, it's always more difficult for the child who's the same sex as the famous parent. In Peter's case my father, Henry Fonda, was his role model, so when Peter was there, he was *literally* being judged. It's just horrible, and I think it's very often why it's the child of the same sex who runs into the greater emotional problems. When you add to that the fact that there's a sibling, I think that makes it really rough."

"For a long time I looked at myself as the third man on a match," Peter reflects. 'It's an old World War I saying: 'Never have three men on a match. In the trench, if you light a match, the sniper sees the match lit and gets the area. The second man, he gets the range. Third man, the sniper takes his head off.' Well, Henry and Jane. Who's third? Everyone looks to shoot me down. I've never been able to shake it. Now that I've been working twenty-two years and made twenty-eight films, I think I'll survive."

In 1962 Peter made his first movie, *Tammy and the Doctor*, which he has rudely rechristened "Tammy and the Schmuckface." Carl Foreman's *The Victors* and Robert Rossen's *Lilith* (in which he appeared with Warren Beatty and Jean Seberg) were more prestigious credits, but they were both box office failures. After his fourth flop, an anachronistic campus caper produced and directed by Samuel Goldwyn, Jr. called *The Young Lovers* (which Peter later said "would have been all right when *he* was in college"), Peter's career had reached a standstill.

His personal life was in a state of flux. In 1961 he had married Susan Brewer, the stepdaughter of Noah Dietrich, Howard Hughes's right-hand man. Soon Peter and Susan had a daughter, Bridget, named after his friend Bridget Hayward, who had committed suicide not long before. Peter and his family lived in Beverly Hills. "I was a conservative, a registered Republican," he later said. "I was into acting out other people's notions about who I should be— doing the right thing, being a member of the right clubs, joining the right party, meeting the right people. Being a socialite, the Blue Book thing—I believed in it. I accepted it."

Another young actor named Jack Nicholson met the Fonda children in the early 1960s. Today he says in amusement, "When I first knew him, Peter was a Republican who thought I was a Communist. He and Jane have both changed quite a bit since then."

As the counterculture blossomed in the years after President Kennedy's assassination, Peter Fonda moved into the vanguard of the new youth movement. In 1966 he was arrested for possession of marijuana. His father flew to Los Angeles to be with him in the courtroom, and the trial ended in a hung jury. During the same period Peter admitted that he had taken [LSD] eleven times. He felt the drug had been therapeutic. "As that first [LSD] trip progressed," he reported later, "I thought about my father and about my relationship with him and my mother and my sister. And suddenly I busted through the whole thing and related to everything. There was no more worry about my father, mother, and sister. I began to feel really on top of all my problems. I had no further relationship with the past; I'd kicked it."

Peter's offscreen behavior began to influence his on-screen persona. His career got a sudden shot in the arm when he went to work for AIP, the studio specializing in low-budget exploitation pictures. His first film for the company, *The Wild Angels* (in which he co-starred with another second generation performer, Nancy Sinatra), was a fast-paced biker melodrama. A hit at the Venice Film Festival in 1966, banned in Denmark because of its violence, the movie stirred controversy wherever it played; even the Hells Angels sued for $4 million for invasion of privacy! In its first few weeks of release, *The Wild Angels* doubled the gross of AIP's previous box office champ, *Bikini Beach*. Posters of Peter astride his cycle became the top-selling poster in campus head shops. Peter's position as emerging cult hero was confirmed by his next movie for AIP, a psychedelic fantasy called *The Trip*, written by Peter's friend Jack Nicholson. Not long afterwards, the *Hollywood Citizen-News* ran a cartoon in which a wide-eyed teenage girl questions her father, "Golly, Daddy, I really don't know whether I'm a Democrat or a Republican. What's Peter Fonda?"

Bruce Dern, who had a supporting part in both *The Wild Angels* and *The Trip*, revealed to Rex Reed the resentment he felt in playing second fiddle to the son of a famous actor: "Suddenly I realized there I was, with solid professional training, supporting Peter Fonda, who had never bothered to take the time to learn how to act." Peter was stung by those words, and he still remembers them. Even today he feels compelled to answer the charge that he owes his career to nepotism. "Bruce Dern commented about me that I never bothered to do my homework," Peter says. "When I read that I thought, 'Wow, did I just skate on up here as Henry's son and Jane's brother? Is that why I'm still here? Did I really not take it seriously and not invest a lot of time?' It's true that I didn't study with Strasberg like Jane did. I went to see Strasberg once. He asked me six questions and told me, 'You don't belong in this class. This is not the way you're going to be acting. Just do what you're doing.' But I really do believe I did my homework."

During that time Peter was the outspoken rebel in the family. Jane was living quietly in France with Vadim; her acts of public defiance were limited to tweaking the bluenoses with her insouciant nude scenes and a few pronouncements on the obsolescence of monogamy. In many ways she began to feel that her younger brother had passed her by. Looking back at that period, Peter remarks, "When Jane came out of Europe and arrived back here in the States, suddenly there was baby brother busted on a marijuana charge, in this cult movie *Wild Angels*, popped on Sunset

Strip during the riots, and seemingly deeply involved in the youth movement. And I think she felt a little bit left out."

In 1968 Peter joined Jane in France to appear with her in one part of the omnibus horror movie, *Spirits of the Dead*. (Their section was directed by Vadim, but the only segment of the film that won any acclaim was the one directed by Federico Fellini.) Peter approached the experience with some apprehension. "I wanted to please Jane," he says today. "She was doing it for me. I was basically broke." Jane berated him for overemoting in one scene. Later when she saw the film, she realized she had been wrong and sent him a telegram apologizing for the tongue-lashing.

During the period he was in France, Peter was thinking about his next project, a screenplay he was writing with his friend, Dennis Hopper. The two had met when Hopper married Brooke Hayward at Jane's New York apartment in 1961, and over the ensuing years they talked about making a film together. An idea finally came to Peter in 1967 when he was invited to speak at a meeting of the Motion Picture Association of America. The first speaker, MPAA president Jack Valenti, sanctimoniously declared that he was weary of the excesses in all the movies about drugs and motorcycle gangs. Waiting in the wings to deliver the next speech, Peter took Valenti's broadside as a personal affront and vowed that he would make the first good movie about drugs and motorcycles. That was the seed of *Easy Rider*. While acting in *Spirits of the Dead* in the south of France, Peter was also working on his new script, which he regarded as the apotheosis of the AIP motorcycle epic. Terry Southern was also on the set of *Spirits of the Dead*; he had contributed to the screenplay of *Barbarella* and was friendly with Jane and Vadim. Peter told him the story of *Easy Rider*, and Southern agreed to polish the screenplay and put it in final form.

Peter recalls, "We were all driving home—Terry and I and Vadim and Jane and Jane's three little dogs. And Terry said to Jane, 'Your brother has a wonderful story.' I hadn't told Jane what I was doing. And when Terry told her the story, Jane was quite skeptical about it. Who can blame her? But after we made the film, she and Vadim came to see a rough cut. It was obviously too long, but she said she loved it."

Peter refused to be discouraged as he labored over *Easy Rider*. But in a sense he had nothing to lose. "I was considered a freak," he recalls. "I was an admitted user of LSD. I wasn't a hot actor. Dennis was and still is known as difficult. But we believed we could make the movie for a price and make money on it. If it hadn't worked, I would have gone back to summer stock and started all over again. It's funny. People felt it was such a personal film. But I was thinking of it in commercial terms. I built the two motorcycles myself. The first thing I put down on paper was the image of the motorcycle I would drive. I wanted to make it attractive to people, like a red-white-and-blue cock."

Fonda and Hopper made the film on location, far from the scrutiny of the Columbia executives who had reluctantly supplied the tiny $360,000 budget. When the finished film was screened for the studio's marketing brass, they were horrified. "Columbia wanted to sell the movie to AIP," Peter reveals. "They thought we had made a drug, sex, and motorcycle movie." To some extent Peter's father shared the executives' disdain. "Henry came to see a rough cut of the movie," Peter reports. "We went back to his house in Bel-Air and he talked to me about it. He swore up until the day he died that the scene I'm about to describe did not happen, but it did."

According to Peter, Henry told him that he seriously doubted any audience would be able to relate to the story. "I had no idea what you were doing or where you were going," Henry said.

"Well, you see where we're going," Peter replied. "Just take the trip."

Henry grew impatient. "That's your generation's language," he complained. "I'm telling you, the audience is going to drop this story because they won't understand what you're up to."

Peter tried to explain the story: "Well, Hopper says he's going to Mardi Gras."

Henry shot back, "I can barely hear it, and its not enough. I don't mean to be angry, but I'm worried for you, son."

"Dad was wrong," Peter says today. "Both Dad and Jane were pleased when the movie turned out to be a success, I think Jane more than Dad. I don't think Dad really understood what it was I had done. Even though he had made so many films, he was a very singular person whose job was, walk and talk. He wouldn't say, 'Could you put that light over there?' His job was to take direction. He wasn't so mild and meek that he would never offer a suggestion. But his job was not to discuss the matter, it was to say the lines. And so he didn't understand what I was doing behind the camera."

Henry was also troubled by one specific scene in the film, when Peter's Captain America takes LSD and, while hallucinating, cries out to a cemetery statue of the Madonna, "You're such a fool, Mother. I hate you so much." The scene had been improvised on location, and in it Peter was clearly trying to exorcise some of his long-dormant feelings about his own mother's suicide.

Peter submitted *Easy Rider* to the Cannes Film Festival, and it was accepted for showing in May of 1969. When Dennis Hopper and he arrived on the Riviera for the annual sun-sin-and-cinema circus, they were understandably apprehensive about the reaction from the first large audience to see the film. After all, it was at that time a completely unknown quantity. Peter recognized that the film's harshly critical view of Southern bigots might find some favor among the European press, which was for the most part strongly anti-American during the Vietnam era. But he felt a pang of terror as the lights went down for the festival screening. His fears evaporated quickly. *Easy Rider* received the most resounding audience response of any film screened at the festival. Afterwards Peter came on stage, and the crowd gave him a standing ovation. Dazed and bemused, he told the audience, "The wine and the grass in the film were real, but not the cocaine nor the LSD." When the festival awards were handed out, *Easy Rider* was named best film by a new director.

After that triumphant showing, Columbia began to realize that it might have a winner on its hands. *Easy Rider* soon swept the country, eventually grossing some $60 million. Peter, who owned eighteen percent of the movie's profits, made a small fortune. Yet Henry Fonda continued to be somewhat bewildered by the film's success. In an interview given to the *New York Times* in 1970, he churlishly attacked director and co-star Dennis Hopper as "a total freak-out, stoned out of his mind all the time. Any man who insists on wearing his cowboy hat to the Academy Award ceremonies and keeps it on at the dinner table afterward ought to be spanked."

Looking back at the film, Jane admits that she, like her father, was dubious about its prospects initially, though she now recognizes its significance as a cultural benchmark. "I think it was a revolutionary film," she says. "Peter's always been ahead of where I'm at, and *Easy Rider* was a little bit ahead of where I was at. I didn't entirely understand it at first. It took me a while. It took other people saying that the film was a milestone for me to go back and be able to view it more objectively."

Easy Rider transformed the Hollywood industry. Before 1969 "youth movies" were a fringe product—beach party romps and biker melodramas made by AIP. After *Easy Rider* all the major studios began to court the teenage and college crowd, though in time the angry social protest movies of the Vietnam era would give way to silly-putty teen flicks not much more sophisticated than the beach party cartoons of the early 1960s.

None of Peter's subsequent movies achieved the impact of *Easy Rider*, but his instincts were frequently prescient. In 1973 he made *Two People*, one of the first Hollywood films to mention the Vietnam war; he played a deserter who falls in love with a fashion model (played by Lindsay Wagner in her first movie role) before deciding to turn himself in. Although the movie failed to click at the box office, it probably had an influence on Jane Fonda, who two years later commissioned her own screenplay on Vietnam veterans—the script that would eventually become *Coming Home*.

By the time *Coming Home* was released, Jane's career had eclipsed Peter's. Her reputation began to take a sharp upward turn in December of 1969, six months after the release of *Easy Rider*, with the opening of *They Shoot Horses, Don't They?* It was a film of stinging social commentary, the first Jane Fonda movie that bore comparison to Peter's *Easy Rider* or Henry's *The Grapes of Wrath*. This stark, engrossing chronicle of a Depression-era dance marathon summoned up the grim mood in post-Vietnam America as well. Jane earned outstanding reviews and her first Oscar nomination for her portrayal of the hard, cynical woman who persuades her dance partner to kill her when she realizes her future is hopeless. Two years later, Jane confirmed her standing as a major American actress with her portrayal of the knowing but vulnerable call girl in *Klute*, the performance that won her the first of her two Academy Awards.

Jane was by then not merely another Hollywood personality; she was a controversial firebrand whose public proclamations against the war and in support of American Indian militants and Black Panthers were grabbing headlines. As Jane became more active politically, her marriage to Vadim broke up, and she began to socialize with a new set of left-wing activists. The one who influenced her most was Shirley Sutherland, an articulate anti-war leader and the wife of actor Donald Sutherland. Jane and the Sutherlands became close friends; several months later the Sutherlands separated, and Jane and Donald began having an affair. Donald and Shirley divorced, and for two years Jane and Donald lived together (reportedly with Shirley's blessing); they also worked together in *Klute*, *Steelyard Blues*, and the irreverent FTA show, a counterculture version of Bob Hope's famous USO tour, which they took around to GI coffeehouses. (FTA stood for either "Free the Army" or "Fuck the Army," depending on one's fastidiousness.)

Jane's high visibility, coupled with her stridency, made her an easy target for right-wing barbs. According to FBI documents released under the Freedom of Information Act, J. Edgar Hoover had a phony letter sent to Hollywood columnist Army Acherd in 1970, alleging that Jane had threatened to kill President Nixon. Jane's 1972 visit to Hanoi inflamed conservatives even more, so much so that at the 1972 Republican convention in Miami, the Young Americans for Freedom circulated a petition demanding that she be tried for treason. A group of Maryland vigilantes threatened to teach her a lesson by cutting her tongue out. The following year, when she attacked returning POWs as "hypocrites and liars," Connecticut Republican Congressman Robert Steele declared on the floor of the House of Representatives, "I would like to nominate Academy-Award-winning actress Jane Fonda for a new award: the rottenest, most miserable performance by any one individual American in the history of our country."

Even with her Oscar, Jane was virtually unemployable in Hollywood. She returned to Europe and made two films there: *Tout Va Bien*, co-starring Yves Montand and directed by Jean-Luc Godard (with Jean-Pierre Gorin), and Henrik Ibsen's *A Doll's House*, directed by Joseph Losey. Although Godard and Losey were leftists whose political views coincided with her own on many issues, Jane's burgeoning feminism created tensions on the set. She tangled repeatedly with the directors and later accused them of having sexist prejudices. Her frustrations on those films were what first prompted her to think about forming her own production company so that her films would reflect her own artistic and political choices.

With the war's end, and Nixon's resignation, Jane began to think about reintegrating herself into the mainstream. She was encouraged by her second husband, former radical leader Tom Hayden, whom she had met at an anti-war rally in 1971 and married two years later, after her affair with Donald Sutherland had cooled. By the mid-1970s, Hayden was seeking a political base of his own, first through his neo-populist Campaign for Economic Democracy and then through his 1976 California Senatorial campaign. Hayden's surprisingly strong showing in the Democratic primary convinced many observers that he was a political force to be reckoned with; ironically, it was because of a desire to curry favor with him that some liberal producers also sent a peace pipe to Jane. Tom shrewdly perceived that if his wife became a major star once again, her status could enhance his political fortunes. Jane felt that the mood of the country was shifting in her favor. As she told the *New York Times* in 1976, "I've changed in the last three years, in the sense that everything has changed. People's attitudes and consciousness have changed. So much is possible now. It was a long, hard winter, but now there's a new wave out there, and it has nothing to do with people who play it safe, people who care only about bucks or trying to build a career."

She returned to Hollywood in a frivolous comedy called *Fun With Dick and Jane*, co-starring George Segal, which was designed to prove, as she said, that she could be "funny and pretty again." This tale of a suburban couple who take to robbery when the husband loses his job was a curiously mixed-up film. While attempting to burlesque American materialism, it ended up happily endorsing any means—including larceny—necessary to stay "in the money." The picture was a box office hit, and it re-established Jane as a bona fide Hollywood star. She solidified her position with a fine performance as Lillian Hellman in *Julia*, one of the most honored films of 1977. In it she worked with her old friend Vanessa Redgrave, for whom Jane's daughter by Vadim had been named. In the film's most moving moment the anti-Fascist heroine, Julia, tells Lillian that she has named her illegitimate daughter Lilly; the scene must have had special resonance for the two actresses.

In the years from 1977 to 1979, Jane reached her peak as an actress. In *Julia*, *Coming Home*, *Comes a Horseman*, *California Suite*, and *The China Syndrome*, she created a gallery of sharply etched characters. She seemed to undergo a remarkable physical transformation from one role to the next; the leathery, self-sufficient ranchwoman she played in *Comes a Horseman* was worlds apart from the smiling, docile anchorwoman she impersonated in *The China Syndrome*. In all these movies, Jane worked with a miniaturist's attention to nuance and detail, and an uncanny responsiveness to women who were often quite different from herself. In *Coming Home* she uncondescendingly empathized with the sheltered military wife who stands at attention even when the "Star Spangled Banner" is played on television. In *California Suite*, by contrast, she played a hard-edged, ambitious *Newsweek* correspondent, and she refused to soften or sweeten the character. Piercing to the core of every character she played, Jane seemed incapable of false or predictable gesture, and her performances won the respect of critics and audiences alike.

Because her newfound popularity gave her greater power than ever before, Jane was able to form her own production company, IPC Films, named for the Indochina Peace Campaign. Jane cites the breakup of the old studio system and her determination to take greater control of her own career as providing the impetus for her creation of the company. "It's more critical, more strategically important today," she says, "for us to become our own producers or to find a producer who will develop projects with us, which is really more true of my case. I'm not really a producer. I found someone to work with me, Bruce Gilbert, who plays that role. I became increasingly dissatisfied with the kinds of things I was being offered. Also, the women's movement raised expectations about the kind of material that we wanted to do and our ability to do it ourselves. But I guess the main thing that prompted me to become an independent producer was that I had very specific things I wanted to say. Had it not been for the Vietnam War, I wouldn't have been interested in making a movie like *Coming Home*. That's what prompted me to form a film company. It's only when you want to say something that other people don't seem to be saying that you're forced to do something like that."

Jane discovered her partner-to-be, Bruce Gilbert, in an unlikely way. Gilbert wanted to break into the movie business but was having little luck. To support himself, he took a job teaching nursery school. One of the toddlers in his class was little Vanessa Vadim. Vanessa's mother took a liking to Bruce, and they discussed movies together. Gilbert told Jane that his interest in filmmaking had been shaped by seeing Peter's *Easy Rider*. According to Jane, "It was *Easy Rider* that convinced Bruce it was possible for young people with a vision to alter cinema. So in that sense the movie had a great effect on me, because Bruce wouldn't have wanted to be a producer. And if he hadn't, I don't know if I ever would have produced."

As Jane and Gilbert drew up their plans for IPC, he conceived the idea of doing movies about ordinary people transformed and even radicalized by their exposure to social inequities. IPC would rework the formula several times—in *Coming Home*, *The China Syndrome*, *Nine to Five*, and the TV movie, *The Dollmaker*. "What interests me most is people's capacity to change," Jane explains. "I guess it's because I've been through so many changes in my own life. I like to start from what is the most universal point, the kind of women that most people can identify with, and then show the heights that average people, that identifiable people, can rise to. I don't make movies about superwomen."

In putting these movies together for IPC, Jane demonstrated a sure commercial touch, which generally meant a conventional, middle-of-the-road approach to controversial subjects. Despite her reputation as a firebrand, Jane seldom risked including anything in her films that might alienate the mass audience. Nancy Dowd's original screenplay for *Coming Home* concentrated on the friendship between two army wives who met in a veterans' hospital. Jane fell out with Dowd when she decided the story should be turned into a male-female love story for greater audience identification. (Two male screenwriters, Waldo Salt and Robert Jones, were called in to revise Dowd's script.) Nevertheless, if neither *Coming Home* nor Jane's subsequent production, *The China Syndrome*, represented radical art, they were both forceful films dealing with social issues that most Hollywood movies had nervously avoided.

The China Syndrome was the first film to expose the unsafe conditions of nuclear power plants and the callousness of corporate officials in the nuclear industry. On that film Jane worked with Michael Douglas, another second-generation actor-producer. "Jane's the most disciplined person I've ever met," says Douglas. "She also accomplishes more in a day than anybody I've ever seen, which I'm sure is a carry over from her background. In thinking back, knowing certain of the periods she went through in comparison to what I did—she was a radical, and I was a hippie on a commune—I'm surprised now at the kind of discipline that I have, and I know hers is beyond mine. I would attribute a lot of that to our fathers."

Both *Coming Home* and *The China Syndrome* were joint ventures between IPC and other producing entities. When Jane's company began to produce on its own, her commercial instinct remained sound at least two of the first three times out. (*Rollover*, a thriller set in the exotic milieu of international finance and co-starring Kris Kristofferson, was a flop.) But the overall quality of her movies declined. *Nine to Five*, a moronic comedy about three abused secretaries (Jane, Lily Tomlin, and Dolly Parton), traded in cartoonish simplifications and degenerated into a kind of distaff S&M fantasy, with the women chortling over scenes in which the chauvinistic boss (Dabney Coleman) is physically tortured. Aiming for the crudest belly laughs, the movie made mincemeat of what might have been a droll, insolent spoof.

Jane's next effort, *On Golden Pond*, which brought tears to the eyes of many moviegoers, was one of Jane's most deeply personal films, for it touched on her relationship with her father. Noble intentions aside, it was a dreadfully mawkish soap opera, with convenient reconciliations and mechanical metamorphoses taking the place of credible drama. Perhaps the most surprising point about both these movies was the weakness of Jane's performances. In *Nine to Five*, she appeared to have lost the knack for comedy she had shown earlier in her career; she was outclassed by Tomlin and Parton, who seemed much more relaxed and natural on the screen. Wendy Kout, a writer who worked with Jane on creating her *Nine to Five* TV series, gives an insight into why Jane's intense, driven nature may block some of her comedic spontaneity: "Jane's so determined and so committed; her whole body, the Workout body, with every muscle defined, is always ready to spring into action. One time, she paid me a high compliment, and inside I was hysterical. During one of our rewrite sessions, she looked me intensely in the eye—she's a very intense woman, as you know—and grabbed my hand. I didn't know what she was going to say to me; I thought maybe she was going to scream or yell. But she said, 'Wendy, this is *very* funny. Okay, on page twenty-seven...' And I'm thinking inside, 'Oh, Jane, just laugh! Come on, lighten up a little bit.'"

If Jane's comic timing seemed shaky in *Nine to Five*, her serious dramatic performance in *On Golden Pond* was no better. She did some of her worst screen acting in that film, alternately stiff and shrill. Perhaps her favorite story of feminine self-realization was growing tired, or perhaps she was spreading herself too thin by doing so many things at once—acting, launching her Workout salons, writing books, and stumping for her husband. Her once high standards seemed to have vanished, as she began lending her name and her presence to so many different ventures. The low point came when she hosted a tacky, unfunny television revue for Showtime's cable network called "Jane Fonda's Celebrity Comedy Fashion Show."

Despite such miscalculations, Jane has remained a superstar at the very top of the Hollywood heap. She heads two separate production companies—one housed at Twentieth Century-Fox, the other at Columbia—and is still one of the two or three actresses considered for almost every female role. As her father said shortly before his death, "Her name is more recognized than mine ever was." In 1983, she completed *The Dollmaker*, a TV movie (aired in the spring of 1984) about an uneducated Appalachian woman who moves with her family to Detroit and is forced to begin a brand new life. She considers this film her finest work and says she wants to do more television acting to bring her social and political ideas to the largest possible audience. Unlike her father, she shuns the theater as being too elitist a medium.

Given all her other interests, one might suspect that she will drift away from acting altogether. Fortunately, Jane recognizes that acting is still her greatest strength. "I'm primarily an actress," she insists. "That's where everything else stems from. It's what fulfills me most and what I think I do best. I know I will be acting up until the time that I die. It's different for women than it is for men. When a man begins to enter his prime ability to play leading roles is when a women *loses* her prime ability to play leading roles. At least that's been true up till now." Laughing slyly, she adds, "I have every intention of changing that, of course."

In describing the movies she intends to make in the future, Jane reveals the same activist zeal that has led her to become such a determined cheerleader for political causes and such an exuberant evangelist for physical exercise. She says, "The kinds of movies I don't like are movies in which you come out feeling more numb or more depressed than when you went in. I like movies that get you going through laughter, through anger, being uplifting, whatever, just so they jolt you. I think comedy is the highest form. You can learn the most, be opened up the most through laughter. But anger is also a very good thing, if it can be constructively channeled. I just don't want something that's numbing. I want to get people thinking and moving."

IN the last decade, Peter's career has stalled while Jane's has accelerated. He has acted in almost thirty movies, but only a few of them have succeeded either critically or commercially. His biggest hit after *Easy Rider* was a low-brow car crash spectacle with Susan George, *Dirty Mary, Crazy Larry*. Most of his other films—including *92 in the Shade*, *Futureworld*, *Outlaw Blues*, and *Split Image*—quietly dropped from sight. As Henry described his son's movies in one of his last interviews, "Peter's mostly are B-pictures that not even he is proud of."

"I'm not the type of actor who wants to wait around for the right part," Peter admits. "If I think I'm going to have a fun time,

I'll go out and make the film." When asked whether Jane and he advise each other on their films, Peter laughs, "Jane has told me, 'Get some eyelashes. Redford does!' I love it."

As an actor, Peter has never caught the spark that distinguishes competent performances from galvanizing ones. In Pauline Kael's words, "He doesn't have a core of tension; something in him is still asleep, and perhaps always will be."

On the other hand, Peter has demonstrated great promise as a director. When he directed his first film, *The Hired Hand* in 1971, it was clear that he had a flair behind the cameras which he had never shown on screen. Photographically, *The Hired Hand* was one of the most stunning Westerns ever filmed. Peter evinced the same visual imagination in the sci-fi fable *Idaho Transfer*, made three years later, and in parts of *Wanda Nevada*, the misbegotten tall tale in which he co-starred with Brooke Shields. Although he never really developed his father's or his sister's passion for acting, he found *his* passion in creating vivid imagery on strips of celluloid. "If I weren't able to shoot movies, I'd go crazy," Peter says. "I'm like a closet cameraman." What may be equally important is that Peter knows how to attract an expert technical team to assist him. *The Hired Hand* was the first film photographed by Vilmos Zsigmond, the brilliant cinematographer who later won an Academy Award for *Close Encounters of the Third Kind*; it was also the first film scored by the gifted young composer, Bruce Langhorne. "My forte," Peter says, "is putting together a crew. My friends say to me, 'You're hanging out with cameramen and sound men. You've got to go out and *schmooze* with executives. That's how you get movies made.' I said, 'No, I'll get a movie when someone gives me money, and those people I hang out with will come and help me make this movie look fabulous and sound terrific."

Yet none of the films Peter has directed has been a box office success. As a result, Peter has trouble convincing the studios to consider hiring him as a director. His Pando Company has developed a number of projects that have yet to find financing. When he contemplates the film business today, Peter calls it "tragic." He reiterates the lament of so many second-generation filmmakers who miss the love of moviemaking that characterized studio moguls in their parents' day: "The people who decide what movies get done today are lawyers and agents; they've never made a movie. More important than the film is the deal. And even more important is where they park on the lot."

Yet Peter claims not to be embittered. He feels fortunate to have accomplished as much as he has thus far. "Making *Easy Rider* was a high point," he reflects. "When I started that, I wasn't taken seriously by anybody in the business. Suddenly, there I was, driving my car, and behind me were all the cars and trucks, the whole movie company. Every dream for every film student, and I got to do it! Then, for my next one, I got to do *The Hired Hand*. Thank you, God. I don't care what happens next or how much heartache or distress goes with the industry. I'm willing to pay the price."

DESPITE the strained relationships within the Fonda family for so many years, both Peter and Jane were able to make their peace with their father before he died. The rapprochement was encouraged by Henry's fifth wife, Shirlee, a former airline stewardess who has always enjoyed a close bond with Peter and Jane. Partly as a result of Henry's illnesses, Peter was determined to effect a reconciliation with his father. In 1977, during a telephone conversation with Henry, Peter suddenly said, "I love you, Dad." Henry hung up in consternation. Peter repeated the phrase the next few times he spoke with his father, and eventually Henry was able to reciprocate.

Howard Teichmann has reprinted a letter Henry wrote to Dorothy McGuire after the death of her husband, actor John Swope. In it Henry reflected on the effect of Peter's words. "I never felt that I have really expressed my great feeling about John," Henry wrote. "But then, that's the story of my life. For reasons that are too deeply buried for me to understand, I have never been able to articulate my emotions. Only recently, Peter has been ending his phone calls by saying, 'I love you, Dad,' And, of course, it forced me to say, 'And I love you, son.' He knew I did. But he was making me say it. And now it's coming easier."

Jane commented, "What Peter did was good, because you can't change *yourself*. Saints and prophets, maybe, but average people—and Dad's average, just as I am—you can't do it by yourself."

In 1978, Peter invited his father to play a brief cameo role in the movie he was directing, *Wanda Nevada*. Henry accepted eagerly and did one day's work as a grizzled prospector. It was a small part in a weak film, but it had great meaning for Peter and Henry Fonda. For the first time, Henry developed genuine appreciation of his son's abilities. He was impressed by Peter's directorial skill, and after returning from the location, he sent Peter a letter that said in part, "I want you to know how proud I am of you. Your whole company so obviously worships you, and it's a beautiful thing to see. And I haven't seen it so often in forty-three years that it doesn't impress me. And you're a very good director . . . You are a thoughtful man, and I love you."

"I can't read that letter without breaking down in tears," Peter says today. "*Easy Rider* was a wonderful experience; the success I had with that was great. But that letter from my father was dynamite. It wasn't until that moment when he actually watched me run a set that he saw that Mommie's little Petey boy—who was ten pounds when he was born but never became the fullback that Dad thought he was going to be, never became the Eagle Scout that Dad was—actually had his shit together. He thought I was nuts. Not nuts, but maybe just about. He thought I didn't make any sense or that I was out of touch with reality. I don't want him to sound like an ogre. But it was tough for him to understand me, and it only happened at that moment when he could see those images that were most important to him, because his whole life revolved around his ability to express himself with his art."

Jane Fonda's sharpest conflicts with her father came during the first years of her involvement in radical politics. In 1967, Henry went on a USO-sponsored tour of Southeast Asia, and defended the American presence in Vietnam when he returned. Jane and he argued about the war, and although Henry eventually came to share her anti-war sentiments, he was troubled by her militancy and by the crowd of hard-core radicals who surrounded her. In an interview with Guy Flatley of the *New York Times*, Henry expressed his dismay that Jane was bringing her whole entourage to stay at his house in New York. Flatley asked how many were in her entourage. "Oh, it's not how many," Fonda replied. "It's how unattractive they all are." Describing Jane to another reporter, Henry said, "She's a bright girl, but she doesn't think for herself. She hears a second- or a third-hand opinion about some injustice, and the next thing you know she's screaming revolution. The trouble is that because I'm her father, other people think I agree with her . . . I get letters calling me a Commie because my name is Fonda."

During one heated argument, Henry told Jane that if he ever discovered she was a Communist, he would be the first to denounce her. Gradually, however, as Jane slipped back into the mainstream, father and daughter grew closer. Jane sees their reconciliation as evolving from her own self-assurance and maturity. "Maybe I was able to allow or facilitate coming closer to my father," she says, "because I was successful in my own right and because I was happy in my marriage to Tom. For someone like my father, the impetus very much had to come from me and not from him. But I think we were always close. I mean, we fought and had some very deep disagreements at various times. But there was always a deep-running current of love and feelings between us. And I think the success of *On Golden Pond* was because of the universality of those kinds of problems—not knowing how to express feelings, not knowing how to step over those barriers. Sometimes it takes maturity. It takes being a parent yourself to forgive and reach out. That, more than anything else, made it possible."

As in Peter's case, Jane and Henry solidified their relationship by finally working on a film together. Jane's company purchased Ernest Thompson's play, *On Golden Pond*, specifically as a vehicle for herself and her father. The play dealt with a woman so intimidated by her imperious father that she is unable to communicate with him. Jane hoped that doing the film would help her to sort out her own relationship with Henry. The first problem she had to confront was the irrational fear she still felt at the mere prospect of working with her father. "I was very nervous," Jane admits. "It paralleled the character I was playing. Chelsea is a woman who says she feels like she owns L.A. When she's away from her father, she's bright-eyed and bushy-tailed and quite successful, but when she's around her father, she becomes a little fat girl. Here I was in the same situation. Weirdly enough, unjustly enough, I had won two Academy Awards, and my father had never won one. I should have felt cocky, right? Not at all. I was absolutely terrified that he would think I wasn't good enough. I was about forty-two or forty-three years old, and I still wanted to prove to him that I had talent. I was scared to death."

Jane was so nervous that she vomited the day before shooting began. Her first morning on the set, she overheard Henry tell director Mark Rydell that she was "doing too much." As the movie progressed, Jane began to feel more comfortable working with her father and Katharine Hepburn. After filming one emotional scene with Henry, Jane reported, "I reached out to take his arm, and I felt him shudder, because he wasn't expecting it. He's not an emotional actor, and everyone on the crew saw it. I took his arm and said, 'I want to be your friend,' and I felt him trying to keep the tears back. It was a moment of such intimacy . . ."

By the end of filming, Jane felt that she had accomplished what she had set out to do. "I feel more grateful for *On Golden Pond* than I can possibly express," she comments. "Grateful because we worked together. Grateful because we had a vehicle that allowed us to express those particular problems and emotions, which I think had all the more resonance because people perceived there was a parallel with reality. Grateful because it was a vehicle that I made possible for him. I produced it for him. And grateful that it did for him what I had hoped that it would do, which is that he won his Oscar, finally and belatedly."

Oscar night in April of 1982 was a highly-charged occasion for the Fonda family. Although Henry was the sentimental favorite to win the award for best actor, his victory was by no means a foregone conclusion. Burt Lancaster had won all the critics' awards for his superb performance in Louis Malle's *Atlantic City*. Henry was too ill to attend the award ceremonies; his coronary problems were worsening, and he had recently undergone a difficult operation. When he was announced as the winner, Jane accepted the Oscar for him and told the crowd, "Father didn't really believe that this was going to happen . . . I know that he's watching right now, and I know that he's very, *very* honored and *very* happy. And *surprised*! And I'll bet when he heard it just now, he said, 'Hey, didn't I get lucky!' As though luck had anything to do with it . . ." Jane went on to acknowledge the various people she felt her father would want to thank and concluded by saying, "I know that lastly but really first he is thanking Shirlee Fonda, who has been his loving support for seventeen years, whom he calls his Rock of Gibraltar." Shirlee told reporters that when Henry watched Jane's speech on television, "he cried like a baby." Henry Fonda died August 12, 1982, four months after winning the Oscar for *On Golden Pond*.

Jane and Peter also plan to make a film together, hoping that it will strengthen their relationship. They had been looking for the right property for a long time, and in 1983 they bought the rights to *Old Money*, a novel by Lacey Fosburgh, the wife of Joan Baez's ex-husband, David Harris. (Fosburgh, a descendant of the Whitney family of New York publishing fame, writes in her novel about a young woman who, like herself, has been disinherited and sets out to discover the source of her father's animus toward her.) The Fondas have made a deal with MGM/UA for Peter to produce the film in partnership with Jane's company; Peter and Jane will co-star as brother and sister.

In the late 1960s, while Jane was still married to Vadim, Roman Polanski, talked to Peter and Jane about doing a film dealing with brother-sister incest, but it never materialized. Peter is still intrigued by the idea, and he has repeatedly teased Jane about reviving it. He laughs as he recalls her horror-struck reaction: "I said to her, 'Jane, it'll mean $40 million in your pocket.'

"The first time I ever shocked her," Peter goes on, "was while she was still living in France and I was staying with her. I read Michael McClure's play, *The Beard*, about Jean Harlow and Billy the Kid. Of course, half of this is theatrical and a joke, but in a sense, you see, it's great business. I ran in and said to Jane, 'Let's do this! We'll film it in Texas or Arizona, and we'll put it into a certain number of theaters, just the way they do with a prize fight. Tickets will be $100 apiece. Jane and Peter in Michael McClure's *The Beard*. With the money we make, you can support whatever cause you want.' So she read the play and got to the end, where Billy the Kid rips off Jean Harlow's panties and goes down on her on stage. Jane said, 'You have got to be kidding!' I said, 'Jane, $100 is a cheap price for those freaks and kinks in the world who would be glad to pay to see that.' Oh well, I can understand how my darling sister would think her brother is slightly out of touch with reality."

In his more serious moments, Peter has suggested that Jane and he do "a comedy with meaning, but not political dogma." He hopes that working together will resolve any unfinished business that still remains between the two of them. "I've never seen a lot of Jane," Peter muses, "but the times we do see each other are extremely special. When we've been separated for a long time and then we come together either on the phone or in person, we don't take on the problem of how long it's been since we've seen each other. It saves a lot of guilt that's not necessary. What we've maintained is a certain recognition code that goes way back to very early childhood. We have a good time together, always have. I've lugged my twelve-string guitar around for years, and every time I'd learn a new song, I'd run down to wherever Jane was and play it for her. I'm kind of embarrassed to play in front of anybody but was always thrilled to play for her."

At times, Peter has shown a sweet if amusing protectiveness toward his older sister. When he spotted a placard reading "Feed Jane Fonda to the Whales" in the Denver airport, he ripped the sign down. Peter was arrested for disturbing the peace and destruction of private property, but the charges were dropped when two prosecution witnesses failed to appear at the trial. "Jane is attacked all the time, and it gets me really pissed off," Peter says. "I took a knife to that sign that said, 'Feed Jane Fonda to the Whales.' In the same area of the airport, there's normally a sign that says, 'Nuclear Power Plants Are Built Better Than Jane Fonda.' Now that's a matter of opinion, protected by the First Amendment. But 'Feed Jane Fonda to the Whales,' that's calling for physical harm. You don't get to say that. I went after the guy, and I prevailed."

In summarizing his relationship with his sister, Peter says, "There are many things we haven't talked about that we should. And I'm hoping that when we work together, we will have that chance. I also know in my ego that when Jane has a chance to see how I operate and work on a set and make things come together and coalesce, she may start to contact me more. I'm not looking to fill up holes in the highway that I already have traveled down. But I *am* concerned with making the forward highway logical, efficient, and smooth."

PETER'S friend Jack Nicholson shrewdly identifies the essence of Henry Fonda's character, which both his children share: "Henry Fonda was never of a mold," Nicholson says. "America came to love Henry Fonda, but he certainly could put steel into his work. I would not call him an Establishment figure, even though he became beloved. Henry Fonda was capable of pissing anybody off at any moment in his life, and that's why I always liked him." Although both Peter and Jane retain some of Henry's Midwestern stubbornness, the same core of conscience and integrity, they seem to represent two different sides of their father. Peter embodies the more poetic and vulnerable qualities of Henry Fonda—the aspect that emerged when Henry played the young, gawky Abe Lincoln or the sweet, ingenuous herpatologist duped by Barbara Stanwyck in *The Lady Eve*. It is the tougher side of Henry Fonda that Jane seems to favor—the rock-hard tenacity that he conveyed, for example, as the authoritarian cavalry colonel in John Ford's *Fort Apache*.

Jane has inspired scorn not just for her militancy but for her fickleness as well. Is there any consistency to the various roles she has played in her lifetime? Can one reconcile the Defense Department's Miss Army Recruiting of 1962 with Hanoi Jane of 1972? The young woman who said she did fashion modeling "because I like the money" with the crusader for economic democracy? Perhaps the unifying force has been her openness to experience, her willingness to experiment. In that respect, Jane is the present generation's counterpart to Clare Booth Luce (who was, coincidentally, once married to George Brokaw, her mother's first husband), a woman who tries to identities the way other women try on shoes, who has an insatiable appetite for public recognition, and who has achieved success in a remarkable variety of fields.

If there is one constant in Jane Fonda's variegated life, it has been the desire to put herself in the limelight. Her father, too, may have suffered from self-absorption, but it was the sort that led him to become a very private man, separating himself from those around him. Jane's egotism has manifested itself in a very different way. From the time she frolicked as a sex kitten in Vadim's nudie flicks right up to her present reign as ubiquitous actress-author-tycoon, she has invariably felt the need to hold center stage. That trait was probably most troubling during her anti-war days, when it caused the greatest friction with her sometime friends and allies. As a movie personality weaned on Hollywood hype, Jane was accustomed to behaving like a prima donna. No matter how fervently she spoke in favor of socialist ideals, she was determined to remain the star, and her fellow radicals were often scathing in their denunciations of her vanity. Veteran activist Saul Alinsky called her "a hitchhiker on the highway of causes." Country Joe McDonald, a folk-rock singer who appeared for a time with her FTA troupe, branded her "simple-minded," "totalitarian," and "unable to work truly collectively."

Dr. Howard Levy, an army dermatologist and anti-war leader who gained notoriety when he was court martialed for refusing to train medics for service in Vietnam, said that Jane "caught a bad case of ego-grandiosity." In Levy's cogent view, Jane was unable to accept the slow process by which social change has always been accomplished in America. She wanted her impact to be felt immediately. "In effect," Levy said, "she tried to start her own version of the movement, which is what a lot of people did, mostly young and not-too-well-educated people . . . Basically, she lost the ability to discuss, to negotiate. I'm not sure she ever had it, mind you, but if she did, she lost it to this sense of moral superiority she has. That's why it's so damaging to have personalities in the movement. In the public's mind, they become the movement itself, and Jane certainly wasn't the movement."

Perhaps it was her brother Peter who had the most sarcastic comment about Jane's metamorphosis from socialite to socialist. In 1974, he said, "Once she was frivolous, empty, without a conscience . . . Then suddenly she became a revolutionary, an intellectual. My sister has never done things halfway. Like all neophytes, Jane would teach revolution to Mao Tse-Tung if she had a chance."

The record of Jane's public posturing down through the years reveals a pattern of naiveté, inconsistency, and downright contradiction. Both she and Tom Hayden voiced sympathy for the Arab cause in the 1973 Arab-Israeli War, for example, then shifted when Tom ran for political office and was out courting the Jewish vote. During the Academy Awards contest of 1978, Jane attacked *The Deer Hunter*—the movie that won out over her own production, *Coming Home*, as best picture—for its "racism," though she admitted that she had not seen the film. After denouncing Joan Baez for criticizing Communist governments in Southeast Asia who had betrayed the Boat People, Jane flip-flopped and adopted the Boat People as a cause of her own. In another embarrassing episode, Jane—the ardent feminist—was sued for sex discrimination by three women employed at her San Francisco Workout salon; the women claimed that they were being paid less than their male counterparts at the gym.

Although a recent Gallup poll named Jane as the fourth most admired woman in America (right after Nancy Reagan), she remains a controversial figure in some pockets of the country. Brian Duff, director of public affairs for the National Aeronautics and Space Administration, was pressured by the White House to resign his post after he invited Jane to a NASA launching in 1983. In addition, several department stores cancelled promotional appearances by Jane to peddle her new line of sportswear after angry callers protested the invitation to the former activist; a Florida department store was even forced to close for an hour after it received a bomb threat. Jane did appear as scheduled at Jordan Marsh in Boston, while two dozen Vietnam veterans marched in front of the store toting signs that read, "Jane Traitor Fonda, we hate you."

At first glance, Jane's current status as both a champion of "economic democracy" and a phenomenally successful entrepreneur would seem to be the crowning paradox. While she assails the inequity of concentrating wealth among a favored few, Jane herself collects several million dollars on every film she makes; in one extraordinary deal, she was paid $2 million for agreeing to star in a prison movie called *Her Brother's Keeper* whether or not it ever went into production. The profits from her Workout salons, books, and cassettes have enlarged her fortune even more.

Jane Fonda's Workout Book was number one on the *New York Times* bestseller list for twenty-one weeks, and sold 1.25 million copies in hardcover alone; her sequel on exercise and diet during pregnancy did almost as well. Over two million of her Workout records were sold. Every week 10,000 people pay seven dollars a class at Jane's Workout salons. The gyms help promote Jane Fonda leotards and Jane Fonda T-shirts in addition to her books, records, cassettes, videotapes, and her fashion collection. "It all caught on like a brushfire," Peter observes. "It baffles her totally. She never thought that she would be this multimillion dollar success. I'm thrilled with it. I even say to her, 'God, Jane, you're making so much money. You know what would be wonderful? If you got so guilty one night about being so mean to me when we were kids that you decided to give me a million.' She just laughs at me."

Jane still describes herself as a "citizen activist." To some, however, she may seem perfectly typical of Hollywood's chic radicals of the Vietnam era who have now settled comfortably into plush executive suites, clinging precariously to humanitarian shibboleths while they bargain for their gross points and tax exemptions. But Jane does try to separate herself from run-of-the-mill capitalists by pouring much of her money into socially progressive projects, such as the Laurel Springs Educational Center, a summer camp that she runs on her ranch in Santa Barbara, where underprivileged children learn the catechism of solar power and nuclear disarmament in between horse-back-riding and lanyard-weaving.

Although Jane's tireless do-goodism sometimes verges on the ludicrous, it is hard to doubt her sincerity. Her husband's motives have always been more questionable. Even during his days in the radical movement, Hayden was viewed by some of his colleagues as a very cold-blooded and calculating organizer. Al Haber, the first president of Students for a Democratic Society, once said, "There was always a question of whether Tom was working for the organization or working for himself." Tom himself has admitted that his first marriage, to civil rights worker Sandra Casey, failed because "I had a way of turning myself off to her needs when they conflicted with what I was doing." Anne Weills, a Berkeley radical and feminist who was briefly involved with Hayden, said, "When I broke up with him, it was not because I didn't love him but because he manipulated everyone—me, the men, the women—in the collective. He is the most manipulative, power-conscious person—obsessed with it—I have ever known." While her view might be considered biased, it was hardly anomalous. Peter Collier, once a *Ramparts* editor who knew Hayden in his radical days, wrote a devastating attack on him in *New West* magazine, recalling that Tom had helped to foment the People's Park demonstrations in Berkeley but stayed away himself. According to Collier, Tom advocated guerrilla violence during the late 1960s but, a few years later, refused to sign an American Civil Liberties Union-sponsored statement decrying the grand jury's attempts to subpoena documentary film material on the Weather Underground because Tom and Jane "wanted to airbrush Hayden's connection with that past radicalism for the upcoming Senate campaign." And his co-member of the Chicago Seven, Abbie Hoffman, once remarked that "Hayden was the only one of all of us who didn't want to go on trial. He had no sense of fun."

Shortly before his death, Henry Fonda was asked about his attitude towards Jane's husbands. He spoke warmly about Roger Vadim, describing him as a civilized, intelligent, compassionate man. When asked whether he had liked Tom Hayden when Jane married him, Henry replied with a three-word answer, a masterpiece of understatement: "It took time."

Jane has been indefatigable on behalf of Tom's political ambitions. In 1982, she personally canvassed the middle-class neighborhoods where he was running for a California-Assembly seat; the story is told of one little old lady who yelled, "Morris, is that you?" when the doorbell rang, only to be met by a most unexpected reply: "No, it's Jane Fonda." A neighbor of the Haydens in Santa Monica reports that although Tom and Jane normally drive a Volvo, Jane rented a Chevy station wagon for a TV commercial plugging Tom's candidacy, apparently deeming it a more appropriate vehicle for an all-American family to display. Over $1.7 million was spent to get Tom elected, some of it coming from the revenues from Jane's Workout salons and some from her motion picture salaries. It was the largest sum ever spent by a candidate in a California political contest, and even more extraordinary considering the piddling position Tom was seeking.

It seems a final irony of Jane Fonda's life that, for all her feminist rhetoric, she has so often allowed herself to be defined or dominated by men. She might argue that these arrangements have been mutually beneficial rather than exploitative. But the pattern has been consistent from the early days when she permitted Voutsinas and then Vadim to mold her performances, through the period when she served as a mouthpiece for radical leaders such as Mark Lane, Fred Gardner, and later Hayden. Her business partner, Bruce Gilbert, has exerted a major influence on her film productions. Even as the reigning Fatima of fitness, she is not quite her own person. Her *Jane Fonda's Workout Book* is not just a show-and-tell manual of scissor-lifts and donkey-kicks but a handbook for selling her husband's brand of economic democracy, a goulash of mini-position papers on corporate greed, food additives, toxic waste, and other assorted horrors. In a devastating critique of the "Adidas socialism" promulgated in the book, Charles Krauthammer wrote in *The New Republic*: "Having ingested the values first of Roger Vadim and now of Tom Hayden, she delivers with mind-numbing seriousness the startling message that one should never take one's values from others and, in particular, that women should never accept sexual stereotypes that make them appendages to men. A curious message for a book that peddles Tom Hayden's ideas wrapped in Jane Fonda's body."

Of the two Fonda siblings, Peter has probably remained truer to the "heretical" values of the 1960s. Of course, it may be slightly absurd to imply that either Fonda is a real social renegade; anyone who earns several hundred thousand dollars a year filming Honda commercials, as Peter does, can hardly be considered a spiritual vagabond. Yet in comparison to Jane, Peter remains an innocent. Stanley Kauffmann described Peter's Captain America in *Easy Rider* as a "Dharma bum," and the description might apply to the real Peter Fonda as well. He thinks of himself as a citizen of the world "who does not wish to be a citizen of the United States or Russia or China or France or England or any nation." He lives on a ranch in Montana and spends very little time in Hollywood. Bewildered by the wheeling and dealing that Jane seems to thrive on, Peter remains haunted by the kind of quirky, personal filmmaking he pioneered with *Easy Rider*. He seems a man out of his time, someone who has opted out in order to remain true to ideals no longer in fashion.

Jane acknowledges the distinction between herself and her brother. "Peter has always been much more visionary than me," she observes. "He's got a sort of cosmic view of major issues. I remember over fifteen years ago Peter would talk to me about the energy crisis and the polluting of our air—before I could even *conceive* that such a thing could happen. Peter's always been ahead of where I'm at."

* * *

PETER and Jane also have different attitudes toward raising their families. For Jane, parenting has sometimes taken a back seat to other concerns. When she went off to Nepal to study with a guru in 1970, she left her infant daughter Vanessa with Vadim. Several months later, when she embarked on a cross-country odyssey with French activist Elisabeth Vailland to observe the conditions of Indians and blacks, she planted Vanessa with Henry. "I got furious with Jane when I thought she was leaving her small daughter Vanessa alone too much while she was off with her anti-war, anti-this, anti-that campaigns," Peter once said. "We had a big blow-up."

Today Peter is more inclined to soft-pedal his criticisms of Jane, but he does reveal how his view differs from hers. "I don't know what prompted me to chastise her in that way," he says. "I don't know if I was trying to lord it over her or whether I was concerned for her children. I do love her children. I think it was based on something she said in the press. When asked about her daughter, she said there were some things that were more important. At that moment she may have been right, but that statement is now *down* in print, and the children will hear about it. I think that was what triggered me off. It's not fair for me to make any kind of critique of her life. We come from the same foxhole, so how could I be an objective critic?"

Jane admits that, in raising her children, Vanessa Vadim and Troy Hayden (named for Nguyen Van Troi, a hero of the Vietnamese resistance), she has made many of the same blunders her own parents did. "There's no question," she says, "that there's a poison passed along from generation to generation. It comes from trauma, unhappiness, wealth, and a lot of other things. You can criticize and blame your parents for errors that they made, and then you find yourself repeating those same errors—a little less, it's true, but I don't want to be self-righteous. I make many of the same mistakes. I try not to live the way we did, although even the way we lived was a lot less ostentatious than the way Joan Crawford's children lived. I know because I went to those birthday parties. Ours was a simpler life. My children's life is a lot simpler than mine was, but is it like the boys and girls next door? No. Some of that's good, and some of that's bad. But it'll take a few more generations to do away with those problems and develop whole new sets of problems. Your parents are your role models. To some extent, it's impossible to be a perfect parent if your parents weren't—to be the ever-present, all-loving and nurturing mother, if yours wasn't. Where do you look for the example? You know, my daughter isn't going to be able to be more than a certain degree better than I am, and her daughter, if she chooses to have children—which she might not, given everything—will be a little bit better. It's a slow process of working out the problems. And yet it couldn't have been all that bad. We're not drug addicts or alcoholics. We have relatively stable lives. I look at my fifteen-year-old daughter, and sometimes I want to flagellate myself. But so far she has two feet on the ground, doesn't do drugs, doesn't drink, doesn't run with some mad pack. Just so she doesn't kill herself, accidentally or on purpose, in the next ten years, she'll be home free."

One thing is certain: Jane is no longer the playful concubine who titillated audiences in the 1960s. Today she takes a deadly serious, almost Victorian view of matrimony, insisting that her union with Hayden must endure because "it would be indulgent for us to allow something to happen to our marriage. It's important to the children. It's important as an example to other people."

PETER's first marriage to Susan Brewer ended in divorce, but it produced two children (Bridget and Justin) who live with him much of the time, along with his stepson (Thomas McGuane IV). His second wife is Portia Rebecca Crockett, who has an impressive lineage of her own; she is a descendant of both Davy Crockett and Louisa May Alcott. She and Peter met when he was filming *92 in the Shade* in 1974. At that time, Portia was married to novelist and screenwriter Thomas McGuane, who was directing the film. McGuane was having an affair with one of the actresses in the film, Elizabeth Ashley, but during filming his amorous attentions shifted to her co-star, Margot Kidder (whom he later married and divorced). Peter, meanwhile, took up with Mrs. McGuane. "I went behind the bleachers for a hot dog," McGuane joked, "and you couldn't tell the players without a program." Despite what may seem like a typical movie-set roundelay, Peter adheres to some traditional domestic values. "Out of the debacle of my childhood, I have not an imaginary family but a real group of children," Peter says. "That is my first priority. There's not a movie I would make or have made that will mean as much to me as what I can do as a parent so that these three youngsters become contributive, are aware and responsible, and take part in the world. It can't be easy for my children. But it couldn't have been so traumatic either. My daughter's quite together. My sons are quite together, difficult but in contact. In this profession, you have to work twice as hard to be a parent. I do with my children."

Peter and Jane's adopted sister, Amy, chose not to enter the arena where she would be compared with the acting Fondas; she is a psychologist living in Colorado. But some members of the third generation are leaning towards performing. Jane's teenage daughter, Vanessa, has not decided on a career, but Jane has already recognized her talent for acting. "She would not say she is interested in acting," Jane comments, "but I watch her, and I know. She's got it. I think I feel about her very much the way my father felt about me. I've seen her act in school, and I think she's got a natural gift, in many ways just like mine. She doesn't know she has it. I don't think she feels comfortable about it. But she's got the temperament of an actress, and I think she would be a very good one if that's the direction she chooses to go in. I would encourage her to study as I did. Here is one difference between me and my father. I am very, very conscious of the problems that come with being 'child of,' and I would be much more wary of those things in trying to help her, more than my father was."

Peter also sees this as a major difference between himself and his father. His daughter Bridget, born in 1964, has been studying drama at New York University and is determined to pursue a career in acting. Peter told her recently, "Bridget, you'll have to climb Everest four times. First for Grandpa, then for Aunt Jane, then for me, and then for yourself. Unless you really pay attention. Because if you really pay attention, you'll only have to climb it once. For yourself." Peter has spoken about one advantage his daughter has: "At least she can talk to me. My father had no inkling of what it was like to be the son of a famous man, so I was never able to explain my problems to him."

Mr. Roberts director Joshua Logan agreed with Peter's assessment of Henry Fonda as a difficult father. "Growing up in the shadow of such a demanding man must have been terribly hard," Logan noted, "but it has made Jane and Peter do extraordinary things they would not have done otherwise." Whether their strength was instilled in them by Henry or whether it was developed as a defense against all the torments of their childhood, Peter and Jane achieved triumphs matched by few other star children. Their careers have gone through major upheavals, and they have been foolish at least as often as they have been courageous. But even if one feels inclined to criticize their occasional fatuousness, one cannot help admiring their resilience. More than most Hollywood progeny, they had a legitimate claim to the moniker "poor little rich kids." But they refused to let self-pity get the better of them.

Peter often ponders the "debacle" of his childhood—the tragedy of his mother's suicide, the long years of estrangement from his father. In 1969, Peter Fonda spoke to a disaffected generation as the nihilistic dropout whose motto was "We blew it." Today the 1960's most emblematic easy rider has arrived at a greater sense of equanimity. He looks back with more understanding than regret, and he looks forward with at least a measure of optimism. "I sometimes worry about the legacy," he admits. "Not just the Fonda legacy, but the legacy of all the famous families in this business. All you hear about are the families cracking up. I have no real explanation of how I've gotten to where I am. The Fonda family motto is '*Perseverate.*' It's the imperative form, and it means, 'Persevere ye!' or 'You *must* persevere.' It's not a suggestion. At my really down moments, I think 'Damn those old Fondas! They must have known that this asshole, me, would be sitting around vacillating at this moment, and he'd need something to kick him in the ass.' The family motto seems to have played a part without my even knowing it. The only reason I'm sitting here now is because I stuck to it. *Perseverate.*"

6

SWEET SUE & COMPANY:
The Ladds

*"...Every star above
Knows the one I love.
Sweet Sue, Just You.
No one else, it seems,
Ever shares my dreams
And without you, dear,
I don't know what I'll do..."*

—"SWEET SUE—JUST YOU"
WRITTEN FOR SUE CAROL BY WILL J. HARRIS
AND VICTOR YOUNG, 1928

OVER the Memorial Day weekend of 1977, Twentieth Century-Fox released a movie that featured a couple of unknown actors and belonged to a genre which, at the time, many Hollywood executives considered box office poison. Soon after opening, this science fiction fantasy starring Mark Hamill, Carrie Fisher, one wookie and two robots was breaking attendance records all across the country. Within months, it had become the highest grossing film in history. The movie, of course, was *Star Wars*—a cultural phenomenon which has since spawned an unprecedented flock of imitations and sequels, revolutionized the American toy industry, introduced a whole new lexicon to the language, and taken a permanent hold on the national consciousness.

The guiding force behind *Star Wars* was its creator, writer-director George Lucas. But the movie's unsung hero was the president of Twentieth Century-Fox Films, Alan Ladd, Jr., who had confidence in Lucas's talent and pushed the project past a skeptical Fox board after Universal (the distributor of Lucas's previous hit, *American Graffiti*) turned it down. Before *Star Wars*, Ladd's track record as an executive had been mediocre at best. In 1975, Fox had attracted a great deal of unfavorable publicity with the release of two expensive turkeys: *At Long Last Love*, Peter Bogdanovich's bizarre musical starring two actors—Burt Reynolds and Cybill

Shepherd—who could neither sing nor dance; and *Lucky Lady*, a waterlogged romantic comedy featuring a most unlikely ménage-a-trois—Reynolds again, sharing a king-sized bed with Liza Minnelli and Gene Hackman. In the wake of these fiascos, Ladd's job at Fox was reportedly in jeopardy, and he managed to hang on only after the *The Omen*, a low-budget horror film with two faded stars, Gregory Peck and Lee Remick, turned into the surprise hit of 1976. The jury on Ladd was still out when the stunning box office performance of *Star Wars* muzzled all doubters.

Star Wars signaled just the beginning of Ladd's year of triumph. A few months after its release, Fox brought out *Julia* and *The Turning Point*, two of the films which inaugurated the new industry cycle of "women's movies." Both challenged the conventional wisdom of Hollywood by tackling serious adult material; *Julia* was based on Lillian Hellman's haunting memoir about her girlhood companion who became a daring anti-Fascist activist, while *The Turning Point* was a penetrating study of friendship and rivalry set against the backdrop of a ballet company. Against all expectations, both movies turned out to be critical and commercial successes; Ladd won further plaudits for his boldness in sponsoring them. Those three films—*Star Wars*, *Julia*, and *The Turning Point*—were among the five nominees for the best picture Oscar of 1977. All told, the three movies earned thirty-two Academy Award nominations, far surpassing the number collected by any other studio. Fox revenues soared from $195 million in 1976 to $301 million in 1977. The company's stock jumped from 8⅝ per share to 26⅝, and Ladd's own earnings climbed to $1.9 million, making him the highest-paid executive in Hollywood.

Before then, there was a widespread suspicion that Alan Ladd, Jr. owed his prominent position to the fact that he was the son of a famous movie star. By the end of 1977, he had established himself as a major force in his own right. He was no longer Alan Ladd's son; he had become *the* Alan Ladd.

ONE of the popular misconceptions about Alan Ladd, Jr. is that he grew up inside a glamorous show business family. In fact, his parents separated when he was just four years old, and Laddie, as he is still called, was raised not by his famous father but by his mother and her second husband—an aircraft technician named William Farnsworth—in the San Fernando Valley. The strongest influence on Laddie's career was probably neither of his natural parents, but rather his stepmother, Alan Ladd's second wife, a former starlet and agent named Sue Carol. She was the member of the family with the sharpest appetite for business, and it was this inclination that Alan Ladd, Jr. seems to have acquired. Although Laddie downplays the resemblances to his stepmother, his half-brother David sees them as quite similar. "Even though Laddie is not my mother's child," David suggests, "he's very much like her. He might shoot me for saying that, but he followed a similar path to hers. He was the only member of the family who had no interest in performing. His interests in the business were her interests."

Laddie's brother-in-law, Los Angeles radio personality Michael Jackson, echoes this sentiment: "We don't always know who the influences are in our lives. Sometimes they provide the wind to our sails, whether we know it or not. It's in the genes, but it's also in the example set by others. I think that Laddie, whether or not he realizes it, was motivated and inspired by Susie."

Sue Carol Ladd may be among the less familiar figures in the Ladd family saga. Yet her story is one of the most fascinating, not simply because of the example she may have set for her successful stepson but because of the successes she enjoyed in her own right. In many ways, she was a woman ahead of her time, a prime personification of unheralded power behind a family throne.

IN early 1927, Evelyn Lederer was a pert, twenty-year-old divorcée from a well-to-do Chicago family. On the rebound from her failed marriage, she was vacationing in Los Angeles with her mother when she was introduced to a handsome movie actor named Nick Stuart. Charmed by her vivacious personality, Stuart used his contacts at the Fox-Movietone Company to get her a screen test, and eventually a contract with the studio. With her name changed to Sue Carol, she was soon being touted as the next Clara Bow. First teamed with Nick Stuart in silent programmers and subsequently starring in a series of flapper talkies—films like *Girls Gone Wild*, *Why Leave Home*, and *Dancing Sweeties*—she developed into one of the more popular players in the Fox stable. If her thespian talent was dubious, her personal appeal was contagious. She was frequently featured on sheet music covers and became one of the first movie stars to boast a fan club with nationwide chapters.

By 1930, Sue Carol and Nick Stuart were married, and Sue made up her mind to relinquish her movie career in favor of motherhood. On July 18, 1932, she gave birth to a daughter, Carol Lee. The child's name was a combination of Sue's stage surname and that of her best friend, Dixie Lee, the starlet wife of an up-and-coming singer by the name of Bing Crosby.

Shortly after her daughter was born, Sue's marriage to Nick Stuart fell apart; they were divorced in 1934. Two years later, she was married for the third time, to a twenty-eight-year-old writer and sometime actor named William Howard Wilson, author of a *succès de scandale* called *Hollywood Doctor* but not much else. On the marriage license, Sue told a white lie and listed her own age as twenty-six, fudging by several years. Perhaps this was the point at which Sue decided to make 1910 her "official" year of birth. She was certainly not the first Hollywood personality to lie about her age, but she may have been doubly sensitive on the issue because of her marriages to younger men. (Her actual birth date has been the subject of some dispute. Alan Ladd's biographer, Beverly Linet, reported that Sue was born in 1903. Her children have called that nonsense; when Sue died in 1982, they listed her age as seventy-two in the obituary they distributed to the press, graciously perpetuating Sue's own version of the truth. A check of Evelyn Lederer's birth certificate at the Cook County, Illinois Department of Vital Statistics lays the minor controversy to rest once and for all: she was born October 30, 1906.)

Wilson's income was unsteady, so Sue tried to resume her acting career. She landed a small part in a 1937 potboiler, *A Doctor's Diary*, but her comeback, like the movie, fizzled. By 1938, Sue Carol, née Evelyn Lederer, was a thirtyish ex-starlet, three times married, with one career behind her, a young daughter to raise, and no immediate prospects.

Fortunately, Sue's natural gregariousness had made her a popular fixture on the Hollywood scene. Her friends—including the Crosbys—were now at the center of the social swirl. At the urging of a woman named Alma Shedd, Sue decided to take her inside knowledge of the business and her special abilities as a confidante and go-between to open a talent agency. Her partner in the venture was Alma's son, Bruce Shedd. Because she was reluctant to cash in on the success of her well-placed friends, Sue concentrated on discovering and representing new talent. Among the first of her discoveries was a radio actor whom she had heard playing two parts on the same show, a crusty old codger and the same character's young grandson.

Sue phoned the actor and invited him to come down to her office for an interview. "She thought I would be sixty years old," Alan Ladd later said of that initial meeting. "We were both glad

I wasn't." Sue's description of that first encounter reads like something out of Raymond Chandler crossed with Kathleen Winsor: "He came into my office wearing a long white trenchcoat. His blond hair was bleached by the sun, and he looked like a young Greek god. His eyebrows and eyelashes were pitch-black over level green eyes which were deep and unfathomable—an actor's eyes. He was for me."

At the time Sue Carol offered to represent him, Alan Ladd's career was not exactly thriving. His versatility in speaking lines had earned him intermittent work on the radio, but most casting directors thought he was too short to make it as a leading man on screen. Sue Carol believed otherwise. She saw something magnetic in his cool good looks, the combination of virility and vulnerability she felt he projected. Alan Ladd became her favorite protégé, and she set out to make him a star.

Sue was indefatigable in arranging meetings with producers and casting directors on Alan's behalf. The joke going around town was that the only part she hadn't sent him out for was the lead in *Charley's Aunt*. She did find bit parts for him in a string of forgettable pictures—as a British soldier under Clark Gable's command in *They Met in Bombay*, as a mutinous soldier in *Captain Caution*, and as one of the Disney animators introduced in the prologue to *The Reluctant Dragon*. He also had a tiny role in *Citizen Kane*, playing one of the "News on the March" reporters sifting through the remains of Xanadu. But his career did not take off until he was cast against type as the ruthless killer in Frank Tuttle's film of Graham Greene's suspense thriller, *This Gun for Hire*. Sue had heard that Tuttle was looking for an unknown to play the part, and she was relentless in cajoling him into testing Alan for the role.

Sue later recalled: "Alan and I went over to see Frank, who said that Alan looked like someone who would say, 'Tennis, anyone?' 'He'd be perfect for a part like that,' Frank told us, 'but this script needs an actor who can play a cold-blooded killer and still come off sympathetically.' Luckily, I'd brought along some mood stills of Alan—you know, with him looking sinister, smoking a cigarette with smoke curling out of his nose. They were quite effective. Alan photographed beautifully. Frank Tuttle studied the stills for a few minutes. Then he looked up at us and didn't say anything for what seemed like ages. Finally he said, 'Let me test him.'"

After reviewing the footage of Alan's screen test in a small projection room, Tuttle turned to Sue and said, "This picture is going to make your client a star." Frank Tuttle's prediction proved to be right on the money. Alan's portrayal of the hired killer Raven set the standard for a new breed of cinematic anti-hero. At once hard-boiled and boyish, cynical and sexy, Raven was a character quite unlike any other that had ever appeared on the American screen. Ladd became, in the words of Richard Schickel, "the first male star to achieve fame by combining beauty and somnambulism like the female of the species. So unemotional was he, with his deadness of voice and feature, that . . . he succeeded in reducing murder to an act as irrelevant as crossing the street."

The sparks set off between Ladd and co-star Veronica Lake in *This Gun for Hire* tantalized audiences. Paramount took advantage of the excitement, teaming the pair in a trio of subsequent films— *The Glass Key*, *The Blue Dahlia*, and *Saigon*—and billing them as Hollywood's hottest romantic twosome. But while the public speculated about a possible romance between the two new stars, the object of Ladd's romantic attention was the woman off camera— Sue Carol. Marjorie Jane (Midge) Harrold, the high school sweetheart whom Alan Ladd married in 1936, and who was the mother of his young son, Alan Ladd, Jr., was no match for the dynamic, determined woman who was guiding her husband's professional interests. Ladd secured a quite divorce from Midge, Sue took up temporary residence in Las Vegas in order to win a quick divorce from William Howard Wilson, and in March of 1942, Sue Carol and Alan Ladd slipped off to Tijuana, Mexico to be married.

Sue's children take issue with the portrait of their mother that emerges in Beverly Linet's biography of Alan Ladd. In that book, Sue is pictured as a conniving home-wrecker who stole Alan away from his first wife, a rather meek and all-too-trusting soul. Linet's version of events relies on the account offered by Midge's sister, who compared Midge to "the sweet, gentle character Joan Fontaine played in *Rebecca*. She had the kind of love for Alan that meant she wouldn't stand in his way." Sue's daughter, Carol Lee, sees things in a quite different light. "I was sitting in the front row, and I can tell you that my mother didn't encroach on that marriage at all," she insists. "Alan was already separated when all this took place. Susie didn't set out to get him. It was something that happened because two people were unattached."

WHEN Sue Carol met Alan Ladd, she may have sensed that a darker, more melancholy streak lay behind his handsome facade.

But she doubtless believed that under her nurturing he could overcome it. In fact, Alan Ladd was haunted by tragedy throughout his life. Born in Hot Springs, Arkansas, on September 3, 1913, he spent his earliest years in poverty; even after he became a wealthy movie star, he could not stand the sight of vichyssoise because it reminded him of the cold soup that was his steady diet as a child. Alan's father died when he was only four. After his mother remarried, the family set out for Los Angeles, where Alan's stepfather hoped to find work as a housepainter. Their trek west was straight out of *The Grapes of Wrath*, Alan would later recall. Everything they owned was tied up on top of his stepfather's jalopy. They slept in tents and worked odd jobs along the way to support themselves. Halfway to California, their money ran out, and Alan and his stepfather hired themselves out as field hands, while his mother was forced to work as a kitchen helper.

The family's fortunes improved somewhat once they had settled into life in the San Fernando Valley. Young Alan continued to work at menial jobs after school in order to help support his parents. In high school, he proved to be a superb athlete, particularly excelling in swimming and diving. His high school diving coach saw him as a possible contender for the 1932 Olympics. An injury, however, dashed his hopes of competing in the games. It was one of the major disappointments of his life.

In 1936, Alan's stepfather died of a heart attack. The following year, his mother also died—but under far more horrific circumstances. On Thanksgiving Day, Alan and his young wife Midge were at home in their small apartment preparing dinner. His mother showed up in the late afternoon, demanding some money from her son so that she could go to the store and "buy something." Still depressed over the death of her second husband, feeling older than her years, Ina Ladd Beavers took the money her son gave her and purchased a small can of ant paste at an all-night grocery. She went into the back seat of Alan's car, swallowed the poison, and died an excruciating death.

"I'm sure my father ended up blaming himself for what happened," David says of that traumatic incident. "It must have provided a source of his unhappiness in later years. God knows, if psychiatric help had been something that someone like Alan Ladd could have submitted to in the 1950s, I don't think that he would have had the problems that he did."

Throughout his life, Alan Ladd was subject to severe bouts of depression, compounded by the physical pain of a chronic ulcer.

The wealth and acclaim he achieved could never quite counter his own sense of personal failure. But Sue Carol had made it her mission in life to rescue her husband from his own despondency and self-destructive tendencies. For a time, her passion and enthusiasm, her unshakable belief in his talent, did help to quell his intense self-doubts. If her victory was always precarious, at least she provided a necessary ballast during his recurrent periods of despair.

The union of Sue Carol and Alan Ladd represents a fascinating variation on a familiar Hollywood pattern. It is not at all unusual to find instances of some older, powerful man taking a beautiful young woman under his wing, attempting to turn her into a star, becoming romantically obsessed in the process, abandoning his wife for his new love, and finally entering into an all-consuming bond in which the lines between personal and professional interests are totally blurred. That is essentially what happened between David O. Selznick and Jennifer Jones, between Darryl F. Zanuck and Bella Darvi. In the case of Sue Carol and Alan Ladd, however, the traditional roles were reversed. The daughter of a Jewish merchant, Sue was seven years Alan's senior, a plucky businesswoman whose salad days as a glamour girl were well behind her. He was (in her words) "like a young Greek god"—a handsome blond athlete on his way to becoming one of the most popular matinee idols in movie history.

Like a distaff Pygmalion, Sue Carol molded her husband into an object to be adored and worshipped. For his part, Alan Ladd was the willing subject, dutiful pupil, devoted companion. In matters of business or career, he would invariably defer to his "Susie"—whose judgment he trusted implicitly. The relationship sometimes exasperated producers and directors. One producer who knew them both likens Sue to a "moat around Alan. If you wanted to talk to Alan, you had to talk to Sue, and that was like leaping into a pit of alligators."

"My mother got the reputation of being tough because she held her ground in negotiations," comments her daughter Alana. "She believed in my father, knew what she wanted for him, and wouldn't budge. And men found that hard to cope with when they were dealing with a woman. Especially one who represented him and was also married to him." Even when she stopped being his agent, Sue sat in on all of Alan's interviews and came to the set every day when he was working; she was intent on making sure that his lighting and makeup were exactly right. When he finished a take, he would often look first to Sue for confirmation and only then to the director.

The trust he demonstrated was evidently justified. Sue was unusually astute when it came to the business side of things. In her hands, Alan's career flourished. He became Paramount's most durable, highly-paid star, a top box-office attraction through the 1940s and early 1950s. His movies of that period, if rarely first-rate, consistently earned a profit. Today most of those movies have been forgotten. With a few notable exceptions—*This Gun for Hire, The Blue Dahlia, Two Years Before the Mast, The Great Gatsby*, and George Stevens's classic Western, *Shane*—the films of Alan Ladd are dated popular entertainments rather than enduring examples of popular art. But Ladd himself always seemed somehow bigger than the movies he was in; he was one of the screen's few icons, "the only tough guy who was also a matinee idol," note Marilyn Henry and Ron DeSourdis in their definitive study of the actor's career, *The Films of Alan Ladd*. Darryl Zanuck called him "the indestructible man," and hoped he could some day lure Alan to Fox. "He stays on top in mediocre films," Zanuck declared. "Imagine where he would be if he were cast in worthwhile and important ones."

Alan's apparent affability off-camera, combined with Sue's predilection for "safe" material, made him an ideal contract player. His personality and his manager-wife's instincts were perfectly in tune with the studio system, which depended on stars' fitting into some particular, well-defined mold and then hewing to their image. The Ladds were always viewed as being among the least temperamental and most congenial of Hollywood celebrities, and the Hollywood press corps adored them for it. Sue Carol cultivated good relations with the powerful gossip hens, Louella Parsons and Hedda Hopper, as well as with the editors of the major fan magazines. Such cooperativeness paid off in the generally glowing publicity accorded them. Alan and Sue were invariably portrayed as Hollywood's "dream couple," raising a happy, well-adjusted brood. The headlines in the fan magazines were treacly: "The Alan Ladds' Million-Dollar Recipe For Marriage" or "Her Heart Belongs to Laddie."

A hint of discord crept into the gossip columns only once. Early in 1955, Alan was starring in *The McConnell Story*, about the first triple ace pilot of the Korean War. His co-star was June Allyson, the popular actress whom the *New York Times* had recently dubbed the "perfect all-American young wife"—a role she had honed to perfection in *The Stratton Story*, *The Glenn Miller Story*, and *Strategic Air Command*. Alan and June struck up an easy rapport. Because of her petite size, he felt more comfortable around her than he had with his taller leading ladies. And besides, according to June, he told her that she resembled his first wife Midge.

In her autobiography, June Allyson has reported that the more they talked, the more she and Alan realized how much they had in common. In particular, both were chafing under the restraints imposed by their respective spouses. June was married to actor-producer Dick Powell, who always expressed firm opinions about June's choices of roles even though he gave her little of the personal attention she craved. "Each of us had someone at home who guided their careers," she has written. "Each of us was suffering in that relationship, but for exactly opposite reasons—I because I wasn't getting enough attention and Alan because he was getting too much." Alan confessed that his role in *The McConnell Story* was a special source of anxiety for him. "Here I am playing the flying ace," he told June, "and I don't fly." What he didn't tell her was that his insecurity about flying was probably exacerbated by the fact that Sue was a fearless aviatrix; she had even been a licensed pilot during the open-cockpit days.

As Alan and June spent more time together, Sue was consumed with jealousy. According to June Allyson, Sue finally called up Dick Powell and asked whether he realized that Alan was in love with June.

"Isn't everybody?" Powell nonchalantly replied.

When Alan got wind of the call, he was furious. He packed his bags and took off for his ranch. The "trial separation," as Sue called it, lasted less than a week. Alan returned to the Holmby Hills mansion, and Louella Parsons breathed a sigh of relief that "Hollywood's most perfect couple" was back intact. "I'd be willing to bet that Sue and Alan Ladd will be happier than ever now that they are over this bad time in their lives," Louella assured her readers. "Sue just isn't going to let anything jeopardize her marriage."

What was missing from Louella's and Hedda's effusive accounts of the Ladd's marriage was not so much the smell of scandal, but a sense of what made the union genuinely exceptional. In celebrating the Ladds' conventional domestic virtues, Hollywood reporters fostered the impression that here were a couple of nice young kids who had fallen in love, made a family together, and were now living happily ever after. For all intents and purposes, the differences in their ages, their previous marriages, even their children by those previous marriages evaporated into thin air. When their son David was born in 1947, one fan magazine conducted a poll of its readers to choose a name for the baby. The overwhelming choice was "Alan Ladd, Jr." Almost no one was aware that there was *already* an Alan Ladd, Jr., who was ten years old at the time. When reporters would show up at the house to do stories on the Ladd family, Sue's daughter, Carol Lee, and Alan's son, Alan, Jr., were routinely shunted off to another room. Hundreds of publicity shots were taken of Alan and Sue together with their two children, Alana and David. But Carol Lee and Alan, Jr. were always absent.

Though feelings of rejection or alienation might easily have resulted from such treatment, neither Alan, Jr. nor Carol Lee appears to carry permanent scars from the experience. Perhaps it helped that both of them were older, able to view the phenomenon with some detachment. Moreover, Alan and Sue took pains to make their step-children feel comfortable in other respects. The occasional invisibility of the older children was treated as one of the inconveniences of the business, like having to be on a set at six in the morning or going off on location for months at a time.

"In those days, actors were not supposed to have children of eleven or twelve from previous marriages," Alan Ladd, Jr. now recalls. "I wasn't supposed to exist in my father's life. I'd have to beat a retreat with my step-sister whenever the reporters would show up at the house. I'm sure I found it somewhat painful at the time, but like all kids, you try to understand. You say to yourself, 'They care about me, so there's probably a reason behind it.' And then when you think back on it, it's a little bit more painful. But eventually you grow out of that, and you begin to accept it."

By all accounts, Sue Carol was almost compulsively devoted to her husband and children. Like many women today who choose to defer the roles of wife and mother until they have pursued a career, she threw herself into those roles with single-minded commitment once she was ready to assume them. She managed her home with much the same zeal that she had formerly spent on her professional life. When her daughter Alana was born in 1943, Sue had already celebrated her thirty-sixth birthday. And when David, her second child by Alan Ladd, was born four years later, she nearly died in childbirth. Although a woman past forty who takes on the task of raising two young children after achieving her own success in the business world might seem like a worthy feminist role model today, in the 1940s the idea was so unorthodox as to be almost freakish. And so Sue Carol's unusual history was set aside in favor of a sanitized, more conventional picture of the innocent young wife and mother. Luckily, Sue looked and acted quite youthful, making it easy to conceal the fact that she was actually old enough to be her own son's grandmother.

Now that they are grown, Sue's children see their parents' commitment to the family unit as one of their more significant legacies. "When my father went to Europe for a picture, it would have been much easier to put us children in a boarding school," Alana observes. "But they didn't want us to be away from them. Wherever they went, we went. We took a tutor with us, and we would have school wherever we happened to be. In the car, on top of the mountain, in the hotel room, in the bathtub—wherever we were, that's where we had school. The other kids I grew up with—the Walkers, the Haywards, the Fondas—were all sent off to boarding school. Those boys used to love coming to my home because there was a closeness, a family unit, that they didn't have. When my father died, I think it was the same day that Peter Fonda's first child was born, and Peter wrote me a beautiful letter relating the one to the other. He said that being with my parents provided some of the happiest times he had during those troubled years."

Even though her family was Sue's major preoccupation, she never abandoned her other interests. At the same time that she was rearing Alana and David, she was also overseeing the family finances. Her son-in-law Michael Jackson contends that Sue's good fortune with business investments derived more from her special personality than from any genius for business. "She was very talented, but she wasn't brilliant," Jackson says. "She wasn't the greatest expert in business investment, but she knew, like a good general, who to call on, how to call on them, how to inspire people to give everything in her cause." Her daughter, Carol Lee, makes a similar observation: "She was very cute about asking different people what they thought at different times, and then she would pool all this knowledge together and do what she wanted. She used every one of her friends, and they knew they were being used."

Sue seemed to have an uncanny knack for putting money into lucrative ventures—everything from fine art and stocks and bonds to a hardware store. Almost invariably, the initial investments soared in value, sometimes spectacularly. In addition to their lavish home in the Holmby Hills section of Los Angeles, the Ladds owned a ranch outside Santa Barbara, a retreat in Palm Springs, and an office building in Beverly Hills. In contrast to his frequent co-star Veronica Lake, whose movie career floundered after her series of early hits opposite Alan Ladd, and who found herself eking out a living as a waitress and dance hall hostess in the 1950s, Ladd remained a top box office attraction through much of his career. Even after his star began to dim, he remained a very rich man indeed.

Yet the acquisition of ever more prominence and wealth held a double edge for Alan Ladd. The more he had, the more he had to lose. Like so many stars whose popularity is attached to a particular image in the public mind, he became reluctant to shed that image and branch out into riskier or more challenging roles. Sue's conviction that he had to sustain his box-office appeal in order to remain psychologically secure reinforced his tendency to play it safe as an actor. The problem grew more and more acute as he got older, when it became increasingly less appropriate for him to play the sorts of romantic leads or tough-guy turns with which he had become associated early in his career. Perhaps because she had masked her own age so effectively, Sue refused to accept the fact that her husband was no longer the beautiful young man she had molded into a major matinee idol. She steered him away from somber, complex parts that might trigger one of his depressions. Though his best performances—as the doomed romantic hero in *The Great Gatsby* and the phlegmatic, melancholy gunfighter in *Shane*—were the ones that drew on his tragic persona, he rarely allowed that side of himself to be expressed on screen.

Alan's inability to make the transition from virile young star to middle-aged working actor was magnified by a decision which Sue and he made in 1955. George Stevens, who had directed him in his best picture, *Shane*, was preparing to film Edna Ferber's Texas saga, *Giant*, a movie that was being touted as the hottest property in town. Alan coveted the role of stolid cattleman Bick Benedict, a part that would ultimately go to Rock Hudson in the film. Stevens originally wanted Alan for Jett Rink, the ranch-hand-turned-vulgar-oil-mogul eventually played by James Dean. Because Sue felt that the Benedict role was the more prominent of the two, she counseled Alan to hold out for it. Stevens rightly argued that the Rink role, though ostensibly smaller, was really the meatier part. In any event, Alan lost the chance to appear in the film and, with it, an opportunity to rise above the routine material to which he had been consigned after *Shane*. In an interview with *The Hollywood Reporter* some years later, Sue said, "It was my fault as much as Alan's. I was used to his being top banana, and we both felt the Jimmy Dean role was a secondary part. It didn't turn out that way. But no matter."

In commenting on the episode three decades later, Alan Ladd, Jr. appears to be equally philosophical: "He went back and forth discussing it with my stepmother. He'd say, 'Well, the Jett Rink part is much flashier, but by the same token, it's less screen time. The Hudson part is duller, but he's there all the time and he's a stalwart character.' A lot of people, including the studio, were telling my father to stay with his image. At times, I could see he had second thoughts about the roles he had turned down, like *Bad Day at Black Rock*. Somebody talked him out of it and said, 'You don't want to play a character part.' And he really did want to play a character part. He turned it down, and later on, when he saw the picture, you could tell that it bothered him. He thought, 'I should have tried to step out of the mold.' I felt personally that he should have gone into character parts at a much earlier time, but who knows? The outcome could have been the same."

Alan Ladd went through a painful period during the 1950s. His movie roles were becoming duller, and the critics were less kind in assessing his performances. Other bad publicity hurt, particularly when it touched on the subject of his height, about which he was always extremely sensitive. When she appeared with Alan in *Saskatchewan*, Shelley Winters complained to reporters about having to stand in ditches for her love scenes with Ladd. Alan was deeply wounded when he saw the clippings, just as he was when he found out that Robert Mitchum had kiddingly described him emerging from a swimming pool and looking "all shrunken up like a dishwasher's hand."

It seemed an appropriate time for Alan to make some major change, especially since his exclusive contract with Paramount had finally expired. In 1954, at Sue's urging, Alan started his own company, Jaguar Productions, under a lucrative agreement with Warner Bros. But the record of Jaguar Productions was lackluster. Ladd tried to capitalize on his success with *Shane* by producing and starring in a couple of pallid Westerns—*Drum Beat*, with Audrey Dalton and newcomer Charles Bronson, and *The Big Land*, with Virginia Mayo and Edmond O'Brien. Both were critical and commercial failures. Though Alan had hoped that becoming his own boss would enable him to branch out and free him from taking routine assignments, he seemed to have no clear sense of just what he did want to do. Part of the problem was that he was still locked in a time warp. Ever loyal to the people who had worked with him during his halcyon years at Paramount, he hired several of them—including Frank Tuttle, who had directed him in his breakthrough picture, *This Gun for Hire*, and the same film's aging cameraman, John F. Seitz—to join him at Jaguar. The result of their collaboration, *Hell on Frisco Bay*, was a creaky throwback to the 1940s melodramas that had been Ladd's staple at Paramount—films like *Lucky Jordan*, *Salty O'Rourke*, *Chicago Deadline*. Ladd also hired the fifty-six-year-old Edward G. Robinson as his co-star in *Frisco Bay*, and he put his old pals William Demarest and Paul Stewart in supporting roles. Around town, Jaguar Productions was jokingly referred to as "the over-the-hill gang."

In April of 1957, Alan's first wife, Midge, died in obscurity. She had moved to Orange County after divorcing her second husband and had taken a job working in a dress shop. Her own diabetes and the cerebral palsy of her young son by her second husband had strained her finances terribly. Despite the fact that they had maintained cordial relations through the years, and Alan had contributed generously to his son's support, it is doubtful that Alan had ever come fully to terms with his divorce. Midge's untimely death, coming at the point when Alan was reluctantly entering middle age and during a period when his screen image was faltering, appears to have reactivated long-dormant feelings of guilt and exacerbated his drinking problem.

Though most of the family disputes David Ladd's theory that his father was an alcoholic, there seems to be little doubt that his drinking did grow worse in his later years, as his career began to decline. According to his son-in-law John Veitch, Alan started drinking to assuage the effects of insomnia brought on by a chronic nasal condition. Whatever the origin, his drinking was almost certainly something he could not fully control. His black moods became more frequent. In 1962, he nearly died of a self-inflicted gunshot wound in the chest. The shooting was reported as accidental, though the facts have never been conclusively established.

The following year, Alan returned to Paramount, the lot that had been his home during his most successful period, to begin work on a picture which both Sue and he hoped would steer his career in a positive new direction. Alan had given up producing on his own, and he desperately needed an opportunity to show that he could still command the screen. Edward Dmytryk (who had directed him twenty-four years earlier in *Her First Romance*, one of his first featured roles) had tapped him to play Nevada Smith in the film version of Harold Robbins's *The Carpetbaggers*. Though it was only a supporting role, the part did provide Ladd with a chance to call on his most reliable trait as an actor—that special combination of impassivity and cynicism—to excellent effect. Alan had prepared for the role by losing weight, and the early rushes showed him looking better on screen than he had in years. Though the movie was released to terrible reviews, the critics gave Alan high marks. It was the sort of performance that might have opened the door to other, better character parts in the future. Besides, it would prove to be his first big hit in years. But Alan Ladd's role in *The Carpetbaggers* was to be his last.

The completion of the film had been something of a letdown. David Ladd suggests that his father thrived on activity. "I don't think he thought too much about his career," David says. "He just liked to work." There was a time when Alan's services were in such demand that he could move from film to film in quick succession, but those days were long past. After *The Carpetbaggers* was completed, and while its fate was still uncertain, he found himself facing another lull. Alan confessed to Sue that he was feeling enervated, and he decided to spend a solitary vacation in Palm Springs. "I knew that more and more Alan was finding his lovely home in Holmby Hills a depressing place to be," his old friend June Allyson observed, "and when it started closing in on him, he fled . . ."

On the afternoon of January 29, 1964, his butler walked into the master bedroom of the Ladds' Palm Springs house. There he found Alan Ladd lying dead in his bed. The coroner's report listed the cause of death as a synergistic combination of depressant and ethanol—sleeping pills and liquor.

IRONICALLY, the most engaging role Alan Ladd played in his last years was one in which he was eclipsed by his son David. In 1956, Samuel Goldwyn, Jr., who was attempting to emulate his own legendary father as a producer, was preparing to shoot a sentimental story called *The Proud Rebel*, about a Civil War veteran who embarks on a desperate search for a doctor capable of curing his mute son. Alan had given David a bit part in *The Big Land*, which Goldwyn had seen and liked. Sam, Jr. tested the nine-year-old David for the role of the boy in *The Proud Rebel* and hired him even before signing Alan for the part of the father.

The movie was directed by Michael Curtiz and co-starred Olivia De Havilland, and it proved to be a modest hit. Though it didn't do much to revise Alan's sagging career, it did give considerable prominence to David, who won rave notices for his portrayal of the mute boy, and immediately received offers to do more movies. In the next several years, he appeared in such films as *Misty* and *A Dog of Flanders*, and was touted as the hottest teen star in Hollywood. The same fan magazines that had once lionized Alan began serving up story after story about David.

Today, David recalls his early star treatment with amusement and not a little revulsion. "I must say that there was nothing worse than having your peer group selling the comic book of your life story during halftimes at football games," he comments. "It was just devastating. All I wanted was to be one of the guys."

In an "open letter" to his son that appeared in *Modern Screen*, Alan Ladd composed (with the help of one of the magazine's veteran writers) a corny, but touching, piece of fatherly sentiment: "You were never a Hollywood kid in the obnoxious sense of that word," he wrote. "You were all boy—jeans, T-shirts, scraps and everything . . . You've never let me down, Davy—not for a minute. Even though all that fan mail you're dragging in makes our secretary, Muriel, work nights, even though you've already copped a lot of awards. Neither all these radio and TV interviews, nor those rock 'n roll records that are wowing the teen-agers, have given you big ideas . . . I know you aren't exactly living it up on a dollar-a-week allowance either. And that twenty-five cents an hour dusting shelves at Higgins-Ladd hardware store in Palm Springs isn't exciting alongside a movie check. But, believe me, those are the things that make it all right with me. I know now I wouldn't have missed doing that picture with you, Davy. Frankly, I didn't want to play your dad on the screen at first. I wanted to *be* your dad, not play him. But not every father gets a chance to start his son off in his own footsteps . . . I say I'd rather be David Ladd's dad than Alan Ladd any day." Even with its fanzine flourishes, that letter offers insight into one of Alan's most earnest concerns. He was always appalled by the prodigality of other Hollywood personalities in dealing with their children, and he made up his mind that his kids would learn the value of a dollar—just as he did during his own impoverished youth.

Robert Radnitz, the producer of *Misty*, and *Dog of Flanders*, recalls another influence that Alan had on David. Alan prided himself on performing his own stunts, and David was eager to emulate him. "I remember a sequence in *Misty*, where we were all worried about David riding a horse," Radnitz notes. "He might have fallen off and hurt himself. But David insisted on doing it, because he said his dad would have done something like that. David idolized his father."

As David's work as a child actor turned him into a celebrity, Alan and Sue were determined to insulate him as much as possible from the uncertainties of the movie business. "They encouraged me to go to a normal school," David says, "to go on to college and complete my education." Sue, who knew the business as well as anyone, was especially concerned that David not become completely seduced by the apparent ease and glamour of Hollywood stardom. Her own experience as a one-time starlet, and Alan's erratic career in later years, must have contributed to the apprehension she felt about David's future. "I was the baby of the family," David explains. "She was always worried about her baby. Nobody in this business wants his kid to go into it, because they all know how tentative it is."

At his mother's behest, David's work as a performer took second place to his education. He followed his father's footsteps not just as an actor but as a champion swimmer as well, and that seemed a greater source of pride to Alan than David's screen accomplishments. Alan Ladd even hoped for a time that David might fulfill his old ambition and qualify for the Olympics.

After graduating from USC, David tried to pick up his acting career. But like so many child stars, he found that the transition to adult roles did not come easily. He appeared in a couple of B-movies and in TV commercials for Arrow Shirts. Obviously, such work represented a considerable comedown from the starring roles he had played as a boy. "I had already had a lot of success, so it wasn't exactly as though I was a struggling young actor," David says. "In some ways, the fact that I had enjoyed so much at such an early age affected me. The later things—guest shots on television shows and the like—that's what made me walk away from it. There wasn't the same joy in it. It was as if I was competing with myself, and I found myself constantly apologizing for doing less than I had done when I was fourteen or fifteen."

Before walking away from it, however, he did appear in one film that would prove important to him personally, if not artistically. The picture was a 1973 potboiler called *The Treasure of Jamaica Reef*. His co-star was a pretty, twenty-two-year-old ingenue from Huron, South Dakota named Cheryl Jean Stoppelmoor, with whom he fell in love. After living together for a year, they were married, and David persuaded Cheryl to adopt her married name professionally. When Aaron Spelling, an old family friend whom Alan had helped get started in television, was casting about for someone to replace Farrah Fawcett in his hit series, *Charlie's Angels*, he gave Cheryl the part. Just as Alan had become an overnight sensation in *This Gun for Hire*, and David had become a star in *The Proud Rebel*, Cheryl was now the latest Ladd to become the instant darling of fan magazines and tabloids. And just as Alan had once come to be known as David Ladd's father, David was now being referred to as Cheryl Ladd's husband.

It was a role that David cheerfully accepted. Though both Cheryl and he were quick to insist that David was not merely functioning as a "househusband", there was no doubt that his new producing career was taking a back seat to her acting career—for the time being. "The fact that, as a man, he can so strongly support what has happened to me is something people can't always accept," Cheryl declared. In article after article, they were pictured as a happily liberated couple, sharing the housework, sharing careers, sharing the responsibility for raising their tow-headed little daughter, Jordan. "David even shared the pregnancy with me," Cheryl cooed. "He had psychosomatic labor pains." It was a portrait of new-style domestic bliss that seemed tailor-made for the readership of *Good Housekeeping* or the *Ladies' Home Journal*, a safely hip update of "The Ladds' Million-Dollar Recipe for Marriage," that paean to Sue and Alan's blessed estate which delighted fans some three decades earlier.

But the storybook romance of David and Cheryl was less durable than that of David's parents. When Cheryl and David broke up in 1979, Sue Carol blamed their separation on "the pressures of working too closely together." David sees a deeper incompatibility stemming from their very different upbringings. "One of the advantages of growing up in the business is that you're not from some little town in the Midwest," he observes. "You know what the realities of the business are. It's very difficult for anyone to suddenly be thrust into the limelight and have everybody in the world telling you that the sun shines out of your ass. It's a distortion of reality. Eventually you come out of it, but while you're going through it, it is your reality. If you've already lived through it, if you've been a part of it, you know it for what it is. You know it's transient. You may be this year's blonde, but next year nobody may want to know your name. I think that's where a lot of fatalities are, both professionally and personally. And I think that we, the second generation, have that edge over the newcomers."

David made some lucrative production deals with ABC while he was married to Cheryl, but over the next several years the deals began to evaporate. (Cheryl's second husband, a songwriter named Brian Russell who was once a close pal of David's, has taken over the job of co-producing her TV movies.) In 1983, David signed on as vice-president for development with the independent production company started by his brother-in-law, John Veitch—an industry veteran who had worked as a Columbia executive for fifteen years. But David indicates that he would be very reluctant to approach Alan Ladd, Jr. with a project. "His standards are so damn high," David says. "There would be nothing worse than going in and pitching something to your own brother and having him say 'No.'"

David's older sister, Alana, also made a stab at acting. In 1960, she appeared with her father in an oafish lumberjacking saga called *Guns of the Timberland*. Frankie Avalon was also making his screen debut in the picture, and Alana was cast as his dewy-eyed love interest. "All the magazines played it up as the big romance of the year," Alana recalls. "In the green room there was a huge photograph of me. About three weeks later, they saw the rushes, and my photograph was taken down." The following year, MGM brought out *Young Guns of Texas*, which boasted as its stars three of Hollywood's biggest names—Mitchum, Ladd, and McCrea. But instead of Robert, Alan, and Joel, the principals were their novice offspring—James, Alana, and Jody. Except for the gimmick of its casting, the movie drew little attention. "A family name will get you in the door, but you better have talent thereafter," Alana remarks. "I was terribly shy, and not terribly talented." She appeared with her father one last time, in a dreary Italian costume epic called *Duel of Champions*, and then retired to get married and raise a family.

Unlike David and Alana, Alan Ladd, Jr. was never drawn by the limelight. "I just think I'm much too introverted to be an actor," he says. To this day, he shuns publicity and is known to be as laconic in person as his father was on screen. His memories of a movie star's circumscribed life may have had something to do with his decision to keep a lower profile. "Being a star means that you really can't go out and do the normal things with your kid that you want to do," he observes. "My father and I never went to any kind of athletic event together because he'd get mobbed if he went out. Even though he was a very good athlete and would like to have gone, it was just something he couldn't do. You couldn't stop by a hamburger joint and have a hamburger together. You couldn't take a walk to a sporting goods store to buy a new football."

Laddie never considered a career outside the movie business, but it was a behind-the-scenes job that he sought for himself. He worked as an agent for a number of years. His boss at CMA, Richard Shepherd, recalls, "Laddie always had an inquisitive mind. Even as a young agent, he asked a lot of questions, but never volunteered anything. After a while, I said to Freddie Fields, 'You know, I think it's a one-way street with Laddie. We're imparting things, but we're not getting anything back.' Laddie's very smart."

Laddie moved to London and produced several films—*The Walking Stick*, *A Severed Head*, and *Villain*, among others—that died at the box office. His wife Patti, a former dental hygienist, opened a boutique in London and helped to support the family. In 1973, Laddie returned home to work as a production executive at Twentieth Century-Fox.

David Ladd recalls the day he first heard about *Star Wars* in 1973. He had stopped by his brother's office at Fox, and spotted George Lucas walking out the door. "I'd gone to USC, and USC kids used to line up for George's student films the way they do for his films now," David reports. "So I knew who he was, and I had just seen a screening of *American Graffiti*. I went in and asked Laddie what George Lucas was doing there. He said, 'I just made a deal with George for the biggest movie ever made. It's about these wookies and this robot called C3-PO.' That's the honest-to-God truth."

With that same synopsis in hand, Ladd did not have an easy time pushing *Star Wars* past the studio's board of directors. Several members of the board despised the project and kept referring to it contemptuously as "that science movie." After Laddie was named president of Fox in 1976, he was finally able to get the $9 million budget for *Star Wars* approved, though there was still a sizable contingent on the board who predicted that it would be his downfall.

The astonishing profits reaped by the movie cemented Ladd's position at Fox, and two years later, the smash success of the outer space horror film *Alien* showed that he had not lost his eye for spotting a blockbuster. But his distinctive achievement as an executive rests as much with some of the other decisions he made during his tenure at Fox. He was the first Hollywood executive of the 1970s to back a whole slate of films about women—not just *Julia* and *The Turning Point*, but also *3 Women*, *An Unmarried Woman*, and *Norma Rae*. These were unconventional because they were films about professional women, powerful women, older women, politically active women. (Even *Alien* fits the pattern— it was the first science fiction epic ever to center on a female character; Ladd was instrumental in having the protagonist of the original script changed from a man to a woman.) Such a slant might not have seemed revolutionary thirty years earlier, but Ladd sponsored these stories at a time when Hollywood was infatuated with all-male buddy movies that consigned women to bit parts as mute wives or tough-talking hookers. Unlike many other studio executives, Ladd had been conditioned to accept the idea of strong, capable women; he had a model close at hand in the person of his stepmother, Sue Carol. In addition, his wife Patti was pursuing a career of her own as an independent construction contractor.

Ladd's prodigious knowledge of movies set him apart from most other executives of his generation, who are notoriously uninformed on the subject of film history. As Paul Mazursky said of him, "He knows everything there is to know about movies—who was the lead, who produced it, who directed it, who did the music, who did the costumes, all the way down to the most obscure credit."

While running Fox, Ladd stood out for other reasons as well. He remained loyal to talented, idiosyncratic directors even if they did not have huge commercial success. Under his aegis, Paul Mazursky made *Harry and Tonto*, *An Unmarried Woman*, *Willie and Phil*, and *Next Stop*, *Greenwich Village*. Ladd backed five films by director Robert Altman at a time when no one else in the industry would hire the maverick filmmaker. He also took chances on several small films without major stars, such as the critical favorite of 1979, *Breaking Away*, a bittersweet comedy about an irrepressible bicycling enthusiast struggling for recognition in an Indiana college town.

For all his executive acumen, however, the record of Ladd's regime was not impeccable. *Damnation Alley*, *Dreamer*, and *The Boys from Brazil* added no luster to the Fox name and contributed little to the company coffers. In addition, there were those who mocked Laddie's monosyllabic oratory, and his soporific personal style. But despite his lack of charisma, he was a leader who attracted staunchly devoted followers.

In the summer of 1979 Ladd became embroiled in a policy dispute with then-Fox Chairman Dennis Stanfill. Ladd believed that Fox's middle-level executives, most of whom he had personally recruited, should share in the enormous profits that were rolling into the company during the post-*Star Wars* boom. He argued that they should be rewarded with substantial bonuses to prevent them from being lured away by other studios. Stanfill, the Eastern-bred Annapolis graduate and Wall Street analyst who had been hired to lend respectability to the company in more troubled times, dismissed Ladd's plan as a needless extravagance. Stanfill's "management by objective" techniques were definitely not of a style to which Hollywood execs had grown accustomed. To Ladd's plea for higher salaries and generous bonuses, Stanfill countered with a far more modest proposal, which Gareth Wigan, a Ladd lieutenant and one of the interested parties, branded as "perversely, knuckleheadedly crass." Unable to reach a meeting of the minds with Stanfill, Ladd announced his resignation as president of the Fox film division. When Rona Barrett broke the news of his departure in one of her early morning broadcasts, the value of Fox stock was sent tumbling $2.25 a share.

Several months later, Stanfill hired Alan Hirschfield, fresh from his own experiences with corporate bloodletting at Columbia in the wake of the David Begelman scandal, to head all of Fox's entertainment operations. Hirschfield named his thirty-five-year-old protégée, Sherry Lansing, to take over as chief of the film division. The flurry of favorable publicity attendant to her appointment as the first female president of a major motion picture company helped to stem some of the bad feeling generated by Ladd's departure. But the record of her regime, which lasted just three years, was no match for Ladd's. Producers who were used to Ladd's forthrightness and plain dealing began to grumble about Lansing's indecisiveness, dubbing her "the princess who sits on the fence." The number of movies made during her reign dwindled; with very few exceptions, those that did reach the screen were among the least audacious and least profitable to come out of Fox since the dark days of the Spyros Skouras-Peter Levathes interregnum of the early 1960s.

Shortly after leaving Fox, Alan Ladd, Jr. signed an enviable production deal with Warner Bros. and set up shop at the Burbank Studios. Warners would distribute films produced by the newly-formed Ladd Company, but Ladd would have complete autonomy in choosing and budgeting his projects. In effect, he would have all the advantages of running a studio without having to answer to a large corporate hierarchy.

From 1980 to 1984, The Ladd Company made five or six movies a year, approximately half the output of a major studio. And Ladd continued to search out unusual material. He talks about the criteria he has invoked in selecting projects, both at Fox and with The Ladd Company: "When you look at the films I've done, there have probably been fewer stars attached to them then at most studios. When I did *Julia*, Jane Fonda was a real no-no. With *Norma Rae*, I liked the idea of taking a chance with Sally Field rather then going back to someone like Jane, who was then a big star again. God knows I didn't do it deliberately, but subconsciously I think our films have been built around the director more than the actor. Sometimes it backfires. Bob Altman is a talented man, but I went with him five times and lost five times. That doesn't mean I wouldn't make another picture with him. Also, I think maybe we're open to a greater variety of material than some other studios."

Ladd Company movies have indeed represented a greater range than the run-of-the-mill products churned out by most of the major studios today: from the sensual mystery thriller *Body Heat* to science-fiction epics like *Outland* and *Blade Runner*; from the exuberant Bette Midler concert film *Divine Madness* to Sergio Leone's gangster saga, *Once Upon a Time in America*; from the unfashionable but haunting mood piece, Fred Zinnemann's *Five Days One Summer*, to light comedies such as *Night Shift* and *Lovesick*. One of Ladd's biggest coups has been the acquisition of the British-made *Chariots of Fire*, a film that every other studio turned down, but that went on to surprise the industry by winning the Academy Award as best picture of 1981.

Interesting though these films were, most of them lost money. In addition, Ladd let two big hits—Lawrence Kasdan's *The Big Chill* and Ron Howard's *Splash*—slip through his fingers. The Ladd Company had, in effect, discovered both directors. Ladd financed Kasdan's *Body Heat* and Howard's *Night Shift*, both of which were well received critically but made no waves at the box office. Subsequently, both Kasdan's *The Big Chill* and Howard's *Splash* were developed at The Ladd Company but were dropped before going into production. Kasdan took *The Big Chill* to Columbia, and Howard found a home for *Splash* at Disney. The *Big Chill* was one of the most successful movies of 1983, and *Splash* turned into the first major hit of 1984—and The Ladd Company lost out on both.

In the fall of 1983, Ladd released two movies that seemed to offer an opportunity to break the box office jinx that had afflicted most Ladd Company films. Bob Fosse's *Star 80* cast a cold but perceptive eye on the life and violent death of Playmate Dorothy Stratten. Not surprisingly, it was too bleak a film to win a large audience, but it represented still another feather in Ladd's cap, proving his willingness to take a chance on a darkly cynical but compelling vision of human nature. Philip Kaufman's *The Right Stuff*, on the other hand, was an ebullient if irreverent tribute to America's ace pilots and astronauts; it was a thrilling aviation melodrama and a smashing piece of epic filmmaking. *Time* and *Newsweek* hailed the movie in cover stories, and it inspired an enormous amount of press pondering the impact the movie would have on John Glenn's presidential aspirations. After enthusiastic previews, Ladd and his minions were gleefully looking forward to their first blockbuster since leaving Fox. Yet despite all the publicity and generally enthusiastic reviews, the movie attracted only moderate business. Several revised advertising campaigns and four Academy Awards could not turn the trick.

What went wrong? Some have speculated that the Glenn connection backfired, conveying the impression that the movie was political propaganda. Others have felt that the subject of the space program seemed too red-white-and-blue square to entice teenagers. Kaufman feels the marketing and promotional strategy were wrong. Whatever the reason, the film's disappointing box office performance was a devasting blow to The Ladd Company. Gareth Wigan, who had worked alongside Laddie for almost a decade, argued repeatedly with his boss over the film's budget, which eventually reached $27 million. Ladd wanted to keep a tighter rein on the costs, whereas Wigan agreed with Kaufman that the expense was justified. This friction strained the relationship between Ladd and Wigan, who resigned his position in late 1983. Shortly afterwards, Ladd's marketing chief Ashley Boone announced that he too was leaving the company, in his case to take a job at Columbia. At the same time that Ladd was experiencing these professional setbacks, his personal life was in turmoil, and he separated from his wife of twenty-four years.

In 1984, The Ladd Company had its first big money-maker—the unabashedly gross comedy *Police Academy*. After all its ambitious and intelligent movies it seemed a sad comment on current audience taste that Ladd should finally strike gold with the porcine romp. In any case, this unanticipated hit came too late to revitalize the company. A few weeks after its release, Ladd and Warner Bros. severed their four year relationship. The Ladd Company was a brave experiment that never quite found its niche. Still, Alan Ladd, Jr. is not one to look back or second-guess himself. "I'd do the same pictures all over again," he remarks. Unlike, say, David Selznick, who vainly tried to duplicate the success of *Gone With the Wind* throughout his career, Ladd recognizes that such megahits probably only come along once in a lifetime. "Quite frankly, I don't anticipate that I will ever do another picture as successful as *Star Wars*," he says. "If I were to go chasing *Star Wars*, I'd drive myself crazy and everybody around me crazy, and after a while, they'd end up carting me off someplace."

His steadiness and even temper are traits that distinguish Ladd from most Hollywood decision-makers, and these qualities may be directly attributable to his second-generation status. The fact that he has been an eyewitness to the industry since childhood and has observed firsthand the fluctuations in so many Hollywood careers, including that of his own father, seems to have given him a longer view of things. Echoing his brother David, Laddie says of his childhood, "It made you aware at a very early age that this is a business of great ups and downs, and you'd better be prepared for it. You can be down today, and tomorrow something good happens. My dad could make a couple of bad movies and then all of a sudden make *Shane*. I realized early on that it was a business of real hard knocks, but you've just got to keep going with it and rolling with the punches. If you don't, you're going to destroy yourself at a very young age. Maybe that's why I've been fortunate in my executive life. When something worked, I said, 'That's great,' and just went on to the next thing. And if something failed, I didn't sit there and moan, because there was nothing I could do about it."

Mel Brooks, who made *Young Frankenstein*, *Silent Movie*, and *High Anxiety* at Fox during Ladd's tenure, once said of him, "The most important thing about Laddie is that he is so handsome. It is such a pleasure to look across a desk and not stare into thick glasses, thick lips, and a drooling mouth." Certainly, this movie star's son does not fit the stereotype of the new-style mogul as Sammy Glick redux. Even more than for his good looks, Alan Ladd, Jr. is highly regarded for his good judgment. In a profession replete with hustlers and jellyfish, he is considered one of the most honorable and coolheaded of executives.

ANOTHER of Hollywood's most respected, if least flamboyant, behind-the-scenes players is Columbia's former production chief, John Veitch, who is married to Sue Carol's daughter, Carol Lee. The story of his initiation into the Ladd family reads like something that even the most gaga publicist might be ashamed to invent.

Though Sue had phased out her agency business to concentrate on family matters and Alan's career, she was always on the lookout for new talent. In 1945, Alan and she were touring military hospitals as part of a campaign to raise morale among wounded servicemen. At one such facility in Utica, New York, they met a strikingly handsome soldier who had been decorated for valor in the war. Sue thought he had the makings of a leading man, and she told him that if he'd like to come to Hollywood, Alan and she would introduce him around the studios.

"I guess I floored them because I said I wasn't interested," John Veitch recalls. He went back to work as a junior executive at General Motors, but the idea of a movie career began percolating in his mind. At last, Veitch came to Los Angeles and called the Ladds, who immediately invited him to dinner. Sue kept her promise of offering him an entrée to the studios. He was signed as a contract player by David O. Selznick, came close to being cast as Tarzan on one occasion and Superman on another. But Veitch soon realized that he preferred working off-camera, as a production manager and assistant director. The Ladds took a continuing interest in his career, and he became a close personal friend. When Sue and Alan were out of town, they would ask Veitch to stay at the house and keep an eye on their kids. An avuncular relationship with young David developed; when Alan could not attend school functions with his son, Veitch would stand in for him.

At the same time John Veitch first appeared at the Ladds' home in Holmby Hills, Sue's daughter, Carol Lee, was all of fourteen years old. In the ensuing years, she had gone on to do some modeling and was married briefly to actor Richard Anderson. After her divorce from Anderson, Carol Lee's friendship with John Veitch developed into a full-fledged romance, and in 1958 they were married. The young soldier whom Sue and Alan had spotted lying in a hospital bed thirteen years earlier would no longer be just an unofficial member of the family. Sue's keen eye as an agent had served her well. Not only could she take credit for "discovering" her husband, but she had found a son-in-law as well.

Though he worked closely with some of the top filmmakers in Hollywood—Ford, Hawks, Hitchcock, Wyler, Wellman, Stevens—and though he acquired a solid reputation for his production skills, Veitch seemed to be stuck in the role of second-in-command. There were those who wondered why he wasn't rising faster and higher in the business. "Part of the reason for that," Veitch says, "is that I had two young children at home, and it was important to me that I spend time with them. My family was at least as important to me as my job, and I think that's something I picked up from being around Sue and Alan, who were always terrific parents. Laddie, Carol Lee, David, Alana—each of them knew their parents were interested in them. While the Crosby boys were running wild and other Hollywood kids were getting into trouble left and right, they were always the kind of kids you could be proud of."

Over the years, Veitch moved steadily through the ranks. He spent fifteen years working in production at Columbia Pictures, an exceptionally long tenure in a business where some executives change employers almost as frequently as they change socks. In 1979, he was named president of production at Columbia. Four years later, he resigned that post to sign an unusual contract whereby he would serve simultaneously as a production "consultant" to Columbia and as an independent producer. In his long career, Veitch has been involved in the making of over 300 movies. While most producers and executives adorn their offices with posters of the various films with which they have been associated, Veitch's suite has none. Instead, the walls are lined with poster-sized pictures of his son and daughter. The only movie star on view is Alan Ladd: a large portrait of the man who was Veitch's friend, mentor, and father-in-law hangs above his desk.

Just down the hall is the office of Veitch's boss, Columbia Pictures president Guy McElwaine, who spent several years married to actress Leigh Taylor-Young, the sister of David Ladd's new wife, Dey Young. Alan Ladd, Jr. describes a family gathering: "John and I can sit down and compare notes. He asks about my company, and I ask about Columbia. It's all kind of incestuous because my closest friend is Guy McElwaine, who only lives two doors from me. We're always together. Now Guy's the president of Columbia Pictures. And his sister-in-law just married my brother. We figured out the other day that now Guy is the second or third uncle to my children. The family tree branches out all over the place."

Such family conclaves as the one Alan Ladd, Jr. describes are not uncommon. "We are the type of family that is together on every occasion," David notes. "And that was in large measure due to my mother." Whenever there was a birthday or a holiday to celebrate, Sue always made sure that the children were with her. Usually it was at the mansion in Holmby Hills. "I've always likened that house and my mother—they are one and the same to me—to a wheel, with Susie and the house as the center hub, and the children as the spokes," says Sue's daughter, Alana.

After her children had left the roost, Sue would take in a UCLA law student each year to live in the house. "She would go up and bring them a sandwich if they were studying late," John Veitch recalls. "She was always checking in on them—to make sure they were studying and keeping up their grades. Bill O'Melveny, who was one of the biggest entertainment lawyers in town, had a crush on Sue before she married Alan. They were great friends—she sort of helped him get started, bringing him Bing Crosby and people like that as his clients. When these kids would graduate from law school, she'd call him up and get them a job with O'Melveny and Myers. There are still lots of lawyers in that firm who got there through her."

After Alan's death, Sue continued to manage the family businesses she had been instrumental in starting. "She was a real doer," David remembers. "She did all the buying for the hardware store in Palm Springs. It was a pretty sizable store, and she would trek off to these gift shows and go down and do the displays herself. Everyone knew that she was having some heart problems. We'd say, 'Slow down.' And she'd say, 'If I slow down, I might as well die anyway.' She would not have been a happy invalid."

In 1981, a faulty pool heater started a fire at the Holmby Hills mansion, destroying half the house. "She actually *catered* the fire," recalls her son-in-law, Michael Jackson. "She sat in a lawn chair—like one of those chairs at Yalta, as if she were Roosevelt or Churchill—with a mink coat and a blanket around her, two dogs on her lap and one at her feet. And while the fire was going on, she was saying, 'Get Colonel Sanders for the firemen, and for the children get Big Macs. Who wants bourbon and who wants Coke? Who wants coffee and who wants wine?'"

"The firemen were marvelously sensitive," adds Jackson's wife, Alana. "They saved everything that really meant something—

every painting, every scrapbook, every film. Later, my mother had the house rebuilt exactly as it had been, the same quality, the same finish. But that fire is what killed her. It just took too much out of her."

A few weeks after the fire, Sue was hospitalized with severe coronary problems. Even in intensive care, she insisted on having a telephone at her bedside, so that she could check in with each of her children on an hourly basis. The flow of visitors created so much commotion that her doctor likened the scene to halftime at the Rose Bowl. Sue was released from the hospital just in time to host her annual Christmas bash in the newly refurbished house. On Christmas Eve, the family gathered to reveal that she had been selected a few days earlier to have her star placed in the Hollywood Walk of Fame. Although virtually anyone who ever toiled in Tinseltown—from Liberace to Lassie—eventually finds his name engraved in brass on the Hollywood Boulevard sidewalk, Sue was delighted with the honor. Still, she viewed it as a challenge. How, she asked ingenuously, could she get the city to dig up the concrete so that her star could rest alongside Alan's?

On February 4, 1982, Sue Carol Ladd died of heart failure. "She possessed all the naiveté of a ten-year-old and the poise of a woman," observed Michael Jackson in delivering her eulogy. "Did you ever dance with Susie?" he asked. "If you did, you'd understand quite a bit about her style, personality, ability. You held her, and it didn't matter how light-footed or how much of a clodhopper you might be. She was with you every step of the way, making you look and feel good. Her Alan Ladd—she was with him every step of the way, insisting that those who could give him a break or a chance must do so. I think she wanted them to love him almost as she did . . . I'm sure it truly never occurred to her, but Sue Carol, Mrs. Alan Ladd, was the binding, the central figure, the mother of what has become one of the most influential families in Hollywood."

The funeral was attended by a throng of mourners, including, of course, Sue's children, and her stepson, along with other leaders of the new Hollywood. Friends of another era were also there, surviving members of Alan Ladd's "Paramount family." In one way or another, they had all lost a matriarch.

7

A LITTLE FAMILY BUSINESS:
The Douglases

"I want my sons to surpass me, because that's a form of immortality..."

—KIRK DOUGLAS

THE Academy Award competition for best picture of 1975 was a true cliffhanger. Oddsmakers had declared the favorite to be the blockbuster thriller, *Jaws*, which was at that moment the highest-grossing movie in history. Among the critics, the top choice was Robert Altman's dazzling panoramic comedy, *Nashville*. The stately eighteenth century romance, *Barry Lyndon*, and the gritty comic melodrama, *Dog Day Afternoon*, were also serious contenders.

The envelope, please. The unlikely winner, a project passed over by every studio on the grounds that it was too downbeat to please the public, was *One Flew Over the Cuckoo's Nest*, adapted from Ken Kesey's novel about an anarchic rebel battling the forces of repression in an Oregon loony bin. Not only did *Cuckoo's Nest* cop the best picture Oscar, it made a clean sweep of the four other major categories as well: best actor (Jack Nicholson); best actress (Louise Fletcher); best director (Milos Forman); and best screen-play-adaptation (Bo Goldman and Lawrence Hauben). It was the first time that a single film had captured all five major awards since another dark horse, Frank Capra's *It Happened One Night*, accomplished the feat way back in 1934.

When he mounted the podium to accept his best picture Oscar, thirty-one-year-old co-producer Michael Douglas became one of the youngest people ever to win the Academy's top honor. It was a gratifying validation for this scion of a Hollywood star. Used to being dismissed simply as "Kirk's boy" (or else confused with the afternoon talk show host, Mike Douglas), Michael had finally come into his own. He was walking off with the coveted prize that had eluded his famous father for thirty years.

As he watched the Oscar ceremony on television that evening in Palm Springs, Kirk Douglas must have had mixed emotions—paternal pride fused with regret and envy. He had been nominated as best actor for *Champion*, *The Bad and the Beautiful*, and *Lust for Life*, but had never won. Besides, Kirk was the one who had bought the rights to *Cuckoo's Nest* when the book was still in galley form; he had played the role of the defiant hero, Randle McMurphy, on Broadway twelve years earlier, and he longed to play it on screen as well. Realizing that he was growing too old for the part and half-believing that the project was a lost cause anyway, he had turned the property over to his son in 1971, hedging his bets by retaining seven-and-a-half percent ownership of the finished film. His share of *Cuckoo's Nest* would eventually earn Kirk Douglas over $15 million, far more than he had ever made from any movie in which he had appeared.

That eye for good properties and that canny business sense had always set Kirk Douglas apart from other movie stars. In fact, he was one of the first actors to become a successful independent producer. When he created his Bryna production company (named after his mother) in 1955, he hope he was creating a family enterprise where all four of his sons could work with him. "I always get a certain nostalgic feeling about the fact that the company is named Bryna," Kirk Douglas says. "A peasant woman comes to America, and a company that's made a few good movies is named after her. I always wanted my kids to work there with me."

KIRK Douglas's attempt to build a family business symbolized his determination to forge a bond with his sons that would be radically different from his troubled relationship with his own father. Kirk's father, an illiterate Jewish immigrant named Herschel Danielovitch, had emigrated to America from Russia in 1910 to escape military conscription. With his wife Bryna, Danielovitch settled in Amsterdam, New York, a small industrial town 150 miles from New York City, where he worked as a peddler with a horse-drawn cart. He was a physically powerful man but completely uneducated and, as Kirk later described him, "totally unskilled and confused in his efforts to make a living." Unable to support his wife, his son, and his six daughters, he eventually deserted the family.

Although Kirk resented his father for this dereliction, he nonetheless struggled throughout his life to win his father's approval. After *Champion* had made Kirk Douglas a top Hollywood star, he returned to Amsterdam and asked his father if he had seen the film. "Yeah, yeah," Herschel Danielovitch replied. And had he liked it? "Yeah, yeah" was the only grudging reply. As Kirk reflected later, "All I wanted him to say was, 'Boy, you're terrific.'" Kirk's second wife, Anne Douglas, commented on the effect of her husband's tortured relationship with his father in an article she wrote for the *Saturday Evening Post* in 1962. She theorized that Kirk was driven by "a monstrous effort to prove himself and gain recognition in the eyes of his father. The old man is dead now — he died in 1954 — but the pattern was set early, and not even four years of psychoanalysis could alter the drives that began as a desire to prove himself."

If Kirk was tormented by feelings of inferiority and also antipathy toward his father, he was openly worshipful of his mother, who held the family together after Herschel left home. It was she who fostered Kirk's yearning for self-improvement. Born Issur Danielovitch (later anglicized to Isidore Demsky) on December 9, 1916, Kirk worked all through his youth to contribute to the support of his mother and his six sisters. While still a boy in grade school, he sold soda pop and candy bars to the men working in the Amsterdam carpet mills. As a teenager, he held a succession of other menial jobs — dishwasher, punch-press operator, cashier, and night watchman. "It's too typical, almost corny," Douglas once said of his youth. "You can almost hear the violins in the background." Sometimes in later years his family would tease him about the horror stories he told of his poverty-stricken upbringing. As Anne Douglas commented, "To hear Kirk tell it, he was the poorest, most miserable child that ever lived. I think it would annihilate him to meet someone who was poorer than he says he was. He wouldn't be able to believe it."

In high school, Kirk's English teacher encouraged him to become an actor. (When he formed his own production company two decades later, Kirk bought a short story that she had written, ostensibly for filming, though it never went before the cameras.) At St. Lawrence University, he worked his way through college as a janitor's assistant, bunking in the janitor's quarters; he also worked part time wrestling in a carnival. But he continued to covet a career in the theater, and after graduation, he joined a summer stock company in the Adirondacks. There he met Karl Malden, another aspiring actor.

"Kirk came up there as Isidore Demsky," Malden recalls. "And it was during our dinners and lunches that we talked about changing our names. I changed my name [from Malden Sekulovich], and I think it was my wife who suggested changing Demsky to Douglas. There was no doubt in my mind even then that Kirk was going to make it. He had something that is just born in you. Some people call it drive. Some people call it magnetism. Even that first summer, when nobody knew who he was, there were always girls around him. He didn't pursue them; they came to him."

In 1939, Kirk went to study at the American Academy of Dramatic Arts in Manhattan. At first, he lived in a settlement house in Greenwich Village and often took his meals in soup kitchens. Gradually, he found work in the theater, but he never appeared in a single hit play. "I never really had ambitions to go into movies," he now says. "My ambition was always to become a big star of the stage." His career was floundering when Lauren Bacall, who had been his classmate at the American Academy of Dramatic Arts, recommended him to producer Hal Wallis. In 1946, Wallis gave Douglas his first movie role, as Barbara Stanwyck's cowardly husband in *The Strange Love of Martha Ivers*.

Although Douglas came to Hollywood reluctantly, it was soon clear that he had found his home in the movies, a medium that he had always considered second-rate. "Kirk's magnetism really didn't come through as clearly in the theater," Karl Malden suggests. "You were too far back. You had to be close to him, and then the camera caught it. Kirk made the right decision in coming to Hollywood when he did."

Douglas's early screen performances, in spicy melodramas like *Martha Ivers*, *Out of the Past*, and *I Walk Alone*, gave him increasing prominence, but none could be considered a star turn. In 1949, he was offered $50,000—his largest fee up to that point—to star with Gregory Peck and Ava Gardner in an expensive MGM costume picture called *The Great Sinner*, a soft-caramel version of a Dostoyevsky story about compulsive gamblers. At the same time, however, a young, virtually unknown independent producer named Stanley Kramer was looking for an actor to play a prizefighter in his adaptation of Ring Lardner's story, *Champion*. Kramer wanted someone with a scrappy physical presence, and since the film's budget was a measly $600,000, he also needed someone who would work cheap. Douglas fit the bill on both counts. Kirk felt that Kramer's film had the potential to be a breakthrough for him, and he angered his agent by turning down the part in *The Great Sinner* to do *Champion* for the lowly salary of $20,000, plus a percentage of the film's gross. But the gamble paid off; the film eventually netted him over $100,000 and, more importantly, turned him into a superstar. (*The Great Sinner*, meanwhile, was branded a fiasco by most critics and died at the box office. It did absolutely nothing for the careers of Peck, Gardner, or Melvyn Douglas, who played the role originally offered to Kirk.)

In *Champion*, Douglas was cast as Midge Kelly, a brutally ambitious boxer who exploits and discards everyone close to him—including his crippled brother (played by Arthur Kennedy)—in his relentless climb to the top. The story was not exactly fresh movie material; much the same pugilistic pulp had been served up in two other movies of the time, *Body and Soul* and *The Set-Up*. But Douglas brought a bruising realism and intensity to *Champion* that compensated for the cliché-ridden script. Kirk's reviews were outstanding. The *Los Angeles Times* called him "quite irresistible." *Look* summed up the critical consensus by declaring that he had become "an important screen star overnight."

Champion established the essential Douglas persona: a ruthless, selfish, fiercely driven upstart. Other actors, to be sure, had evinced similar qualities—Humphrey Bogart conveyed a cruel sense of cynicism, John Garfield suggested the tough disillusionment of a man bred in poverty, James Cagney and Alan Ladd showed the sexual allure of violence. But no other actor before or since has drawn so boldly on the dark, unsavory side of himself to become a star. Douglas himself has frequently commented that "virtue isn't photogenic," and he has relished playing the heel. His attitude is not typical. Most movie stars try to make their characters as lovable as possible; their own hunger for acceptance leads them to soften and sentimentalize the characters they play. Douglas, by contrast, has worried when his occasional sympathetic roles might be construed as too endearing. In doing the acclaimed anti-war drama *Paths of Glory*, for instance, he complained that his character as written was "too noble" and "too sanctimonious." As he has said, "I've made a career, in a sense, of playing sons-of-bitches."

Some of Douglas's co-workers have found striking parallels between the actor and the characters he played. Throughout his career, he has made his share of enemies because of his abrasive, belligerent manner. When gossip columnist Hedda Hopper told Kirk that he had changed after *Champion*, he shot back impudently, "I was an SOB before I did *Champion*, and I'm still an SOB, only I was too unimportant for you to notice it before."

Whether or not the characters always reflected the man, the fact is that over the next thirty years Douglas gave many of his most memorable performances in roles which Hollywood would now brand "unsympathetic." For example, in *Detective Story*, he played a self-righteous and authoritarian cop so unforgiving that he repudiates his wife when he learns she once had an illegitimate child; it was one of the first movies to criticize police fanaticism, and Douglas bravely highlighted the character's psychosis. His portrayal of the megalomaniacal, self-destructive producer in *The Bad and the Beautiful* was equally daring and dynamic. Douglas's hard-edged roles also included the ruthless race car driver in *The Racers*, the diabolical murderer in *The List of Adrian Messenger*, the neurotic Naval officer who rapes a nurse in *In Harm's Way*, the callous advertising man in *The Arrangement*, the amoral outlaw in *There Was a Crooked Man*, and the opportunistic marshal in *Posse*. Probably his single most brilliant performance was in Billy Wilder's powerful study of human venality, *Ace in the Hole*. For many years, Wilder had wanted to make a movie about the exploitation of Floyd Collins, who was buried alive in a Tennessee cave in 1925; the trapped man's plight had turned into a carnival-like attraction, drawing thousands of spectators to the disaster area. Wilder despaired of finding an actor who could play the antihero he had in mind until he saw Douglas in *Champion*. Then he tailored the role of reporter Chuck Tatum for Douglas. The actor gave an uncompromising performance as the unprincipled newspaperman who manipulates another man's tragedy to resuscitate his own sagging career, and the film still stands as one of the most astringent movies ever made in Hollywood, indicting journalistic opportunism as well as the obscene voyeurism of the mob. *Ace in the Hole* was not a popular success, but over the years it has been recognized as a mordant classic.

Although such fiercely unsentimental characters as Chuck Tatum may have been Douglas's most striking and original roles, he was a versatile enough actor to command the screen in many different parts—the idealistic slave leader in *Spartacus*, the Bix Beiderbecke-like musician in *Young Man with a Horn*, the urbane schoolteacher in *A Letter to Three Wives*. But all of his best performances were marked by an extraordinary emotional intensity. That was the quality that linked the cads he played in *Champion* and *Ace in the Hole* to the more sympathetic characters he played in *Paths of Glory* or *Lust for Life*, where he gave a vivid and compassionate portrayal of Vincent Van Gogh, one of Hollywood's few convincing renditions of a great artist.

His histrionic intensity has made Douglas an unfashionable actor in some quarters today. Even at the peak of his success in the 1950s, stand-up comedians parodied the clenched-fist rage that was his specialty, and the *Harvard Lampoon* named him worst actor of the year three consecutive times, eventually dubbing its boobyprize the Kirk Douglas Award. His style of acting was diametrically opposed to the cool detachment of the Ivy League's favorite star, Humphrey Bogart. But fashions change, and Douglas's best performances are sure to be rediscovered. There is a moment at the end of *Champion* that epitomizes his acting style at its best: Badly beaten and dying, Midge Kelly suddenly forgets where he is and conjures up a happier time in his youth; he surrenders to a childlike reverie so vividly evoked that we, too, lose our bearings and enter his troubled consciousness. His pain is so raw and truthfully rendered that we feel almost embarrassed to witness it.

If Douglas invariably conveyed great passion on the screen, his work was also marked by great discipline, which may help to explain his professional longevity. "Some actors," he comments wryly, "are unable to separate make-believe from reality. I never thought I was Spartacus. Someone said to me, 'I saw you in *Lust for Life*, and, my God, you were so lost in the role' I said, 'No, no, *you* were lost in the role. That's my job. I had to keep the passion of the thing and at the same time hit certain marks. I had to seem to look in the mirror when I cut off my ear, though I couldn't really see the mirror because the camera had to see it.' A movie actor has to have discipline."

Douglas's biggest mistake was not his intense style of acting but his indiscriminate choice of roles. Partly because of his poverty-stricken childhood, he has always been terrified of not working. His fear of inactivity has led him to accept roles in dozens of terrible movies that have tended to dilute the impact of his best performances. Billy Wilder once likened Douglas to "the man who committed suicide because he couldn't dance at two weddings at the same time."

Kirk's phenomenal energy is matched by his ferocious self-reliance. He has always been known for his independence. After he made his first two movies for Hal Wallis, the producer offered to sign Douglas to a seven-year contract. Douglas asked Wallis exactly what projects he envisioned for him. "He was rather gruff," Douglas recalls. "He said to me, 'Look, you either sign for a seven-year contract, or I drop you.' I said, 'Okay, drop me.'" A few years later, after the success of *Champion*, Kirk's agent persuaded him to sign a nine-picture contract with Warner Bros. But Douglas was dissatisfied with the first three films—*Young Man with a Horn*, *Across the Great Divide*, and a flat-footed adaptation of Tennessee Williams's *The Glass Menagerie*. He felt all three movies were seriously compromised, and he agreed to make a fourth, an insipid Western called *The Big Trees*, for no salary if the studio would let him out of his contract. From then on, he has never been tied to a single studio.

That same spirit of independence has led him to strike back at anyone he suspects of taking advantage of him. In 1954, while he was making *20,000 Leagues Under the Sea* for the Disney Studio, Walt Disney invited Kirk and his sons Michael and Joel to come over to his home one Sunday afternoon. Walt had a small locomotive in his back yard, and Kirk and the boys took a ride on the train, while Walt shot home movies of the family outing. Two years later, the footage turned up in a television special promoting Disneyland. Kirk sued Disney for $415,000 for invasion of privacy, charging that he had never agreed to permit those home movies to be used for promotional purposes. Eventually, Douglas and Disney reached an understanding and the lawsuit was dropped.

WHEN Douglas formed the Bryna Company in 1955, part of his motivation was to give himself a stronger base in the industry. "I never had any idea of becoming a tycoon," he asserts. "It's just that I've always liked to participate in the creative process. I like to study the script and express my ideas. If I am an actor only, some people don't appreciate it. I only want the director to listen. If he listens and then rejects my ideas, okay. He's the boss. But sometimes in the old days, I used to get in trouble because they'd say, 'Oh, a thinking actor.' That was a contemptuous remark."

If there were practical reasons for setting up The Bryna Company, there were sentimental ones as well. "My mother was illiterate when she came to this country," Kirk explains. "I taught her how to write her name, B-R-Y-N-A. And when I came back from Hollywood to see her, she would always say, 'America is such a wonderful land. My boy—the whole world knows him. My son's name is in lights.' I said to her, 'I'll put *your* name in lights.' And a year later, I got a big limousine and took her to Times Square in New York. I parked across the street, and there was a marquee almost a whole block long. And in big lights, it said, 'BRYNA presents SPARTACUS.' I said, 'See, Ma, there's your name in lights.' 'You know,' she said, 'America is such a wonderful land.'"

Douglas formed the Bryna Company at a time when the authority of the major film studios was on the decline. Fewer and fewer stars were under contract; they were making their own independent production deals and forcing the studios to bid for their services. In 1955, a whole slew of stars besides Douglas announced their move into production, including Frank Sinatra, Robert Mitchum, Cornel Wilde, Joan Crawford, Henry Fonda, and Rita Hayworth. Burt Lancaster's Hecht-Hill-Lancaster Company became a viable and active producing entity; as for the other stars, they produced a movie or two, and then their companies expired ignominiously. If Kirk Douglas succeeded as a producer where most of these other actors failed, it was partly because of his intelligence, partly because of his boldness in selecting material and talent, and partly because he was a prudent businessman. He was shrewd enough to balance thoughtful, offbeat projects such as *Paths of Glory* and *Lonely Are the Brave* with strictly commercial ventures such as *The Vikings*.

His most expensive and successful production, *Spartacus*, came into being because of a movie role he didn't get. MGM was preparing its $16 million remake of *Ben-Hur*, at that time the most expensive movie yet made, and Douglas craved the title role. However, director William Wyler—who had made *Detective Story* with Douglas—felt that Charlton Heston, then the movies' leading Biblical hero, was the right actor to play the stalwart Judah Ben-Hur. Wyler offered Douglas the choice role of the villainous Messala, Ben-Hur's childhood friend and adult antagonist. After all the colorful heels Douglas had played, it seemed to be a role tailor-made for him. But Kirk could not cotton to the idea of playing second banana, and so he refused the role of Messala, which went to Stephen Boyd instead.

Miffed at losing the title role to Heston, Douglas resolved to make his own spectacle set in ancient Rome. He admitted, "That was what kind of spurred me to do [*Spartacus*], in a childish way, the 'I'll-show-them' sort of thing. They can't do that to *me*." Kirk was determined to do Wyler and Heston one better. His choice of story was characteristically audacious; rather than dusting off another Biblical tale or remaking an old warhorse, he purchased the rights to Howard Fast's passionate, controversial novel about an early Roman slave revolt. To write the screenplay, Kirk selected Dalton Trumbo, a blacklisted writer and one of the "Hollywood Ten," who had been jailed a few years earlier for refusing to cooperate with the House Un-American Activities Committee's witch-hunt. Douglas helped to destroy the blacklist when he allowed Trumbo to use his own name rather than an alias on the film's credits. Rabidly right-wing Hedda Hopper (who had once applauded the deportation of Charlie Chaplin by writing "Good riddance to bad rubbish") denounced Douglas in column after column for the perfidy of hiring Trumbo. The American Legion threatened to boycott *Spartacus* and posted pickets at the Los Angeles premiere. "We are against the Commies coming back in the movie world or anywhere else in the U.S.," declared one of the protestors. Despite this virulent opposition, Douglas promptly signed Trumbo to write two subsequent movies, *The Last Sunset* and *Lonely Are the Brave*, one of the first contemporary Westerns chronicling the demise of the cowboy in an urbanized technological society.

Douglas often chose to work with talented new filmmakers, such as Stanley Kubrick, who directed both *Paths of Glory* and *Spartacus*. Kirk hired another rising young talent, John Frankenheimer (who had directed many of the most acclaimed *Playhouse 90* dramas on television), to film *Seven Days in May*, a gripping melodrama about an attempted military coup in the United States. The Bryna Company also produced Frankenheimer's *Seconds* (in which Douglas did not appear). This fascinating tale of a middle-aged man who undergoes radical plastic surgery—John Randolph reborn as Rock Hudson—bombed when it was released in 1966, but it has since turned into a cult favorite. Bryna's 1968 production of *The Brotherhood*, a gangster melodrama directed by Martin Ritt, prefigured *The Godfather* in chronicling the changes within the Mafia as the older generation bound by family loyalty gives way to a corporate-style criminal syndicate presided over by bloodless organization men. All these films demonstrate Douglas's taste for unconventional, provocative material—one of his greatest virtues as a producer.

DESPITE their occasional conflicts, the Douglas family never approached the Gothic extremes of discord and disintegration that typified the lives of so many other movieland dynasties. Even more than the Ladds, who endured their patriarch's recurrent periods of despair and his untimely death, the Douglas family chronicle unfolds in sunlight rather than darkness; there have been no grotesque tragedies or long-standing feuds tearing the family apart. All four of Kirk Douglas's sons appear to have come to terms with the mixed blessing of having a famous name, and all are "functioning," to use their father's word. "I see what has happened to a lot of kids in this profession," Kirk comments, "and so when I look at my kids, it's something to be very grateful for. Selfishly, I'd like to think that maybe I had something to do with it, or their mothers did. Who the hell knows? I don't want to question it. I want to be grateful for it."

If the family can be counted among the surviving, successful Hollywood clans, it may be because Kirk Douglas approached the challenge of raising his children with the same intensity and gusto that he brought to his acting. "He may have been accused of trying too hard as a father," Michael Douglas notes. "He always did everything with great energy." It was almost as if he *willed* the family to be happy, and though reality sometimes tarnished the perfect image he had in mind, that act of will ultimately triumphed.

In 1943, Kirk married Diana Dill, an aristocratic young actress whose background was radically different from his own. Her father had served as Attorney General of Bermuda, and Kirk was mesmerized by her elegant bearing, her slim, willowy figure, and her upper-crust British accent. "I used to follow Diana around just to hear her talk," he once said. The couple had two sons—Michael, born in 1944, and Joel, born in 1947—but the marriage began to sour soon after the family moved from New York to Hollywood. Diana was also acting in movies; her credits included supporting parts in *The Late George Apley*, *House of Strangers*, and *Storm Over Tibet*. The competition to make a name in Hollywood seems to have placed a strain on the relationship. "It's difficult to work out a marriage when both parties are professionals," Diana later said. "There's a conflict of egos there. My wanting to act was an assertion of my own independence." She and Kirk finally separated in 1949, the year of *Champion*'s release.

Kirk regarded the breakup of his marriage to Diana as a crushing personal failure, for it reminded him of the collapse of his parents' marriage. After the divorce, Michael and Joel went to live with their mother back east. Kirk took off for Europe for an extended period and initiated a series of hit-and-run affairs with starlets, the most serious of which was with Pier Angeli, the petite brunette with whom he appeared on screen in *The Story of Three Loves*.

In 1953, he met Anne Buydens, a chic, intelligent, thirty-year-old Belgian woman who served as production coordinator and publicist on two of his European movies, *Act of Love,* a romance co-starring Dany Robin, and *Ulysses*, a gaudy Technicolor rendition of Homer's *Odyssey.* Anne was born into a wealthy Belgian family; her parents separated when she was a child, and her father died soon afterwards. During the German invasion of Belgium, her family lost its fortune. Anne was married briefly during the war, but after separating from her first husband, she had to go to work in order to support herself. The languages she had learned in finishing school enabled her to land jobs writing subtitles for films in Paris and then working as production coordinator for American film companies shooting abroad in the early 1950's; her first major assignment was on John Huston's biography of Toulouse-Lautrec, *Moulin Rouge*, starring José Ferrer. Anne also produced a short-lived television series on French fashions and worked for several years as assistant to the director of the Cannes Film Festival.

Anne found herself attracted to Kirk when she met him, but she was determined to keep her distance. She says today, "I had been working too long in the business not to see that these romances can be very nice when you're on location, but they usually don't last. It's like the shirt that you buy in Mexico. It looks terrific when you're on vacation, and you buy a dozen. By the time you come back to Los Angeles to wear your Mexican shirt, it just looks funny. I did not want to be a Mexican shirt."

Nevertheless, Kirk continued to court Anne even after he returned to America. The couple carried on a trans-Atlantic love affair and were finally married in Las Vegas in 1954. During the early years of their relationship, Kirk was respectful of her professional achievements, but her linguistic ability intimidated him. He recalls seeing her in action at the Cannes Film Festival one year: "I'd hear her talking with someone in Italian and switching to someone else in German, then talking to someone else in French or English. I was quite impressed. That's one of the things that got me learning languages, because I wasn't going to sit there like a dummy while she ordered the meals."

If Kirk's natural competitiveness made the sparks fly in their relationship, it helped that there was no direct career rivalry between them. Anne herself feels that the fact she is not an actress has contributed to the durability of their marriage. They have two children—Peter Vincent (the middle name was for Van Gogh, whom Kirk was playing at the time), born in 1955, and Eric, born in 1958. At her husband's urging, Anne gave up her career while her sons were young and devoted herself to motherhood.

In 1956, Diana Dill Douglas also remarried; her second husband is William Darrid, a New York actor and theatrical producer. Diana and Bill Darrid have remained friendly with Anne and Kirk Douglas. Michael Douglas believes this ongoing cordiality between his parents helped his brother and himself adjust to the divorce. "It was very fortunate," he says. "I remember when we moved back east and my father came to pick us up once, I saw him and my mother kiss each other hello on the cheeks, and I thought, 'It's okay.' They were very careful not to be bad-rapping each other. When each of them remarried, Anne was very good at dealing with us, and my stepfather, Bill Darrid, was extraordinary in the responsibility he took on. And my father was smart enough and understanding enough to appreciate how lucky he was that his past wife remarried this wonderful guy. So to this day, the four of them get together once or twice a month for dinner, with or without the kids. For me and my brother Joel, that was a tremendous plus, because there was a continuity and a dialogue."

Anne Douglas also agrees that the comfortable relations among the present and former spouses has contributed to the well-being of the family. "I was not the person who got in the way of my husband's first marriage," she points out "Diana and Kirk were divorced four years when we met." Anne recalls that when Kirk was casting his first Bryna production, *The Indian Fighter*, he came to her with an unusual request: "Kirk said to me, 'Would you mind if Diana played my wife in the movie? She would be ideal for it.'" Anne agreed that Diana would be perfect for the part. "I was pregnant with Peter at the time," Anne reports. "Michael and Joel stayed with me while Diana was in Oregon making a movie with Kirk. It's really rather amusing. But it started very well. I like Diana very much. She's a terrific lady."

Anne fully understands her husband's motivation for wanting to stay on amicable terms with his former wife. As she once put it, Kirk "has a sense of loyalty and responsibility to his family that borders on a guilt complex. You don't have to be a psychiatrist to realize that this is a compensation for his father's lack of loyalty and responsibility."

Though this friendship among former and present spouses seems genuine, the spectacle of their working and socializing together may appear to some to have an absurdist quality, like something out of a Paul Mazursky movie. Kirk and Anne and Bill and Diana often go to Palm Springs together, and Anne reports, "We have tennis matches, the former and the present Mrs. Kirk Douglas. And Michael and Joel are rooting for their mother, while Peter and Eric are rooting for me. It becomes very amusing, but we do see each other a lot, and there's a very good feeling among all of us. When Michael and his wife had a little boy, Kirk's first grandson, they made me the godmother which I thought was very nice."

Anne's talents for diplomacy have served her well professionally and personally. Still a svelte and elegant woman in her early sixties, she presides over some of the most fashionable parties and charity galas in Hollywood. Now that her children are grown, Anne has resumed her career in the film business as well. She had always kept an eye on Kirk's investments and felt that he was not being well served by his business managers. In time, he came to agree with her. "A person becomes an actor," Kirk comments, "and suddenly he's making money that he never dreamt of, and he's dying to give it to somebody more knowledgeable to take care of. There are many unscrupulous people ready to handle your finances. My wife has a much better business sense than I do. She was the first to begin to see it."

In the late 1960s, Anne took control of business at The Bryna Company. She personally supervises all matters pertaining to the finances of the company and the investments of Kirk's earnings. Their son Peter explains, "My father has fairly vast holdings in real estate, oil and gas investments, in addition to his perpetual profit participations in his films. So my mother handles all of that—rolling it over from one account to another, managing the funds, investing in different kinds of companies. My mother isn't highly educated in those areas, but she's very bright, and she's extremely capable socially. She's able to find and meet the right people—this person who is particularly good with bonds, another person who is good with real estate. She is primarily responsible for cultivating those contacts. She was able to build a very good group of advisors, but she would always second guess every one of them with other people's opinions. She checks and double checks and triple checks everything.

"I think it all goes back to her background. She came from a very wealthy background, but when the Germans raided Belgium, for years she had absolutely nothing. So here is a woman who was very rich, had it all taken away from her, and gradually worked her way back up, and now with my father is rich again. All the more terrifying to ever wind up being poor again. When you've had money, lost it, and finally got it again, you don't ever want to lose it. I think what she learned during that whole period of time was that he who has the gold makes the rules. And I think that's something she used quite shrewdly in business. There is a very animal cunning that she has, and I don't say that contemptuously at all. It's needed in this business particularly, and I think that is a big contribution that I received from her."

As Anne began to assume a pivotal role in the family business, Kirk deferred to her judgment more and more. In 1971, he went to direct his first film in Yugoslavia—*Scalawag*, a failed attempt to create a pirate adventure movie for children. While they were on location, Anne ended up producing the film after Kirk fell out with the original producer. Today, Anne is president of The Bryna Company.

Like Alan Ladd's wife Sue Carol, Anne Douglas has a strong head for business and has managed to parlay her husband's earnings into a sizable fortune. But unlike Sue Carol, who made creative decisions for her husband as well as business ones, Anne Douglas limits herself to financial dealings and does not try to oversee the creative aspects of her husband's career. Their responsibilities are evenly divided, and each basically steers clear of the other's area of expertise. Kirk selects properties, chooses the roles he wants to play, works on the scripts with the writers. "I rarely call on Anne to read a script," Kirk says. "Occasionally, but rarely. She has a point of view, sometimes rather harsh in her judgments of my work. That's her right."

Anne confirms: "I don't have a gift for reading scripts. That is not where my capabilities are. If there's something about a contract or financing that I don't know, I can call up fourteen people, and they all help me to make my decision. Whereas Kirk can call up fourteen people, and they will all give him different reasons why he should do a movie or shouldn't do it. It only gets him more confused. I feel my job is a lot easier."

For his part, Kirk is reluctant to intrude on Anne's handling of business matters. "I have no interest in that area," he insists. "Sometimes I have an idea or two, but I would much rather spend the whole day working with someone on a script. I think *I* have an easier time of it. I try to get Anne to ease off, let somebody else take care of those responsibilities. But she's very conscientious, and I think it fulfills something within her."

* * *

IN relating to their famous father, the sons of Kirk Douglas have faced problems similar to those of other stars' children. Kirk was an extraordinarily demanding parent. "He was tough, really tough," Michael notes. "There was a question of whether you could ever be the man that your father was. I think ultimately that toughness has been a benefit to all his sons, although it was a real close call. Some of that quality that was larger-than-life on the screen—that presence, that anger—was carried over into his own life. We were in awe of his anger. That was definitely one side of him. On the other side, he had an enthusiasm and love and energy. I was amazed at his incredible energy level, his phenomenal stamina. Surprisingly, I wasn't in awe of him as a screen fixture. Only on a couple of occasions. When I was very young and saw *Champion*, the performance was so intense that it gave me a visceral feeling that Dad's hurt. And I remember when we saw *Lust for Life*, my brother Joel ran out of the theater. He was devastated by it and really thought Daddy cut off his ear."

As they grew older, the Douglas boys were subjected to the same envy and resentment that other celebrities' children have protested. "If someone meets me and knows who my father is," Michael says, "it allows that person to presume a lot of things about me—where I grew up, what my economic background is, who my friends are. And the assumption is, 'Well, he's got to be an asshole, so I'm going to ignore him.' I went around smelling my armpits, thinking, 'What did I do?' Then later I realized it had nothing to do with me."

Ten years later, Michael's half-brother Peter faced similar problems. "In my teens," he recalls, "I found a lot of resentment toward the fact that my family had money, resentment toward the glamorous world that they thought I moved in." He contrasts his reaction to Michael's: "I focused on the benefits of my upbringing. I'd traveled all over the world, met all kinds of people, been fascinated by many different things. And so when I was a teenager, I found myself drawn to older people. That was probably a defensive reaction, anticipating the reactions of my peers, and finding it much more comfortable to feel aloof. I chose not to belong."

As they grew older, Michael and Peter again responded in different ways to the natural urge toward independence and self-expression. Michael went through what he calls a "hippie period" in the 1960s. During his first year at the University of California, Santa Barbara, he flunked out of school. For a while he lived in a commune, made pottery, meditated, smoked pot, and experimented with LSD. A decade later, Peter also dropped out of college, but in his case it was because he had an obsessive desire to make his own living, an appetite for work not unlike his father's. Peter had jobs as a photographer while still a teenager, and he established himself as something of an entrepreneur. "For example, I did a feature story for *Cosmopolitan*, 'Camping the Baja Peninsula By Air,'" he recalls. "The real basis for that was that I was a pilot and I wanted to fly a twin Beechcraft and just couldn't afford it. So I put together a deal with Beechcraft and *Cosmopolitan* and Coleman camping gear to do this expedition. I guess what I'm saying about myself is that I never considered myself such a great photographer as I did a concept-maker, a deal-maker. I really wanted to work. I was thrilled with the prospect of being able to make my own money. To a certain extent, that came out of a desire to establish my own identity, though I wasn't consciously aware of it at the time."

The commitment to work seems to have characterized all the Douglas sons. Even Michael outgrew his "hippie phase" in record time. After his parents demanded that he support himself, he took a job pumping gas and soon won an award as "Mobil Man of the Month."

One of the amusing perplexities of the Douglas family is how thoroughly the sons inherited their father's drive and compulsive desire to achieve, even though they grew up in a radically dissimilar environment. "I've often said to my kids that they did not have my advantages," Kirk Douglas reflects. "I had the advantage of being born in abject poverty. I had nowhere to go but up. If my father was Kirk Douglas, a rich movie star, I don't know what I would have done. I might have become a playboy, a polo player—who knows? I have great admiration for my kids because they all have a drive. Maybe I contributed in some way. I remember once telling Eric, 'I don't know what's the matter with you kids today. When we were young kids, we'd steal a couple of potatoes, make a little fire in the gutter, roast the potatoes, and have a ball.' And he said, 'Oh, Dad, I'd love to do that. I can just see it, making a fire in the gutter in Beverly Hills. The police would be here so fast.' He's right. I sometimes make those trite remarks about poverty, and once Eric said, 'Listen, Dad, if you wanted me to know how it is to be poor, why didn't you bring me up that way?' That's a brilliant remark. A kid can't be penalized because he sees Gregory Peck and Burt Lancaster coming over to the house when he's growing up."

Unlike many self-made men, Kirk Douglas tends to scoff at the idea that poverty builds strength of character. "I'm against a boy having to work his way through school the way I did," he has said. "It's a waste of precious time . . . It took me years to concentrate on being a human being—I was too busy scrounging for money and food, and struggling to better myself." He wanted his own children to have the benefits that he could afford to give them. At the same time he was leery of making things too easy for his sons. To this day, he believes unquestioningly in the work ethic.

Peter describes the "double messages" he received while growing up: "We had a beautiful house, beautiful cars, the swimming pool, and the tennis court. Then when I was in college living on my own, I asked, 'Should my parents maintain my standards, or should they say you're on your own now?' Those areas became difficult for me. And my parents were confused by it, too. They were concerned that, by giving me everything, I would have no motivation. And yet they didn't want to deprive me. Quite often I felt manipulated because the approach was not consistent. At times they would indulge me and at other times cut off the support. It was sort of a yo-yo. They never denied me the help. But it wasn't given without a lecture or two: 'Sure, we'd be delighted to help, but . . .' It made me feel very insecure. I wanted to make it on my own, but sometimes it wasn't all that easy. Sometimes I had to compromise and take money from them. All of that confusion created a lot of conflicts. I went through a rough period with my parents in my later teens, when I was just starting to go out on my own. Ultimately there was only one resolution, and that was independence."

KIRK discouraged his sons from acting. "I always warned them that it's a heartbreaking profession, so full of rejection," he explains. "But if I could talk somebody out of going into this profession, then they shouldn't be in it. Nobody could talk me out of it. People said to me, 'Are you crazy? What are your chances?' Either you want to do it or you don't."

Despite his father's warnings, when Michael returned to UC Santa Barbara, he entered the drama department and found a vocation that inspired him. Before long, he invited his father to see him in a production of *As You Like It*. After the performance, Michael gingerly asked Kirk what he thought. "You were terrible,"

Kirk said bluntly. "I couldn't understand a single thing you were saying."

Kirk recalls now, "I thought, 'Well, that'll take care of that. He'll become a lawyer.' A couple of months later, he called me to come and see him act again. I was surprised; he had improved and really was very good. He won a best acting prize and a directing prize, and so he came into the profession."

Michael found work in regional theater and co-starred in a CBS TV movie called *The Experiment* opposite Ann Sothern's daughter, Tisha Sterling. That led to a contract with the network's newly-formed (and short-lived) theatrical film unit, Cinema Center Films. "We all have our brief gaudy hour," Michael notes sardonically. His first picture was a tepid anti-war drama called *Hail, Hero!* which, Michael jokes, "still has the record of the lowest attendance of any picture to play at the Radio City Music Hall." At many showings, the Rockettes outnumbered the paying customers.

Michael was quickly typecast as a brooding young man pitted against the Establishment—in Cinema Center's *Adam at 6 A.M.* and in *Summertree*, another anti-war play based on a play he had performed in Connecticut. The film of *Summertree* was produced by The Bryna Company; while doing it, Michael fell in love with his co-star, Brenda Vaccaro, with whom he lived for several years. (They never worked together in another film, but Brenda received an Academy Award nomination when she appeared with Kirk Douglas in *Jacqueline Susann's Once Is Not Enough*.) Soon after Michael and Brenda broke up, Michael met a pretty, twenty-one-year-old Georgetown student named Diandra Luker at Jimmy Carter's inaugural ball. Michael and Diandra were married a few months later.

Michael's early bid for stardom fizzled. His performances in *Adam at 6 A.M.*, *Summertree*, and in a stiff little Disney picture called *Napoleon and Samantha*, were callow and unmemorable. The films were all box office duds, and as Michael admits, "My gaudy hour was over." When the movie offers stopped coming, he turned to television. He had appeared in an episode of *The FBI* for producer Quinn Martin, who remembered him when casting his new police series, *Streets of San Francisco*, in 1972. The star of the series was Karl Malden, who had worked with Michael's father thirty years earlier. "The first time I met Michael," Malden recalls, "I was coming in to try on some clothes for Quinn Martin. Michael was in the office. Quinn introduced him as Michael Douglas. I said, 'Kirk's son? That's good enough.' He got the part. I think he learned how to act doing that series. After the first season, I went to the producers and writers and said, 'Give Michael more to do. Michael can handle it. If the show's going to last, they'll get so damn tired of me.' And the second year, they started to give Michael more. Television is the best training an actor can have, because you learn all the tricks, and you can see your mistakes and correct them the next week."

The validity of Karl Malden's observation about television as a training ground for actors is made clear by comparing Michael Douglas's performances before *Streets of San Francisco* with his performances afterwards. While he may not have become an inspired actor during his four seasons on the series, he did become a professional—relaxed, assured, completely credible on camera. "When you're in television, you get an unbelievable amount of weekly attention," Michael says. "Knowing how to handle that comes from at an early age watching your father handle autographs in restaurants, learning from him how to get through a crowd, ways to handle yourself diplomatically and yet efficiently. Also, it helps that all your life you've seen major stars and heads of agencies or heads of studios as real, silly people with their own vulnerabilities, no matter what their position might be. There is no larger-than-life impression."

After a few seasons on *Streets of San Francisco*, Michael decided to follow his father's example once again and try his hand at producing. It is worth emphasizing that Michael's biggest success as a producer, *One Flew Over the Cuckoo's Nest*, grew out of his father's shrewd instincts more than his own. It was Kirk who bought the stage and film rights to Ken Kesey's novel in 1962, when Kesey was an all but unknown writer. Kirk brought the play to Broadway in November of 1963, savoring the role of the misfit McMurphy waging war against the authoritarian doctors and nurses in a mental hospital. Kirk was supported by a cast that included William Daniels and Gene Wilder as follow inmates in the asylum. The reviews were mixed. Not a single one of the New York critics seems to have been familiar with Kesey's novel; they all admitted that they had not read it, and several had not even heard of it. Writing in the *Herald Tribune*, Walter Kerr denounced the play for "the extraordinary tastelessness with which it has been conceived." Howard Taubman of the *New York Times* struck the same note when he called the play's jokes, "either embarrassing or in appalling taste."

A few reviews were more favorable, but critics and audiences alike seemed bewildered by Kesey's irreverent approach to mental illness, a subject which had previously been treated in only the most solemn terms. Kesey's book was one of the first to popularize the Laingian notion that what psychiatrists label "schizophrenia" may simply be unconventional or socially undesirable behavior. In 1963, *One Flew Over the Cuckoo's Nest* had not yet achieved its cult status and become a favorite text in high school and college courses. (The book would eventually sell eleven million copies.)

"When I did the play on Broadway, I realized that New York in many ways can be provincial," Kirk Douglas now observes. "I don't know whether the tall buildings block them in, but very often I find that they don't have as much of a vision as they think they have. There's a certain snobbery in the literary group in the East. If Ken Kesey had been an Eastern writer, I think he would have been treated differently. He's from Oregon. His father is in the dairy business. To be accepted then, you had to be in a loft in Greenwich Village. I don't think the critics knew how to deal with *Cuckoo's Nest*. I remember Mia Farrow was just sixteen or seventeen then and used to come over quite often to see the show. Her mother, Maureen O'Sullivan, was in a hit play across the street, *Never Too Late*. And at the same time, the *New York Times* would write about Walter Kerr's wife's play, *Mary, Mary*. I said to my wife, 'Goddammit, years from now they'll forget about those two plays. I brought a classic to Broadway, but they don't know it.' "

The play ran less than six months, and Douglas returned to Hollywood, determined to put *Cuckoo's Nest* on film. He hit a roadblock when the author of the play, Dale Wasserman, claimed legal rights to the film and stage version. Wasserman and Douglas tangled in a lawsuit that was not settled until 1966, when Douglas won the film rights while Wasserman retained stage rights.

That delay undoubtedly hurt Kirk's chances of making *Cuckoo's Nest* into a film. All the major studios considered the material dangerously offbeat and depressing, but by the end of the decade, the book was developing a strong campus following, and other filmmakers, including Peter Fonda, expressed interest in buying it from Douglas. He held on to the property, although he recognized that he was getting too old to play McMurphy himself. "After ten years, I didn't know what to do with the project," Kirk says. "And Michael said to me, 'Dad, can I try to run with it?' I said, 'Go ahead. We'll become partners. See what you can do.' Of course, he found no studio would put up the money, and eventually he found outside financing. I always loved the project, but I don't want to give the impression that I was smart enough to predict that it would be the tremendous hit that it was. I thought on a low budget it would do moderately well. I didn't expect it to gross $200 million. So we all did well on that, and I realized that Michael had a talent for production."

Michael's main contribution as producer was his persistence in the face of repeated rejections. Eventually, he persuaded Saul Zaentz of Fantasy Records to put up the money for the film. When Zaentz and Douglas saw a rough cut of *The Last Detail*, they decided Jack Nicholson was the only actor who had the right magnetism and physical energy to embody McMurphy. As it happened, Nicholson was a fan of the book, and he eagerly signed on. With Nicholson in the lead, the film's budget jumped from $1.5 million to $3 million, but it was still a relatively inexpensive film for the time. (That Jack Nicholson should have inherited the role from Kirk Douglas is logical, for Nicholson is one of the few actors of his generation keeping Douglas's extroverted, no-holds-barred style of acting alive.)

Although *Cuckoo's Nest* can be criticized for its simplistic ideas about madness and sanity, and for its misogynistic portrait of the tyrannical Nurse Ratched, there is no arguing with its skillful direction and superb ensemble acting. Of his father's reaction to his success with the project, Michael now says, "There were some mixed feelings. There had to be since he had bought the novel and played the part on Broadway. The only thing that counteracted his disappointment was the fact that it was a good picture. My father had enough appreciation of the picture that turned out. He was a *mensch* about it, and a major supporter of Jack Nicholson, as Jack was of him. We all knew his love for the project. Plus, he had a percentage of the film and did very well. I still joke with him about the initial negotiations when I was first acquiring it. He's a very tough deal-maker."

After *Cuckoo's Nest*, Michael went on to produce *The China Syndrome*, demonstrating a shrewd dramatic and commercial instinct of his own. In 1976, he had read a script about the nuclear power industry by a documentary filmmaker named Mike Gray. Gray was based in Chicago and operated far outside the Hollywood power structure; his previous effort, *The Murder of Fred Hampton*, was a stark exposé of police persecution of the Black Panthers. Douglas immediately recognized the potential importance of a film pointing up the dangers of nuclear energy. Originally, Douglas cast Richard Dreyfuss as a documentary filmmaker who unlocks the cover-up of a nuclear accident. But Dreyfuss dropped out because he wanted more money and because he felt the story had lost its urgency. ("Now that Carter is President," Dreyfuss ingenuously remarked, "we don't have to worry about nuclear power anymore.") Some Columbia executives suggested to Douglas that there might be a way of combining his project with one Jane Fonda was developing about Karen Silkwood, the young woman who was killed in a mysterious automobile accident after she threatened to go public with information about dangerous conditions at the plutonium processing plant in which she worked. Fonda was having trouble securing the legal rights to the Silkwood story; Douglas suggested that the male documentary filmmaker in his script be changed to a female TV reporter so that Fonda could play the role. She was excited by the premise of Douglas's movie and agreed to co-star with Jack Lemmon in the production.

The China Syndrome might have been a better film if Douglas had stuck with Mike Gray's original script and hired Gray as director, as he had first planned. But Fonda argued for a more mainstream approach to the subject than the gritty, documentary-like style that Gray envisioned; she wanted the film to be accessible to the largest possible audience, and a less audacious filmmaker, James Bridges, was brought in to replace Gray. Despite Bridges's lackluster direction, the inherent power of the subject matter and the gripping narrative remained intact. Michael Douglas's original approach might have been stronger artistically, but Jane Fonda's instincts were well-grounded commercially, and there was no denying that the movie helped to stir public concern over nuclear proliferation.

Spokesmen for the nuclear industry mounted a full-scale publicity campaign to challenge the film's message. Before its release, Southern California Edison charged that *The China Syndrome* had "no scientific credibility and is, in fact, ridiculous," while General Electric withdrew its sponsorship of a Barbara Walters television special that contained an interview with Fonda. On March 27, conservative columnist George F. Will attacked the film in *Newsweek* for perpetuating the myth that nuclear power plants were unsafe. The very next day, at the Three Mile Island nuclear reactor outside Harrisburg, Pennsylvania, a devastating accident took place which almost exactly duplicated the scenario for disaster prophesied in *The China Syndrome*: a "turbine trip" occurred, caused by a stuck valve and a vibrating cooling pump. But unlike the accident portrayed at the fictitious plant in *The China Syndrome*, radiation actually escaped into the atmosphere at Three Mile Island, forcing a massive evacuation of the area. The disaster happened just twelve days after *The China Syndrome* opened, providing a grim verification of the film's ominous warning. Michael Douglas was at home in Santa Barbara the morning of the accident; his wife Diandra heard the news on the car radio and rushed back to inform Michael. "It was the closest thing I ever had to a religious experience," he said afterwards. "I was stunned, scared, shaken up. You heard your script on the news. And you felt like it was ordained. You felt some logic. It went way beyond being a coincidence."

The movie went on to become one of the most talked about and financially successful films of the year, grossing more than $60 million. With his profits from *The China Syndrome* and *Cuckoo's Nest*, Michael Douglas has acquired a substantial fortune of his own. His father tells a wry story to describe Michael's transformation from hippie dropout to wealthy tycoon. "In college, Michael lived like a bum," Kirk recalls. "He had an old, ramshackle place near the University of California in Santa Barbara. I remember when I went up to visit him once, he slept on the floor, and he had me sleep in his single spring bed. I finally said to him, 'Michael, I spent my whole life trying to get *out* of a place like this. Next time I'm going to be at the hotel. If you want to see me, you can visit me there.' Today, Michael has a big estate overlooking the Pacific, not far from that ramshackle place in Santa Barbara. But I think he can handle it. I wrote a note to Michael once after he did *Cuckoo's Nest* and *China Syndrome*. Very simply, I said, 'Michael, I want you to know that I'm more proud of how you have handled your success than I am of your success.' That affected him. He understood the compliment."

MICHAEL'S three brothers are less firmly established in the movie industry. They have had to follow not just a successful father but a successful older brother as well. Kirk's second son, Joel, has understandably kept a lower profile, working behind the scenes as a production manager and associate producer on a number of television shows and films (including *One Flew Over the Cuckoo's Nest*). In 1983, he bought a small studio in Mexico and produced a low-budget romantic melodrama, *Torchlight*.

Peter Vincent Douglas, the first son born to Kirk and his second wife Anne, comments on his own response to Kirk's and Michael's success. "It doesn't intimidate me," Peter claims. "It motivates me. I find what it's done is make me tough, and I am not by nature a very tough individual." Peter came into the industry very early, and of all the Douglas sons, he has spent the most time working with his father. When he was nineteen, he served as post-production supervisor on Kirk's movie, *Posse*. Around the same time, Peter persuaded his father to buy the rights to Ray Bradbury's fantasy novel, *Something Wicked This Way Comes*, for The Bryna Company. Both father and son responded to Bradbury's tale of a sinister carnival troupe that comes into a small midwestern town and disrupts the placid life of the community.

There were to be many delays before *Something Wicked* finally reached the screen, but in the meantime Peter produced his first film for The Bryna Company, *The Final Countdown*, starring Kirk and Martin Sheen. That was in 1978, when Peter was twenty-three. It was he who conceived this rather ridiculous story about a nuclear aircraft carrier sailing through a time warp and transported back to Pearl Harbor on the eve of the Japanese attack. "It was a film that I got into because of my love for flying," Peter explains. "I wanted to have a ride in an F-14 off the deck of a carrier. So I came up with a film that would give me the chance to do that." Whether or not that is a reasonable motivation for making a $12 million movie is certainly open to question. In any event, the picture turned out to be a turgid, unconvincing potboiler.

During the filming of *The Final Countdown*, Peter found himself embroiled in family quarrels that eventually led to his leaving The Bryna Company. The most bitter conflicts were not with his father but with his mother. Anne Douglas claims that the friction developed because of her refusal to countenance Peter's extravagance. "Peter was actually producing the picture," she says, "whereas I was holding the purse strings. I was getting Peter's pre-production expense accounts, and I said to him, 'I'm sorry, I will not permit that. At your age, I don't feel one has to go to '21' for lunch or to stay at the Dorset Hotel like your father. You want to be hired again by these people. They're putting up $12 million, an awful lot of money. I want you to prove to them that you're going to hold the budget down.' When he was on location, he insisted on having his own apartment while the rest of the crew was living at a little motel. I wanted him to live with the crew at the motel. I didn't always get my way, but at least I made the point. By now, Peter is older, and I hope that he knows on his next picture he'd better stay with the crew. That's where he belongs."

Peter, however, sees the tension deriving from his mother's own position in The Bryna Company and her fear that her son might usurp it. "My father has visions of all his sons together in this family dynasty, and yet what he forgets in those visions is my mother, who's an equal partner and who may at times not agree and may even resent some of his views," Peter says. "When I was working at The Bryna Company, my father gave me a great deal of freedom, and this led to major rows between him and my mother, who felt that I was getting too much. She was concerned as a mother that maybe I was experiencing these things too soon and too fast, and that I might find myself in other situations expecting the same freedom. But beyond that, I suspect she was also a little bit threatened. My mother enjoyed her position in the company. It was a base of control and power for her, not only in the family, but in the industry, the town. None of this was discussed. I think my father felt that my mother would like to be out of the company and be relieved of all the burden. And my mother did act with that pretense. She presented that point of view, but I think that while there *was* a burden and while she might like to alleviate the burden, she derived satisfaction from her position that she was not yet willing to let go of. Unfortunately, that was never communicated. I suppose if there is one single issue that created the most problems with my family, it was the lack of honest emotional communication. Emotions were always hidden in my mother's case. She is very emotional but would keep it all inside, and it was therefore hard to understand just what was going on. My father would explode and get it all out."

Eventually, Peter decided that he had no choice but to sink or swim on his own. "Everything was becoming a fight," he says of his last days working for The Bryna Company. "I was getting involved in a lot of areas that belonged to my mother, and she didn't want that. My mother was a much more complex matrix in this whole scenario than even my father realized at the time. He has gradually become aware of it. So, in a sense, I feel good that, with all the rows that ultimately caused me to leave, it promoted a better understanding between my mother and father. They're closer now than they've ever been."

As part of the agreement reached when Peter left the company, he took *Something Wicked* with him and eventually produced it at the Disney Studio. Jack Clayton, a perfectionist director who had not made a movie since *The Great Gatsby* in 1974, was so painstakingly slow that the budget for the film (which had first been set at $6 million) eventually leapt to $22 million. The result, panned by most critics, was a commercial catastrophe. Disney listed it as a $21 million loss.

Peter has had several other projects in development. Of his position in the industry, he says, "I'm not making a fortune, but I'm making a comfortable living. Now that I'm on my own, I have the self-confidence and the independence necessary to be friends with my parents. And I guess, more specifically, I accept them for who and what they are. I don't try to change them, and I'm not crushed by their wanting to change me."

Unlike his three older brothers, Kirk Douglas's youngest son, Eric, has shown no interest in producing movies. Instead, he wants to be an actor. He has appeared in a few off-Broadway plays, and had a small part in his father's TV movie, *Remembrance of Love*; he played Kirk's character as a boy. The resemblance between father and son is not merely physical. "Eric very often irritates me," Kirk says, "because I see so much of myself in him. Parts of myself that I don't like—his volatile temper and all that. Eric was interested in acting from an early age. He was the only one." There is, of course, one crucial difference between Kirk and Eric Douglas. One is the child of a junk peddler, the other of a famous movie star. Kirk understands this, but he refuses to let Eric feel sorry for himself on account of his pedigree or allow him to use it as an excuse for failure. "Recently, Eric said to me, 'Dad, you don't know how difficult it is being the son of Kirk Douglas.' So I said to him, 'Then change your name. I changed mine. You think it's that tough, don't be Eric Douglas, be Eric Smith. You have my permission.' I'm not going to take any of that crap. Being the son of a movie star has its advantages, and it has its disadvantages. That's life."

NONE of the Douglases is completely free of professional problems. Kirk and Michael certainly have no financial worries, but their careers are in a state of flux. In the last decade Kirk's reputation has been hurt by an unfortunate selection of poor roles in worse movies—*Once Is Not Enough*, *The Fury*, *Home Movies*, *The Villain*, and *Eddie Macon's Run*. If Kirk has continued to hold his position as a major star, it is mainly because of his appeal overseas. His most successful project of the last decade came in 1982. He appeared in a small Australian film, *The Man From Snowy River*, a box office hit all over the world. Kirk owns fifteen percent of the U.S.-Canadian grosses (which have reached over

$20 million), but in September 1983 he filed suit against the film's producers, claiming that he had not been paid all monies due him.

His wife Anne would prefer that Kirk work less often now and hold out for films of quality. "I don't want him to do anything any more because he has to bring in the bread," she notes. "I'd rather invest the money in a different way. I feel he has earned the stripes now. He can afford to say, 'No, thank you, this part is one I've already played so many times. I'm waiting until that big plum falls off the tree right in front of me.' I think he should do that. On the other hand, he's very unhappy when he doesn't work."

Kirk Douglas's predicament is one that many aging stars have faced. As his son Peter says, "He's a good-looking guy in his sixties who still has a physique of a thirty-year-old man. I'm embarrassed to take my shirt off around him in Palm Springs. And yet he doesn't fulfill the needs of the studio's leading men. He's lost his perspective on what the audience accepts or wants to see him as. For any actor whose prime was as a young rebel, it's hard to forget that you're no longer a young rebel, that you're now an elder statesman who can't play those same roles."

Early in his career, Kirk Douglas gave up his dream of Broadway stardom and reluctantly embarked on a career in the "second-rate" medium of the movies. Lately, his feature film roles have become less and less distinguished, and he has made another career move—to the third-rate medium of television. *The Moneychangers* and *Victory at Entebbe* were both hits on the small screen, and *Remembrance of Love*, the Holocaust soap opera in which he starred with Pam Dawber, even beat out Monday Night Football in the Nielsen ratings. Nonetheless, though television may give him the chance to keep on working, it is doubtful that it will ever offer the opportunity to perform the kinds of memorable roles he played earlier in his career. For one thing, the material is weaker, and for another, there aren't great directors like Billy Wilder, Joseph L. Mankiewicz, Stanley Kubrick, or Elia Kazan with whom he can collaborate.

THOUGH he is twenty-eight years younger than his father, Michael Douglas has also had some trouble retaining his standing in the industry. He produced one movie right after *The China Syndrome*, a piece of post-*Rocky* jock schlock called *Running*, in which he starred as a middle-class loser trying to race his way out of oblivion (which is where the movie itself promptly landed.) Other projects he was hoping to produce failed to win studio approval. In 1983,

Michael finally began his first production in four years, a light-hearted adventure film called *Romancing the Stone*, from a script submitted to him by a Malibu waitress. The movie was obviously influenced by *Raiders of the Lost Ark*, but re-written from a woman's point of view. The central character is a romance novelist (played by Kathleen Turner) who gets embroiled in a treasure hunt in the jungles of Colombia. Michael's skills as a producer show in the spectacular effects he achieved on a skimpy $9.5 million budget. The film grossed over $95 million to become one of 1984's biggest hits. Michael was also executive producer of Columbia's science fiction thriller, *Star Man*, with Jeff Bridges and Karen Allen.

Michael's biggest dilemma has been in deciding what kinds of films he wants to produce. "I have these two films of socially redeeming value [*One Flew Over the Cuckoo's Nest* and *The China Syndrome*] staring me in the face," he notes. "I have not found anything that can match those. I remember after we finished *Cuckoo's Nest*, Milos Forman said to me, 'Mikey, it's all downhill from here on.' You've got to be a fool not to see that."

Michael has now chosen to concentrate more on acting, where he still feels the need to prove himself. "In acting, I feel I haven't yet come close to doing what I'm capable of doing," he explains. His father has advised Michael to devote more time to acting than producing, for he recognizes that a producer's "talent" may be hard to identify and build upon. "Michael hasn't really scratched the surface of his abilities as an actor," Kirk says. "He's an excellent producer, but I don't really know what a producer is. I've been making movies for over thirty years, and I still wonder, what's a producer? You know, sometimes a guy says he wants to be in pictures. So you ask him 'You got $10 million? You're the producer.'"

The only problem with Michael's decision to focus on acting is that he has had difficulty establishing any distinctive talent in that area. He has given competent and likable performances in *Coma*, *The China Syndrome*, and *It's My Turn*, but he seemed indistinguishable from many other blandly good-looking, stolid leading men. He has yet to demonstrate the magnetism that made his father a star of the first rank. Writing in *The New Yorker*, Renata Adler noted that Michael "doesn't have the presence, the controlled intensity and magnetic isolation, of a true cinema maverick."

One reason why Michael may not have come into his own as an actor is his fear of competing with his father. At least that is his own theory. "I censored a part of myself which I felt was similar to my father—the part of me that had his anger," Michael says. "I don't know if it was a mistake. But now I'm more open. I've gone over that hurdle. It's interesting that, before *Champion*, my father played five or six 'sensitive young man' roles. Recently, I've seen a similar progression in my own career. I've played those sensitive roles. Now I'm looking for what I call a prick role or a very physical role—something I know I could do easily and I would enjoy doing, but which I shied away from for a long time. My father always teases me that I'm the biggest killer of the family cloaked in this diplomatic style. I think he's right. If I have to turn killer, I can do it." In concealing that part of himself, Michael may well have stifled his most exciting potentialities as an actor. His lusty, hard-edged performance as the soldier of fortune in *Romancing the Stone* suggests that he is taking his father's prodding seriously. It is his most charismatic piece of acting to date, and it is the performance in which he most clearly emulates the unbridled energy of his father.

Yet in some fundamental way, one suspects that Kirk and Michael are different personalities. "Michael has an awful lot of his mother in him," Karl Malden suggests. "His mother is charming, generous, soft, and that's where Michael gets a lot of those qualities." These differences between Kirk and Michael may also have something to do with their respective upbringings. Kirk Douglas is still in a hurry, still a workaholic, always driving himself and others, as if desperate to prove that he is not just the son of a junk dealer from Amsterdam, New York. As one of his directors, Melville Shavelson, wrote, "The hungry, restless battler of *Champion* is still fighting, several million dollars later, slugging his way toward some invisible championship that continues, apparently, to elude him."

Michael says of his father's generation, "My father came out of poverty and subscribed to the work ethic. It's admirable in many ways. He worked hard, achieved, and was successful. The bad side of it is that all he knows how to do is work. Once he achieved success, it was hard for him to enjoy it, to savor it. I had a different background, so I feel more like a surfer waiting for waves; there are going to be lulls. And that's the way I approach things; I don't try to force them. I've been trying to tell my father for a long time to simplify his operation. I tell him, 'You don't have to run through airports; you can walk, smell the flowers.'

That's where he thinks I'm lazy. Yeah, I'm lazy. I'm open to other perspectives.''

If the Douglas boys all seem to have inherited some of their father's drive, Kirk may also have learned something from their more easygoing manner. Michael recalls a conversation he had with Kirk not long ago: "My father and I have been getting along really well lately, and he said to me, 'Well, Michael, you've finally changed. You've grown up.' I said, 'Did you ever consider the fact that maybe *you've* changed? Maybe you've mellowed out, maybe you're more relaxed, maybe you're not pushing so hard?' He told a couple of his friends what I said, and they said, 'No shit, Kirk, he might be right.' But he has a style, which is the offensive, go-for-it, aggressive tone. It's not mine, but I've come to be really amazed and impressed by him.''

Kirk's feeling for his sons is the glue that binds the family together. As his wife Anne says, "To this day, Kirk's one desire and one love is to be with his four sons. Actually, women could disappear until they're called in. His best times are when his sons take him out for a birthday, and there are just the four boys and him. That is his greatest joy, and I think in a way they all feel that. They know they are very important to their father, and he would do anything for them.''

Given his feeling for his sons, Kirk is understandably disappointed that they have all left The Bryna Company to work on their own. "It's difficult for kids to work for their father," Kirk sighs. "It's a normal love-hate thing. Every son wants to kick his father in the balls at least twice. Sometimes I think I've got it three times. My four sons have all worked for me, or with me, for short periods of time. But I don't think they particularly liked working with me. They'd rather be on their own. I understand the desire to express themselves. They don't want to be just Kirk Douglas's sons.''

Looking back on the failure of Kirk's dream to create a family business, Anne Douglas says, "I never felt it would work, not because they don't love each other very much, but in a way all four of the boys see their father as bigger than life. There's no way they could compete with that, so they have to find their own identity and make their own niche. If it's The Bryna Company, a family enterprise, they feel everybody will say, 'Oh, that's Kirk Douglas's company.' I understand that fully. Maybe one day before we are too old, when they have all made it on their own, they might say, 'Now we are ready.' And then people won't say it's

Kirk Douglas's company. They will say it's The Douglas Company. That is really Kirk's biggest dream. I hope we get to see it."

In the final analysis, Kirk Douglas's greatest legacy to his sons may not be a place in the company he created but the spirit of independence which inspired them to leave it. "My father was the first actor to set up an independent company," Michael notes. "And he's always had a vision that his sons would take over his company and continue it. That is practiced in every other business, whether it's a plumbing company or a law firm; sons take over from their father. But I always try to explain to my father that he should take it as a great compliment that we all went into his business, and that he was able to give us enough of an incentive that we wanted to do it on our own."

The Douglases disprove Tolstoy's famous statement that all happy families are alike. This is a group of distinctive, complex, competitive individuals who have fought hard at times but have managed to survive the petty squabbles and occasional breaches. Despite their conflicts, they have found the maturity to remain friends—the greatest challenge and achievement for a family. Their separate fates in the movie business may still be unresolved, but at least they *have* succeeded in resolving the internal tensions that plague so many other Hollywood dynasties.

8

HOUSE OF STRANGERS:
The Mankiewiczes

"For people who have never learned to communicate to each other, it's curious that we love communication so much. Other families who are far more taciturn and less verbal succeed in communicating love and more basic emotions better than we ever did."

—CHRISTOPHER MANKIEWICZ

AROUND the time that a little boy named Jackie Cooper first stole the hearts of American moviegoers, the Man of Steel from the planet Krypton made his debut in the pages of Action Comics. Half a century later, Jackie Cooper was playing Perry White, the irascible editor of the "Daily Planet," in the all-star movie version of *Superman*. During a break in the shooting, Cooper turned to Tom Mankiewicz, the movie's "creative consultant" and the last in a string of highly-paid screenwriters. "I just realized something," Cooper confided to Mankiewicz. "I've been in the business for fifty years. And if I get hit by a bus tomorrow, the first picture I ever made was written by your old man, and the last one will have been written by you." That first picture, *Skippy*, was released in 1931, and was among the earliest screenwriting credits of Tom's distinguished father, Joseph L. Mankiewicz.

Tom's cousin, Don Mankiewicz, tells another anecdote to illustrate the professional longevity of this exceptional family. In 1982, while working as story editor on ABC's hit TV series *Hart to Hart*, Don was accosted by an aged Arab extra hired to play a sheik for a scene set in a gambling casino. "Mank!" the Arab cried.

Don stared at the extra and drew a blank.

243

"Don't you remember me?" the Arab persisted. "I am Abdullah! From Paramount."

Don Mankiewicz had never been employed at Paramount, but his father Herman, to whom he bore an uncanny resemblance, was under contract there in the 1920s. "I began to understand," Don says. "Abdullah must have worked on *Son of the Sheik* or something like that at Paramount, where my father wrote about 150 silent pictures. This guy was only fifty years out of sync!"

The Mankiewicz clan has been a fixture in Hollywood from the silent days right up to the present. This in itself is remarkable, but what may be even more remarkable is the nature of their accomplishments. They are a family of wits and intellectuals in an industry overrun with dunces and boors. Consider their credentials: Herman Mankiewicz won a screenwriting Oscar for co-authoring *Citizen Kane*, frequently cited as the greatest film ever made. His brother, Joseph L. Mankiewicz, has the unprecedented distinction of winning four Academy Awards in the space of two years—for writing and directing *A Letter to Three Wives* and *All About Eve*, a pair of acerbic comic masterpieces. Joseph's son Tom contributed not only to *Superman* but to several of the stylish James Bond movies of the 1970s. Herman's son Don wrote a prize-winning novel, *Trial*, was nominated for an Academy Award for co-writing *I Want To Live!*, and created several long-running TV series. His brother Frank was Robert Kennedy's press secretary, director of George McGovern's presidential campaign, a syndicated columnist, and head of National Public Radio. Their sister Johanna was a novelist and a writer for *Time* magazine until her accidental death in 1974, and Johanna's husband, Peter Davis, produced and directed such highly regarded documentaries as *Hearts and Minds* and *The Selling of the Pentagon*. Frank's son Josh is an ABC TV correspondent, while Don's daughter Jane is a *New Yorker* writer and his son John is a budding young screenwriter. Even a distant cousin from the Canadian branch of the family, Francis Mankiewicz, won the Canadian equivalent of the Oscar for directing a film called *Les Bons Debarras*.

Of course, other families of writers have worked in the movies— the Benchleys, the Kanins, the Goldmans. But the Mankiewiczes may be unique for the number of writers they have produced and for the sophistication of their best work. Another second-generation writer, Jill Schary, succinctly defined the special status of the Mankiewiczes in movieland: "The family was wonderful to know and impossible to compete with . . . They did not have the money of the other major Hollywood families and the kind of power that such money brings, but they had the power that comes from quality and class and style." As Tom Mankiewicz says, referring to both his pride in the family heritage and the burden of living up to its standard, "Mankiewiczes are meant to be excellent: in fact, 'Mankiewicz' is almost synonymous with the word 'excellent.' Our family was never a villa-in-the-south-of-France family or a Rolls Royce family. We always lived comfortably, but not in an ostentatious way. The pride always came from the achievement."

IN a business largely created by semi-literates, the Mankiewiczes have a distinctive pedigree. Like many of their colleagues, they were descended from European Jews, but their roots are in Germany rather than the ghettos of middle Europe. German Jews have traditionally considered themselves intellectually and culturally superior to refugees from the "shtetls" of Poland or Latvia. Certainly, the family patriarch, Franz Mankiewicz, who emigrated to New York in 1892, was a breed apart from Goldwyn, Zukor, and Mayer. A newspaper reporter and editor, Franz went back to school in his forties, eventually earned his Ph.D., and became a professor at New York's City College. He edited the *Modern Language Quarterly* and founded a luncheon round table for German-born intellectuals, including Albert Einstein. Through their father, the Mankiewicz children were exposed at an early age to academics, artists, scientists, and political thinkers.

By all accounts, Professor Mankiewicz was a brilliant man but an unyielding, tyrannical father. He was especially hard on Herman, who was twelve years older than Joseph. Although Herman was an "A" student, nothing he did seemed to satisfy his father. If he scored ninety-two on a test, the Professor wanted to know why he had missed eight points.

The Professor's two sons responded to his domineering character in opposite ways. Herman was always reckless, irresponsible, and self-destructive, squandering his gifts as if to defy his demanding father. Joseph was more disciplined and more driven, determined to rise to the top of his profession and win his father's respect. Herman once speculated about the effect their father had on his brother and himself: "Pop was a tremendously industrious, brilliant, and vital man. A father like that could make you very ambitious or very despairing. You could end up by saying, 'Stick it, I'll never live up to that. I'm not going to try.' That's what happened to me. Joe, however, was fiercely ambitious as a kid."

Both boys inherited the Professor's interest in language and the life of the mind. Herman and Joseph each entered Columbia University at age fifteen and graduated before the age of twenty. In 1920, at the age of twenty-three, Herman went to work as a foreign correspondent in Berlin, then was hired as a publicist for Isadora Duncan. A few years later, he returned to New York, wrote theater reviews for the *New York Times* and *The New Yorker*, and co-authored two Broadway plays.

Joseph followed in his footsteps. After graduating from Columbia, he was sent off to Europe to attend the University of Berlin, with the understanding that he would return to Columbia to teach literature. "That was my father's idea, but not mine," Joseph says. "When I hit Berlin in 1928, I was dazzled by the theater." Although he vowed then and there to pursue a career in the arts, Joseph always felt a pang of guilt for having abandoned his father's profession. In one of his early triumphs, *A Letter to Three Wives*, Joseph made a hero of the learned, cynical schoolteacher played by Kirk Douglas; undoubtedly, Joseph meant this character to serve as an homage to his father. Douglas portrays a man of taste and principle who despises the hack writing that his wife (Ann Sothern) does for radio soap operas. A strict grammarian, Douglas chides Sothern in one scene for saying "Those kind" instead of "This kind."

Exasperated, she shoots back, "There are men who say 'those kind' who make $100,000 a year."

"There are men who say 'Stick 'em up' who make a lot more," Douglas counters wryly. "I don't intend to do either."

IN the late 1920s, successful writers were often lured to Hollywood by the promise of easy money and the excitement of working for the popular new medium of the movies. When these writers migrated to California, they set off in defiance of certain powerful voices within the New York literary set. *New Yorker* editor Harold Ross, for example, constantly disparaged Hollywood in the pages of his magazine, not just because of its vulgarity and excesses, but because he knew that his magazine could never compete with the lavish salaries which the studios were offering his writers. *The New Yorker* was losing some of its brightest contributors—including the young Herman Mankiewicz—to the cultural wasteland.

If some East Coast intellectuals scorned the hedonism of Hollywood, Herman Mankiewicz surrendered to it instantly. Upon arriving in Los Angeles in 1926, he purchased a big Cadillac and promptly joined a country club. Herman lived high, drank heavily, and gambled recklessly. His son Don recalls, "My father told me once that he believed he always had the advantage in gambling because everything was even money. I watched him play poker and bet $1000 that the top card in the deck was a spade. He said it was even money, because it would either come up a spade or not come up a spade. He never grasped the fallacy of that thinking."

A year after he came to Hollywood, Herman was named head of Paramount's scenario department, earning $1250 a week. Even before that, he had sent a telegram to one of his New York cronies, fellow reporter Ben Hecht: "Will you accept three hundred per week to work for Paramount Pictures? All expenses paid. The three hundred is peanuts. Millions are to be grabbed out here and your only competition is idiots. Don't let this get around." A bon vivant, Herman was renowned for his scabrous wit—Hecht called him the Central Park West Voltaire. His wisecracks have become legendary, and he was capable of supplying them under even the most uncomfortable circumstances. During a dinner party at the home of Arthur Hornblow, Jr., a stickler for the niceties of etiquette, Herman imbibed a bit too much and threw up at the table. Though still green around the gills, Herman promptly reassured the host, "Don't worry, Arthur, the white wine came up with the fish."

Herman worked on dozens of movies at Paramount, including several of the early Marx Brothers classics—*Monkey Business*, *Horse Feathers*, and *Duck Soup*. Before long, Herman sent for his brother Joe, arranging a job for him as junior writer at Paramount. Hollywood seemed like a boom town, and by 1930 the brothers were so heady with their success that they placed a full-page ad in the trade papers: "Herman and Joseph Mankiewicz, writers at Paramount. How about Erna?" Their twenty-nine-year-old sister accepted the invitation and joined her brothers on the Paramount lot. But Erna lacked her brothers' drive and their talent, and she left the film business after two years and moved back east.

It was an era of extravagance, and the outrageous, sybaritic style of the town could easily prove intoxicating to the newcomers. When Joseph Mankiewicz looks back on those early days, a sense of wonder fills his voice. "As a young writer, I used to wander around the studio at night," he says. "That's when the sets were built. There was all this activity, lights blazing. It was fantastic.

The commissary was open twenty-four hours a day. Every day at five o'clock, the barber shop was locked, and only executives could use it. You went in if you were one of the privileged. Louis B. Mayer had a manicure every day, and had the blackheads squeezed out of his forehead. The ministering that went on at that barber shop! It was such a completely different world.

"You never left the lot for anything," Joseph adds. "When you were at the studio, you were not only safe from the outside world, you could participate in any part of the outside world that you wanted to. If you wanted to register to vote or renew your driver's license, they came on the lot. At Christmas time, the department stores used to bring stuff over to your office to show you. Once I wanted some toys, and I had my secretary call Robinson's downtown. They said they couldn't bring the toys over, but they told her, 'If Mr. Mankiewicz would like to come down some evening, we'll keep the toy department open for him and have a saleslady there.' I went downtown, and we were the only two people in Robinson's department store. That's beyond belief now, but that's the way it was."

When Joseph first came to work in Hollywood, he was often confused with his older brother, and he resented living in Herman's shadow. "I now know what they will put on my tombstone," he once commented. "Here lies Herm—I mean Joe—Mankiewicz!" Fiercely protective of his own ego, Joseph was especially sensitive on the issue of screen credits. When the *Los Angeles Record* mentioned that Herman, not he, had written the dialogue for *The Social Lion*, Joseph demanded a printed retraction. Another controversy developed over the 1932 comedy classic *Million Dollar Legs*, starring W.C. Fields. Herman was producer of the film and supervised Joseph and his co-writer, Henry Myers. The authorship is still contested. In 1978, Joseph told his biographer, Kenneth Geist, "I don't think Herman, throughout his entire life, mentioned *Million Dollar Legs* as something he'd been connected with." Herman's widow, Sara Mankiewicz, disputed this, saying, "Herman always boasted about *Million Dollar Legs* and regarded it as one of his happiest and most delightful pictures." In *The Citizen Kane Book*, Pauline Kael accepted Sara's claim and pronounced Herman to be the author. (To confuse matters even further, the forgotten co-writer, Henry Myers, insisted that *he* wrote a lot of the picture without help from either Mankiewicz.)

The pettiness of this credit dispute suggests the rivalry that was to consume the Mankiewicz brothers throughout most of their lives. Joseph once remarked, "Everyone else has a mother or father complex, but I have a Herman complex!" He knew that Herman was always better liked than he was. Herman was generous to a fault and adored by a galaxy of friends. By contrast, Joseph is known to this day as a tightwad. His son Christopher refers to him as "miserly."

Money was a particular source of tension between the brothers. In his first year in Hollywood, when Joseph's salary reached the then-respectable figure of $125 a week, Herman made him put a fifth of it into a savings account; six months later, Herman "borrowed" all the money to pay off one of his gambling debts. Some years later, Joseph refused to borrow on his life insurance to meet more of Herman's debts. Furious, Herman ordered Joseph to come to screenwriter Charles Lederer's office. When Joseph got there, Herman turned to Lederer and fumed, "Now will you kindly tell this little SOB what a brother is—that everything he has is mine."

Today, Joseph tries to downplay the rivalry between Herman and himself. He does admit, however, that they squabbled over finances. "Herman sometimes made demands for money that I couldn't meet," Joseph says. "There was a little friction about that. But we weren't competing for work. People forget that my brother Herman was a generation older than me. I was this tiny little fellow surrounded by giants—articulate, yelling giants. I turned to my brother for help. Perhaps later on, when he was in desperate straits, he said things he may or may not have felt."

As Joseph's career ascended and Herman's started to wane, the relations between them grew increasingly strained. The roles they had played in their first days in Hollywood were reversed, and Herman was galled by Joseph's success. He began referring to Joseph as "my idiot brother." For his part, Joseph denigrated Herman's abilities as a writer, arguing that he was essentially a raconteur who did not always succeed in committing his wit to paper.

In 1934, Joseph moved from Paramount to MGM to take advantage of a more lucrative contract. One of the first movies he wrote for MGM was *Manhattan Melodrama* (which has earned a footnote in history as the picture John Dillinger went to see on the night he was shot). The chronicle of two childhood friends, one a reckless gambler who destroys himself while paving the way for the other's rise to professional eminence and power, the story bears a certain parallel to the histories of the two Mankiewiczes during the 1930s.

In 1935, Joseph began producing films for MGM. One of his first productions was *Fury*, a powerful anti-lynching drama starring Spencer Tracy and directed by Fritz Lang. Then, as now, strong social protest dramas were commercially risky propositions. "I've got to prove to you right away the facts of this business," Louis B. Mayer told Mankiewicz. "I'm not only going to let you make *Fury*, but I promise in writing, every penny that Irving [Thalberg] spends on *Romeo and Juliet*, I will spend exploiting *Fury*. It will get great reviews, and it will go on its ass."

"He kept his word," Joseph reports. "He had skywriting over New York City promoting *Fury*. And his prediction came true. It got great reviews, and it went on its ass."

Joseph went on to produce a number of more profitable movies at MGM, including *Three Comrades*, a wartime romance starring Margaret Sullavan and Robert Taylor, and two of Katharine Hepburn's most memorable films: *The Philadelphia Story* and *Woman of the Year*. But at the same time that Joseph Mankiewicz was earning greater prominence, Herman's career was faltering. Herman was continually in conflict with producers and studio executives, who had scant patience for his irrepressible sarcasm. In a fit of pique, Irving Thalberg threw him off the Marx Brothers comedy *A Night at the Opera*, though L.B. Mayer continued to believe in Herman's talent and kept him on the payroll. It was Herman's gambling, rather than his impudence, that troubled Mayer. He advanced Herman $30,000 on a new contract on the condition that Herman never gamble again. The very next day, Mayer came upon Herman engaged in a high-stake poker game on the MGM lot. Herman was gone from MGM that afternoon.

When he was hired at Columbia, Herman was warned not to say anything that might alienate his new boss, the feisty Harry Cohn. Shortly after reporting for work, Herman found himself at the same table with Cohn in the executive dining room. As related by Bob Thomas in *King Cohn*, the studio chief began pontificating about some mediocre movie he had seen the night before. "When I'm alone in a projection room," Cohn told the assembled flunkies, "I have a foolproof device for judging whether a picture is good or bad. If my fanny squirms, it's bad. If my fanny doesn't squirm, it's good. It's as simple as that." The underlings nodded deferentially, but after a moment, Mankiewicz broke the silence.

"Imagine," he exclaimed, "the whole world wired to Harry Cohn's ass."

Cohn was not amused, and Herman rejoined the ranks of the unemployed.

Herman's son Frank once said of his father, "There was something self-defeating about his being in Hollywood. I guess that's why he drank too much and insulted people who could help him. He was a gambler, and he probably was an alcoholic, but those are not sins. He never stole from the poor, he never fired anybody on Christmas."

In 1941, Herman pulled himself together for one last blaze of glory. A decade earlier, he had been a frequent guest of William Randolph Hearst at San Simeon. Since Hearst allowed his guests only one cocktail before dinner, his mistress, Marion Davies, had a secret cache of booze for heavy drinkers like Mankiewicz. But Herman usually managed to stay reasonably sober, and when the company sat down to dinner, Hearst would always place Mankiewicz to his immediate left so that he wouldn't miss a single one of his guest's witty ripostes. What Hearst did not realize was that Herman was taking his own mental notes of everything he observed at those glittering dinner parties. Later, Herman suggested to Orson Welles the idea for a movie to be called *American*—an exposé of a powerful American press lord over a period of fifty years. In framing the concept, he drew on many details he had gleaned from his friendship with Hearst and Marion Davies. The resulting movie, *Citizen Kane*, earned Herman an Oscar as well as the undying wrath of his former host. Hearst was not the only person displeased by the film. When Herman won the Academy Award that year, his brother Joseph lamented to his wife, "I don't think I'll ever win an Oscar . . . He's got the Oscar and I'm a producer at Metro, goddamn it!"

With *Citizen Kane*, Herman Mankiewicz's career had reached its zenith. In some sense, Herman Mankiewicz and Orson Welles were not just etching a portrait of William Randolph Hearst in the film, but expressing their own private fears as well. At one point in the movie, Charles Foster Kane says to his childhood guardian, "If I hadn't been very rich, I might have been a really great man." One would guess that line was written by Herman Mankiewicz. Herman always believed that he had sold out his talent for the financial rewards of a screenwriting career in Hollywood. He continued to fantasize about pursuing the serious writing of which he believed himself capable. Though he completed an epic-length screenplay about evangelist Aimee Semple McPherson, the project never came to fruition, and he hated himself for accepting yet more hackwork assignments.

His downfall was abetted by the most famous target of his satire, William Randolph Hearst. The newspaper magnate viewed *Citizen Kane* as a personal betrayal, and he tried everything in his power to block the release of the movie. Hearst's attorneys unsuccessfully sought legal grounds for an injunction. Hearst columnist Louella Parsons denounced the film repeatedly before its release, and she persuaded Nelson Rockefeller, then thirty-three years old, to cancel the film's booking at Radio City Music Hall, threatening that Hearst's *American Weekly* would run an exposé on him unless he complied. In addition, Hearst's friend Louis B. Mayer offered $842,000 to RKO president George J. Shaefer if he would destroy the negative. All of these tactics failed, and Hearst waited to find some other means of avenging himself. His opportunity came in 1943, when Herman, on the way home from a late-night binge, smashed into another car just outside Marion Davies' residence in Beverly Hills, where Hearst was staying at the time. Two passengers in the other car were slightly injured. Mankiewicz was charged with a felony and had to stand trial. Worse, Hearst saw to it that the accident was trumpeted as front-page news in all his papers across the country. On March 14, 1943, the *L.A. Examiner* ran a major page one story—"Felony Charge Filed Against Mankiewicz"—about the accident, which had resulted in nothing more serious than a bruised knee. Inside the paper was a full-page spread of photographs, together with a "diagram" of the collision. Hearst refused to let the story die. He flogged Mankiewicz several times a week; he also used the incident as a pretext for launching a series of follow-up stories about the degenerate lifestyle of Hollywood. Eventually, Mankiewicz appealed to the American Civil Liberties Union for help in putting a halt to the harassment. But the studio brass, always sensitive to bad publicity regardless of its merits, were terrified to hire him.

Herman's screenwriting output dwindled over the course of the decade, and by the end of the 1940s he could barely find work at all. As his politics shifted to the right during the last years of his life, he became even more of a pariah. His son Don believes that his ideological conversion was motivated mainly by his distaste for the knee-jerk liberalism that masqueraded as political conviction in Hollywood. "He resented not so much the idiocy of the political points of view that were being pressed on him, but the liberals' unwillingness to *do* anything in support of their values," says Don. "Dorothy Parker and Alan Campbell spent thousands of dollars in a campaign to free Tom Mooney [a radical labor leader unjustly imprisoned on a murder charge and later pardoned], but it was my father who spent two dollars a week to buy him the ice cream that he needed for his stomach ailment.

"There were people in the Hollywood Ten who claimed—I think falsely—to have been partly responsible for the death of Trotsky. There is no doubt that the assassin spent time in Hollywood before going down to Mexico to kill Trotsky. My father used to rage, 'What kind of people would boast that they were involved in a plan to put a mountaineering axe into the head of a seventy-five-year-old man, and then tell *me* that I lack humanity?'"

Don recalls a particular incident at the family home one evening. A fellow came to the door collecting money so that Sam Ornitz, one of the Hollywood Ten, could get work. Herman said, "That's very interesting. Why is Sam Ornitz not getting work? He has no credits worth mentioning and he has never written anything worth reading, but still I would hate to feel that the man's out of work."

"He's been blacklisted," the fundraiser explained. "Nobody will hire him."

"Nobody will hire *me*," Mankiewicz replied. "Is anyone contemplating setting up a fund on my behalf?"

"Well, no," said the visitor, "because your problem is not political."

"Are you saying that there is to be a fund to get Sam Ornitz a job because Sam Ornitz is demonstrably subversive?"

The fellow squirmed. "I wouldn't put it quite that way, but that's about it."

Herman looked at him and said, "Well then, let me assure you, if you could see into my secret heart of hearts, you would think Sam Ornitz was a patriot! Good day to you, sir!"

Don remembers the simmering rage his father felt as he reached the end of his life: "There is a celebrated story of his breaking into tears, drunken tears, and being able to say nothing but 'Goddamn it, I am a better writer than Bernie Hyman." Bernie Hyman was a script supervisor of some sort who was sitting in judgment on him. My father was out of work almost all the time in those last years. He was totally overqualified for what he was doing. He was totally overqualified not only for the work he was in, but for the conversations that went around the dinner table. He told me once that one of the most important aspects of American policy was the influence of Thomas Marshall during Woodrow Wilson's illness. And he said, 'I have to discuss this with people who think Thomas Marshall's the fellow who started a high school in Burbank.'"

No doubt Herman's bitterness during those last years was magnified by Joseph's growing success and status. Joseph began directing in the late 1940s, and showed promise in his first films at Twentieth Century-Fox, such as *The Ghost and Mrs. Muir*, a supernatural comedy with Gene Tierney and Rex Harrison, and *House of Strangers*, starring Edward G. Robinson and Susan Hayward and centering on the conflict within an Italian banking family (supposedly based on the Gianninis, founders of the Bank of America and major financiers of the movie industry). After collecting his four Oscars for *A Letter to Three Wives* and *All About Eve*, Joseph was universally recognized as the premier writer-director in Hollywood.

All About Eve remains Joseph L. Mankiewicz's masterpiece, probably because it touched deeply personal chords. Sexual jealousy is a common theme in movies, but only a very few films have dealt with professional jealousy and rivalry, and that is what makes *All About Eve* so distinctive and provocative. It was the kind of drama Joseph understood from firsthand experience and was therefore in a position to illuminate. He drew on his unresolved feelings about his relationship with Herman in framing the story of the aging Broadway star Margo Channing (Bette Davis) who is betrayed by her protégée, the treacherous young upstart Eve Harrington (Anne Baxter). "You gather I don't like Eve?" Joseph once asked in an interview. "You're right," he confessed, "I've been there."

According to Herman's biographer, Richard Meryman, "In Herman's mind the successful Joe had become self-important, ruthless, and somehow fraudulent." As Joseph won more and more kudos, Herman took satisfaction in reminding himself that almost all of Joseph's triumphs (including *A Letter to Three Wives* and *All About Eve*) were adaptations of other writers' stories and that Joseph had never written an original screenplay that could hold a candle to *Citizen Kane*. Once, a correspondent for *Theatre Arts* magazine was exposed for plagiarizing a speech from *All About Eve* in one of her articles. When Herman heard about the incident, he professed relief. "Oh, she stole it from you," he needled Joseph. "I was afraid it was the other way around." Joseph recalled the last time he saw Herman, just after the release of Joseph's film of *Julius Caesar*. Herman was uncharacteristically effusive in praising the film, probably because the screenplay represented little more than a faithful rendering of Shakespeare's play. "Quite understandably," Joseph admitted, "he found it much easier to like my direction than to like my writing."

FOR all the intellectual qualities they may have shared, Herman and Joseph were polar opposites in their personal lives. Despite his heavy drinking and reckless gambling, Herman seems to have been a devoted husband and father. In fact, Joseph used to tease Herman for his prudishness; he claims that, while working at MGM, he was frequently called upon to rewrite the stiff, unconvincing love scenes in Herman's screenplays. Joseph was much more disciplined than Herman in every area but sex. Joseph is known for his series of love affairs with well-known actresses, including Joan Crawford, Gene Tierney, and Linda Darnell. Pamela Mason, former wife of James Mason and a friend of Joseph's, has described his womanizing as a manifestation of "ego and competition." His sexual conquests "were all famous," she remarked. "It had to be a brand name."

His affair with the young Judy Garland was particularly tempestuous. Louis B. Mayer was furious about the relationship, as was Judy's mother, who believed that Joseph was poisoning her daughter's mind by urging her to seek psychiatric care. Mayer and her mother tried to persuade Judy to break off the affair, but she ignored them both. According to Mankiewicz, Mayer once berated him for seducing Garland and then tried to placate him by saying, "You have to understand. I have the welfare of all my players at heart, and I'm talking to you like a father."

"No, you're not," Mankiewicz replied. "You're talking like a jealous old man."

Needless to say, Joseph left Mayer's employ soon afterward.

It was Joseph himself who finally ended the liaison with Garland. She tried to hold on by telling him she was carrying his child, but when the pregnancy tests proved negative, he stopped returning her calls. "I really wanted to marry Joe," Judy told her daughter Liza. "I wanted him to leave his wife."

Joseph thought of himself as something of an amateur psychologist—he had a lifelong infatuation with psychoanalysis—and his biographer Kenneth Geist reports that he frequently used psychoanalytic techniques in his relationships with women. He acted as their confessor and healer, an approach which drew many insecure young actresses to him. His son Christopher says, "When I got married, my father said to me, 'You know, of course, you're marrying your mother.' This is a guy who really wanted to be a shrink, and I guess he had great success with women, particularly movie stars, by dealing with them on a psychological level. Rather than saying, 'You have great tits, my dear,' like everybody else was saying, he found a new tactic."

Joseph's first marriage, to actress Elizabeth Young, quickly ended in divorce. His second marriage was to Rosa Stradner, a gifted actress who came from Max Reinhardt's theater in Vienna. It was Louis B. Mayer who brought her to Hollywood, where she made her American film debut playing James Stewart's wife in *The Last Gangster*. She married Joseph in 1939, but the relationship was rocky from the start.

Joseph wanted her to abandon her acting and devote herself to being a homemaker, probably the one role she was least capable of playing well. The Hollywood social scene bored her, and she was far too intelligent for the mindless activities to which Hollywood wives were being consigned. "My mother was terrifically frustrated," Chris says. "She always felt cheated that my father had said to her, 'You're going to give up your career.'"

Chris remembers his mother coming home one night and saying, "Oh God, I had to go to another dinner party last night."

"What was so bad?" Chris asked.

"I had to sit next to Jack Benny again," Rosa moaned.

"But Mom," Chris interjected, "I hear Jack Benny on the radio, and he's terribly funny."

"Well, maybe he is if somebody else is writing his material," she replied, "but, God, he's boring if you have to sit next to him at a dinner party."

According to Dr. Frederick Hacker, a psychiatrist and a friend of the family, Rosa believed that she had the potential to be a Garbo or a Bergman, and that she had forsaken a promising career to marry Joseph. She drank heavily whenever her husband was working. In 1942, Rosa fell into a catatonic state and spent nine months at the Menninger Clinic. When she recovered, Joseph did give her a chance to try acting again, casting her as the mother superior in his production of *The Keys of the Kingdom*, a sanctimonious religious drama starring Gregory Peck. It was to be Rosa's last movie role. In 1948, she attempted to resume her stage career in a play called *Bravo!* She traveled east, full of excitement.

But she was replaced during the Boston tryout, and her acting career was over.

IN 1951, Joseph moved his family to New York, feeling that the atmosphere there would be healthier for all of them. "I never could stand the city of Los Angeles," he explains. "At birthday parties, as you came through the door, the kids would say, 'What movie are you going to show? How many clowns you got? Only *one* clown? We had a tightrope walker at *my* birthday party.' I had seen too much of that going on. I did not want my kids growing up in that environment. And I felt if I didn't get out then, when I had just won four Oscars in two years, I'd never get out. Nobody was going to say that I left because I couldn't get a job."

After he moved back east, Joseph saw less of Herman, and relations between the brothers remained fairly distant for the rest of Herman's life. In his last years, Herman had only two screen credits—*A Woman's Secret*, a forgotten melodrama adapted from a trashy novel by Vicki Baum, and *The Pride of St. Louis*, a biography of Dizzy Dean that is a pale imitation of his earlier tribute to Lou Gehrig, *The Pride of the Yankees* (the Gary Cooper tearjerker that was to set the standard for sports "affliction dramas," a subgenre later taken up with a vengeance by television). Herman's career was washed up, the drinking and the disappointments had taken a physical as well as an emotional toll. Photographs taken of him in his last years show a dissipated, wizened figure, in shocking contrast to the ebullient, rakish young man caught in snapshots twenty years earlier.

Herman looked far older than his fifty-six years when he died in 1953. He succumbed to a series of ailments—heart trouble, uremic poisoning, and liver infection—brought on in part by his heavy drinking. Shortly before his death, he said, "I don't know how it is that you start working at something you don't like, and before you know it, you're an old man." That chilling line sums up the disillusionment of so many Hollywood writers when they look back at all the aborted and bastardized projects that form their list of credits.

When Herman died, Joseph and Rosa flew to Los Angeles from New York for the funeral. On the day of the funeral, the couple had one of their ugliest quarrels and Joseph stormed out of Herman's house. Sara, Herman's widow, told her nephew Chris what happened later that evening. "In the middle of the night, my mother came into Sara's room and cried, 'Sara, I'm miserable. Please come sit with me.' And so Sara spent the whole night sitting up with my mother and comforting her. Finally, Sara said to herself, 'Wait a minute, *I'm* the one who should be comforted. People should be sitting on *my* bed. I just put my husband in the ground today. What am I doing sitting on the bed listening to Rosa talk about *her* problems?' The next morning, my father returned, and my mother and he went off to the airport as if nothing had happened. To me, this just epitomizes the total self-involvement of people in Hollywood."

The strained relationship between Joseph and his wife did not improve. They spent more and more time apart. Their quarrels grew more violent, and Rosa's hold on reality became more tenuous. Finally, in 1958, Rosa Mankiewicz committed suicide by swallowing an overdose of sedatives. "The night my mother died," Chris recalls, "I was at the all-night movies in Times Square. It was my freshman year at Columbia. I rushed over to the apartment when I finally got the message, at three or four o'clock in the morning. Later on, as we were going down the elevator, the family psychiatrist said to me, 'What are your feelings at this moment?' I said, 'This may seem strange to you, but I feel intensely happy, that a great weight has been lifted off my shoulder. The agony of my mother is finally over, and at least there will no longer be that terrible tension.' He said, 'That's the first honest emotion I heard expressed here tonight.'"

ALTHOUGH not all of Joseph L. Mankiewicz's films succeeded at the box office, he was still regarded as one of America's most prestigious moviemakers throughout the decade of the 1950s. His Waterloo came when he started work on *Cleopatra* in 1961. It was a project which he reluctantly took over in mid-course and foolishly believed he could salvage. The financial temptations were overpowering. In addition to an extravagant salary, Fox paid Mankiewicz a $1.5 million fee to purchase his production company. At the time, it was the highest sum ever paid to a movie director.

In other respects, this misbegotten project was an unfortunate harbinger—the first example of a film that came into existence because of an irresistible "deal." Elizabeth Taylor never wanted to star in the movie, so she made a salary demand that she was certain would be rejected—a $1 million fee, against ten percent of the gross. To her astonishment, Twentieth Century-Fox, then under the management of Spyros Skouras and Peter Levathes, accepted her terms. It was the highest star salary ever paid and set in motion the steadily escalating costs of the entire project. It also established a precedent for the exorbitant star salaries which have since become routine.

Shortly after production began under director Rouben Mamoulian, Taylor was hospitalized with influenza; her health deteriorated rapidly, and she required an emergency tracheotomy to save her life. When Mankiewicz was hired to replace Mamoulian, Fox had already poured $6 million into the picture without producing a foot of usable film. Fox kept shifting the location from Hollywood to London to Rome and back to Hollywood again. The studio's European representative was described by Mankiewicz as "only capable, with difficulty, of ordering a ham sandwich." But Mankiewicz plunged in, telling himself that this monumental mess could be transformed into an artistic masterpiece. He tried to write dialogue in the style of Shakespeare and Shaw, but he was waging a losing battle. There was simply not enough time to get the screenplay in shape, and with costs rising every day, Mankiewicz had to write as he filmed, relying on drugs to keep up the pace. Joseph has described his daily ritual: "Someone would wake me up at five-thirty or six in the morning, and I would gulp down a Dexedrine. I was given a shot after lunch to keep me going through the afternoon. Then I was given a shot after dinner so I could write till two in the morning, and then I got a final shot at two so I could go to sleep."

Joseph's difficulties in keeping the movie under control were exacerbated by the extra-marital escapades of his two stars. Ironically, it was Mankiewicz who was indirectly responsible for the off-camera shenanigans, since he was the one who urged casting Richard Burton to replace Stephen Boyd in the role of Antony. (Mankiewicz also pressed for Rex Harrison to replace Peter Finch as Caesar.) Before long, Mankiewicz was embroiled in a drama almost as juicy as the one he was filming. As Kenneth Geist has written, "The saga of Liz and Eddie and Richard and Sybil, the tabloids' favorite real-life soap opera, became an added drain on Mankiewicz's sorely taxed energies, much as he enjoyed his role as confidant and marriage counselor to the participants."

The romance of Taylor and Burton generated wild press reports. At one point, an Italian paper printed a front-page story claiming that Burton was merely pretending to be Taylor's offscreen paramour in order to conceal the real romance between Taylor and Mankiewicz. Impatient with the ridiculous rumors and unable to resist an impish joke, Joseph countered by calling in the publicist and declaring, "The real story is that Richard Burton and I are in love and Elizabeth Taylor is being used as our cover-up." To prove it, he turned to Burton, kissed him on the lips, and walked off the set. The incident was reported with utter solemnity by the Italian press.

By the time *Cleopatra* limped to completion in 1963, Twentieth Century-Fox was under a new commander. Darryl F. Zanuck had returned to Hollywood, seizing power from Spyros Skouras, and Zanuck and Mankiewicz renewed an old battle. A decade earlier, Mankiewicz had left Fox and gone independent because Zanuck resented all the attention being showered on the brilliant writer-director. On most Fox pictures Zanuck was credited as producer or production executive, but on Mankiewicz films, Mankiewicz himself received almost all the glory. Zanuck once wrote him a memo, vigorously complaining that he was being "lost in the shuffle." The two men locked horns again during the editing of *Cleopatra*. Zanuck recut the film over Mankiewicz's protests, defiantly stating, "I would rather go back to another job than leave picture-making totally in the hands of an artist."

"Zanuck rode over the movie with a bulldozer," Mankiewicz recalls twenty years later. Mankiewicz's four-hour cut was chopped to three hours soon after its release; crucial plot points and evocative scenes were left on the cutting room floor. According to Mankiewicz, most of Zanuck's excisions were designed to make Marc Antony seem less of a weakling. "If any woman treated me like that," Zanuck told him, "I would kick her in the balls." There has been talk ever since of restoring the lost footage and reconstructing *Cleopatra* into the two three-hour films Mankiewicz had originally envisioned.

In a state of exhaustion after the ordeal of *Cleopatra*, Mankiewicz did not undertake another feature film for three years. He returned with *The Honey Pot*, an ingenious contemporary variation on Ben Jonson's *Volpone*. Despite some wonderfully urban repartee between Rex Harrison and Maggie Smith, *The Honey Pot* was coolly received by both critics and audiences. Mankiewicz's next picture, a slyly cynical Western, *There Was a Crooked Man* (starring Kirk Douglas and Henry Fonda), fared no better.

Mankiewicz recouped somewhat with *Sleuth*, released in 1972. Although it was no more than a faithful transcription of Anthony Shaffer's hit play about the deadly battle of wits between a jaded mystery writer and his wife's lover, Mankiewicz won an Academy

Award nomination for his stylish direction, and both Laurence Olivier and Michael Caine were nominated for their performances. It remains Joseph L. Mankiewicz's last film. His son Tom believes that, since *Sleuth* was a commercial as well as a critical success, Joseph may have wanted to leave well enough alone rather than risk another failure. "He's a man filled with immense pride," Tom suggests. "I think he's very concerned about ending his career on a good note."

MANY of the conflicts and patterns played out between Herman and Joseph Mankiewicz were reenacted by their sons. Just as Herman and Joseph had been opposite types as youngsters, so were Herman's sons, Don (born in 1922), and Frank (born in 1924). While Frank was highly competitive as a boy and always a diligent, vigorous achiever, Don was overweight, deeply introverted, sloppy, and given to bouts of indolence.

Frank went to journalism school but ended up switching to law and politics. For a time, he too was drawn to show business; he worked as an entertainment lawyer in Beverly Hills from 1955 to 1961. But one day he called his uncle Joe and said, "I can't take this any more." He resigned his $28,000-a-year job and took a job for half that salary working as director of the Peace Corps in Lima, Peru. As Frank explained this dramatic career change, "My wife Holly and I decided that if I stayed with the firm, within ten years we'd have this terrific house and a lot of money, but nobody would care if we had lived or died, except perhaps our mothers."

His stint in the Peace Corps introduced Frank to Robert Kennedy, and he worked as RFK's press secretary from 1966 to 1968. Frank was with Kennedy on primary night in California when the candidate was shot by Sirhan Sirhan in the kitchen of L.A.'s Ambassador Hotel; Frank had stepped back to help Ethel Kennedy through the crowd when he heard the gunshots. The next day, it was Mankiewicz who had the sad task of announcing Kennedy's death. Four years later, Frank helped guide the presidential campaign of George McGovern. The campaign was a bust, but Mankiewicz had a revenge of sorts by later writing two scathing books on McGovern's opponent, Richard Nixon. In 1977, Frank was named president of National Public Radio. During his six years in that post, he enhanced the station's prestige and increased its number of listeners with a literate mix of news and commentary, but he also significantly increased its deficit. In 1983, he resigned under pressure as the financially beleaguered NPR struggled to stay afloat.

Frank's older brother Don followed an opposite course—he first enrolled in law school but dropped out during World War II to join the army and eventually began writing. "During the war," Don recalls, "I wrote a very short piece in about an hour and a half, which I sent to *The New Yorker*, and I believe they gave me $185. I calculated what that would be for a forty-hour week, and I said, 'My father was right. This has got to be the easiest business that ever was!' Then I went for many years without a sale of any kind." When his Harper Prize-winning novel, *Trial*, was bought by MGM in 1955, Don moved back to Hollywood to write that screenplay. (Glenn Ford and Anne Francis starred in the movie version of *Trial*, a McCarthy-era melodrama about a well-meaning liberal lawyer duped into becoming a pawn of the Russians.) Later, Don rewrote *I Want To Live!*—a strong tract against capital punishment—for his Uncle Joe's company, Figaro Productions; the film brought him an Oscar nomination and won an Academy Award for its star, Susan Hayward. Her electrifying portrayal of a woman unjustly executed in San Quentin marked the high point of Hayward's career.

During the 1950s, Don began writing for such television series as *Studio One* and *Playhouse 90*. Later he created the pilots for *Marcus Welby, M.D.* and *Ironside*. Although he made out well financially from his TV work, he does not conceal his contempt for the medium. He describes one experience he had with *Ironside*, the police series which starred Raymond Burr as a crippled wheelchair-bound detective. "After we did the pilot for that show," Mankiewicz remembers, "NBC called and said, 'We're ordering the series, but we want to know one thing: When does Chief Ironside walk?' Now the whole purpose of putting the guy in a wheelchair was to demonstrate to the audience that he must have solved the mystery with his brain, because he couldn't have solved it with his body. The network hadn't perceived that."

In 1982, Don took a job as story editor on *Hart to Hart*, the suspense-adventure series starring Robert Wagner and Stefanie Powers, which his cousin Tom helped create. Don's work on the show served as another painful reminder of the lowly position writers occupy in the Hollywood pecking order. "When you write a book," Don says, "what finally goes on the page with your name is what you wrote. Here in Hollywood, that's not the case. If I get a call saying, 'I just read your script, and in Act III, the fellow shouldn't kiss the girl, he should kiss the cow,' he's gonna kiss the cow. My father wouldn't do it. When they told him to toe the line and he wouldn't, they put him on a Rin Tin Tin picture, and it's literally true that he wrote a script in which at the beginning Rin Tin Tin is frightened by a mouse and runs away, and at the end the dog carries a baby out of a burning house. I don't go that far.

"Of course, my father came to this business out of the newspaper business and the theater. Those are two businesses where you don't make much money and you get kicked around a lot, but goddammit, what you write is what they say or what they print. Movies are a team act. Now you get a great many advantages as a result of that. Imagine how long it would take me to write a novel if I had to describe what takes place off Diamond Head when the fleet rendezvous. But when I work on a picture, I write, 'Ext. Diamond Head. Wide. The fleet passes in review.' And then everybody does the rest of that—what might be 8000 difficult words for me—and does it *better*, because there's no way I could evoke what people are going to see. But in return for that, you pay a terrible price, at least if you don't like characters who use 'hopefully' as if it meant 'I hope,' or who say 'I could care less' when they mean 'I couldn't care less.' On *Hart to Hart*, the actors say what they goddamn please, and it quickly infects the day players and the director, and there's total anarchy. I want my name on the series to establish that I worked there, but I sure as hell don't want my English teacher to know what I was doing. Television is a trash medium. It is trash. You can't get away from it."

Don seems to have acquired not just his father's cynicism, but also his distaste for the party line thinking of so many show business liberals. "What I inherit from my father," he suggests, "is some degree of talent, but an even greater degree of rage at all these humorless, symbol-oriented people."

Through his brother Frank, Don became involved in George McGovern's campaign for the Presidency in 1972. But he soon drifted away from McGovern because he had no patience for some of the candidate's humorless compunctions. "At the convention, McGovern asked me to write a self-deprecatory joke to start his address to the Women's Caucus. And I wrote, 'I have been a fighter for human equality all my life, but the demands of this caucus would test the ingenuity of Persondrake the Magician.' He wouldn't say it. The moment I realized he wouldn't say it, I realized he was not for me."

That kind of mischievous wit might enrich the movies, but Don has had very little opportunity to demonstrate it in the film and television work he has done. Today Don seems to feel some of the same bitterness that tortured his father, Herman Mankiewicz, during his last years. "My father kept saying that it is not a good business and it will destroy you," Don remarks. "But he always said that he had never in his life succeeded in talking anybody out of it, and he did not expect to talk me out of it, either. He did warn me, 'Try to understand that whatever they pay you, A) you will earn it five times over, and B) it will not suffice to pay your psychiatrist bills.' And he was basically right."

JOSEPH'S sons, like Herman's, were always opposite types. Christopher (born in 1940), was more moody and withdrawn. Tom (born in 1942), was more affable and sociable, dubbed "fun-loving Tom" by his father, though he was subject to psychosomatic asthma attacks as a result of the pressures he felt at home. Chris and Tom responded to their father's influence in different ways, just as Joseph and Herman diverged in response to *their* father. "Tom went out to seek approval, love and attention by excelling," Chris says. "I went out to do the opposite. I wanted to hurt my father by being the worst kid. The more I fucked up, the more I figured I was giving him pain and hardship. And I guess that's what I wanted to do."

Chris mentions the title of one of his father's movies—*House of Strangers*—to evoke the atmosphere he felt at home. "I was always envious of families where the members were friends," Chris says. He and his brother were kept apart as children, sent to separate boarding schools, and were never very close.

Joseph Mankiewicz was a very demanding father, much as his own father had been when he and Herman were growing up. Chris remembers the evening his father picked up two Academy Awards for *All About Eve*. His parents came home from a post-Oscar party, and his mother told him of what had transpired. A guest had come up to them and burbled, "Joe, congratulations!"

Mankiewicz looked at him quizzically and asked, "Do I know you?"

The man said, "No, actually we've never met."

"Then why do you call me Joe? Please call me Mr. Mankiewicz."

Chris says, "That was a moment, a flash, which reminded me of how intimidating my father was to me as well, and I guess that's why I've never forgotten it. I remember a couple of years later, when he was shooting *Julius Caesar*, we were out in California for the summer and were staying in Norma Shearer's beach house. I'd gotten some bad grades. My father berated me, and I started to cry. When he saw me crying, he really heaped on the abuse. I realized that I had opened myself up, and he was just merciless. Right then, I made a determination that I would never break in front of him again."

Because Joseph had little time for his son's problems, Christopher was shunted off to psychiatrists from the time he was thirteen until he graduated high school. Chris remembers the experience as one of the rites of growing up in Hollywood: "What all of us seemed to have in common was constantly going to the shrink. Most of us progressed from nannies to nurses to housekeepers to psychiatrists. There was always a surrogate parent around. The attitude of my father and others was, 'I'm too involved. You and I could never talk these things out. I think it would be a good idea if you had somebody you could talk to freely and openly.' So that they didn't have to interrupt their careers and their lives and deal with the issues that fathers and mothers should be confronting with their children, we were shipped out to professionals. That has got to be somewhat unique to the Hollywood experience. I can't think of a group of kids who more frequently were going to shrinks in the forties and fifties. The idea of just sitting down and rapping with your parents was inconceivable in my family. But the shrinks were always there."

Chris's own time on the couch did not cause him to look kindly on the psychiatric profession. He recalls one day when he had gone to his regular session with his analyst, Dr. Lawrence Kubie: "I left his office, came home to our apartment, and my father happened to be home. As I passed through the hallway, he said, 'Chris, come in here a minute. What do you mean telling Dr. Kubie that I'm never around?' Here's a guy who didn't wait two minutes before calling my father to report on everything I told him. So much for the sanctity of the shrink's office!

"Once I was eighteen, I stopped going, and I've never been back. There are only so many times that psychiatrists can betray your confidences. And after all, when you see how unsuccessfully they treated your parents, it's not a great confidence builder in the art form."

* * *

BOTH Chris and Tom found the lure of show business irresistible when it came time to carve out their own careers. "You grew up as a kind of aristocracy," Chris explains. "You knew that everybody was interested in you. It made you something special because what your folks did was special. I don't know if that's a good thing. In retrospect, I feel some of us are as useless as the czar's children. Anything that suggested routine, although it might be clinically quite healthy for us, seemed repellent. We had never seen our father or mother leave every morning and come home every evening at the same time. Where's Dad? Dad's in Turkey shooting a picture. Or Mom is in New York doing a play. That's the kind of thing you're used to. So when you get out of high school and start to think of what to do with your life, you look around and most things look pretty dull in comparison to show business. Even if you have no particular talent for writing or directing, that's what you gravitate toward."

For a time, Tom thought of being an actor. But his father quashed that ambition after going to see Tom perform in a summer stock production. Joseph Mankiewicz came backstage and told his son, "I've always said to you that you can be anything you want. If you want to be a dentist, be a dentist. If you want to run a gas station, fine with me, whatever makes you happy. But in terms of being an actor, I beg you—eat with them, sleep with them, marry them, divorce them, talk to them, fight with them, fuck them, but please don't *be* one."

Tom heeded the advice. After working briefly as a production assistant, he wrote a few TV shows and films, as well as the book for a short-lived musical called *Georgy* based on the hit film *Georgy Girl*. Writing intimidated Tom at first because of the inevitable comparisons he knew he would face. "For me," Tom admits, "there was something terribly frightening about writing a screenplay when you have the last name of Mankiewicz. You say to yourself, 'Oh, shit, no matter what I write, it sure ain't any *All About Eve*, is it?' It takes a long time to get over that. When I first came out here, everybody said, 'Give my regards to your old man, will you, and by the way, if there's anything I can do for you . . .' On the one hand, all of that is very nice and tremendously advantageous. On the other hand, it sort of robs you of any sense of achievement. It's a real double-edged sword. And it wasn't until I had been asked back several times and, as awful as it sounds, for a lot of money, that I could finally convince myself that these people really want *me* because they think that I'm the best person to write the script."

All things considered, Tom admits, the benefits of being a Mankiewicz easily outweighed the drawbacks. For one thing, there was the stimulation of growing up in a literate, sophisticated household. "That was one of the greatest advantages I ever had as a writer," Tom remarks. "Dad was a very interested man, with all of his problems. He was a genuine intellectual." Besides that, the family name provided a valuable entrée into the business. "My God," Tom says, "it was great to be able to come out here as I did from Yale and call anybody and say, 'This is Tom Mankiewicz,' and if they hadn't met you, they would call you back just to see which Mankiewicz you were."

When Tom was hired to do a rewrite of the James Bond movie, *Diamonds Are Forever*, the direction of his career was set. He was on the path to phenomenal success, even if it was not the kind of success he had once envisioned for himself. He worked on several more Bond movies—*Live and Let Die*, *The Man With the Golden Gun*, *The Spy Who Loved Me*— and a couple of pictures for the English mogul, Sir Lew Grade (whom some refer to as Sir Low Grade), *The Cassandra Crossing* and *The Eagle Has Landed*. Tom became known as a reliable script doctor and rewrite man, though he found that role increasingly thankless. When director Richard Donner called him from Paris and begged him to rewrite the script of *Superman*, Mankiewicz initially declined. Donner was dissatisfied with the earlier drafts by Mario Puzo, Robert Benton, and David and Leslie Newman, and he desperately needed Mankiewicz's help to get the script in order. He sent two massive screenplays to Mankiewicz's home. Tom read through the scripts and again decided to turn the project down. As he tells it, "The doorbell rang the very next night. I opened the door, and there was Dick Donner in a Superman suit. He said, 'You've got to do the picture.' He was very persuasive. I rewrote both those scripts from top to bottom, and I've never worked so hard in my life."

After *Superman*, Tom's friend, TV producer Leonard Goldberg, asked him to rewrite the pilot for *Hart to Hart*. In return, Tom was given the chance to direct the two-hour pilot as well as several of the episodes of the long-running series. He was credited as creative consultant and has a piece of all the syndication sales. Although the tabloids have linked him romantically to the show's co-star Stefanie Powers, Tom jokingly dismisses the published reports that they had wed: "We were married in the *Enquirer*, divorced in the *Star*, and divided up the community property in the *Globe*," he laughs. "It's amazing how many people who claim never to read those papers were coming up to congratulate me."

Tom has also written the script for an expensive new screen version of *Batman*. Tom Mankiewicz is Hollywood's reigning king of comic strips and capers; he has made his reputation writing special-effects spectacles and feather-weight adventures. Ironically, this is exactly the sort of product his father always detested. Chris comments pointedly on Tom's success: "For years, my father has predicted that special effects would take over and movies would become circuses. What he predicted has happened, and the fact that my brother is so successful in writing *Superman* and James Bond movies must confirm to him pitifully that Tom is an exponent of what he regards as the mindless entertainment that passes for films. If my brother were a more open kind of person— he isn't, unfortunately—he would admit that he's had real problems in terms of competing with his father. I don't think in a million years that he would conceive that he has ever written anything or even could write anything as good as *All About Eve*. But he's extraordinarily successful. He signed an incredible deal with Warner Bros. for an unbelievable amount of money, at a time when most people are out of work, including me. For whatever reason, he's the flavor of the month or the flavor of the year."

Tom insists that he needed to establish financial independence from his family as a first step towards artistic maturity. He felt he could achieve that independence best by mastering a genre that was as far removed as possible from the typical "Mankiewicz movie." He elaborates, "I wanted to be able to say to my father, 'Listen, I've got my own area over here. This is my part of the yard, and you don't do this kind of thing. Maybe I'll do one of yours some day, but I don't need any money, thank you very much. I'm standing right here on my own.' That gives you a kind of confidence and security. I think I've got my own identity, and I've established a good base camp."

Nevertheless, Tom recognizes what he has achieved and what he may have sacrificed along the way. "I'm under no illusions when I walk into Warner Bros. that they're saying, 'Here comes another Noel Coward.' They say, 'Dollars and cents, here he comes.'"

But what about the standard of excellence with which the Mankiewicz name is supposedly synonymous? "I think Dad is probably

PICTORIAL PARADE (2)

ABOVE: Henry Fonda with second wife Frances Brokaw at the Biltmore Bowl, Hollywood, early 1940s. BELOW: Jane Fonda, age twenty-one, in a publicity still for her appearance in the play, "No Concern of Mine," 1959.

LEFT: *Jane with Roger Vadim in California shortly after their marriage, 1965.*
ABOVE: *Peter Fonda with first wife Susan Brewer in London, 1962.*

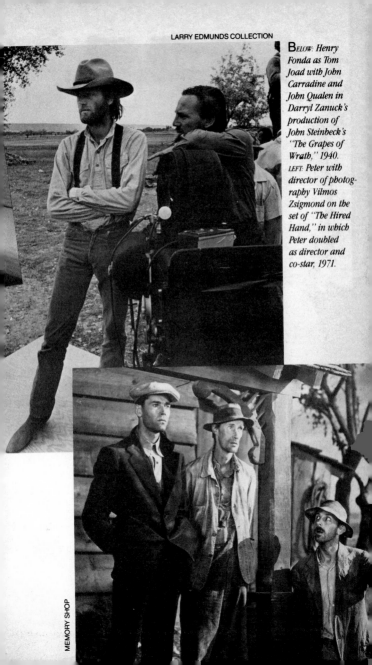

BELOW: *Henry Fonda as Tom Joad with John Carradine and John Qualen in Darryl Zanuck's production of John Steinbeck's "The Grapes of Wrath," 1940.*
LEFT: *Peter with director of photography Vilmos Zsigmond on the set of "The Hired Hand," in which Peter doubled as director and co-star, 1971.*

ABOVE: *A rare picture of the entire Ladd clan, (from left) Alana, Alan, Jr., Alan, Carol Lee, Sue Carol, David, 1952.*
LEFT: *Alan Ladd and wife Sue Carol read fan mail, 1946.*

Pinups, then and now.

RIGHT: *Cheryl Ladd in "Charlie's Angels," 1977.* BELOW: *Alan Ladd as Raven in his breakthrough film, "This Gun For Hire," 1942.*

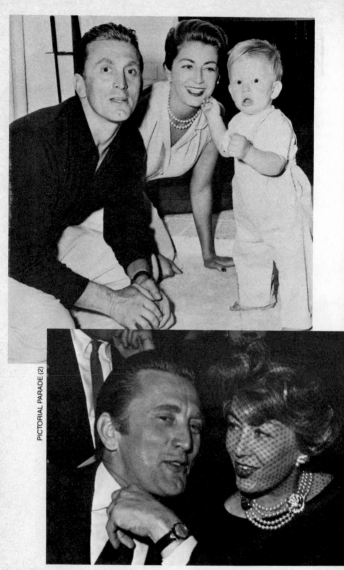

ABOVE: *Kirk, Anne, and Peter Vincent (the middle name was for Van Gogh, whom Kirk was playing at the time), 1956.*
BELOW: *Kirk and Anne Douglas at a movie premiere, Hollywood, 1958.*

Kirk as his favorite character-type, the "heel."

ABOVE: *As reporter Charles Tatum in the Billy Wilder cult film, "Ace in the Hole," 1951.*
BELOW: *With Paul Stewart in the film that made him a star, "Champion," 1949.*

ABOVE: *Father and son at an American Film Institute tribute to Henry Fonda, (from left) Anne and Kirk, Michael with wife Diandra, Hollywood, 1978.*
BELOW: *Second-generation co-stars—Michael Douglas with Jane Fonda in "The China Syndrome," 1978.*

Joseph L. Mankiewicz with his sons, Christopher and Tom, 1944.

ABOVE: *Director Joseph L. Mankiewicz with Sir John Gielgud and Greer Garson during rehearsals for M-G-M's production of Shakespeare's "Julius Caesar," 1953.*

RIGHT: *Joseph's wife Rosa Stradner on the set of "Keys of the Kingdom," 1944. Oscar-winning films from the Mankiewicz brothers.*

OPPOSITE ABOVE: *Often cited as the best American film ever made, Herman's "Citizen Kane," with Orson Welles, 1941.*

OPPOSITE BELOW: *Anne Baxter, Bette Davis, Marilyn Monroe, and George Sanders in "All About Eve," Joseph's acerbic masterpiece, 1950.*

KANE

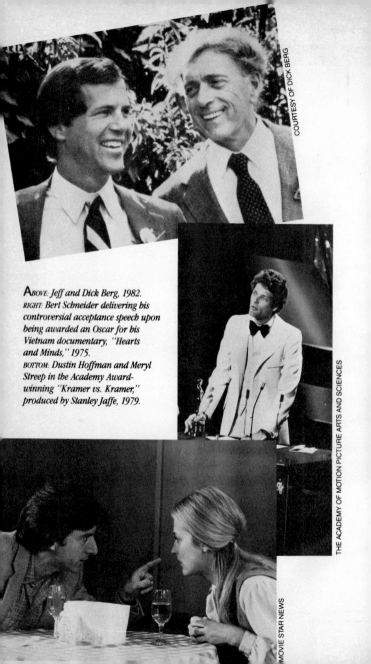

COURTESY OF DICK BERG

ABOVE: *Jeff and Dick Berg, 1982.*
RIGHT: *Bert Schneider delivering his controversial acceptance speech upon being awarded an Oscar for his Vietnam documentary, "Hearts and Minds," 1975.*
BOTTOM: *Dustin Hoffman and Meryl Streep in the Academy Award-winning "Kramer vs. Kramer," produced by Stanley Jaffe, 1979.*

THE ACADEMY OF MOTION PICTURE ARTS AND SCIENCES

MOVIE STAR NEWS

Aʙᴏᴠᴇ: *Lisa and Paula Weinstein with Jane Fonda at an awards dinner honoring their mother, the late Hannah Weinstein, April, 1984.*
ʟᴇғᴛ: *Richard Greene, the star of Hannah's acclaimed English television series, ''The Adventures of Robin Hood,'' 1955.*
ʙᴇʟᴏᴡ: *Diahann Carroll, who starred in another of Hannah's uncommon productions, ''Claudine,'' 1974.*

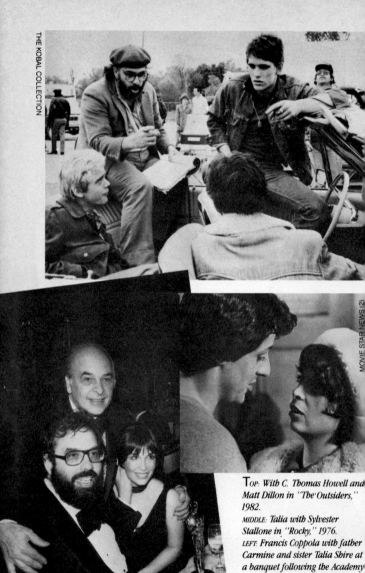

TOP: *With C. Thomas Howell and Matt Dillon in "The Outsiders," 1982.*
MIDDLE: *Talia with Sylvester Stallone in "Rocky," 1976.*
LEFT: *Francis Coppola with father Carmine and sister Talia Shire at a banquet following the Academy Awards ceremonies, at which Francis picked up three Oscars and Carmine one for "The Godfather II," 1975.*

Francis at work.
ABOVE: *With Marlon Brando in "Apocalypse Now," 1979.*
RIGHT: *With daughter Sofia on the set of "The Godfather II," 1974.*

THE ACADEMY OF MOTION PICTURE ARTS AND SCIENCES

Leaders of the non-family networks of the New Hollywood.

ABOVE: *Director George Lucas with Sir Alec Guinness on the set of "Star Wars," 1977.*
BELOW: *Director Steven Spielberg on the set of "Close Encounters of the Third Kind," 1977.*

MOVIE STAR NEWS (2)

disappointed that I have not worked up to what he considers to be, and I must say I consider to be, my creative potential," Tom admits. "He's never said he's disappointed, but I know he is, and I know that come Oscar night some year, he would love to see some wonderful film that I wrote and directed being honored."

"I do share Tom's disappointment," Joseph L. Mankiewicz affirms when talking about his son's career. "Or put it this way: he came to share my disappointment. On the other hand, I understand completely. I wrote for W.C. Fields. I wrote Westerns. I wrote anything when I started out. The point is, Tom sold his stuff. Now I happen to think he's better than that. Tom found it a little too easy. Instead of shooting the fourth draft of his screenplay, they shot the second. I have said to him, 'I don't think the second draft is good enough, Tom. You can do better.' But he didn't have to do better, and that was a pity. You see, Tom didn't have half a dozen very good producers sitting on his tail."

Joseph compares his own rigorous training as a novice writer-director with the laxity that his son has encountered: "The first movie I wrote and directed was *Dragonwyck*. Lubitsch was the producer, and he ate my ass out! I'll never forget one day when he pulled me aside. The day before, I had directed a scene where Vincent Price, the lord of the manor, followed his wife, Gene Tierney, into a bedroom. She threw herself on the bed crying, and he tore into her, bawled her out. Lubitsch had seen the dailies, and he looked at me and said, 'How stupid can you be? This man did not close the door! You think he's going to let the servants hear this?' He was right. I had made a booboo! I had the same thing happen with my screenplays. When I started out as an apprentice, I had some great writers like Percy Heath and Grover Jones in story conferences. And they would always say, 'Let's make it *better*.' And that ingrained in me the desire to put intelligent, adult material on the screen. I think if Tom had had to be more critical of his own work, he would have been, and he could have been."

"Maybe I wasn't hungry enough in the past," Tom admits. "When things are going well, you can get lazy with the best of intentions. If you can make a very good living writing James Bond—and God knows there's nothing wrong with it, people love the pictures and the money is good—then when somebody asks if you want to do another one, the easy thing to do is to take it. When I started out, I sort of thought of myself as an enormously sensitive young writer who wanted to do these deeply personal films. I don't know how many years ago that was. But I still intend to be."

In 1982, Tom signed a multi-picture deal with Warner Bros. allowing him to write, direct, and produce both films and television. He has resolved to take greater control of his own career, and he is determined to branch out beyond the comic strip movies that are his trademark. He claims to have several "personal" projects on his agenda, films that would attempt to revive the kind of literacy that his father and his uncle brought to films. One of them is a satire of the medical profession called *The Practice* (somewhat reminiscent of his father's *People Will Talk*, which starred Cary Grant as an iconoclastic doctor). "If I do it properly," Tom remarks, "I'll never be treated by a physician again in my life.

"To do another one of those pictures I've done," Tom adds, "is like eating another peanut. At this point, it would just drive me crazy if I keep heading off into the sunset doing exactly what I've been doing. I'd love to think that I'm still thirty-two years old, but I'm over forty. I've been writing for the last fifteen years. It turns out suddenly to be a long time. I don't want to end up like those guys who crank out scripts whenever Irwin Allen or Dino De Laurentiis is in trouble. In this deal with Warners, I will finally be able to fall on my ass or make it on my own. I'm cutting myself free of everything else now, and I'm just going to try and see if I'm as good as I believe I can be."

FOR all his disappointments, Tom Mankiewicz has at least established himself as a well-paid Hollywood writer. His brother Christopher has faced a more difficult passage, perhaps because he is one of the rare Mankiewiczes who is not a writer. He is articulate and intelligent, but he has not yet proven his creative talent. His father helped him to get his first job in the business at Columbia Pictures, and he subsequently pursued the executive route, working for various independent producers, as well as at middle management jobs for United Artists and Columbia. He has also tried to direct and produce films on his own, so far without much success.

In discussing his career choices, Chris admits that he has been inhibited by the fear of competing with his father. "When the opening and the opportunity presented itself," he says, "I went into being what we laughably call an executive, rather than perceiving myself to be a writer and working in an area where I would be in a direct *mano-a-mano* competition with my father. I tried to write a couple of things, and I thought they were terrible. I didn't want to give up my right to criticize other people's work. Or maybe it's simply because it's much easier not to compete and not to write. I hope that isn't the case. I've gotten to an age and to a point where the fact that I will be a footnote in the history of the cinema doesn't bother me at all. I just don't have the drive.

"Every kid dreams that one day he can be president. But when you grow up in a family like mine, you can't have that dream, because your father already *is* the president. It would be too extraordinary for a family to presume that it could pass the presidency along from generation to generation. In a way, you rob a child of his dream if the dream is already being fulfilled by his parent. That's very ball-cutting."

His father, however, dismisses the notion that a family name creates some sort of paralyzing obstacle to success. "That's a problem that's as old as the hills, isn't it?" asks Joseph L. Mankiewicz. "I felt the same thing. When I was seventeen years old and a student at Columbia, my brother was getting known around New York City. He was an Algonquin wit. And he was George Kaufman's assistant at the *New York Times* drama department. Well, I wanted to write. I started writing things and sending them off to magazines under the name of Joe Mason. And I remember when I got my first check for seventeen bucks. I sold something I had written. I don't think it's a valid point that Chris makes. I've encouraged him in the sense that I've gotten him positions. I got him all sorts of jobs, and he didn't keep them. He fought a lot. Chris is very opinionated. I have always told Chris he should strike out and work in the area in which he has the greatest knowledge. Chris has the most incredible knowledge of recorded music, which he's never used really. I told him there's a lot of money to be made in musicology and a lot of prestige. But suddenly, he got the bug to make movies. I don't know how or why. Unfortunately, he wanted to start off at the top, as a director. Chris has been trying to make it; he's having a rough time. I hope he gets his act together."

At times, Chris has come close to seeing his films produced, but they always seemed to be jettisoned at the last minute. Once he was hired to direct a film with Alan Bates, but the deal collapsed. *Yellowbeard*, a pirate spoof he developed, was finally made with several members of the Monty Python troupe, but he claims that he was squeezed out before the movie was shot. "That was a piece where I typed the treatment on my own typewriter," Chris declares bitterly. "I've reached the state in my life where I can no longer run after straws. When you've put in twenty years, as I have, and have seen your hopes cruelly dashed time and time again, I just can't bear to go through the exercise."

In 1983, Chris formed a partnership with Rafael Bunuel, the son of legendary Spanish director Luis Bunuel, to produce low-budget movies with Mexican financing. Most of them are cheapie thrillers with titles like *To Kill a Stranger* and *The Killing Touch*.

Chris's career frustrations have undoubtedly put a strain on his relations with both his father and his brother. Certainly one hears a measure of resentment when Chris talks about Tom's successes, and Tom definitely feels that Chris's failures have affected their relationship. "I don't think Chris has found exactly what he wants to do," Tom suggests. "And if you're a Mankiewicz who doesn't know what you want to do, especially if you're in the film business, you're kind of an eyesore. Chris is still searching for a base camp. He is at a lower level on the mountain, not as a human being or not with his intelligence. And so I think it still gnaws at him. I always thought how hard it would be to be Lorna Luft. Not only is Judy Garland her mother, but Liza Minnelli's her sister. Chris isn't saddled with that with me because I'm not the most famous guy in the business. He's saddled with it a little bit in that I *am* successful in the business. God, I wish Chris could get that picture to direct. I wish he could get that one big score that's always eluded him. If he got it, I think he'd be damn good. I have no competitive feelings with him at all. I wish to Christ he'd win the Oscar next year. It would make his life a lot easier. It would make our relationship a lot easier, too. I think he feels the family pressure much more than I do right now."

Tom's metaphor about his brother's position on the "mountain" is more than merely figurative. Tom himself lives in a big house perched atop Beverly Hills. He can see the entire city from his terrace, and the physical elevation symbolizes his professional status. Chris lives in a modest bungalow just above Hollywood Boulevard, before the hill starts to rise. Inside his living room, a pet cockatoo squawks occasionally, stirring memories of the bird that shrieked in the climactic scene of his Uncle Herman's classic, *Citizen Kane*. It is almost an unconscious reminder of the fabled family past that weighs on Chris today.

Echoing his father's criticism, Tom feels that one of his brother's difficulties is his lack of diplomacy. "Chris doesn't suffer fools gladly," Tom observes, "but he will also call a lot of intelligent people fools and shouldn't. Part of it is tremendously admirable, because he calls a spade a spade and is very honest. But the overkill sometimes is incredible. And it is true in show business that when you're in a position like Chris—an executive at various companies—and you treat people with what they perceive as disdain, all of a sudden when you need a job, those people are delighted not to cross the street to help you."

Chris once had a position with producer Martin Ransohoff, and Tom has told an amusing story of how he asked Ransohoff what it was like working with Chris.

"Chris was easily the most intelligent man I've ever had working for me," Ransohoff replied.

"Then why did you let him go?" Tom asked.

Ransohoff chuckled slyly. "Why should I pay a guy $2,000 a week to look at me like I'm an idiot?"

THAT story sums up an essential truth about this remarkable Hollywood family. Whether successful or not, the Mankiewiczs are clearly far more intelligent than most of the people who have worked in the movie industry. No doubt most of them have been "overqualified" for their jobs, as Don Mankiewicz said of his father. Their travails are typical of those experienced by other intellectuals in Hollywood down through the years. Their love-hate relationship with the movies parallels the ambivalence expressed by many other gifted writers, from Dorothy Parker, William Faulkner and F. Scott Fitzgerald to Joan Didion and John Gregory Dunne. Even as they are seduced by the money and the glamour of the film capital, they feel the need to apologize compulsively for their movie work. Joseph Mankiewicz often has referred to himself as "the oldest whore on the beat." Although he lent his talents to more high-quality projects than almost any other writer-director, he always dreamed of working in the theater and felt that he had failed to realize his full artistic potential by devoting himself to picture-making.

As Chris observes, "My father always had this kind of ambivalence about making money in Hollywood. He had this constant need to put on a hair shirt. It didn't stop him from fucking all the pretty girls and making money and having a terrific career. But there was a side of him that knew there was a more serious world out there."

Considering his impressive list of screen credits over a forty-year span, Joseph Mankiewicz has a curious way of describing his own career. He speaks of filmmaking as if it were only a part-time avocation rather than his life's work. "I was never committed to Hollywood," Joseph insists. "I was never committed to film, either. Nor was Herman, for that matter. My brother's greatest talent was his knowledge of the American political scene. If he had written a political column, Herman would have been far greater than Walter Lippmann ever was. As for me, yes, I've worked in films, but I also directed for the Metropolitan Opera. I'm writing a book on the history of the performing woman, the actress, how women came into the theater. I'm working on a play. I'm a writer, not a Hollywood writer. There's a difference between families in the film business like the Goldwyns and the Selznicks, and our family. If there were no film business, you wouldn't have those other families, but you would still have the Mankiewiczes. We'd still be writers. Late in life, I have a daughter who's now attending Williams College. There's no doubt in her mind that she's going to be a writer of some kind. That's a genetic tendency, but I don't think it was formed by Hollywood. It's just that writers came to Hollywood because Hollywood used to be one hell of a market for writers."

Joseph has seen that market dry up, and he is dismayed by the gradual erosion of standards in the movie community. A decade ago, Mike Frankovich, who was then a top producer with Columbia, called Joe to discuss a new novel he had optioned. He did not mention the title, but he wanted Joe to write and direct the movie version. They met for lunch, and Frankovich rather sheepishly pulled out the manuscript: Jacqueline Susann's *The Love Machine*. "Now, Joe, I know what you're going to say," Frankovich mumbled defensively. "But in your hands, it could be something special."

Mankiewicz insisted that he was open to considering the project. He was willing to make a step-deal, as Frankovich had suggested. He asked $50,000 for the first step.

"That sounds reasonable," Frankovich said eagerly. "Now just exactly what will that first step entail?"

"Reading that piece of shit!" Mankiewicz replied, as he pointed at Miss Susann's manuscript.

No further steps were taken, but that encounter foreshadowed Mankiewicz's mounting frustration over the last decade. "I've turned down a lot of crap," Joseph asserts. "But on the other hand, my name just doesn't come up out in Hollywood any more. Maybe they think I'm too old. Over the years the characters at the studio change, so no matter who you are, you have to manufacture a certain amount of personal hype, and that is something I've never done. I never had a press agent. It's very easy if you're not there for your name to be forgotten. I'm on the public mailing list for Filmex [the Los Angeles International Film Exposition]. They send me mimeographed handouts addressed 'Dear Friend of the Film' or 'Dear Film Buff.' I once got an invitation from the American Film Institute, when they voted on the best films of all time. *All About Eve* was in the top ten. And I got a mimeographed letter inviting me to buy a ticket for $350 and come and mingle with the men who had made those films. I had made one of them! I called Elia Kazan because *On the Waterfront* was among the top ten, and I asked him, 'Did you get this same form letter and the $350 request?' He said, 'Are you out of your mind? I got free tickets.' I said to him, 'I'm on the public mailing list!' "

That comment reveals Mankiewicz's confusion. At the same time that he scoffs at Hollywood and mocks its values, he still craves obeisance from the town that once revered him. He remembers a time when his intellect won him the respect of his inferiors. In a more melancholy, reflective mood, Joseph comments: "I don't think there are that many good writers in Hollywood today because the demand for good writing isn't there. What they want today is quick writing. I have a screenplay that was aborted simply because I took too much time in writing it. You have to understand that none of my films were ever blockbusters. Never. I was the kind of filmmaker whom studios could afford. Most of the films I wrote and directed made a profit—not through the roof, but they got their money back and some profit. I don't think I could get *All About Eve* financed today. First of all, it takes longer to write. And it takes good acting and careful direction, not of lenses but of the people. The big films today are like cartoon strips, and the dialogue is the kind that you read in balloons. I don't think they'd be impressed by a Faulkner in Hollywood today. The old moguls were really impressed to know that Lion Feuchtwanger and Aldous Huxley and Thomas Mann were living in Pacific Palisades. They actually bought Franz Werfel's *40 Days of Musa Dagh*. They reached for things in those days. Even Bernard Shaw came out to look around. I don't think he'd visit Hollywood today."

At least in the past, there was some place in the movies for the Mankiewiczes' wit and intelligence. Joseph may have felt impotent when his films were recut by Mayer or Zanuck; Herman may have been even more embittered by his failure to do the serious work of which he knew he was capable. Nevertheless, their names are on some of the brightest, classiest movies of all time: *Monkey Business*, *Million Dollar Legs*, *Dinner at Eight*, *Citizen Kane*, *A Letter to Three Wives*, *All About Eve*, *Five Fingers*, *The Honey Pot*. Nowadays, where are the acerbic adult stories which a Joseph or a Herman Mankiewicz might enrich?

The sad fact is that no forum exists for the literate, sardonic writing that the Mankiewiczes have always done. If they do work, it is on *Hart to Hart* or James Bond or *Superman*, where their special talents are almost completely wasted. And for some of them, there is less work altogether. Don has not been able to get a feature made in years; his last screen credit was on a lame George Segal comedy, *The Black Bird* (1975), and in 1983 he wrote a pallid, scaled-down TV version of *I Want To Live!*, with Lindsay Wagner feebly essaying the Susan Hayward role. His Uncle Joseph is living on a farm in Bedford, New York, working on his book, his play, but unable to find a movie project that he and the studios can agree on.

Tom Mankiewicz recalls the one time, in 1972, when he and his father both happened to be working on the same lot, Pinewood Studios outside London. It was at the tail end of the period when London was a major film capital that drew American filmmakers to English sound stages. Joseph L. Mankiewicz was directing *Sleuth*, his last film to date. Tom was working on his second James Bond movie, *Live and Let Die*.

"The Bond movie had eleven sound stages," Tom says, "and my father had one. Of course, it was the classiest stage you would ever want to see, with Olivier and Michael Caine and Ken Adam designing the sets and Ozzie Morris photographing. My father used to come out at night after finishing shooting. The Bond picture would be going late, and he used to open the door to E Stage and there were girls in bikinis and machine guns and underwater battles. It seemed so crazy to him. He'd say, 'What are you doing in here all day long? I don't understand any of this. I'm working with two guys and a camera.' Sometimes he and I would walk part of the way back to the Connaught Hotel. And he would say to me, 'You know, I don't think I'm ever going to do another picture.'"

Perhaps Joseph L. Mankiewicz sensed that it was the end of an era. The invincible James Bond had won yet another battle for supremacy. His ear-splitting artillery had silenced a more civilized voice.

YOUNG TURKS

9

MANHATTAN TRANSFERS:
The Schneiders, The Jaffes,
The Weinsteins, The Bergs

*"I don't wanna live in a city where the only cultural
advantage is that you can make a right turn on a red light."*

—WOODY ALLEN COMMENTING ON LOS ANGELES IN *ANNIE HALL*

THE moguls who cast dreams on celluloid were themselves the
stuff of legend—intrepid showmen given to grand gestures and
fierce vendettas. The companies they ran were indelibly stamped
with the personalities of the men at the helm. Darryl Zanuck *was*
Twentieth Century-Fox, Louis B. Mayer embodied MGM, Warner
Brothers really meant Jack, and Harry "King" Cohn reigned supreme
at Columbia. They were the undisputed rulers of their studio
empires.

Or so it seemed. Because the Hollywood potentates presented
themselves as larger than life, it was hard to imagine their answer-
ing to anyone. But the fact is that most of them were always
accountable to others. High-sounding titles have come to be so
debased in the corporate ranks of most movie companies over the
last decade—with a president of production under a president of
the film division under a president of the corporation under a chief
executive officer under a chairman of the board—that it is easy
to forget how sparingly authority used to be delegated. Louis B.
Mayer was long considered the single most powerful man in Hollywood, but the entire time he ran MGM he never rose above the
rank of vice-president. Nicholas Schenck, the president of Loew's
New York office and the financial controller of MGM, always
held sway over Mayer in the corporate pecking order. At the

family-run studios like Warners and Columbia, flamboyant impresarios Jack Warner and Harry Cohn were kept in check by their conservative older brothers, Harry Warner and Jack Cohn.

When the movie business was in its infancy, it required a certain boldness to make the trek west. Unsurprisingly, within the family-owned movie companies, the most adventurous members were the ones who migrated to Hollywood first and built the stages where movies were actually made. The cautious brothers remained behind, preferring to take charge of the financial books and balance sheets. They held forth in New York, where budgets were set and invoices paid. When the studios became publicly owned corporations and thus subject to regulation by the Securities Exchange Commission, they suddenly turned into "legitimate" big business; they had to play by the government's rules and be responsible to their shareholders, rendering the role of the New York financiers even more pivotal.

Just as their Hollywood brethren surrounded themselves with loyal underlings, so did the New York money men. These anonymous, colorless figures arranged the loans, held the purse strings, and doled out the dollars that kept the machinery of production operating. They developed a style markedly different from that of their Hollywood counterparts—prudent and guarded rather than extravagant and volatile. And gradually, as the first generation of movie magnates died out, the New York organization men began to infiltrate all aspects of the business, moving from financing and marketing into production as well.

Like the wildcatters who first conquered Hollywood, most of their successors were Jews, but more conventionally assimilated Jews; they lived in the suburbs, played golf on weekends, and subscribed dutifully to the Philharmonic. They aspired to be respectable pillars of the community, and they tried to transmit to their children a sense of commitment to worthy causes.

They also passed on their knowledge of the movie business and sometimes passed on their jobs as well—in the hallowed tradition of show business nepotism. Yet there was one crucial difference between the founding fathers of Hollywood and the men who took charge of the industry in later decades. Legendary moguls like Carl Laemmle, Jack Warner, Harry Cohn, and David O. Selznick proved a hard act to follow, and their children sometimes floundered in attempting to carve out careers in the industry that their irrepressible, piratical fathers had created. On the other hand, it was not so intimidating to follow in the footsteps of a methodical accountant in a pin-stripe suit; the children of these latter-day executives had a much better chance of matching and even surpassing the achievements of their parents.

AT no studio was the battle between east and west more intense than at Columbia. The brothers Cohn were almost never on speaking terms, and Jack Cohn seems to have understood that if the company was to survive the internecine warfare that raged between his brother Harry and himself, he would have to staff the New York office with men who were not just loyal to him but whom his brother would also perceive as above reproach. He found two who fit the bill in Abe Schneider and Leo Jaffe, young accounting students hired out of New York University who survived both Cohn brothers and ultimately rose to the very top of the Columbia hierarchy.

While Harry would snidely refer to Schneider and Jaffe as "bookkeepers"—which, of course, they originally were—he still admired their financial savvy. An inveterate tightwad himself, he was secretly pleased that they kept their eyes glued to the ledgers, and he would often invoke their admonitions about cost overruns to support his own negotiating position with outside producers and agents. Although Harry Cohn, a born huckster and ex-song plugger, viewed the circumspect, subdued Schneider and Jaffe as an alien species, he ultimately granted the New York "bookkeepers" his grudging respect.

Schneider, especially, had a gift for diplomacy which made him an invaluable member of the management team. He had come to work as an office boy for Jack and Harry Cohn and their partner, Joe Brandt, when the company they owned was still called CBC Film Sales. That was in 1924, when Schneider was seventeen years old. He moved on to the bookkeeping department while working his way through night school at NYU. When Columbia Pictures graduated from Poverty Row and went public in 1933, Schneider was appointed treasurer and, a year later, was elected to the board of directors. After Jack Cohn's death in 1957, he took over as chief financial officer and was subsequently named president and chairman of the board, retiring as honorary chairman in 1975.

Throughout his long career at Columbia, Schneider maintained a low public profile. His subordinates respected him for his even-handed style of management; one of them nicknamed him "Sitting Bull" in tribute to his ability to preside calmly over the warring tribes that made up the company. "He even looked like an Indian chief," the former aide notes, "and so did his wife." Schneider's marriage to Ida Briskin, the stern-visaged sister of Harry Cohn's general manager, Sam Briskin, certainly didn't hurt his standing with the front office.

Abe and Ida Schneider had three sons, Stanley, born in 1929, Berton, born in 1932, and Harold, born in 1939. The boys grew up in suburban New Rochelle, New York, in a well-ordered home not unlike that of other affluent Jewish families. Despite Abe's involvement in the film industry, he and his wife turned up their noses at the glitter of Hollywood. They were known as rather stuffy members of the country club gentry; the most passionate preoccupation of the family was not movies but golf. When Stanley and Bert vied for the championship of the Fenway Country Club, the wheels of government in Columbia's New York offices came to a grinding halt.

Despite Abe's remove from moviemaking, his sons Harold and Bert were both eager to enter production when it came time for them to decide on their own careers. The oldest son, Stanley, was more the replica of his father; like Abe, he was a cool, detached money manager who avoided the bedlam of Hollywood. He was hired to work in Columbia's international division in 1956 and, over the next decade, was given a succession of steadily more important jobs. In 1969, he was named president of Columbia, at the same time that his father was serving as chairman of the board.

Like his father, Stanley tried to play the Indian chief—a man above emotion, the perfect corporate manager. He even took on Abe's starchy mannerisms and snobbish air. He seemed to be the "model son," but the image his father had defined for him proved increasingly constricting. In 1973, he became an independent producer under the terms of a lucrative contract with the studio, and finally had the means to liberate himself from parental domination. A year later, he began shooting his first project, *Three Days of the Condor*, a taut melodrama about warfare within the Central Intelligence Agency, starring Robert Redford as a renegade agent. By January of 1975, the production was running weeks behind schedule, and Stanley, who suffered from high blood pressure, was becoming extremely anxious about delays and spiraling costs on the picture. Accustomed to keeping close tabs on the cashbook from his experience in the financial office, Stanley had trouble coping with the daily unpredictability of production. On January 22, 1975, five days before his forty-sixth birthday, he was stricken with a fatal heart attack at his New York hotel suite. Abe Schneider was devastated by his son's untimely death. He resigned as honorary chairman of the company a few months later and retired permanently from the movie business.

Abe's youngest son, Harold, has been overshadowed by his more prominent older brothers. After graduating from college, he held jobs at several of the Columbia subsidiaries, then co-produced movies with his brother Bert and his brother's friends, Bob Rafelson and Jack Nicholson. In 1982, he was brought in to take over *WarGames*, which turned out to be the biggest hit with which he has been associated. Liked for his unpretentiousness and his rambunctious sense of humor, Harold has a reputation as a knowledgeable line producer, but he has so far had little luck initiating significant projects of his own.

Both Stanley Schneider, the stolid bureaucrat, and Harold Schneider, the reliable job-filler, fit familiar patterns for the sons of a top film executive. The most mercurial member of the family has been the middle brother, Bert, who set a rather singular course for himself. Jack Nicholson, whose professional fortunes were aided considerably by his association with Bert, suggests one of the reasons for Bert Schneider's determination to play the maverick: "Bert was the middle brother in the family, and not the kind of guy who likes the number two position anywhere in life. And since it was his brother Stanley he was dealing with and this wasn't *Macbeth*, he decided to step out of the system and not be competitive, even though it was a competition that he might easily have won. As it happened, everybody did well. Stanley wound up running the studio, and Bert wound up being the most influential producer of films in America in the sixties and seventies."

Bert had shown signs of defiance even as a youth. Instead of socializing with his suburban peers at the Fenway Country Club, he used to hang out with the caddies and the waiters. He enrolled at Cornell but was expelled for, in his words, "bad marks, gambling, and girls." By indicating on his selective service form that he supported various dissident political groups, he managed to avoid the draft, and went to work for Screen Gems, the television arm of Columbia Pictures. There he played the corporate man long enough to move up in the organization—with what he called "a healthy assist from my family background."

Yet even then, Bert differed from his brother Stanley. "Stanley was very pompous and prickly and generally hated by everybody," recalls Christopher Mankiewicz, who went to work in Columbia's

New York office in 1963. "Bert, on the other hand, was charming. He always had his coat off, and you could go into his office and sit on the side of the desk. They were two radically different individuals." Despite his informal manner, Bert was well on his way to following his father and older brother into the upper echelons of the Columbia power structure. "I was into the American dream," he said. "I wanted a family, career, money, the whole bit."

But the dream soon tarnished. Bert responded early on to the rebellious spirit of the 1960s. Leo Jaffe's daughter Andrea had known the Schneider boys while growing up, and she recalls how Bert seemed to change almost overnight: "The executives in the eleventh-floor command were all very conservative men, with neckties and gray suits. Bert used to look exactly like they did. But then one day, in he walks with a leather jacket, open shirt, and beard."

Bert became the first member of the Schneider family to leave the New York fold. In 1965, he departed Screen Gems, set up shop in Los Angeles with his friend Bob Rafelson, and created a group of Beatles facsimiles called The Monkees. Raybert Production's television series starring the synthetic four lasted a few seasons and earned Rafelson and Schneider enough money to do what they really wanted to do—make movies. With the addition of a third partner, ex-agent Steve Blauner, the company changed its name to BBS (for Bert, Bob, and Steve) and, in 1968, produced a psychedelic fantasy film called *Head*, starring The Monkees, co-written by Jack Nicholson, and directed by Rafelson. A year later, BBS hit pay dirt with *Easy Rider*, the Peter Fonda-Dennis Hopper road picture that inaugurated a cycle of hugely profitable low-budget youth movies. In the wake of the unanticipated hoopla over *Easy Rider*, Bert used his family connections at Columbia—where his brother was now president and his father was sitting as chairman of the board—to seal a unique multi-picture production deal with the studio. Columbia would bankroll BBS as long as its budgets were held to $1 million per film, and BBS would have complete creative control over its own productions. No one at Columbia would see a foot of film until a BBS picture was ready for release.

Bert Schneider bridged the gap between Hollywood's executive establishment and the hip young filmmakers who were energizing the industry. At one moment, he could play the hard-driving, no-nonsense mogul, and at the next he could take on the mellower style of an Esalen guru. He was the first of a new breed—the whole-earth wheeler-dealer—and his personal charm drew the brightest rising talents to BBS. Explaining why Schneider's company seemed like a creative haven to young filmmakers, Jack Nicholson notes, "We all knew that Bert was the roof and the foundation of BBS. We didn't have to deal with anybody but Bert, and he set it up so *he* didn't have to deal with anybody else. Obviously, he never made a *Star Wars*. But in its combination of quality-intentioned films and commercial success, BBS was probably the best production unit in town."

By 1971, BBS was riding high, in more ways than one. Columbia executives were reportedly alarmed when Schneider would nonchalantly light up a joint in their presence. Still, it was hard to fault the head of a company that was responsible for so many low-budget hits when Columbia's more expensive products—*Lost Horizon, Nicholas and Alexandra, Oklahoma Crude*—were coming up croppers. BBS productions not only enriched the Columbia coffers, they enhanced the studio's prestige as well: Rafelson's *Five Easy Pieces*, an evocative, tough-minded character study of a contemporary drifter (brilliantly played by Nicholson), and Peter Bogdanovich's *The Last Picture Show*, a more conventional but affecting panorama of small-town Texas life, both collected a bevy of Oscar nominations. In the vanguard of the new "personal" style of filmmaking ushered in by *Easy Rider*, BBS was probably the first major American producing entity to adopt an *auteurist* line as a matter of stated policy. "We do not care what the story content of a film is," Bert Schneider declared in 1970, "who the stars are, or if there are stars involved. We are concerned only with who is making the film. If his energy and personality project something unique, he is given the freedom and help to express himself. We'll gamble that the films will express those personal qualities."

The gamble paid off handsomely with *Easy Rider, Five Easy Pieces*, and *The Last Picture Show*. But by 1972, BBS was already running out of steam. *A Safe Place*, directed by Henry Jaglom, *Drive, He Said*, directed by Jack Nicholson, and *The King of Marvin Gardens*, directed by Rafelson, were box office duds. The last two films at least did have flashes of eccentric brilliance, but *A Safe Place* was a murky time-jumbled love triangle, which critic Judith Crist suggested Jaglom had assembled "by blindfolding himself and cutting strips from hither and yon among the plethora of soggy dreams" of the film's flower-child protagonist, Tuesday

Weld. It epitomized the perils of directorial self-indulgence that were inherent in the BBS philosophy.

Bert was not the only Schneider having troubles at the time. His brother and his father were being challenged inside the Columbia boardroom by a group of dissident directors, led by two major stockholders—Geritol magnate Matthew W. "Matty" Rosenhaus and Herbert Allen, whose Allen Brothers investment banking firm was attempting to acquire a controlling interest in the company. The board offered Stanley Schneider a six-figure production deal to buy him out of his contract, and, eager to try his hand at moviemaking, he resigned his post as Columbia president in 1973. He was replaced by former agent David Begelman. Aligned with the Rosenhaus-Allen faction of the board, Begelman could hardly be counted on to give the same support to BBS that it had enjoyed under Stanley Schneider's regime. Bert Schneider's conflicts with the new management were only the first of the problems that would confront him in the years ahead.

When the anti-war movement swept Hollywood in the late 1960s, Bert had taken the plunge into radical politics. He sponsored fundraisers on behalf of imprisoned Black Panthers and became friends with Panther honchos Huey Newton and Bobby Seale, who were talking about making a *Superfly* ripoff to be written by Newton and in which Seale would star. (It never came to fruition.) As the anti-war, anti-Nixon fever mounted in Hollywood, Schneider decided to do a documentary about the Pentagon papers. Bob Rafelson, who by this time had left BBS to direct pictures on his own, suggested that Schneider hire a young filmmaker named Peter Davis to work with him on the project. Davis's television documentary, *The Selling of the Pentagon*, had been praised for its hard-hitting exposé of the Defense Department's questionable image-building practices. (Davis had Hollywood connections of his own. His parents were screenwriters, and he was married to Herman Mankiewicz's daughter, Johanna.) Although Davis liked the idea of Schneider's documentary, he thought it should be expanded to consider the whole question of American involvement in Vietnam. He left for Indochina in the summer of 1972 and began collecting footage for what would ultimately become *Hearts and Minds*.

As the film was being put together, Schneider tangled repeatedly with the two editors, Susan Martin and Lynzee Klingman, both young anti-war activists who considered the producer little more than a limousine liberal. Under pressure from the Columbia management to deliver a rough cut of the film before year's end, Schneider ordered the two women to complete their work by December 15, 1973. They labored day and night and did meet the deadline, but when they called Schneider to inform him that the job was done, he was off skiing in the Rockies. The coup de grace came when Schneider's then-girlfriend, Candice Bergen, turned up at a holiday party on the arm of "public enemy number one," Henry Kissinger. In a stinging *Esquire* piece, Bo Burlingham skewered Schneider for his high-handedness in dealing with the crew: "He ran his employees ragged while he lived like a king and then quoted Chairman Mao in their faces. The *chutzpah*!"

Once *Hearts and Minds* was finally completed, Schneider faced obstacles from other quarters. At that point there had never been a Hollywood film directly criticizing America's involvement in Vietnam. The new Columbia management was growing nervous, not just about the film's political stance but about its commercial prospects as well. David Begelman owed nothing to the Schneider family, and after viewing the film, he dropped support for its release and demanded that the Columbia logo be removed from its titles and advertising. Bert Schneider did not mask the contempt he felt for his brother's successors at Columbia. "The new management is a whole other kettle of fish," he remarked at the time. "And as my grandfather used to say, a fish stinks from the head down."

In May of 1974, over Columbia's objections, Schneider took *Hearts and Minds* to the Cannes Film Festival, where it won tremendous acclaim. BBS sued Columbia to win back ownership of the film, and Warner Bros. took over the distribution rights. Schneider opened it in Washington, where it became the hot topic among press and politicos alike. Cashing in on the rave notices from Cannes and cleverly making Columbia's renunciation appear to be politically motivated, Schneider was able to promote the film as a major media event. He arranged to have it play in Los Angeles for a week in December in order to qualify for the Academy Awards.

But before the film could go on to an extended run, Schneider hit another snag. Former presidential adviser Walt Rostow had reluctantly agreed to be interviewed for the film, but upon seeing the finished product he was livid. Rostow claimed that the scenes showing him pontificating about American policy had been so selectively cut that his position on the war was grossly misrepresented. In short, Rostow felt he was made to look like a posturing nincompoop. He filed suit to have his interview excised, and a Los Angeles judge issued a temporary restraining order against further showings of the film. The order was lifted a few weeks later, and Rostow's motion to have the movie permanently enjoined was denied.

In focusing public attention on *Hearts and Minds*, Bert Schneider had done his job well. Critics compared the film to the impassioned political documentaries of Marcel Ophuls and, despite opposition from the conservative wing of the Motion Picture Academy, it was a shoo-in for best documentary honors.

Although Schneider had earned a reputation for outspokenness within the Hollywood community, his name and face were virtually unknown in the country at large. That all changed on Oscar night in April, 1975. Accepting the best documentary award for *Hearts and Minds*, Schneider paid homage to his recently deceased brother. Then he read a message from the Provisional Revolutionary Government of Vietnam (the political ·arm of the Viet Cong) which contained "greetings of friendship to all the American people" from Ambassador Dinh Ba Thi, chief of the PRG delegation to the Paris peace talks. Before the assemblage of Hollywood luminaries could catch their collective breath, Schneider went on to extol the "liberation" of South Vietnam by the PRG. His ringing endorsement of the Communist victory in Vietnam (which led to the humiliating departure of American military forces) set off a firestorm backstage. Phone calls and telegrams—both pro and con—started flooding in, and emcee Bob Hope took it upon himself to write a rejoinder which Howard W. Koch, the show's producer, quickly approved and which Frank Sinatra read before the television cameras. Sinatra bleated that the Academy "wasn't responsible for any political references on this program, and we're sorry they took place." That statement, issued in the name of the Academy but actually ratified by only three members, turned out to be as controversial as Schneider's acceptance speech.

Schneider's critics later argued that the Awards telecast was an improper forum for transmitting a political message. "It's incredible to think that *any* forum is inappropriate to bring a message of peace from people you've been bombing the shit out of for fifteen or twenty years," Schneider countered. "It's interesting that we often see so-called Communists exhibiting the finest Christian ethic of turning the other cheek."

The day after the Oscar telecast, the Motion Picture Academy issued a statement supporting Hope's position. "My remarks were not supposed to be anything but my remarks," Schneider scoffed. "I never claimed to be speaking for the Academy. Sinatra and Hope had no right to use the name of the Academy in their protest. That is an attempt to put an official stamp of approval on right-wing politics."

Nevertheless, Schneider confessed that he "loved" the Sinatra-Hope statement. "They are like Walt Rostow in terms of heightening consciousness," he said. "Rostow helped the movie and helped the peace movement by trying to censor our film; he made sure that people knew more about it. And Sinatra and Hope are wonderful for the same reason. They call attention to the issues. The more air time that I can take advantage of, the better, because it all helps the cause." The controversy also helped *Hearts and Minds* at the box office. Grosses tripled in Los Angeles the day after the Awards and almost doubled in New York.

Although Schneider must have felt vindicated by his Oscar and by the commercial and critical success of *Hearts and Minds*, he soon announced plans to curtail his moviemaking activities. "Movies can make you very insulated," he decided. The public controversy created by his Oscar night performance may have been the most immediate reason for his retreat. But there were more private, personal reasons as well. He was reeling from a series of traumas that had befallen him in the preceding year. His long-term affair with Candice Bergen had ended. He had grown close to Peter and Johanna Davis during the preparation of *Hearts and Minds* and was badly shaken when Johanna was run over and killed by a taxicab in Greenwich Village during the summer of 1974. A few months later, Huey Newton, whom Schneider described as his "best friend," was arrested in Oakland, jumped bail, and dropped from sight. On the night of January 17, 1975, Los Angeles police raided Schneider's Benedict Canyon home and arrested him for allegedly holding a marijuana bash at which twenty-six juveniles were present. (The charges were later dropped when Schneider paid a trespassing fine; his guests' cars had blocked some neighbors' driveways.) A week after the Benedict Canyon bust, his brother Stanley died of a heart attack in New York.

And then there was the eerie tale of Artie Ross, a Berkeley graduate and Schneider protégé who socialized with Bert and Candice in Big Sur and introduced them to Arica, a short-lived fad of the "human potential movement" of the 1970s. In return, Bert entertained Artie in Benedict Canyon and offered him an entrée to the Hollywood scene. Artie penned a screenplay called

West Coast, about a leftist film producer, his movie star girlfriend, his hippie protégé from Big Sur and his clique of radical pals, one of whom he tries to smuggle into Cuba. (Rumor had it that the story was based on Ross's own true-life adventures with Huey Newton—who had by then surfaced in Havana—and Abbie Hoffman, who was still on the lam.) A few months after the Oscar brouhaha, Bert was supposed to have dinner with Artie Ross. That evening, Bert was called and told that his friend had strapped his face to an oxygen mask and accidentally inhaled a lethal overdose of laughing gas—Artie's latest recreational drug.

In the space of six years, Bert Schneider had gone from triumphant maverick to jinxed castaway. His personal life was a shambles, and he seemed to be buckling under the pressure. His closest friends had either disappeared or died, the family support structure which had bolstered his professional standing was pulled out from under him. And the mood of the country was changing, too, rendering his position as a spokesman for the psychedelic "youth movement" and the radical coterie of Hollywood increasingly obsolete.

When he closed down BBS in 1975, Schneider had one more completed film to distribute, a documentary about Charlie Chaplin called *The Gentleman Tramp*, which chronicled the legendary comedian's film career and his vilification by the right-wing press. It had limited theatrical release and was shown on public television. In 1978, Schneider made a brief comeback when he produced *Days of Heaven*, Terrence Malick's elegiac pastorale about a trio of young vagabonds (Richard Gere, Brooke Adams, and Linda Manz) who attempt to break free of their treadmill existence by scheming to relieve a dying farmer (Sam Shepard) of his estate. As their plan collapses, the lives of all the participants are tragically transmuted. Like many of Schneider's BBS productions, *Days of Heaven* was a directorial tour-de-force. Malick and his cinematographers, Nestor Almendros and Haskell Wexler, created a milieu of awesome grandeur—a stunning, painterly landscape captured in a series of breathtaking tableaus. (The movie won the best cinematography Oscar for 1978.) The movie also resembled Schneider's earlier films in its portrayal of rebellious, disaffected young people and in its strong concern for social injustice. But *Days of Heaven* was a carefully framed period piece, more distanced in style and more contemplative in mood than the BBS movies. That was mostly the result of Malick's studied visual effects, but it also reflected Bert Schneider's growing detachment from the contemporary world. In its pessimistic conclusion, the film suggested Schneider's own apprehension that the ideal community he once tried to create had come apart.

With the disbanding of BBS, Schneider has lost his footing in the industry, as have many of the gifted directors—such as Rafelson, Hopper, and Bogdanovich—whose careers he helped launch. Those filmmakers have had trouble doing business with the more conventional, less venturesome production companies that dominate the industry today. Their experiences at BBS gave them a taste of creative freedom that the studios could never satisfy. Bert Schneider still lives in Los Angeles, but he has gone into a state of semi-seclusion, declines to be interviewed by the press, and, according to friends and former associates, has become increasingly remote and quiescent. His odyssey from corporate heir apparent to outspoken rebel to isolated eccentric was one of the strangest in the family annals of American moviemakers.

WHEN Abe Schneider stepped down as Columbia board chairman in 1975, he was succeeded by Leo Jaffe, who had been his successor in virtually every post he held. To those who worked with them, Schneider and Jaffe functioned as a team, almost as inseparable as Siamese twins. They spoke with one voice, and if there was any disagreement between them, their colleagues and associates never got wind of it. Their only visible competition was on the golf links or at the gin rummy tables.

Hired by Schneider to work in the Columbia bookkeeping department during the summer of 1930, Jaffe stayed with the company for more than half a century. Like Schneider, he worked his way up the corporate ladder in the New York office, developing a reputation as one of the shrewdest financial experts in the business. It was Jaffe who came up with the idea of cutting costs by consolidating Columbia's production facilities with those of Warner Bros. at the Burbank Studios.

A diffident, conservative man, Leo Jaffe eschewed publicity all his life. If his name turned up in the pages of *Variety* or *The Hollywood Reporter*, it was invariably in connection with the kudos bestowed upon him at a B'nai B'rith dinner or by one of the multitude of philanthropic causes he supported. Observes one long-time Columbia aide, "He's the sort of man who was born to win the Jean Hersholt Humanitarian Award"—an honor he did receive from the Motion Picture Academy in 1979. Unlike his friend Abe Schneider, Jaffe had few cultural pretensions. He was essentially a *hamish* family man from New Rochelle—not so different from a well-to-do haberdasher living in the suburbs of Cleveland or St. Louis.

With his sacerdotal demeanor and his reputation for probity, Jaffe became known as the "conscience of Columbia." That title must have been severely tried during his days of dealing with the shifty manipulator who ran Columbia's West Coast operations, Harry Cohn. But it was not until years later that Jaffe's performance as a moral arbiter was put to the sternest test, during the David Begelman scandal that suddenly rocked the company in 1978.

Begelman, the dapper ex-agent who replaced Stanley Schneider as Columbia president in 1973, forged several checks during a period of financial and emotional instability. When the crime was discovered by corporate officers, it stirred an internal battle over how to handle the matter. Some board members and studio executives argued for Begelman's immediate ouster, but an even larger contingent—headed by Herbert Allen and producer Ray Stark—wanted to let Begelman stay on. As chairman of the board, it was Jaffe's duty to mediate the dispute and keep Columbia on course during this turbulent interlude. In David McClintick's best-selling account of the episode, *Indecent Exposure*, Jaffe emerges as the board's sole voice of reason, keeping his head when all around him were losing theirs. Amid the welter of palace intrigues and professional backstabbings, he made a desperate effort to protect the company's credibility. To Begelman's *mea culpa* before the board and the claim that he was now "cured" of the "abberational behavior" which had led to his embezzling funds, Jaffe responded, "In his heart, David wants to do as well as he can. But there are certain things you can forgive a man for doing as a human being, but that have no place in a publicly-owned company . . . What do we say to the next person who steals? Do we give him a second chance? Do we have a double standard? Executives can steal, but employees at a lower level can't?"

"My father was always known for his integrity," remarks Leo Jaffe's daughter Andrea, now a Hollywood publicist. "When I was working for an insurance company and got gifts from a law firm," she recalls, "my father screamed at me for twenty minutes, insisting that I return them." Andrea also remembers how the family's normally tranquil life was upset during the Begelman affair: "I was living alone in Los Angeles at the time. Somebody called up my father and said, 'We want "x" amount of dollars, or we're going to cut up your daughter.' It happened right around the time they were printing all these stories about the Columbia board. Then they called again and said David Begelman and I had been in some kind of deal together, and they wanted the money. I was the only one in the family who didn't even know David Begelman. Once the brakes on my car were tampered with. This went on for a long time until my father, over seventy, was actually coming out here wired. Nobody ever showed up for the money, and we still don't know who was threatening me. It could have been anybody who had a script rejected, of course, but it was pretty unsettling."

While Leo Jaffe's strict sense of right and wrong earned him the respect of his co-workers, there were times when morality would slip over into moralizing—to the detriment of the company. Screenwriter Gerald Ayres, who once worked under Jaffe as a junior executive, tells a revealing story about how Columbia lost the film rights to Hair, the groundbreaking musical celebration of the 1960s counterculture: "I had spent two months wooing two of the *meshugenah* guys of all time, James Rado and Gerry Ragni, who had a big hit on Broadway called *Hair*. They had agreed after many, many months to have me produce it as a movie, but they were still skittish and nervous because they knew all the stories about Hollywood boiling you alive.

"When the day came to close the deal, Rado and Ragni brought along their lawyer, their manager, their guru, and their tarot reader to Columbia's New York headquarters, and we all sat there opposite the studio lawyer, who had a face chiselled in granite. Suddenly, I was called into Abe Schneider's office, where all the top executives were assembled, purple with rage. They had obviously been arguing among themselves all morning. Abe said, 'On a project of this importance, for this amount of money, it's not a majority rule; there has to be unanimity, and Leo changed his mind overnight.' Leo looked at me and said, 'Gerry, I'm sorry, I can't help it. If Columbia Pictures ever produces a film which uses the word "fuck" while I'm still president, I'll jump out that window.' He was standing next to the eleventh floor window. Abe let the conversation run for a while, and Leo didn't budge." As a result of Jaffe's veto, the Age of Aquarius would not dawn on the silver screen for another decade. (Ironically, when Milos Forman's rendering of *Hair* did finally reach the nation's moviehouses in 1979, it was rated PG. By then, the film seemed like a quaint period piece and attracted no audience.)

Jaffe's puritanism colored his attitude toward filmmaking generally. In a "State of the Industry" address delivered to the Motion Picture Pioneers Foundation banquet in 1972, he declared that "showmanship is still the name of the game." (A year earlier, he had penned a similar essay for a trade paper declaring that "banking is still the name of the game"—indicating either that he had difficulty coming up with clever turns of phrase or that showmanship and banking were interchangeable terms in his mind.) At the same time that he was ostensibly celebrating the virtues of "showmanship," Jaffe exhorted his fellow executives to "demonstrate that we are capable of restoring confidence in our audiences. This can be accomplished by a succession of pictures that have entertainment rather than carnal values. Great discipline must be exercised to achieve this goal."

In part, Jaffe's disdain for "carnal values" was a reflection of his lifelong distance from Hollywood, which he tended to view with suspicion, if not contempt. Like his boss Jack Cohn, who deplored the profligacy of his brother Harry, Jaffe held firm to his New York base and his New York values. He had a few close friends among the creative set—Joan Crawford, Sidney Poitier, producer Sam Spiegel—but the perimeter of his social circle seldom stretched to the West Coast. Though he had offers from Harry Cohn to join the Columbia production team in Los Angeles, he always turned them down. "I never wanted to get into production," he insists. He recognized that his areas of expertise were administration and finance, and he also felt that Hollywood was a treacherous place to raise a family.

Leo Jaffe's revulsion toward the Hollywood scene was most intense when it threatened to corrupt the lives of his five children. His daughter Andrea recalls one occasion when a producer suggested to Leo that she audition for a part in a film. "My father started screaming at him," Andrea says. "He told the man, 'Not my daughter, never!' He made it perfectly clear that he didn't find it complimentary to him, and there was no way one of his children would ever be an actor or actress."

If acting was out of the question, moviemaking *per se* was not. All of Jaffe's five children have been involved in the film business in one way or another. Andrea is a vice-president with PMK, a major Hollywood public relations firm, and her client list includes some of the hottest young actors in the business—Tom Cruise, Sean Penn, Eric Roberts, and Timothy Hutton. Leo's other daughter, Marcia, is married to Eugene Margoluis, an executive with

ABC Motion Pictures. His youngest son, Ira, is president of the music division of Polygram Films. His oldest son, Howard, has been a producer, working with his brother Stanley on *Man on a Swing* and *Taps*.

One family friend has observed that Leo's "Gemini personality" was split down the middle with respect to his two older sons, Howard and Stanley. All of Leo's gentle, avuncular qualities seem to have been passed on to Howard, while all the hardheadedness and determination were inherited by Stanley. Howard has occupied a succession of mid-level executive positions and producing jobs— serving as story editor with Filmways and Donna Reed's production company, working as an associate producer for his father's friend Sam Spiegel on three of Spiegel's least notable films, *The Swimmer*, *The Night of the Generals*, and *The Happening*. Howard briefly ran a production company in partnership with Charles Feldman, but when Feldman died, the company died with him. In 1975, Howard produced a thriller called *A Reflection of Fear* (which has the dubious distinction of being one of the first and only Hollywood features about a hermaphrodite) but could never get it widely shown. Over the years, he has tried to write and develop other projects on his own, so far with sparse results.

By contrast, Stanley Jaffe quickly established himself as a potent force within the industry, first in the executive suites and then as an independent producer. He is clearly the most aggressive member of the family—a tireless, short-tempered street fighter, certain of his own abilities and determined to land on his feet. "We have a real sense of family honor," he notes. "If somebody fucks me over, he gets one shot, and then I know how to play samurai."

In his cockiness and self-confidence, Stanley is not unlike other second-generation movie brats. He comes out of a somewhat different family background than most of them, however, and he followed a different route to the top. Instead of observing the moviemaking process firsthand on the studio lot as Richard Zanuck or Alan Ladd, Jr. did, Stanley Jaffe picked up the intricacies of management and commerce from his accountant father, and then went to study economics at the Wharton School of Finance. After graduating in 1962, he took a job with Seven Arts, a production company run by two of his father's cronies, Eliot Hyman and Ray Stark. Stanley already knew the financial end of the industry. Under the tutelage of Hyman and Stark, he acquired a more practical understanding of production.

In 1968, he bought an option on Philip Roth's comedy of nouveau Jewish manners, *Goodbye, Columbus*, for the modest sum of $2500. ("I wanted to make the picture because I felt I could just go with a 16mm camera to my country club and have a great time making a movie," he jokes.) Roth's novella had won the National Book Award for fiction in 1960, but the book stirred little interest in Hollywood. Stanley Jaffe strongly identified with the story, however, partly because its two main characters so vividly reflected aspects of his own personality. In both Brenda Patimkin, the spoiled "Cliffie" weakly rebelling against her parents' puritan smugness, and Neil Klugman, the arrogant skeptic who looks down his nose at the Patimkin family's life of conspicuous consumption, there were qualities which Stanley Jaffe not only understood but shared. Soon after Jaffe optioned *Goodbye, Columbus*, Roth's *Portnoy's Complaint* was published. It became an instant literary sensation and was sold to producer Ernest Lehman and Warner Bros. for $300,000. By that time, Jaffe was already preparing his production of *Goodbye, Columbus* at Paramount, with two screen newcomers, Ali MacGraw and Richard Benjamin, set to star. "It was luck," Jaffe insists. "You know and I know that the day after *Portnoy's* was out, there's no way anybody could have touched anything else Philip Roth had written. I did *Columbus*, it was a hit, and because it was for Bob Evans and Paramount, we got into conversations. Charlie Bluhdorn [chairman of Gulf and Western, the company that owns Paramount] asked me if I wanted to run the company, and I did."

That was in 1969, when Stanley Jaffe was twenty-nine years old, making him one of the youngest men ever to head a major studio, especially one that wasn't controlled by the young man's father. Jaffe concedes that his early success may have gone to his head. He told a reporter in 1976, "If you're that age and someone like Charlie Bluhdorn hands you a half-billion-dollar corporation that is not feeling well and says, 'You be the doctor,' you bet you get a little cocky." The fact that he managed to help turn the ailing company around only inflated his already oversized ego. "When I took over Paramount," he noted, "we substantially reduced the overhead, came out with *Love Story* and had *The Godfather* on the way. It just never occurred to me that I wouldn't win and win and win."

Although Stanley Jaffe made numerous enemies with his arrogant manner, there was at least one person who could be counted on to put him in his place: his father. Stanley recalls attending a meeting of the Motion Picture Association of America in 1969, just after he had been named president of Paramount. "Here I was, all of twenty-nine, going with Charlie Bluhdorn to this MPAA board meeting. Dickie and Darryl Zanuck were there representing Fox, and there was Skouras representing a group of exhibitors along with Joe Levine, and Lew Wasserman and Sid Sheinberg from Universal. You name them, they were there. And I'm looking around at this assemblage, and all I wanted to do was ask for their autographs, because these were people I'd heard about all my life. Anyway . . . I was in an accident as a kid—my legs were run over by a truck—so I always try and elevate my legs. I proceeded to put my feet up on the side of the table, and I was rocking back and forth. My father was sitting across the table from me as the president of Columbia, and he looked straight at me and mimed the words, 'Get your feet off the table.' It didn't matter that I was running a studio and he was running a studio. He was my father. There was no discussion: it was bad manners."

On another occasion, father and son, along with other film industry major domos, were called down to San Clemente to meet with President Nixon. "We shared a car with [Columbia production head] Mike Frankovich," Stanley reports, "and when the limousine pulled up to the Coast Guard station, the guard asked, 'Who shall I say is calling?' Mike said to him, 'Mike Frankovich and Leo and Stanley Jaffe.' The guard got on the phone and said, "Mike Frankovich and the Jaffe brothers are here.' I looked at my father and said, "I don't know if I look that bad or if you look that good.'"

Stanley Jaffe had deliberately avoided going to work at Columbia when he was starting out as an executive. "I made a conscious decision not to work for my father, because I felt very strongly that that was not good for me," he says. But his attitude changed a few years later. First, he left Paramount in 1971 to return to producing; among his films were *Man on a Swing*, a murder mystery starring Cliff Robertson as a cynical cop and Joel Grey as an oddball psychic, and *The Bad News Bears*, the popular Little League comedy starring Tatum O'Neal and Walter Matthau. Then Stanley was called back to the executive suite—as the production head of Columbia, where his father was presiding as chairman of the board. To this day, Leo Jaffe is an unabashed admirer of his son's talents. "He's a perfectionist who works hard at his trade," says the elder Jaffe. "His record speaks for itself."

Stanley claims that when he took charge of the production unit at Columbia in 1976, he did so because "the timing was right." He still had doubts about the wisdom of working under his father but was finally convinced it was an offer he couldn't refuse. "David Begelman said a very sage thing to me," Stanley recalls. "I said, 'I'm not sure if I can work there. My father's chairman of the board.' He said, 'Look, it's not your fault if you have a terrific father.' And it made really good sense to me. My father shouldn't be penalized because I'm good at what I do, and I shouldn't be penalized because he's good."

At Columbia, Stanley oversaw the production of *Close Encounters of the Third Kind*, *The Deep*, and Peter Bogdanovich's abortive *Nickelodeon*. But before long, he once again grew restless in the role of studio executive. Unlike his father, he was too independent-minded to feel fully at home in the corporate world. He enjoyed the challenge of rescuing a company on the brink of ruin and then returning to his true love, making movies of his own. Upon leaving Columbia, he acquired the rights to *Kramer vs. Kramer*, Avery Corman's slick, affecting novel about a highly-charged custody battle and the emotional awakening of a single father. To adapt the novel and direct the film, he hired Robert Benton, with whom he had worked on Benton's first directorial effort, *Bad Company*, an offbeat Western about Civil War draft dodgers that charmed critics but went largely unseen by audiences.

Kramer vs. Kramer proved a watershed film in the careers of both Jaffe and Benton; it also gave added impetus to Meryl Streep's rising fortunes and reestablished Dustin Hoffman—on the rebound from a pair of box office flops, *Straight Time* and *Agatha*—as a star of the very first rank. What made the film consistently interesting was its clear-eyed portrayal of a morally ambiguous situation. It would have been easy to load the case against either of the parents involved in the custody battle, to create a single sympathetic protagonist for the audience to cling to. But the filmmakers chose the difficult course of showing a more complex truth. Each of the boy's parents is guilty of selfishness, neglect, cruelty—and so is the boy himself. Yet none of them is seen as incapable of changing, and that is what lends credibility to their separate plights and makes their colliding interests so agonizing to reconcile.

Jaffe, Benton, Hoffman, and Streep were all rewarded for their work with Oscars in 1980. For his part, Stanley Jaffe was established as one of the preeminent producers in Hollywood, a position solidified a year later with the box-office success of *Taps*, the gripping melodrama about a student revolt at a military academy, which starred Timothy Hutton and George C. Scott.

Certain patterns have taken shape in the course of Stanley Jaffe's filmmaking career. For one thing, he has been predisposed to work with other second-generation talents: director Larry Peerce (son of opera singer Jan Peerce) in *Goodbye, Columbus*; Joel Grey (son of comedian Mickey Katz) in *Man on a Swing*; screenwriter Bill Lancaster (Burt's son) and Tatum O'Neal (Ryan's daughter) in *The Bad News Bears*; Jeff Bridges (Lloyd's son) in *Bad Company*; Timothy Hutton (Jim's son) and Sean Penn (son of director Leo Penn) in *Taps*; Penn again and Nicolas Cage (nephew of Francis Ford Coppola) in *Racing With the Moon*. In addition, Jaffe's movies are laced with certain artistic and cultural pretensions—not just in the choice of material but in the stylistic trappings and details of setting and locale. *Kramer vs. Kramer* is the quintessential Upper East Side New York movie; the Vivaldi on the soundtrack, the elegantly-framed compositions, and the geometrical editing style all contribute to the film's tony veneer. Jaffe aimed for a similar style in his first directorial effort, *Without a Trace*, the story of a divorced mother (forcefully played by Kate Nelligan) searching for her lost child. It is worth noting that the protagonist was no ordinary housewife but a professor of literature at Columbia University and a classical pianist to boot. With such flourishes, Jaffe lets the Hollywood hoi polloi know that he is attuned to a more cultivated world than the freeway-and-burger culture that spawned *them*. He does not conceal his disdain for the ambience of Hollywood. "In New York, substance is much more important than style," he remarks. "But in California, the fact that you're doing lousy work or can't pay the rent is less important than that you drive the right car and get the right table."

There seems to be a central theme running through Stanley Jaffe's productions, from *Goodbye, Columbus* to *Bad Company* to *The Bad News Bears*, *Kramer vs. Kramer*, *Taps*, *Without a Trace* and *Racing With the Moon*. All of these pictures deal with young people groping toward maturity as well as with the complex relations between children and their parents, especially divorced parents. "The one thing that almost all the pictures I've been associated with have in common is that they do deal with children, but more important, they deal with children in the context of their families," Jaffe affirms. "Even *Taps*, which mainly spoke about children, had as much to do with parents that you didn't see. It has to do with how we delegate the responsibility of bringing up our children. To be a parent in this world is very hard."

It could be argued that Jaffe's affinity for such stories derives from his own experience as the son of a close-knit Jewish family. Unlike second-generation moviemakers who grew up in Hollywood and for whom divorce and domestic upheaval were so routine as to seem almost banal, Jaffe was raised in a household that hewed to the traditional ethic about the sanctity of matrimony. When Stanley's first marriage, to his college sweetheart Joan Goodman, ended in 1973, it was a traumatic event in his life. "First my marriage fell apart, then my head fell apart," he once remarked. The verities he grew up believing in had been shattered, and perhaps that explains the intense and genuine anguish in his films about the children of divorce. As he has testified, his divorce alerted him to the dramatic possibilities of *Kramer vs. Kramer*, which before its release was hardly considered blockbuster material among the Hollywood prognosticators.

Stanley Jaffe's instinct for strong dramatic subject matter has consistently set him apart from other Hollywood producers. His track record is not flawless, but he can take pride in both the intelligence and the commercial success of most of his films. He is a less idiosyncratic and adventurous moviemaker than Bert Schneider, but he may be the one producer of his generation who has a chance to match the records of such old-fashioned "prestige" producers as Selznick, Goldwyn, or his father's close friend Sam Spiegel (who did *On the Waterfront*, *The Bridge on the River Kwai*, and *Lawrence of Arabia* during his long association with Columbia). Jaffe acknowledges that Spiegel is "the person I've tried to emulate most as a producer."

In 1983, Jaffe formed a new company with Sherry Lansing, who was leaving the presidency of Twentieth Century-Fox after a disappointing three-year reign. Jaffe's *Taps* had been one of her few hits for the studio; she had previously struck up a close bond with the producer during the filming of *Kramer vs. Kramer*, which she supervised at Columbia. There was speculation that Jaffe had offered Lansing the chance to go into partnership to give her a way of saving face before the new Fox owner, Marvin Davis, could fire her. But those who observed the working relationship between the two former studio heads on the set of their first joint effort, the 1940s romance *Racing With the Moon*, concur that Jaffe probably joined forces with Lansing because he needed her gifts as a mediator and conciliator. In dealing with cast and crew, Jaffe and Lansing enact a kind of "bad cop/good cop" scenario, with the brusque, opinionated Jaffe badgering and demanding, while the soft-spoken, smiling Lansing does the ego-stroking and fence-mending. Jaffe-Lansing is an unusual company, a latter day version of BBS in its relationship to the studio with which it is affiliated. In an arrangement similar to that between Columbia and BBS, Paramount supplies financing for the Jaffe-Lansing movies, but the producers retain creative control so long as budgets are kept low. From Jaffe's standpoint, it is an ideal setup in more ways than one; Lansing can oversee operations in California, while Jaffe is based in New York, where he learned about the movie business in the first place and where he still feels more fully at home.

THE same year that Stanley Jaffe picked up his Oscar for *Kramer vs. Kramer*, his partner-to-be, Sherry Lansing, was named president of Twentieth Century-Fox Films. Her selection as the first female head of a major studio was widely trumpeted as a sign that women were finally coming into their own in the movie industry. For years, feminists and their supporters had griped about the inferior position to which women were traditionally relegated in the business. Lansing's rise was taken as an indication that things were finally changing.

While it was assumed that movie moguls would groom their sons to enter the industry, it was all but unthinkable for any of them to steer a daughter in that direction. For the most part, women executives who have risen to positions of influence in the movie business have not been the daughters of tycoons; rather, they have worked their way up through the ranks, usually beginning in the studio story department, the traditional domain of the so-called "literary ladies." In many cases, women like Lansing who lacked family connections compensated by striking up relationships with powerful male mentors. (In Lansing's case, she started out as a starlet-protégée of producer Raymond Wagner, then moved on to form ties with Daniel Melnick, Alan Hirschfield, and finally Stanley Jaffe.)

The second woman to head a major studio followed a similar pattern—with one added twist. Former United Artists president Paula Weinstein has had her male sponsors over the years, including Mike Medavoy, David Begelman, and Alan Ladd, Jr., but she also had bloodlines. They reach back not to a famous or powerful father but to her mother, an independent producer named Hannah Weinstein. With her sister Lisa, who has also worked in the business as a producer and story editor, Paula is the youngest of a distinctive group of women, perhaps the most striking example of a behind-the-scenes movieland matriarchy.

Hannah Weinstein, who died of a heart attack in March of 1984, made her mark at a time when female producers were a rarity. She began in television during the 1950s with sophisticated British-made shows like the popular *Robin Hood* series, then emerged as a full-fledged film producer two decades later. Her special commitment was to making realistic films about the lives of black people, movies that were notably distinct from the exploitation pictures in vogue at the time. *Claudine*, a family drama which won an Academy Award nomination for Diahann Carroll in 1974, was one of the first American features to be made with a predominantly black cast and crew, and one of the few films about black life to "cross over" and appeal to white audiences as well. Weinstein went on to produce two movies with Richard Pryor—*Greased Lightning* in 1977 and the smash hit *Stir Crazy* in 1980. "She was," Pryor says admiringly, "a woman who had her shit together."

That may sound like an odd description from an unlikely source, considering that the subject is a diminutive Jewish grandmother who looked as if she would have been more comfortable roaming the aisles of Bonwit Teller than wrapping up a movie deal. But Hannah Weinstein was never one to pay much attention to what the rest of the world thought she should be. From an early age, her self-confidence propelled her toward challenges that other women never dreamed of undertaking. "It didn't even occur to me that I couldn't do things," she said in an interview held shortly before her death. "I had always done what I wanted to do."

Hannah Dorner was born in New York City in 1911. Her mother died when she was still a teenager, and she was forced to assume the responsibilities of raising her two younger brothers. Her father, who owned a fur business, spent much of his time in China, and Hannah was put in charge of the household. She studied journalism at NYU and, in 1927, left home to work as a reporter for the *New York Herald Tribune*, a decision which precipitated the only quarrel she remembered having with her father. "He didn't talk to me for two weeks because I took the job," Hannah said. "He was afraid people would think he couldn't support me." Her father's anger quickly turned to pride when her first byline appeared in the paper, and he gave Hannah his blessing to pursue her career.

In 1938, Hannah married a fellow writer by the name of Isidore

Weinstein. Unlike Hannah, an ambitious overachiever who threw herself into her career, her left-wing causes, and the rearing of her three young daughters, Isidore was essentially a loner who, according to his daughter Paula, "never wanted to have the responsibility of a family and kids." Paula describes her father as a dashing figure, a romantic drifter who had been a successful journalist as a young man "but just didn't go anywhere in his midlife. He didn't have the drive my mother had."

Hannah and Isidore Weinstein separated in 1950. Isidore moved to Brooklyn Heights, took a job in advertising, and then settled in Mexico in the 1960s; he died in San Diego in 1969. "I remember them separately," Lisa says of her parents. "I don't really remember them together—except on the day the Rosenbergs were executed, because that's one of the most vivid memories of my childhood." Paula, the youngest of the three daughters, can recall only two occasions when her parents were together in the same room. "Both times I did the strangest thing," she says. "I introduced them, as if they didn't know each other. I had no concept of their having had a relationship."

The breakup of the Weinsteins' marriage triggered a whole new adventure for Hannah and her girls. "It says something about my mother that when she and my father were having a hard time and decided to separate," Lisa comments, "she didn't just move across town, she took us to Paris. She was dead broke, but she always remembered that year and a half she spent in Paris as the most fun she ever had in her life." Hannah and her daughters lived in a small hotel on the Left Bank with other expatriate Americans, most of them leftist writers and artists, some of them refugees from the Hollywood blacklist. Because the Weinsteins were the only ones with heated rooms, their suite became a favorite gathering spot, alive with political debates and literate conversation. "We always had a very extended family," says Paula. "Our place was full all the time. We didn't just have a mother. We got to have lots of other people who parented us."

It was never a part of Hannah Weinstein's agenda to become a movie producer, she fell into it, in her words, "quite by accident." She was sitting with some friends at a Paris cafe when one of them told the story of a furtive wartime romance between a young Parisian civilian and a member of the French underground. Weinstein was intrigued and suggested they make a little film based on the story. She raised $7,000 for the project with her friend, expatriate American director John Berry, and together they shot the movie with actors from the Comedie Française and other Parisian theater groups. She took the finished product, titled *Faits Divers à Paris*, back to the United States, screened it for various American television companies, and finally succeeded in selling it to one called Ziv. It was shown on the *My Favorite Story* series, hosted by Adolphe Menjou. Hannah decided that the whole operation had been so much fun that she would like to try making a living at it. She once again packed up her three daughters, moved to England, and embarked on a career as a producer of series television, starting with a three-part mystery about a cunning London detective called *Colonel March of Scotland Yard*, with Boris Karloff in the title role.

During the early 1950s, commercial television was in its infancy in England, and Weinstein was able to parlay her modest success with the Karloff series into a profitable string of deals. Hannah explained how she became involved in the development of her next major series: "A few organizations were getting together to apply for licenses from the Postmaster General, who was in charge of communications in London. One group was made up of Lew Grade and his brother Leslie, who were then agents; their partners were Littler, who owned all the theater real estate in the West End, and Val Parnell, from the London Palladium. The Grade brothers and their consortium approached me and Official Films and we became equal partners."

Their maiden effort was the long-running *Robin Hood*, the first British-made series ever to air on an American network. Starring the swashbuckling English counterpart to Tyrone Power, Richard Greene, *Robin Hood* was one of the classiest shows ever to appear on commercial television. Hannah attributed the program's high quality to the acting talent she was able to draw on from the Old Vic, the Royal Shakespeare, and other distinguished British theatrical companies. In addition to Greene in the title role, the cast included such highly regarded stage performers as Ian Hunter playing King Richard, Bernadette O'Farrell as Maid Marian, Rugus Cruikshank as Little John, and Donald Pleasence as Prince John. "I would go around the country recruiting actors," Hannah recalled. "London was very barren as far as writers were concerned, but there was a wealth of fine actors eager for work. They weren't like Hollywood actors who wouldn't do television unless they were out of work and desperate."

Hannah's main stumbling block was finding performers whose locutions could be understood by American audiences. "We were always looking for a mid-Atlantic accent," she noted, "which was hard to find then—even though most British actors have mastered it by now. But when we started out, an actor like Hugh Griffith, with his heavy Welsh accent, sounded like gobbledygook in the States. Once they realized they *could* understand the actors, American audiences were pleased, and when the networks finally cancelled the show, parents wrote very sharp letters of protest, saying, 'Our children have been hearing English as it should be spoken.'"

Hannah sold the rights to *Robin Hood* and her subsequent shows to American companies for a tidy sum, while keeping production costs down by filming in England. She remained in London for ten years and produced some 435 episodes of television, including such series as *The Buccaneers* with Robert Shaw and *Four Just Men* with Jack Hawkins, Dan Dailey, Richard Conte, and Vittorio De Sica.

During this period in England, Hannah lived in luxury. She leased a lavish country house where *Robin Hood* was filmed and where she and her daughters lived. In the summers, the girls would come back to the United States to visit their father in Brooklyn Heights. There they were treated to what Paula calls "a regular life"—a far cry from their mother's house in the English countryside with its seventeen bedrooms and stables for the horses. "I always felt ambivalent about that," Paula says of her mother's baronial estate. "There was something very appealing about my father's regular life. We'd go to Bohack's to buy food, and he'd make dinner for us. I loved the feeling of just being a regular kid." Those annual journeys from the manor house in England to the apartment in America created a divided attitude toward wealth that stayed with the Weinstein girls all of their lives.

In the mid-1960s, Hannah herself suffered a financial reversal. "Production in England was always very sporadic," she explained. "Even the Korda studio had to be taken over by the government." Flushed with the success of *Robin Hood* and her other series, Hannah had bought a studio of her own in Walton-on-Thames. But as the vogue for Westerns and cop shows began sweeping American television, the networks turned thumbs down on the costume dramas and more literate fare that Hannah was producing in England. With the evaporation of the American market, she was forced to sell her studio at a huge loss and close down her company.

With her bank account depleted, Hannah returned to the United States and devoted herself to various political causes. She headed the arts unit of Eugene McCarthy's presidential campaign and, in 1970, led a group called Senators for Peace and New Priorities, which was working to elect anti-war Democrats running for the Senate.

Around this time, a black writer she knew mentioned that of 6,000 members of the various technical unions in New York, very few were blacks. Weinstein investigated and found that only five were black (while only two were Hispanic). She relayed this information to four black actors with whom she had worked in civil rights causes—Diana Sands, James Earl Jones, Brock Peters, and Ossie Davis—and suggested that together they try to find a way of rectifying the situation. "Diana and I went to Washington and searched out all the government agencies until we found Manpower Career Development, which agreed to sponsor our on-the-job training for blacks and Hispanics," Hannah recalled. Some of the trainees found work under the auspices of her newly formed company, Third World Productions, which was producing its first feature, *Claudine*. (Diana Sands, the movie's star, died of cancer shortly after filming began, and she had to be replaced at the last minute by Diahann Carroll.)

The story of a single parent trying valiantly to raise a brood of children on her own, *Claudine* bore a certain resemblance to Weinstein's personal experience as a single mother, even if her background was considerably more exotic than that of the characters in the film. Although *Claudine* made money, studio decision-makers dismissed it as a commercial fluke. They were not eager to produce more pictures with black themes. Only after Hannah was able to secure the services of a hot young actor-comedian named Richard Pryor did her next feature under the Third World banner, *Greased Lightning*, begin shooting in 1976. It was a lackluster biography of Wendell Scott, the black man who became a champion stock car driver in the South at a time when the sport was completely dominated by red-necks. The movie gave Pryor his first starring role, but it fared poorly at the box office. Weinstein and Pryor had better luck four years later when she produced *Stir Crazy*, the prison comedy (in which Pryor co-starred with Gene Wilder) that earned over $80 million worldwide.

Although her films were more earnest than inspired, Hannah's aggressive determination, her resilience, and her sense of social commitment, made her a most uncommon Hollywood producer. In a letter written shortly before Hannah's death, on the occasion of an award bestowed upon her by the Liberty Hill Foundation,

Hannah's close friend Lillian Hellman wrote of her, "One of the most remarkable things about Hannah is that in this shabby time when either nobody believes in anything or has long given up, hope, she does believe and she does carry out what she believes in."

WITH Hannah for a role model, it is not surprising that all three of her daughters were motivated to seek careers of their own. The eldest, Dina, has never showed any interest in entering the movie business. She has worked in advertising like her father and now owns a catering business in New York; she is divorced and has a young daughter. Lisa, the second child, went to work for producer Joseph Papp's Shakespeare-in-the-Park, became a stage manager off-Broadway, then a production assistant for Dick Cavett's interview show. In 1970, she moved to Los Angeles (over her mother's objections) to try to break into the movies. She developed projects for writer-director Paul Schrader and later for producer Leonard Goldberg. She also worked for a time with her mother on *Greased Lightning*, an experience she remembers as "difficult." She admits that when she took the job with Hannah, it was against her own better judgment. Lisa explains, "Part of my wanting to come to California in the first place had to do with the need to be on my own. I wanted to forge my own way and not be around Mother all the time." Lisa describes Hannah as having been "a very dominant personality, which means she was never a very easy mother— a wonderful mother but not easy."

Paula followed her sister to Los Angeles after studying at Columbia, where she had been a leader of the radical anti-war movement of the late 1960s. She was introduced to Jane Fonda through her mother, who was trying to put together a movie deal with Fonda and Donald Sutherland in 1970. (The story, which was never filmed, traced the love affair between an ex-nun and a defrocked priest accused of aiding Marxist guerrillas in Guatemala.) Jane hired Paula to read scripts for her, and the two women became close friends. After Paula went to work as an agent at CMA, she took Jane along as her most prominent client. "I needed a job; and Mike Medavoy hired me because he thought I'd get Jane to go to work," Paula candidly states.

Paula quickly realized that, far from being a hindrance, her political connections could be useful in advancing her career. "It's a fine line between using your politics to make yourself successful and having your politics," she says. "I had politics, so I got clients who shared those politics. What made me different—my feminism, my politics—is what made me stand out. People's heads would turn, and they would remember me, and I'd begin to attract attention."

Paula's striking looks and confident bearing also helped her attract the attention of male executives who were searching for a few token women to join their management teams. In the mid-1970s, Paula left her job as an agent and moved into a series of executive positions with Warner Bros., Twentieth Century-Fox, and The Ladd Company. "I got on a path and just got more and more successful at it, working for people whom I loathed," she says. "I kept asking, 'Why am I an agent? Why am I working for a studio?' I kept changing jobs because I knew there was always something wrong about it. I like things about it, but I always felt out of it."

As she rose through the executive ranks, Paula developed a reputation as a tough, combative negotiator. She got ahead, it was said, not by playing the supportive, maternal role that marked Sherry Lansing's relations with filmmakers, but by playing hardball—the way the men did. While her brusque, abrasive style won her the respect of the management types who paid her salary, it sometimes infuriated the filmmakers whose projects she monitored. Although her own understanding of film technique was limited, that did not prevent her from expressing firm opinions. In supervising the prison melodrama *Brubaker*, she nixed the cinematographer (Vilmos Zsigmond) whom director Bob Rafelson wanted to use; she considered Zsigmond a perfectionist who was sometimes difficult to work with. Rafelson tried to defend his choice by referring to Zsigmond's special skills at "depth of field," but he was flabbergasted to find that Weinstein did not know the term. He later said, "I had to give her a primer course explaining depth of field and deep focus." In the end, Rafelson lost the battle—and the film. He was replaced by Stuart Rosenberg.

The projects with which Paula had the best luck were those in which the filmmakers involved were not strangers. She engineered the deal with Fox to do Jane Fonda's *Nine to Five*, and she was also instrumental in putting together *Julia*, in which her friend Jane portrayed Hannah's friend Lillian Hellman. When the chance came to initiate a project of her own, Paula was less adept. She seized upon an inane script about a small-time loser who bowls his way out of obscurity, nursing it to the screen under the title *Dreamer*. It turned out to be a commercial and critical gutter ball, and Paula now admits her mistake in backing it. "I hated it and knew we shouldn't do it," she confesses, "but I was desperate to get a movie on. I would never do that again. I don't want to be involved with movies that I don't care about."

Alan Ladd, Jr., her boss at Fox, was indulgent enough to overlook Paula's miscue with *Dreamer*. He respected her decisiveness and her willingness to take hard stands—qualities which Paula herself attributes to her days in the radical student movement of the late 1960s. "You had to organize people around ideas and decide whether to take positions or not," she once commented about her SDS experience. "After a bayonet's stared you up your nose, what's to be scared of taking risks?"

After Ladd departed Fox in 1979, she followed him to his new production unit at the Burbank Studios. She oversaw *Body Heat* for The Ladd Company in her capacity as vice-president for creative affairs. "Once I'd been involved with *Brubaker* and *Nine to Five* and *Body Heat*, I'd done the best I was ever going to do as a studio executive," Paula says. "I'd made hit movies, and there was almost nothing left to do except to be the head of a studio and finish the cycle."

That opportunity came in 1981, when David Begelman offered her the presidency of United Artists. She had known Begelman from her agent days at CMA, and she remained on friendly terms with him even after his embezzlement of corporate funds made him persona non grata among many of her associates. Paula went to UA expecting to take charge of the studio and revitalize the beleaguered company. But the lines of authority were so tangled within the corporate structure that developed after MGM merged with (and eventually absorbed) UA that Paula's authority was undermined. Despite her impressive title, she still had to answer to Begelman, UA Chairman Frank Rosenfelt, and MGM Chief Executive Officer Frank Rothman. When Begelman left MGM/UA in the summer of 1982, her own days at the studio were numbered. MGM/UA underwent yet another organizational shuffle when Freddie Fields was named president of the studios' newly-created joint production divisions. Weinstein was hung out to dry. In October of 1982, she claimed that the studio breached her contract by undercutting her power to make production decisions. She took the unusual step of issuing a public statement claiming that the studio's reorganization was tantamount to having her fired. "I felt the powers and responsibilities of my position had been so usurped that I was unable to do the job for which I was hired," she declared. Rather than go gentle into the good night of "indie production" like most other dismissed executives, she threatened to file a breach-of-contract lawsuit and eventually submitted her case to arbitration; the acrimonious dispute has lingered on. Although some in the industry admired Paula's defiant stance, they wondered whether she was irreparably damaging her career by refusing to exercise the customary cowardly "tact."

One of the most complex controversies to occur during Paula's brief tenure as UA president involved the movie *WarGames*, which her sister Lisa had been signed to produce. Lisa had developed the story about a young computer freak who practically triggers a nuclear war, and she had worked for two years with the two first-time writers, Lawrence Lasker (the son of actress Jane Greer) and Walter Parkes, to shape the script. To direct the movie, Lisa and her boss, Leonard Goldberg, had recruited Martin Brest, a talented young filmmaker with a reputation for fastidiousness in choosing his projects. (He had made a stunning student film called *Hot Tomorrows*, then scored a mild hit with his feature debut, *Going in Style*, an offbeat caper about a trio of larcenous senior citizens—Art Carney, George Burns, and Lee Strasberg; after that film's release in 1979, he turned down every other script he was offered until *WarGames* came along.) As they worked on preparing *WarGames* at Universal, differences developed between director Brest and the two screenwriters, Lasker and Parkes. Brest favored a more realistic and less cartoonish approach to the subject; Lisa sided with Brest. Meanwhile, Universal executives were nervously eyeing the movie's mounting costs and decided to drop the project. Goldberg had close ties to MGM/UA head David Begelman, and Lisa, of course, had even closer ties to UA president Paula Weinstein. A few days after *WarGames* was abandoned by Universal, the project found a new home at United Artists. But as shooting was about to commence, Leonard Goldberg's enthusiasm for Martin Brest began to wane. By this time, Lisa had become something more than a professional ally of the director; she and Brest were romantically involved. Goldberg and new MGM/UA president Freddie Fields got together to view the early rushes, and they turned thumbs down on the footage they saw. Goldberg and Fields resolved that Brest would have to go. It fell to Paula to hire Brest's replacement, director John Badham (who had just finished making *Blue Thunder* for Columbia). Goldberg did not communicate with Lisa or with Brest. George Justin, the head of physical production at UA, informed Brest he was being fired, and in an act of solidarity, Lisa walked off the production with him.

Lisa had worked on *WarGames* for almost four years, shepherding it through an obstacle course of studio doubts and pre-production delays. Now her breakthrough project, the picture she hoped would give her the credibility of a top-flight producer, was out of her hands. When the movie finally reached the screen in the summer of 1983, co-producer Harold Schneider garnered producing credit for the picture, which turned out to be one of the year's biggest money-makers. Lisa received no credit at all.

There were reports of arguments between the two Weinstein sisters during the *WarGames* imbroglio, but both Lisa and Paula deny any bad blood. "I think Paula is the only decent studio executive who ever existed," Lisa states emphatically. "The best you can ever expect from production executives is that they're passionate about your movie," she says, adding that her sister is one of the few who are capable of generating such enthusiasm. Though the experience on *WarGames* was painful, Lisa claims that it has made her tougher and certainly wiser. "A lot of people respect me for the choice I made on *WarGames*, and I'm sure a lot of people think I was a schmuck," Lisa says philosophically. "It was destined to be a successful film, but I have no regrets about my decision. I no longer have any naiveté about the creative process, because I've been up against men who don't give a shit about the creative process or creative people." Lisa is now developing other projects, some in association with Brest and some on her own.

AT the same time that Lisa has chosen to follow in her mother's footsteps as a producer, she makes it clear that she does not—and probably cannot—emulate Hannah completely. "I don't want to be my mother," she says. But she admires her mother greatly, describing her as "the bravest person in the world, always seeking out adventure, taking chances. She had more energy than all the rest of us put together." If there is one aspect of her mother's personality that Lisa does try to take after, it is her tenacity. "She was someone who just never gave up," Lisa says. She recalls that after Hannah submitted Bruce Jay Friedman's final draft screenplay for *Stir Crazy* to Columbia boss Frank Price, he lost confidence in the project and cancelled Columbia's backing. Undaunted, Hannah personally recruited Richard Pryor and Gene Wilder to star and Sidney Poitier to direct. She returned to Price with the package, and he changed his mind. "She'd go on fighting as long as she could, because she liked winning," Lisa says of Hannah. "And even though she complained about it, I think she liked all the tumult and *geshrying* of the business. She went through a lot of ups and downs in her life, and she never felt like stopping."

If Hannah Weinstein ever had doubts about her role as a single parent, she never revealed them to her children. Not did she fret about balancing a career with motherhood. "I don't think my mother ever deprived herself of any of her career or her fun for us," Lisa says. Paula strikes a similar note when she says her mother was "a very remarkable woman in very unconventional terms. If she'd had to be a mother full-time, she'd have been a horror. She was able to lead a very balanced life—being a good mother and an enormously successful woman. She would never have been good at *just* being a mother; it would have made her very frustrated and unhappy. But having us around gave her a different perspective. When she thought about what she wanted to do, she had to consider it in terms of other people."

For a long time Hannah was distressed that Lisa and Paula did not have families of their own. Hannah's prodding did not go unheeded. After leaving the presidency of United Artists in 1982, Paula spent a lot of time trying to sort out her priorities. Her speedy rise to the top levels of the executive hierarchy had given her money, power, and considerable self-confidence. But she felt a gnawing emptiness about her life and a certain revulsion toward the system which had so amply rewarded her. "I don't ever again want to do movies on a full-time basis," she now says. "I think it's important to try and have a whole life, establish a relationship. It won't happen if all I'm thinking about is myself and what I'm going to do and who I'm going to win over or what movie I'm going to make. If 'I' is in front of every sentence, it ain't gonna happen."

Paula recalls a fight she had with her mother when she was eighteen and announced that she was going to leave home. "I told her I wanted to go learn how to live alone," Paula reports. "My mother said, 'That's the odd thing about your generation. Every other generation has wanted to learn how to live together, and you guys want to learn how to live alone.' The older I get, that remark of hers has haunted me more and more. What a distorted view we had—that a sense of independence and freedom was to be gained from having our own apartments, our own money. We mistook material stuff for independence, instead of learning how to be cooperative with other human beings. She was right, but it took me years to understand it."

Hannah was hardly delighted that both Paula and Lisa chose to pursue careers in the movie business. "It's a rough, rough business," she said. "I think there are more rewarding fields for young people—law, psychiatry—but it was their decision." She was especially apprehensive for her daughters because she believed that Hollywood was such a sexist bastion. "There's this 'clubby' atmosphere about the way the men operate here," Hannah said. "There was none of that when I was working in London. It was much easier there; nobody seemed to care that I was a woman. I certainly didn't." In fact, Hannah insisted that she never really encountered much prejudice as a working woman until she came to Hollywood. "I never had any feeling of being misused or being made fun of, and nobody ever made a pass at me when I was working in New York or in London," she said.

Paula, too, felt an abrupt change in the way men related to her professionally once she migrated to California. "New York people are much more sophisticated," she says. "The language of the feminist movement had certainly reached the executive offices in New York, and a man there would blush to say some of the things I heard when I came out here. I felt the sexism enormously at the beginning, but I didn't pay much attention to it. I had a mother who did what she did and never talked about it. It just never occurred to me that there was a job that 'women did.' When I got involved in politics, I knew I was going to be on the Central Committee; there was no way I was going to lick envelopes. It wasn't until I came here and I felt the foot on my head that I began to look for some sort of support system."

Because an organized feminist movement did not exist in Hollywood, she joined a group of women writers, executives, and other professionals called Women in Film. "I thought it was going to be a women's meeting," Paula says, "but it turned out to be the 'ladies who lunch.' We'd sit around and talk: 'Oh, yeah, she got engaged,' that sort of thing. The women in Hollywood were all extremely jealous of one another." Eventually, she realized that the encouragement and friendship she needed from other women were not to be derived from these occasional kaffeeklatches. In fact, many women in Hollywood disliked Paula intensely—perhaps out of envy, perhaps out of a distrust of her peremptory manner.

Isolated from most of her peers, Paula concentrated on developing relationships with a few other young executives who shared her perspective and concerns—Warner Bros. vice president Lucy Fisher, Goldie Hawn's producing partner Anthea Sylbert—as well as with two of the most important female stars in the business, Jane Fonda and Barbra Streisand. Describing the women she likes and respects, she says, "We are by and large very serious women in a town where there are an enormous number of casual women and casual liaisons. The men who are in these jobs don't respect the women; most of them are ambivalent because they want to be the center of attention, and yet they know that the kind of woman who makes them the center of attention isn't enough, so they finally divorce her or throw her over. There's no man I'd respect who would let *me* be the center of attention. If I want to make a serious relationship, I have to view my work and myself in different terms. I don't mind that I'm not in the limelight any more. In fact, I feel relieved, and I think I'll do better work."

After leaving United Artists, Paula kept a low profile for over a year. Finally, her name appeared in the trade papers in an unexpected way. In May of 1984 she married Mark Rosenberg, the newly appointed president of Warner Bros. That union was a Hollywood first—the marriage of two studio presidents. Rosenberg had assumed the Warners vice presidency that Paula vacated in 1978 when she went to work at Fox. He was a longtime friend of hers from SDS days, and she had encouraged him to come to Hollywood, where he, too, started out as an agent. Some friends felt that Rosenberg had always carried a torch for the statuesque, charismatic Weinstein—even during his previous marriages to writer Tracy Hotchner (the daughter of Hemingway's cohort A.E. Hotchner) and producer Lauren Shuler.

If Paula's vociferous public statements upon leaving UA injured her standing in the industry, her marriage to Rosenberg certainly facilitated her reentry into the circle of power. Before formally tying the knot with Warner president Rosenberg, Paula set up shop on the Warner Bros. lot. In partnership with Gareth Wigan, a former associate from her executive days at Twentieth Century-Fox and The Ladd Company, she formed a production company there in 1984. Their first joint project was a film called *American Flyer*, to be directed by John Badham—the man Paula had hired to replace Martin Brest on *WarGames*. Her sister Lisa also secured a production deal with Warner Bros. in early 1984.

Looking back on the changes in the movie industry and in her own life over the past decade, Paula is at once regretful and hopeful: "For me, the greatest sadness is that it is still as potentially exciting as it is, and yet people relate very little to the work and enormously to the money. Something is broken by how much money everything costs. It's a stomach turner." The huge salary she herself was earning as a studio president distorted her own sense of values, she admits. "I was seduced by the income," she says. "I started working for $140 a week, and it seemed great to me. And then, when I got $50,000, I thought, 'Oh boy, am I getting a lot of money!' And now I think that's no money at all. The value of money and the exchange of money for hours spent don't mean anything after a while."

Paula says that she is grateful to be out of the executive rat race. She realizes that she was becoming increasingly isolated from the rest of the world—and from the moviegoing public whose tastes and interests it was presumably her job to understand. Before she was pulling in an exorbitant salary and enjoying a multitude of executive perks, she had lived quite modestly. "I used to worry about my extravagances," she says. "I watched what my income was. I thought before I'd make a big purchase." But as her salary rose, her attitude changed. "It's a very different feeling going into a store, handing over your credit card, and not even asking how much things cost," she says. "There's no way that doesn't affect you. It puts you in a class of people who are out of reach, out of touch with their environment. I had a guy who watered the plants. I had a guy who brought flowers once a week. I had a maid who came to clean the house two times a week. I didn't even go to the market; I would call Jurgenson's and have them deliver groceries to the office. I hired a young woman who would go to the laundry for me three times a week. I did nothing to make my life—not my work, my life—run. I had other people running every part of my life. Well, if you don't water the plants, then you never develop any relationship to the plants. If you don't go to the market and choose the food, then you don't realize how much things really cost. And you start to become more and more rarefied. Then, all of a sudden, I was out of a job, and I didn't have two secretaries and all those people *shlepping* for me. I realized I'd become a weakling. You ask if I'm ready to have a family. How can someone nurture a family if she can't even water a plant?"

Paula compares her own dizzying rise to the top with the financial roller coaster her family rode when she was a child. Though her mother acquired a small fortune producing television series in England, she suffered a reversal when the American networks stopped buying her product. And before that, she had been flat broke in Paris. Through it all, however, a sense of pride in her work came first for Hannah, and the money came second. "I can remember living in the house with seventeen bedrooms and horses and servants and the Rolls Royce," Paula says. "And then I had to go to work because we didn't have any money. Still, my mother never measured her success by the seventeen-bedroom house. After she lost it, she started over. She struggled for a terrible ten years and made it happen. When she produced *Claudine*, she wasn't just trying to do some trick thing that she thought would be successful. She made something happen that she could also feel good about. I grew up in the fifties, when my mother's friend Lillian Hellman had no money because she was blacklisted and Hammett was dying and Paul Robeson was living at our house in England. I saw that what loomed larger than the income was the talent and the personality. And that is what my mother always said to me about Hollywood and doing a job: If you love it, then go be chairman of the board, but if you don't love it, take less money and go lead a life that has meaning for you. Do what you want to do, but be the most successful at it that anybody can be. My mother never had a burning desire to make movies. She liked ideas. She wanted to make ideas, not movies. She liked to make movies because they had something to say."

Indeed, almost all the movies with which the Weinsteins have been associated have had "something to say," occasionally to the point of message-mongering. *Brubaker*, which was one of Paula's projects during her stint at Fox, and Hannah's production of *Stir Crazy* both exposed the wretched conditions of American prisons; Hannah's *Claudine* and *Greased Lightning* were briefs against racial prejudice; Paula's *Nine to Five* was an indictment of male chauvinism and sex discrimination on the job; Lisa's *WarGames* was a cautionary melodrama about the perils of nuclear proliferation. Yet all these movies were slickly packaged commercial entertainments. The Weinsteins believe in making the ideas in their films palatable and accessible. "I think it's stupid to go out and make a movie that has something to say and not make it in the most mass-appealing way possible," Paula declares. "We're not the French film industry, where you can make a small movie about the Algerian problem. People here don't pay that kind of attention." She cites her friend Jane Fonda as the "master of mixing ideas and commerciality."

Though they take pride in making movies, the Weinsteins recoil at the idea that anyone might construe them to be a "Hollywood" family. "We grew up with great contempt for this environment," Lisa says, "because most of the people we knew in England were refugees from Hollywood and we would hear these terrible stories about what it was like to be here. Now we feel like we're here, but we're not here permanently. We're not a part of the Hollywood family tradition." Paula is even more adamant on the subject. Explaining why it was almost inevitable that her mother's producing career began overseas, Paula says, "She could never have become successful here, when all her friends were blacklisted. My childhood had very little to do with Hollywood. It had to do with a lot of Hollywood people who were blacklisted who told me stories of Hollywood—wonderful, gay, funny Hollywood. But it was always anti-studio, because they were political people who were in the movies; they never thought of themselves as being in the *business*."

As women in a male-dominated profession, as politically committed individuals dealing in the currency of showbiz, the Weinsteins see themselves as strangers in a strange land. Paula says of Hollywood, "I came here nine years ago, and everybody I came here with got to be very successful. It's a very mediocre town, and it's wonderful, and I don't know anywhere else in America where the possibility for success is as great." That statement may sound slightly schizophrenic, but how could a studio head who claims to loathe the studio mentality sound otherwise? The very word "success" is such a staple of Paula's vocabulary that one wonders whether she can evaluate life experience in any other terms. Her preoccupation with success, that obsession which William James once described as "our national disease," may not be conscious, but it betrays Paula's fundamental alliance with the community whose values she professes to abhor.

PAULA Weinstein's swift ascent began when she was working as an agent—a job which has served as a springboard for many other top executives and producers in the new Hollywood. In the early days of the film industry, movie studios protected their sovereignty by signing their stars, writers, producers, and directors to ironclad contracts. After that system was challenged in the courts and the studios' stranglehold on talent was broken, major agencies—such as William Morris and International Creative Management (ICM)—filled the vacuum. Arranging multi-million dollar deals through the "packaging" of their clients, agents have become the industry's true power brokers.

Jeff Berg, the young president of ICM, describes this change in the power structure: "In the thirties and forties, agents didn't have the same effect on what got made as they do today. At that time, the studios were making fifty films a year, and they had their own pipeline of material. Agents sold it to them, but they didn't have that much influence on what got made, because most of the talent was under contract. Now it's much more freelance and project-by-project, which I think is healthier for both sides. It makes everyone work a little harder."

Critics have charged that the agents' rise to dominance has adversely affected the quality of films, making the deal more important than the script and reducing everything to a matter of economic percentages. Like it or not, however, the agent is cock of the walk in today's Hollywood. And as president of the town's largest agency, Jeff Berg is clearly one of the industry's most influential figures. Named to the presidency of ICM at the age of thirty-three, Berg is one of the youngest tycoons in the movie business. He earns several hundred thousand dollars a year and presides over 100 agents representing more than 2200 clients from offices in Los Angeles, New York, Paris, London, and Rome.

Outsiders who hear about Berg's rapid rise from the mailroom to the presidency might be tempted to describe his story as a latter-day Horatio Alger saga. But Jeff Berg is not an entirely self-made man. He is the oldest son in one of the less visible but most accomplished Hollywood dynasties. The Berg family migrated from the East Coast when Jeff was eleven years old, and like other Eastern-bred families who have come to play a prominent role in the movie business, the Bergs hold themselves somewhat aloof from Hollywood even while embracing its riches and rewards.

Of all the Eastern transplants, the Bergs may be closest to the Mankiewiczes, both in their love-hate relationship with show business and in their literary ambitions. All the Bergs are either writers or aspiring writers. Jeff's father, Dick Berg, began in the business as a writer, and Dick's second son, Scott, is a biographer and sometime screenwriter. Even Jeff, the superagent, and his younger brother Tony, a musician, dream of one day turning their attentions to writing prose. "Writers were always important to our family,"

Scott Berg notes. "They were our parents' closest friends. We lived in a house where the books on the shelves actually got read."

The family patriarch, Dick Berg, found himself drawn to the entertainment world even when he was growing up in the suburbs of New York City. He acted in high school plays and, he says, "felt very much at home in the extended family that show business has always provided for me." In the early 1940s, immediately after graduating from college, Dick came to Hollywood with the hope of breaking into the movies. He worked briefly at Republic Pictures but made little headway. Dick moved back east and, in order to support his wife Barbara and his young sons, opened a paint store in Westport, Connecticut. (His father had been a paint manufacturer.) The store eventually evolved into an art gallery called Poor Richard's and, as Dick says, he "became very smitten with the art world." He befriended the artists and writers—Rod Serling, Max Schulman, Peter De Vries—who lived in the Westport area and joined their social circle.

At the same time, Dick kept his writing hopes alive. In 1955 he came up with an idea for a TV pilot, a dramatic series called *Most Likely To Succeed*, about the diverse fates of individuals who have been awarded that appellation at some point in their lives. He was convinced that only one actor could play the leading role in his script: Claude Rains. Berg resolved to place the script in Rains's hands. He went to the office of Rains's agent in New York but could not get past a protective secretary. Undaunted, Berg waited for her to leave her desk and quickly copied Rains's address from her address book. At last he located Rains and gave the actor his script. "I promised him that if he would do it," Berg says, "I would name our third child—who was about to be born—after him."

Although many novices may dream of launching their careers with such a bold gambit, Berg actually pulled it off. Rains was tickled by the fledgling writer's resourcefulness; he also liked the script and agreed to star in the pilot. Dick lived up to his part of the bargain. "Originally, my birth certificate said Claude Berg," says Tony Berg, Dick's third son. "And my mom said, 'I can't live with the name Claude!' So instead they made my middle name Rains. What was best about it was being able to say that Claude Rains was my godfather. I didn't really know him well. The last time I saw him, which was shortly before he died, he had unfortunately become a pretty religious man. And the last thing he asked my dad was, 'Does Tony *believe*?' I think my dad said yes, knowing full well that the answer was no."

In the interim, Claude Rains's participation had introduced Dick Berg to film production. "While I never sold that pilot," Dick says, "I was invigorated by the experience of making the film and being involved with marvelous people—Franchot Tone was in it, along with Rains. It was an altogether delightful experience in which a cousin of mine who financed the film unfortunately lost a lot of money. But it was a launching platform."

There was no turning back for Berg. He moved his family to California and wrote forty original dramas for such TV series as *Playhouse 90*, *Studio One*, and *Kraft Playhouse*. His fourth son, Rick, born in 1959, was in and out of hospitals during his infancy, and Berg decided to take a studio job to stabilize his life. He became a contract producer at Universal for much of the next decade. Since then, he has worked primarily as a producer, though as he notes, "there was a lot of time spent rewriting scripts. The typewriter and the pencil were never put aside." Dick produced a few unmemorable feature films, including *Banning*, with Robert Wagner as a golf pro, and *Counterpoint*, with a miscast Charlton Heston as a symphony conductor in Europe during World War II. But Berg's primary success was in television. During the 1960s, he produced the most acclaimed dramatic series of the era—*Bob Hope's Chrysler Theatre*—and worked with many major actors (Robert Redford, George C. Scott, Anne Bancroft) and directors (Sydney Pollack, Mark Rydell) early in their careers.

Later Berg left Universal and formed his own company, Stonehenge Productions, housed for a time at Lorimar, then at Metromedia, then at Paramount. He has remained one of the most active producers in television, responsible for two-hour movies and miniseries, including the adaptations of Philip Caputo's Vietnam exposé, *A Rumor of War*, Ray Bradbury's *The Martian Chronicles*, Irving Wallace's *The Word*, and his most ambitious production—a multipart rendition of James Michener's *Space*.

David Manson, who worked as Berg's assistant and then coproducer during the 1970s, says of Dick, "He's been producing for twenty-five years, and he is still able to get enormously enthusiastic at the smell of a deal. That's exciting and stimulating to other people. I think he also has a very fertile mind. He's well educated, and he reads a lot, so there are a lot of ideas. He has such energy when he presents them that you have to be able to separate good from bad and not be overwhelmed by the rush of energy. What is producing? Most of the time it's taste and the ability to motivate other people. And in both those areas, I think Dick has talent."

Fay Kanin, a writer, producer, and past president of the Motion Picture Academy of Arts and Sciences, wrote her first TV movie, *Heat of Anger*, for Berg. When he read the script, he sent Kanin a large bouquet of flowers. She was flabbergasted, for she had never heard of a producer commending a writer with such a chivalrous gesture. "That's the kind of producer Dick was," Kanin says. "He's a great enthusiast. That was a difficult film because we started with Barbara Stanwyck and she got ill, so we had to start all over with Susan Hayward. But Dick never lost his enthusiasm."

Dick Berg has consistently demonstrated a yearning to be attached to high-toned material. Over the years, he has struggled to bring serious novels such as Norman Mailer's *The Deer Park* and Joyce Carol Oates's *Bellefleur* to television. Yet more often than not, these demanding projects failed to win the green light at the networks, and Berg fell back on more exploitable fodder like *Rape and Marriage—The Rideout Case*; *Someone I Touched*, a story about VD starring Cloris Leachman; and *Firehouse*, the pilot for a series about life in a fire station. Dick has affection for some of his television work but says frankly, "Nobody has any great cause to be that pleased with the body of his work in this community. I feel some pride in what I've done, but most of what's done is very second-rate."

David Manson probably knows the different sides of Dick Berg and his family as well as anyone. Manson first met the Bergs when he and Tony attended high school together; the boys became fast friends, and Manson soon developed a rapport with the entire family. "It was sort of like being taken in by Jewish gentility," he says. Yet as he came to know Dick better in the six years that he worked alongside him, Manson perceived something beneath that genteel, cultured facade. "Dick has a very, very strong showbiz side to him," Manson suggests. "When you get past that veneer and education, Dick is very much a Jewish *tummeler*. Even the Yiddish phrases start coming out. I think that is less extant in his sons. You have almost no sense of the sons' Jewishness, but with Dick you do. In my mind, I associate that side of him with the Carnegie Deli—that enjoyment of *tummeling*, being in the midst of action and activity."

Dick Berg recognizes that there is something of a contradiction in his personality, though he tends to downplay it. Unlike Joseph L. Mankiewicz, he does not despise show business. "My approach to the mass media cannot be elitist," he says. "I like to think that we bring a level of taste to our work, but essentially we're in show business, and to attempt to make it more didactic would be a mistake. The work should have a mass appeal. Otherwise, I should be working off-Broadway or writing poetry or teaching on some campus, which I once thought of doing when I was a very young man. If there is a gap between the creator and the audience, there's nothing wrong with that. I think the tension and the anguish that the artist experiences, the alienation frequently triggered by the marketplace and the investors, is both an irritant and a stimulus."

While Dick Berg succeeded in the TV marketplace, he never became entirely *of* Hollywood. He was primarily a family man whose happiest times were spent with his wife and four sons at their sprawling home in Brentwood. "When we were growing up," Scott says, "Dad's friends were writers and writer-producers. We rarely had actors in the house." One actor who was invited to dinner was young Tony Bill, who had made his film debut playing Frank Sinatra's kid brother in *Come Blow Your Horn* and was starring for Dick in a segment of Chrysler Theatre. But Bill was a poet as well as an actor, and he had respectable academic credentials to boot. For his part, Bill found Dick Berg something of a novelty in Hollywood. "I was particularly drawn to him," Bill says, "because he reminded me of my teachers from prep school and college. He was thoughtful, literate, and educated, almost professorial. And that's what I enjoyed about his sons as well."

THOSE who know the family agree that Jeff Berg was a late bloomer; when he was growing up, he gave no hints of being a budding business whiz. "Up until college, Jeff was really a nondescript character," his brother Tony says. "He wore a leather jacket and drove a Lambretta. And then he went to college at Berkeley and became a great student. He became curious, which he'd never really been before."

At Berkeley in the late 1960s, Jeff became active politically and also discovered movies at the revival houses that specialized in American and foreign classics. That newfound passion, combined with his family background, led him into the film business. During one summer vacation, his father helped him to get a job in the mailroom at Ashley Famous, which became International Famous Agency. He soon progressed to being a script reader. "By the time I graduated from Berkeley in 1969," Jeff says, "IFA made me an offer to come to work as a literary agent, which I did. That seemed the logical thing to do in light of the four prior summers I had spent apprenticing. I loved movies, and I liked the idea of being a part of the overall fabric in some way."

Shortly after going to work at IFA, Jeff was spirited away by its larger rival, CMA. (In 1975, the two agencies would merge to become ICM.) There he became the protégé of the agency's co-founder, Freddie Fields, a colorful, ostentatious go-getter who represented top stars such as Judy Garland, Al Pacino, and Woody Allen. When asked what he saw in young Berg, Fields commented tersely, "He was certainly attractive, and he spoke well."

Although Jeff credits Fields with advancing his career, their personal styles were quite different—Fields ebullient and expansive, Berg cautious and contained. While Fields was primarily an actors' agent, Berg chose to be a literary agent. "It's no accident that I wound up being a literary agent rather than a talent agent," Jeff admits. "My father's background as a writer encouraged me to lean toward writers and writing."

There was also a more pragmatic reason for Jeff's decision to represent writers. "When I was starting out," he says, "I saw other people in my company who were representing actors and actresses very successfully. I had to try to create a niche for myself, and I thought the literary side would be more effective for me. It was also a period when there was a whole new generation of talent entering the business out of the film schools and the American Film Institute. A lot of the early people whom I represented came from those schools."

Jeff settled into his job the summer that *Easy Rider* swept the country and triggered the Hollywood "youth revolution." He shrewdly sensed that young writers and writer-directors were the up-and-coming force in the industry, and he cornered the market by aligning himself with many of the hot ones: Paul Mazursky (*Bob & Carol & Ted & Alice*, *Harry and Tonto*), Paul Schrader (screenwriter of *Taxi Driver*, writer-director of *Blue Collar* and *American Gigolo*), John Milius (writer of *Jeremiah Johnson* and *Apocalypse Now*, later the director of *The Wind and the Lion* and *Conan the Barbarian*), Hal Barwood and Matthew Robbins (*The Sugarland Express*, *Corvette Summer*, *Dragonslayer*), Walter Hill (screenwriter of *The Getaway*, one of the producers of *Alien*, director of *The Warriors* and *48 Hours*), Terrence Malick (writer-director of *Badlands* and *Days of Heaven*), novelist-screenwriter

Peter Benchley (*Jaws* and *The Deep*). Berg also represented a promising young filmmaker named George Lucas. Lucas's mentor, Francis Coppola, was a client of Freddie Fields at CMA, and Berg, too, worked closely with Coppola for a number of years.

On behalf of these clients and others who joined him later, Jeff put together some of the most lucrative deals of the 1970s. He sold Peter Benchley's *The Deep* for $500,000, then pulled off an even greater coup by winning $2.15 million for Benchley's *The Island*—the highest sum ever paid for the movie rights to a novel. The picture went on to be a commerical catastrophe, for Zanuck/Brown and Universal, but Benchley and Berg smiled all the way to the bank.

In 1977, one of Berg's clients, screenwriter Walter Hill, happened on the script for a sci-fi monster movie that had been kicking around the studios for years. He was intrigued by the story, did a quick rewrite, and Berg sold the project to Twentieth Century-Fox. The original writers, Dan O'Bannon and Ronald Shusett, ultimately demanded an arbitration before the Writers Guild and forced Hill's name to be removed from the writing credits. Nonetheless, Berg successfully negotiated for Hill and his partners, David Giler and Gordon Carroll, to become producers of *Alien*. He also won them a hefty percentage of the movie's profits, and although they had to sue Fox for an accurate accounting, they all made a fortune on the $100 million bonanza.

It was Berg who arranged the deal for George Lucas to develop *American Graffiti* at United Artists. When UA rejected the script, Berg took it to Universal. Executives there were hesitant to put up the tiny $750,000 budget required to make the movie until Berg persuaded CMA client Francis Coppola (fresh from his triumph on *The Godfather*) to lend his name as producer. *American Graffiti* remains one of the two or three most profitable films in history, eventually grossing more than 100 times its modest cost. Universal nonetheless passed on Lucas's next script, a comic book adventure set in outer space, and Berg sold *Star Wars* to Alan Ladd, Jr. at Twentieth Century-Fox. ICM received not just ten percent of Lucas's salary but ten percent of his share of the profits. When the earnings were finally tallied, ICM had made over $4 million on the behemoth blockbuster.

At that point, however, Lucas decided that he no longer needed an agent. He left Hollywood, and retreated to Marin County, where he plotted the *Star Wars* sequels and *Raiders of the Lost Ark*. Lucas terminated his representation agreement with ICM, but Berg believed the agency was still entitled to commissions on all sequels to *Star Wars*, since he had made the original deal for the movie. Lucas disagreed, and the matter went to arbitration. ICM lost its case and all profit participation—amounting to millions of dollars— in *The Empire Strikes Back* and *Return of the Jedi*.

Despite their legal battle, Berg insists that he and Lucas remain on cordial terms: "I have no ill feelings toward George, and I don't think we're adversaries in any sense of the word. I think the years we did work with each other were very positive ones and productive ones commercially and professionally." No matter how successful he is, any agent inevitably loses clients over the years. Describing his feelings when this happens, Berg comments, "It can be painful, because you've put an enormous emotional investment into the relationship, and when it ends, invariably you ask yourself, 'What did I do wrong, and why doesn't he like me?' I tend not to ask those questions any more. I don't take it quite so personally as I used to when I was twenty-four or twenty-five. There is ebb and flow in the client business. You lose a client, and you ask yourself, 'How can I get a new one?' "

At the same time that many of his colleagues at ICM were leaving the agency to become producers or studio executives, Jeff resolved to stick with the company. Freddie Fields became a producer in 1973 and offered Jeff a job with his new production unit, but Jeff chose to remain an agent. Over the years, he has been offered studio jobs; he was rumored to be the first choice for the position that Sherry Lansing ultimately assumed at Twentieth Century-Fox. His former boss at CMA, Richard Shepherd, notes, "I don't think Jeff wants to be anything other than a very good agent, and that's why he has succeeded."

At a time when very few studio chiefs hold their jobs for more than two or three years, Jeff's innate conservatism probably kept him from joining the executive shuffle. He explains his decision to remain at ICM: "My attitude was and remains, if you love something, continue doing it and find ways to grow and improve upon it. I never really saw the agency business as a springboard to passing to another life. I've stayed at ICM over the years because I think it's the most interesting company in the entertainment industry. It's in every aspect of the arts. You can work on a movie project or something in television, you can get involved in a concert act, you can be involved in the sale of a book. That mix can't be found anywhere else besides the agency business. It works for my personality."

Because of his loyalty to the agency and the phenomenally lucrative deals he negotiated, Berg was rewarded with the ICM presidency in 1980. Yet it says a good deal about him—and about his family's obeisance to literature—that even while he was climbing the ladder at ICM, he was taking night classes at USC toward his M.A. in English. He still has to complete his thesis on revolution and politics in twentieth century literature; the focus of the thesis is Andre Malraux, author of *Man's Fate*. "My masters project is five years late," Jeff says in some dismay. "I would love to have that out of the way. It would give me a sense of accomplishment."

One of his clients, writer-director James Toback, comments on these contradictions in Berg's personality. "The major distinction between Jeff and other executives," Toback notes, "is that you have the feeling with him that, even if he has to go through the motions of favoring mainstream commercial movies, he really likes more ambitious, offbeat, and original films. He got into movies because of his excitement over Godard's films. You're not going to hear David Begelman say that *Pierrot le Fou* is one of his five favorite movies."

Berg has been fanatically loyal to Toback, the writer of *The Gambler* and the writer-director of *Fingers*, *Love and Money*, and *Exposed*—not one of which has made a nickel in profit. But this is typical of Berg, and atypical of agents in general. "He's ready to continue to work enthusiastically for people who have not enriched the coffers of ICM or the studios," Toback says in amazement and gratitude.

His family tends to tease Jeff about his loyalty to some of his more eccentric clients. "Jeff and I agree about most films, aside from the fact that his own loyalty to clients is monumental," his father says with a chuckle. "I don't suffer that problem." Jeff's brother Tony is more outspoken in questioning Jeff's unstinting devotion to such clients as John Milius, the perpetrator of the moronic paean to surfing, *Big Wednesday*, and the blood-soaked comic strip, *Conan the Barbarian*. "Jeff is so devoted to his clients that it's insane," Tony says. "He'll see some garbage movie that one of them has made—a real piece of crap—and he'll insist that the movie is good. Jeff's attracted to funny guys. Milius and he are very close. Jeff finds the heart in these guys that the rest of us would not discern. Now I think *Apocalypse Now*, which was written by Milius, is a great movie. There's an intelligence in that film, and I think Jeff has found that in Milius. On the other hand,

Milius can make the worst trash. *Big Wednesday* is maybe the worst movie ever made."

Jeff Berg belies the image of an agent as a slick, sycophantic charlatan with tinted glasses, body shirt open to the navel, and fingers encrusted in silver and turquoise. He favors charcoal gray suits and dark ties, is immaculately groomed, precise in his syntax, and can be brusque to the point of rudeness.

Berg has made his share of enemies in the line of duty, but as Freddie Fields once said in his defense, "What excuse do you have, what defense against a proper negotiator, when you've been bettered? You call him a killer, a cold-blooded guy. They're all overused terms. There's no such thing as a sweet, warm, adorable good negotiator."

His brother Tony characterizes Jeff sympathetically but accurately. "He's not afraid to say 'Fuck you' to somebody when it's appropriate. He's very abrupt with people, and I know a lot of people think of him as a kind of Sammy Glick, but he's the antithesis of Sammy Glick, because Sammy Glick was single-minded and devious. Jeff is neither of those things. I think Jeff has less pettiness than almost anyone I know. He hates small talk, hates petty resentments; he is the most straightforward of anyone in the family. Scott will remember that seven years ago he was slighted by someone in a bar, whereas with Jeff each day is starting over. He doesn't care about things like that. He's really got a good sense of himself. This is a typical Jeff conversation. He'll call me at seven in the morning and say, 'Hi. What's going on?' And I'll say, 'Well, nothing. It's seven in the morning.' And he'll say, 'Okay, got to go. Bye.'"

Like most agents, Jeff Berg conducts much of his business by phone. "If Jeff has a flaw," says Paul Mazursky, "it's that he watches the phones too much. If I really want to talk to him, I arrange to meet him away from the office." Berg's spacious ICM office has three extensions, each with eight lines, and his two secretaries keep the calls coming in. A lull of even a few minutes puts him on edge, and during an early-morning meeting at his home in Pacific Palisades, he is slightly disgruntled when two phone calls in a row are for his wife, a psychologist. "My wife is more popular than I am," he says in consternation.

Like his father, Jeff stays out of the Hollywood fast lane. His aloofness has sometimes been taken for hauteur, and some of his colleagues have nicknamed him "Ice Berg." "Jeff has this cold, efficient business channel," says James Toback. "But there's another side of him that comes out with a few friends. He has a wacky sense of humor, but most people don't see it. He's succeeded by keeping people at arm's length. Unlike most other people in Hollywood, he does not say 'I love you' ten times a day; he does not kiss everyone on the cheek. I suspect that may come from his family. My feeling on seeing the family together is that there's a certain amount of containment. They're a close family, but they're not a demonstrative family."

If Berg's cool, impersonal style generally enhances efficiency, there are those who believe it may have hurt his company. In the last few years, a smaller agency in town, Creative Artists Agency, has suddenly established itself as a rival to ICM and William Morris. Started by five renegade agents from the Morris office, CAA has snapped up many of the superstar clients—including Paul Newman, Robert Redford, and Dustin Hoffman—once represented by either William Morris or ICM. And some observers feel that Jeff Berg's chilly personality has hurt ICM in the competition for big-name talent. One colleague of Berg's says, "CAA represents most of the heavyweight clients in the business, and it's because they're really a family. They cover you like a blanket; you can't sneeze without them saying, 'Gesundheit!' At ICM, agents are all battling each other. I think Jeff has a problem in getting everybody within the agency to row in the same direction. They're like separate little companies looking out for their own people and no one else. If Jeff had different personality traits, he'd shake those people up and get them to help each other. That's the only way to sign more people and represent them more effectively."

Jeff has heard these criticisms, and he answers: "If those rivalries do exist here, it's not something I concern myself with. CAA may have developed a more familial approach towards business. But I don't like working in highly-structured, paternalistic corporations. I think in a company you should create an environment where individuals can grow and develop on their own." That is not unlike the environment Dick Berg sought to create for his own family—an atmosphere of healthy competitiveness rather than blind loyalty.

Jeff Berg seems impervious to criticism of his agency or agents in general. One of the most common complaints leveled against big agencies like ICM is that they try to maximize their income by stuffing as many of their clients—actors, writers, producers, and directors—into a particular film, whether or not the clients are well suited to the project. "It does occur," Berg admits. "But finally the studio doesn't have to accept the project, so ultimately no one's being forced or coerced into doing anything." A *Wall Street Journal* reporter, Stephen J. Sansweet, sat in on a regular agents' meeting at ICM in 1982 and noted that, when a junior agent announced that a non-ICM actress was about to be signed for a big-budget film scripted by an ICM writer, Berg directed the agent to "try to knock her out of it" and substitute an ICM actress.

Perhaps the criticism that draws the most vehement rebuttal from Berg is William Goldman's blunt statement in *Adventures in the Screen Trade* that agents and ex-agents have one common characteristic: they lack passion. "I don't believe that," Berg retorts. "I care deeply about what I'm doing. To me, it's not just commerce. I have a feeling for the work. I also have a relationship with people I've been working with over the years. You become not only the economic conduit, but what you do also relates to the ability of an artist to express himself. So it's a very profound mandate, and serious agents don't take that lightly."

ONE cannot help wondering whether Dick Berg ever harbored the sort of jealousy toward his son that has more frequently been felt by children toward their successful parents or siblings. "It must have been strange for Dick," his former associate David Manson muses. "Here his son was under thirty years old and enjoying a kind of celebrity within the same business that he was working in. Besides, Jeff was involved in creating major films at a time when we were trying unsuccessfully to move into that area. But I don't think jealousy is an accurate word. Their relationship is complex, but I think Dick takes enormous pride in Jeff." Scott Berg admits that the family had some difficulty adjusting to Jeff's sudden success. "It was a little rough on my father when Jeff started to rise," Scott says candidly. "Jeff was in the eye of the hurricane, in the center of power. I sensed some tension when I came home in 1971. But that didn't last very long. Dad was always extremely proud of Jeffrey." Today, on the wall in Dick Berg's office is a framed copy of the issue of *Variety* announcing Jeff's appointment to the presidency of ICM.

In comparing the accomplishments of father and son, one must take into account that they are men of somewhat different temperament. Although Dick Berg admits that at times he has fantasized about running a major company, he also recognizes that he is probably not ideally suited to such a position. "I don't want to be a power broker," he says, "and I'm not sure that I would be content with that kind of situation. Once you're responsible for a volume of product, as you would be in running a network or a studio, you must turn out an awful lot of crap. I'm sure Grant Tinker has this problem running NBC. His imprint is on *Cheers* and *St. Elsewhere*, but he's also got to allow—not only allow, but encourage—*The A-Team*. And I don't want to be identified with *The A-Team*."

In other words, Dick's fastidiousness probably kept him from reaching the very top rungs of the ladder. Jeff seems to have no such compunctions. Although he may personally favor Godard, he must bring the same enthusiasm to *Conan the Barbarian*. There are other crucial differences between father and son. "Jeff can be much less tolerant than my dad," Tony Berg suggests. "My dad would never make someone real uncomfortable by pointing up that person's inadequacies in some department. Jeff would."

One other difference is that Dick came into the business much later in life—at the age of thirty-five, when he already had a family. His priorities were different from those of a twenty-two-year-old dynamo just starting out. "My dad was always closer to his family than to his work," Scott says. "That's why I think he has had a quieter career than some people. I like his career, and he likes it. But we always knew we came before his job. If he had to go to New York on business, he called home twice a day. He and my mother have been married thirty-seven years, and they're closer today than ever."

All the Berg sons were gently steered toward lives of high achievement. The second son, Andrew Scott, was the most disciplined student and pursued the family's literary inclinations most directly. By the time he was a teenager, Scott's course had been set. "I did a tenth grade report on Fitzgerald, at my mother's urging," he says. "I became obsessed with Fitzgerald." He was delighted that he shared his hero's middle name, and decided to highlight the fact by calling himself A. Scott Berg. "Scott was a Scott Fitzgerald freak as a teenager," his brother Tony says. "It's a sick notion, but he was."

Scott wanted to follow his idol's example and enroll at Princeton. "When I was sixteen," he says, "Princeton, New Jersey seemed to me the most glamorous place on earth. To me, academicians were stars. Movie people weren't." At Princeton, Scott studied Fitzgerald's papers and those of his editor at Scribner's, Maxwell Perkins. He became an undergraduate protégé of Hemingway's biographer, Carlos Baker. But he also retained a lingering attraction to show business. He had acted in high school, and in college he participated in the Princeton Triangle Shows. His parents were horrified when he threatened to quit college to become a professional actor. It was not the life they had envisioned for any of their sons.

That was merely a rebellious gesture, however; before long Scott returned to the preordained path. "The truth is I always felt being an actor was nothing compared to being a writer," he says. After graduation, Scott decided to expand his senior thesis into a full-scale biography of Maxwell Perkins, the New York editor who had nurtured the careers of Fitzgerald, Hemingway, Thomas Wolfe, and other major literary figures. His parents were so relieved that he had abandoned the notion of acting that they agreed to support him as he completed the project. He lived at home for seven years after graduation while he labored over the book. He had no other job. Scott explains, "My parents felt if I had wanted to be a doctor, they would have sent me to medical school. This was my medical school."

Carole Serling, the widow of Dick's close friend Rod Serling, says of this interlude, "A lot of parents, if they had a kid at home writing a book for seven years, wouldn't have been able to tolerate that. First of all, a lot of families couldn't afford it financially. But even if they could, most parents would say, 'Hey, kid, get yourself a job.' I know I would. So Scott had a very unusual situation."

"Scott spent seven years completely isolated," Tony Berg says. "I'm sure you can be engaged in something like that, but to do it for seven years bordered on sickness. I know at a certain point about six years into the book, he didn't know if what he was doing was any good at all. And when it finally came out and received all the attention it did, there was this sense of freedom for him. He has since become very social."

Max Perkins won the American Book Award, and Scott decided that it would be the first in a series of biographies of major cultural figures he wanted to write. But first he was waylaid by the movies. His father suggested to him that he try to write a few screen stories, and he came up with one that was immediately salable—an up-to-the-minute romantic drama about a married man confronting his homosexuality. Scott proposed the notion to his friend Barry Sandler, the screenwriter of such Hollywood baubles as *Gable and Lombard* and *The Duchess and the Dirtwater Fox*. Together they took the notion to Claire Townsend, an old Princeton classmate of Scott's, and a second lieutenant under Sherry Lansing at Twentieth Century-Fox. With Townsend's support, the studio bought the story and signed Daniel Melnick—a mentor of both Townsend and Lansing—to produce the film. Scott concedes that his brother also played a part in bringing *Making Love* to the screen. "Jeff did shepherd *Making Love* unofficially," Scott admits. "He and Dan Melnick are very close."

His first moviemaking experience turned out to be less than happy for Scott. Because of its bold subject matter, the movie—which starred Michael Ontkean as the bisexual doctor, Kate Jackson as his unsuspecting wife, and Harry Hamlin as Ontkean's lover—received a barrage of publicity while in production. But the finished film was attacked by most critics as a laughably tepid treatment of the theme. *Making Love* did very little for the reputation of anyone connected with it. Nevertheless, Scott continued to dabble in the movies; he provided the story for another project developed at Fox (but dropped when both Townsend and Lansing left the studio) and worked on a screenplay with director John Frankenheimer, a client of his brother's and a friend of the family. Scott insists that his movie deals are merely diversions. "I don't want to have a motion picture career," he insists. "Movies are extracurricular to me, and I think they always will be."

In recent years, Scott's main project has been his work on the definitive biography of Samuel Goldwyn. It is probably no accident that Scott should have chosen Goldwyn as the subject of his second book, for Goldwyn epitomized Hollywood's aspiration to cultural respectability. A born salesman who strove for "good taste" and literary prestige while immersing himself in the vulgarity of the movie business, Goldwyn bore the divided sensibility that characterizes the Bergs as well.

The third son, Tony, was probably the most free-spirited of the Berg children. In junior high, he tuned out of school work, grew his hair long, began smoking grass and playing rock and roll guitar. "I was the one son who had a real bad period with my folks for about two years," he says. Outsiders see even that period of rebellion as rather mild compared to the conflicts other families endured during the 1960s. As David Manson says in amusement, "Given the battleground of most of my friends' parental relationships, Tony's relationship with his family seemed relatively placid. He was actually one of my straighter friends. I'm sure when he put an earring in his ear, everybody looked askance for a moment. But Tony could always go home."

Still, Tony did choose the most unconventional route of all four sons. He went to college for two years but dropped out when he got an opportunity to work as musical director at the Mark Taper Forum, the experimental theater attached to the Music Center in Los Angeles. After that, Tony spent a year in the orchestra performing with *The Rocky Horror Show*. He scored Robert Altman's movie, *A Perfect Couple*, arranged music for a daytime variety show and a number of TV movies, including one score he wrote for his father's film, *An Invasion of Privacy*, which starred Valerie Harper and Jerry Ohrbach. "That worked out well," Tony says. "The network loved it, and the participants loved it. But I don't think I'd work for my father again. There's an implicit pressure on him for me to do well, and that kind of pressure shouldn't be placed on anybody. I appreciate that he hired me to do it, but I think all of us got some gray hairs from it."

Perhaps the high point of Tony's career has been the three years he spent as Bette Midler's musical director, from 1979 to 1982. "I wrote all the arrangements for her," he explains, "rehearsed the band, chose the material with her, and engaged in a lot of arguments with her. Bette thrives on conflict. Everything has to be taken to its limit before you get a rise out of her, and then you get a lot of juice from her. But who wants to go through that angst all the time? She had musical directors before me, like Barry Manilow, who were more sweet and accommodating. I was neither of those things. She and I locked horns all the time, but I think some of the best stuff each of us has done came from that."

When he left Midler, Tony decided to form his own rock and roll band. He looks down on the idea of film scoring and has little desire to work in movies or television. "The whole concept of film scoring is a phony notion," he says scornfully. "It's this artifice in the midst of something that aspires to be so naturalistic. For the most part, the filmmaker attempts to portray reality as best he can, and then he hires 101 strings. It's a stupid concept. Besides, television and film never really fascinated me. I think they're both facile media. Film especially can take a mediocre project and by virtue of its size attempt to elevate it to something it's not. I hate that." Taking a dig at one of the most successful clients his brother's agency has ever represented, Tony goes on, "To me, a Steven Spielberg film is a classic example of third-rate melodrama elevated way beyond its depth. I can't think of a filmmaker whose stuff I like less. His work is so manipulative."

Instead of aspiring to a career in films, Tony one day hopes to write novels. The Bergs' youngest son, Rick, has so far avoided show business altogether. But he, too, is doing remarkably well as an aide to Senator Christopher Dodd in Washington, D.C.

Like the Douglas family, the Bergs engage in the kind of sparring one expects to find in a male preserve; all of them are articulate and highly opinionated. As one family friend observes, "You'd be sitting in their kitchen, and somebody would come in and give an opinion about a film, which would immediately set off five other opinions, many of them totally hyperbolic. Scott will tell you he never goes to see a foreign film, that his favorite movie of all time is *Pride of the Yankees*. Is that a pose, or is it a real opinion? The point is that it produced lively debate."

Despite their periodic arguments, the Berg brothers do not bear the scars of any intense sibling rivalries. Their parents deliberately sent the boys to different schools so that they would not face comparisons with the others' achievements. This is not to say that their relationships have been conflict-free. Scott and Jeff are radically different in personality. "Scott loves tradition, loves anything musty," Tony points out. "Jeff loves immediacy." As Scott defines their differences, "Jeff always felt I was very much into my ivory tower. He likes to make fun of me and say I came back from the east with a phony accent. He loves action, loves to have nineteen things going at once. I hate that. I'm a monomaniac, a plodder. I concentrate on one thing at a time."

Tony also went through a period of intense conflict with Jeff when he was about twenty. "Jeff was a successful agent," Tony recalls, "and I was just starting to get work as a musician. There was a real resentment of what each guy did. I think he was envious of the fact that I was doing what I *wanted* to do, and I was envious of the fact that he had reached the pinnacle of success in his particular profession. There was this budding antagonism. He would say things like, 'You don't have any thoughts.' And I would say, 'That's an odd comment coming from a guy who spends his life selling other people's material.' For a few months, we had a hard time, and then we resolved it in the course of conversation. When he drew a spade, I drew a spade, and that's all that mattered."

There were times when Dick Berg, like Kirk Douglas, fantasized about having all his sons work with him, but he professes to be happier now that they have gone their separate ways. They try to keep their business and personal lives separate. "I've managed to dissociate my professional activities from my brothers," Jeff says. "I care about what they're doing, and I would like to be helpful wherever I can, but I really believe in keeping a separation." They all feel that their closeness as a family depends on each of them maintaining his independence.

The force holding the family together is Barbara Berg. At least Dick feels that his own influence on his sons has been "by osmosis," but that Barbara "really assumed the burden of rearing these four young men and did a noble job." There is no question that she is an ambitious, accomplished woman in her own right, and in that sense she provided a parental model just as significant as her husband's. When she was in her late forties, Barbara returned to college at UCLA—with classmates who were younger than her children—and graduated Phi Beta Kappa and summa cum laude. Her next challenge is to work toward her doctorate in contemporary European history. That extraordinary sense of discipline and drive to achieve have been inherited by her sons.

Among Hollywood families, the Bergs seem to have been particularly privileged, yet David Manson raises a provocative point when he identifies a possible inadequacy in the second generation: "To a certain extent, their lives have been adversity-free. Each one of them has been blessed. Generally, you find a certain balance of the cursed and the blessed, as with the Kennedys. Scott had this sort of pastoral existence, and I would say it allows him to have a very romantic point of view. It allows for a certain kind of glibness in all of them, because what do they know? Not poverty, not deep loss or sense of death. You wonder what will happen when that does come into their lives. Often, original talent that forces you to create comes out of a certain pain or desolation. In a sense, the Bergs' talents are all interpretive talents. Jeff's talents are definitely in that area. Tony is primarily an arranger rather than a songwriter. Scott is a biographer rather than a novelist. I guess it's the consequences of too much happiness. Dick grew up in a more complex past, and I think he's experienced certain kinds of pain that none of the boys have yet. As a result, he is a very visceral personality. The sons are less so."

There is no question that Jeff Berg embodies a breed of executive quite unlike the passionate, explosive showmen who started the movie business in a few empty warehouses. Jeff epitomizes a new generation of college-educated, meticulous corporation men. They know how to engineer lucrative deals, and they have their enthusiasms certainly, but they are a more careful and controlled species than their predecessors. Yet even if one regrets the depersonalization of the entertainment business, there is no turning back the clock. "The original moguls brought creative energy to a new business," Jeff Berg says. "But people entering it today are bringing their own creative energy. There exist pioneers in every generation."

10

LA FAMIGLIA:
The Coppolas

*"I want to thank my son Francis, because without him I
wouldn't be here. But then if I wasn't here, he wouldn't be
here, either."*

—CARMINE COPPOLA ACCEPTING THE OSCAR, 1975

FROM the outside, the mansion on Bellagio Road looks like almost
any other Bel-Air estate—an electrified fence surrounding the
grounds, a perfectly manicured lawn, several expensive foreign
cars parked in the circular driveway. But once inside the house
where Talia (Coppola) Shire lives with her second husband,
lawyer-turned-producer Jack Schwartzman, the aura of aristocratic
gentility quickly disappears. Talia may have the wealth of a Bel-
Air matron, but she still has the personality of a slightly discom-
bobulated *paisana* whose motor runs a little faster than normal.
Although she has a Mexican housekeeper and a personal secretary
at her command, she is reluctant to give up the responsibilities of
a regular suburban mom. She drops a Chick'n Stick in the Cuisinart
for her baby's lunch, but the gadget regurgitates the food in indi-
gestible lumps. So she throws that away and opens a can of mush-
room soup instead. With a welcoming smile, she invites a visitor
to have a seat, then notices that the wicker chair she has designated
has a gigantic hole made by another son.

Later, Talia shifts gears to confer with a production assistant
who is also working at the house. Talia and her husband are
preparing for the release of their first co-production, the James
Bond adventure movie *Never Say Never Again*, which is billed as

"A Taliafilm Production" in the credits. But Talia the movie producer, Academy Award-nominated actress, and sister of genius-mogul Francis Ford Coppola, is also the frazzled housewife who has to rush off in her station wagon to pick up her oldest son at school; it is her day for car pool, and the urgent business of making movies will have to be put on hold for the rest of the afternoon.

Over the hill in the San Fernando Valley, a similar mood reigns in the more modest ranch-style home of Talia's parents, Carmine and Italia Coppola. Knickknacks line the shelves of the cluttered living room, and brightly-colored pillows lie helter skelter on the sofa. In the kitchen, Italia is grilling toasted cheese sandwiches for lunch. "Carmine, you've got to keep Pepsi in the house!" she screams as she rummages through the refrigerator. Married for over fifty years, Carmine and Italia bicker like a Mediterranean Maggie and Jiggs. An outsider would probably be surprised to learn that this unpretentious couple head one of movieland's most successful families. Yet there on the coffee table, right next to the vase of artificial flowers, is the Oscar that Carmine won for scoring *The Godfather, Part II*, which was written and directed by his son. And although the wedding picture over the mantelpiece looks like an ordinary blowup from the family album, it is actually a still from the famous opening scene of *The Godfather*; their daughter Talia is the bride, but she is flanked by her celluloid family— Marlon Brando, Al Pacino, James Caan, and Diane Keaton. It is an almost surreal touch, suggesting the constant interplay of theatricality and domesticity within this vibrant Italian clan.

Three thousand miles away, the godfather himself, Francis Coppola, is also mired in chaos as he struggles to complete his latest movie, *The Cotton Club*, a gangster melodrama set against the backdrop of Harlem's most famous night club. Predictably, the film is weeks behind schedule and millions of dollars over budget. It has been delayed by a series of well-publicized crises; once Francis walked off the set for two days because producer Robert Evans had not paid his salary. The movie, which stars Richard Gere, Gregory Hines, and Coppola's nephew Nicolas Cage, could end up costing an outlandish $42 million in all, meaning that it will have to gross something like $175 million just to break even. Once again, Francis Coppola is flirting with disaster. As Paramount chairman Barry Diller had said, "Francis likes living on the brink."

After visiting with his sister and his parents and then reading about his latest turbulent production, one might conclude that

Francis's propensity for disorganization is somehow hereditary. Francis himself has said, "I bring to my life a certain amount of mess," a statement which might almost serve as the family motto. Certainly there is much more to the Coppolas than this love of "mess," but the first impression is that they are a passionate, boisterous group—anomalies among the more repressed, methodical drones who dominate today's movie industry.

"My family is still into the whole Italian thing," Talia Shire notes. "Come over and cook pasta. We do that as anchors. We love children. We love to keep the world *al dente*, if you know what I mean. I'm sure that the Selznick family got very chic. We never do. I remember once seeing Francis after *The Godfather* was making all that money. He went into Tiffany's to buy silver, and they were going to throw him out; they didn't know what to make of this strange, overweight man playing with the silver. The men in my family love dishes and silver. Francis once looked at me and I looked at him, and he said, 'You know, we'll never be able to coordinate our clothes. It's genetically impossible.' It's true. We're never going to pull that off, and that's what saves us. We're still a very earthy family."

Observing his in-laws, Talia's husband, Jack Schwartzman, is reminded of his own roots in Brooklyn: "This is not unlike a Jewish family," he says, "where things are always cooking. The pot is stirring all the time, the emotions are vying. There's a tremendous amount of energy."

Indeed, the Coppolas hark back to the peasant Jews who started the movie business. Francis is the one leader of the new Hollywood who bears comparison to the buccaneer-tycoons of days past. It is he, not the cautious, frightened men now running the studios, who carries on the legacy of Selznick, Warner, and Cohn. He has the same unbridled egotism, the gambler's instinct, and the carnival barker's love of showmanship. He also shares the old moguls' love of movies, which is something else that sets him apart from today's colorless executives. His brother-in-law Jack Schwartzman says, "Those old guys—no matter how they talked, no matter how big the cigar they chewed or how tough they were—loved film. They loved it the way a tailor loves the cloth. Today you have people who are very skilled and adept at doing their job, but they're not in love with the product. Francis is in love with the product. He's a throwback."

The Coppolas evoke the legendary Hollywood clans in one other crucial respect: no other latter-day dynasty has formed such an extensive network of working relationships. Not since Universal's founder Carl Laemmle populated his studio with a horde of relatives from Bavaria have so many family members worked together so frequently. The novelty in the Coppola family is that the son rather than the father is the prime mover and shaker. Francis made it on his own, but once he was established in the movie business, he proceeded to hire his father, his sister, his nephew, and his children at one time or another.

Although it was Francis who launched the filmmaking dynasty, he had an artistic tradition behind him. His father, Carmine Coppola, is a musician and composer. Carmine was born in New York in 1910, the son of Italian immigrants. At an early age Carmine took up the flute. He describes himself as "kind of a boy wonder."

When he was nine or ten years old, Carmine had an encounter that would later be dramatized in his son's most famous film. Carmine's father was a machinist who had once worked as a gunsmith in the Italian army. Occasionally some of the small-time hoods who hung out in New York's Little Italy would bring him their pistols and tommy guns to repair. One evening, young Carmine was with his father in the machine shop when a few shady characters walked in and told the senior Coppola to bolt the door. They dropped a cache of machine guns on the table and instructed the machinist to oil the weapons. Suspiciously, they asked who the young boy was, and Carmine's father answered, "It's all right, that's my son. He is studying the flute." The gangsters asked to hear him play, so Carmine performed a solo while his father worked on the machine guns. When they left, the mafiosi gave the boy $100 to continue his studies. Years later, Carmine told *his* son of the incident, and Francis wrote the scene into *The Godfather, Part II*; it was eventually cut from the theatrical release version of *Godfather II* but was restored when the entire *Godfather* saga was shown on television.

That was one of the few times in which the Coppolas crossed paths with the Mafia before Francis made *The Godfather*. Talia Shire says, "We're very proud of the fact that we were Italians who were cultured, who dug our way out of the subways of New York." After finishing high school, Carmine received a scholarship to The Juilliard School, where he continued his musical studies. There he struck up a friendship with a fellow student, a trumpet player named Pennino, who brought Carmine home to meet his family. Carmine fell in love with his friend's sister Italia. Her father, Francesco Pennino (for whom Francis was named), also had a musical background; he had started out as a pianist in Naples. "He was playing at a certain cafe," Carmine reports, "and many times a young tenor would come in and sing for a handout. That was Caruso. He and my wife's father became friends." Pennino became a popular songwriter—his daughter calls him "the Irving Berlin of Italy"—and he also wrote plays; an excerpt from one of them appears in *Godfather II*, in the scene in which Vito Corleone (Robert De Niro) first meets the leader of the Black Hand whom he will later assassinate. Pennino also arranged for the first Italian films to be imported into America, and during the silent picture days, he had an offer to work at Paramount Pictures (the studio that would later produce *The Godfather*). He turned the offer down. "He said he didn't want his children in Hollywood," Italia notes with a sardonic shrug.

Even today, Italia resents the assumption that her son Francis was the first family member to become involved in movies. She also resents the notion that her children's artistic aspirations derive solely from Carmine's side of the family. She and her husband still argue about whether the Coppolas or the Penninos were the more musical family. "From some of the things Carmine says," Italia protests, "you get the impression that if I had married a barber, my sons would be a bunch of stupid barbers. But there's more music on *my* side of the family than on his side."

"Now I resent what *you're* saying," Carmine interjects. "Yours was not a musical family. You didn't talk about symphonic music and about opera, which I did."

"No, my father didn't sit home and talk to his kids about opera," Italia concedes. "But he gave us all piano lessons. Carmine's mother was in awe of my father; she wanted to meet him. She remembered his song 'Goodbye to Naples.' So music comes from both sides," she concludes emphatically.

After graduating from Juilliard, Carmine played for a time with the orchestra at Radio City Music Hall. The Coppolas' first son, August, was born in 1934. Soon afterwards, Carmine took a position as first flutist with the Detroit Symphony Orchestra, and the family settled in Detroit. Francis was born there in 1939. Then, in the early 1940s, Carmine was hired by the NBC Symphony Orchestra under the direction of Arturo Toscanini. He moved the family back to New York, where the youngest child, Talia, was born in 1946. Carmine spent ten years as first flutist with Toscanini. "I learned so much from Toscanini in balance and musicianship and how to conduct," Carmine says today. "He did not rehearse a lot. He was fast; he came in tremendously prepared. He knew exactly what he wanted to do. There wasn't a wasted movement."

Yet Carmine was not fully satisfied in his work for Toscanini. He also wanted to write music; he composed some symphonic pieces that received little exposure and an opera that was never performed. He fantasized about conducting.

In 1951, Carmine left Toscanini to seek other opportunities. He arranged music for the Rockettes at Radio City Music Hall, worked on one film for Paramount called *The Stars Are Singing*, and later conducted musicals on the road for the David Merrick Organization. He worked on *Kismet*, *Stop the World . . . I Want to Get Off*, and *110 in the Shade*, among others. But from 1951 to 1971, his career was very unstable. He was constantly uprooting his family, rushing off in search of new opportunities that rarely materialized. Francis has called his father "a very frustrated man . . . he felt that his own music never really emerged." Talia once described this restless time in her father's life by saying, "He was a flutist of genius, but he *loathed* playing the flute . . . My father has such *wanderlust*. If you were in a room with him, and a train whistle went by, his face flushed."

Today Talia feels that her father suffered a mid-life crisis during this period. "My father was very successful when he was younger," she says. "Then there was a decade when things were shit, and that was the decade I was growing up. He was conducting on the road, or he was staying home and being isolated and depressed. I watched him sabotage himself. I watched him be afraid. I watched him be glorious. I traveled on the road with my father when I was nine years old. I saw his face flush when he got some applause. I knew that would make him happier than anything I could do. My father was in love with that moment."

Her attitude toward her father during this trying period shaped the way in which Talia would relate to men throughout her life— with a mixture of protectiveness and self-denial. "I would have done anything for him," she says. "That should have been the decade of my development, the time for having a friend over, and it got lost in the concern for my father. I still have a feeling for male artists and their vulnerability. I was practically an autistic child—I had a terrific inner world, but I was too far inside. I don't know if it came from the Catholic Church or something I picked up from my mother, but I felt that everything must be done *for* someone. Sacrifice is a very big and exciting thing. And it carried forth in my work, the need to sacrifice myself on camera. I became an excellent partner to an overwhelming male, but I never wanted the camera for myself."

This unstable period in Carmine's life also had a profound influence on Francis. As a child, Francis always ended his prayers by saying, "Let Daddy get his big break." At fifteen, he was working at Western Union and made up a phony telegram from Paramount Pictures that read, "Dear Mr. Coppola, you've been made the composer of *Jet Star*, please come to Hollywood immediately . . ." Carmine was overjoyed at the news, then heartbroken when his son told him that it was no more than a thoughtless jest. "At least you know why I was so delirious when [my father] shared the Oscar for best musical score with Nino Rota," Francis said after *Godfather II* swept the Academy Awards in 1974.

Francis felt the family's financial instability keenly. "As a kid, I never knew where the family stood," he told author Gay Talese. "One minute we had a little bit of money, the next my father was saying he couldn't afford the mortgage. It was tempestuous." Some children might have responded to that insecurity by resolving to live their adult lives as cautiously as possible. But Francis came to a different conclusion; he decided that security was always ephemeral and that there were more important things than money. "I think most people regard money as a vital element of life," he has commented. "You hold onto it and don't jeopardize it. My attitude toward money is that it is just something to use."

From Carmine, Francis inherited a bohemian indifference to financial stability as well as a yearning for artistic achievement. But the ego strength that enabled him to achieve spectacular success at an early age probably came from his mother, a woman of tremendous drive whose primary obsession was protecting the family. "Of the whole family, my mother is the most powerful one," Talia insists. "And yet the message she got was that it all had to be for Carmine. It would have been better for us if she had been a working woman and was allowed to express herself."

Talia believes that her own development suffered as a result of her mother's expectations. "My upbringing was to be a good, quiet Catholic girl. I wasn't allowed to have strong impulses. I wanted to be a choreographer for a while. But I always felt guilty about expressing a dream. That was a masculine thing."

FOR the Coppola sons, there was no such message of sacrifice or self-denial; they were to go after what they deserved. August was a handsome young man, an outstanding student, and a charismatic figure to everyone around him, including the members of his family. "Augie was sort of a Renaissance prince," Talia says. "In his heyday, there was nothing quite like this sort of Tyrone Power guy coming up with these wonderful ideas. He was a true visionary, a pioneer, a philosopher, a cultured man. He told me to read Anaïs Nin when I was twelve. He was always very supportive. Augie is a natural teacher. He would want to see Francis improve and would want to see me improve. He's constantly wanting to teach."

Italia says even more emphatically, "August was my first son, and he set the example. If it wasn't for August, Francis would be nothing. He encouraged Francis; he was the one who was always helping Francis and doing things for Francis. Carmine was very busy, involved with himself, and so Francie turned to Augie. This is a hard thing to say, but I'm going to say it: If Francis had been my first son, the family wouldn't be this famous today. Augie was a straight-A student, and that made Francie try to get it. If Francis had been the firstborn and had a D on his report card, Tallie and Augie wouldn't have given a damn, either. Augie is brilliant. I thank God he was the first."

Francis has certainly confirmed the influence of his older brother. He said of his youth, "I was funny-looking, not good in school, near-sighted, and I didn't know any girls. My mother called me the affectionate one of the family. My older brother was handsome, brilliant, the adored one of any group." It was August who first inspired Francis to try his hand at writing. Francis said, "He was a great older brother to me and always looked out for me, but in addition, he did very well in school and received many awards for writing and other things, and he was like the star of the family and I did most of what I did to imitate him. I even took his short stories and handed them in under my name when I went to the writing class in high school myself. My whole beginning in writing started in copying him, thinking that if I did those things, then I could be like he was . . . I would say that my love for my older brother formed the majority of aspects of what I am, and the other part was formed by my father in terms of my attitude toward music . . . I think that a lot of what I'm like is from the fact that I was the audience of the most remarkable family."

August continued to excel as he grew older. He was awarded his Ph.D. in comparative literature in an unusual program designed for "Renaissance men and women" and sponsored by the Ford

Foundation. He taught at California State University Long Beach and created the tactile gallery at the Exploratorium in San Francisco under a grant from the National Endowment for the Arts. In 1978, he published a murky stream-of-consciousness novel called *The Intimacy*, the meaning of which was somewhat impenetrable, even if the main female character was not ("He heard her breathing, her body expanding, the wet sounds, his penis taprooting for all that was there . . ."). In 1982, California Governor Jerry Brown wanted to have August named chancellor of the California State University system, but the controversial appointment was scuttled after a number of prominent academicians dismissed his innovative educational philosophy as impractical.

August continues to write and pursue his work as an educator, but clearly the roles played by the brothers during their childhood have been reversed; August has been eclipsed—at least in the public mind—by his once-undistinguished younger brother. August refuses to speak about his feelings. "He's been questioned about this," Talia says, "and he's very sensitive to it. I don't think he wants to deal with it. He doesn't want to be asked if he feels damaged. I'm sure these thoughts occur to him, but he is a success. He is a remarkable man." Talia contrasts the intense competition her brothers felt with her own situation, and she finds at least one advantage in being the baby sister: "What stopped me is also what protected me. Being a woman is a tremendous way to blossom at your own speed, because nobody is looking at you. You don't get the crown; it goes to the boy. So you have more opportunity to be dismissed *and* to experiment. I'm sure there was much more pressure for Augie."

Not surprisingly, the theme of the complex, competitive relationship between brothers has been central to many of Francis Coppola's movies, from his very first feature, *Dementia 13* (a horror film about a torch-wielding sculptor and his murderous younger brother), all the way up to *The Cotton Club*. In both *Godfather* movies, fraternal rivalries are central to the story. In *The Godfather*, Sonny (James Caan) is the charismatic leader among the sons; his younger brother Michael (Al Pacino) recedes whenever he is in the same room with the more domineering, hot-blooded Sonny. Only after Sonny's death does Michael come into his own. One of the most compelling and overlooked aspects of *Godfather II* is the relationship between Michael and his weakling older brother Fredo (John Cazale), who betrays the family and allies himself with the rival mafiosi who aim to eliminate Michael.

There is a moving scene late in the film when Fredo tries to explain to Michael what led to his act of disloyalty. "I'm your older brother," he exclaims, "and I was passed over." One cannot help wondering whether Francis was imagining what it must have been like for August to see his younger brother surpass him in fame, fortune, power, and influence.

Francis's film of S. E. Hinton's *Rumble Fish* more directly suggests the roles played by the Coppola brothers when they were growing up. The film centers on teenaged Rusty-James (Matt Dillon), who worships his mysterious, glamorous older brother, the Motorcycle Boy (Mickey Rourke). Francis dedicated the film "to my older brother, August Coppola, my first and best teacher." Rusty-James is alternately worshipful and resentful of the attention his brother receives. "You ain't going to be like him," another character tells Rusty-James. "Your brother is a prince." Rusty-James is secretly jealous that his mother preferred his older brother. Eventually, the Motorcycle Boy dies so that Rusty-James can find his liberation; it is a fable that may recall Francis's own fantasies as a youth.

DESPITE his musical background, Carmine Coppola never encouraged his sons to pursue careers in the arts. Perhaps because of his own frustrations as a working musician, he wanted his sons to have a more stable life. "If anything," Talia says, "I think my father tried for us not to express ourselves creatively. Augie was to be the doctor. Francis was to be the engineer."

However, Francis's artistic gifts blossomed after he contracted polio at the age of ten and was bedridden for a solid year. Carmine recalls, "I got him some marionettes to while away the time, and he started to make up plays." Francis's interest in theater grew, and at Hofstra College he began directing in the drama department. "I don't think he did any homework," Carmine notes with a chuckle. At Hofstra, Francis met two aspiring actors, James Caan and Troy Donahue, both of whom he would one day cast in his movies. (Donahue was the campus heartthrob whom Coppola envied; later Francis did Donahue a "favor," at a time when the actor's career was on the skids, by casting him as the opportunistic gigolo who marries Connie Corleone in *Godfather II*.).

Francis came to do graduate work at the UCLA film school in 1960, just before the country's film schools began to attract publicity and throngs of applicants. "My idea," he said, "was you're working on the films and drinking wine at night, and there are beautiful girls who are working on the films and you're all in it together. It wasn't like that. It was very lonely and nowhere near as much fun or as satisfying as my theater experience had been. I found that the other film students were not really interested in film as a more complete humanistic art form. They were just interested in the technology."

At that time, Roger Corman, a producer of low-budget exploitation pictures, had a penchant for hiring UCLA film students because they would work cheap and fast. Coppola jumped at the chance to sign on with Corman. His first assignment was to take a Russian space picture, do the English translation, and transform it into a monster movie. "I got something like $200 for a million weeks work," Francis says. Still, he was determined to impress his boss. "I'd deliberately work all night," Francis recalls, "so when Roger would come in the morning, he'd see me slumped over the moviola." The strategy paid off, and Coppola was given the chance to direct a quickie horror picture, *Dementia 13*, for Corman. While working on the movie in Ireland in 1962, he met and married an American artist named Eleanor Neil.

Coppola also directed a couple of soft-core nudie pictures, then graduated to a screenwriting contract with Seven Arts, the company that would eventually buy up Warner Bros. He toiled on a number of screenplays, including *Reflections in a Golden Eye*, *This Property Is Condemned*, and *Patton* (which later won him his first Oscar, in 1970), though in all cases he was one of a team of writers, and the finished films contained only snatches of his work. The frustrations of seeing his scripts rewritten made him "horny to direct a film," and he persuaded Seven Arts to back a low-budget feature, *You're a Big Boy Now*, one of the spate of psychedelic youth movies of the late 1960s. Although it seems somewhat dated today, the film remains a lively treatment of Coppola's favorite theme of family relationships; it concerns a young man (Peter Kastner) trying to break free of his parents' influence, only to fall under the spell of a sadistic temptress (Elizabeth Hartman), an younger and more demonic version of the protagonist's overbearing mother (Geraldine Page).

Francis's next project for Warner Bros, *Finian's Rainbow*, came about partly because he wanted to impress his father. "I decided to do *Finian's Rainbow*," he says, "because I remembered the show. My father had conducted musicals. And it was a very romantic idea—wouldn't my father be happy if I did a big musical?" Francis excitedly phoned Carmine, who was conducting a road-show company version of *Half a Sixpence* at the time; he offered his father a job writing some of the orchestrations for the movie. That was what brought the senior Coppolas to California for good.

The movie turned out to be a disaster—though luckily not a very expensive disaster. It starred Fred Astaire, Petula Clark, and Tommy Steele, none of whom appeared to be at ease roamin' through the gloamin'. The score was still lovely but the story—a mishmash involving a leprechaun, a mute girl, and a Southern bigot all searching for a pot of gold—was as creaky as it was cockeyed. Although Francis tried to give the movie a freeform, improvisatory feeling, he failed to camouflage the weaknesses of the script. He recognized even then that the project was doomed. "The fact that it was all shot on the back lot disturbed me," he says. "I couldn't shoot on location. Basically, *Finian's Rainbow* was a cheat. It was an absurd idea to take a $3.5 million musical and send it out to compete with fucking *Funny Girl*, where they had rehearsed the musical numbers for two months. On *Finian's Rainbow*, I improvised all the dancing, and I know nothing about dancing."

Francis is amused, however, in recalling the studio's high expectations for the film: "Ironically, everyone at Warners thought it was going to be a big hit; they were just wild about it. This is the joke of the movie business because no one knows *anything*. The movie was a disaster. But before it was released, they were counting their millions. They decided to blow the picture up to seventy millimeter and make it a road-show picture. And when they did that, they blew the feet off Fred Astaire when he was dancing. No one had calculated the top and bottom of the frame."

This unpleasant experience proved significant in at least one respect. It was while working on *Finian's Rainbow* that Francis met George Lucas, a USC film-school graduate who came to Warner Bros. under an apprenticeship program and was assigned to be Francis's assistant. The association helped to launch Lucas's career and tied the two men's professional lives together for a number of years. Lucas again worked as Coppola's assistant on his next film, *The Rain People*.

Disillusioned by the experience of making a big-studio musical, Coppola resolved to film *The Rain People* far from the pressure-cooker atmosphere of Hollywood. He persuaded Warner Bros. to give him a $750,000 budget for the film and then convinced the unions to ease some of their restrictions so that he would work with a small twenty-two-person crew. The company filmed on location, and Coppola rewrote the script on the road to take advantage of the flavor of the places they visited.

The story was ahead of its time. It concerned a married woman (Shirley Knight) who learns that she is pregnant; she leaves her husband on a sudden impulse and embarks on a cross-country journey to try to clarify her own identity and decide whether she wants to become a mother. (*The Rain People* was made in 1969, the same year as *Easy Rider*; it was definitely the year for cross-country voyages of discovery.) The film reveals a good deal about Coppola, his intense commitment to family, and his ambivalence toward strong women. At the beginning, Coppola seems sympathetic to his heroine's longing for independence. But the movie abruptly shifts gears in the middle and begins to condemn the character as a selfish, monstrous harpy. She picks up a hitchhiker, a brain-damaged football player (played by James Caan, Francis's old college friend). The athlete is clearly meant to be symbolic of her unborn child; her conflicting responses to him mirror her contradictory feelings about becoming a mother. "I never really resolved it," Coppola admits. "I ended the movie with a *deus ex machina* and a very emotional plea to have a family. She comes to the conclusion that somehow her destiny is to be a mother and that there is something overwhelming about that which is not demeaning to her womanhood."

Feminists rejected the conclusion then and might reject it today, but Coppola insists that he was really affirming the idea of family rather than derogating women. Still, the film failed to define the motivations of its own protagonist. One reason for the failure was Coppola's stormy working relationship with Shirley Knight, who fought with him continually over the interpretation of her role. Francis responded by trying to shift the emphasis to James Caan's character—an evasion of the film's central theme. *The Rain People* remains the only movie by Coppola that focuses on a woman's sensibility.

The Rain People did not succeed with either critics or audiences, but it was a fascinating experiment, and it was the first film to reveal Coppola's superb skill at directing actors. In addition to Knight, James Caan and Robert Duvall (both of whom would later be recruited to work in *The Godfather*) delivered vivid performances early in their respective careers.

After making *The Rain People*, Francis decided not to return to Hollywood. In 1969, he and George Lucas moved their base of operations to San Francisco and started a film company of their own called American Zoetrope as an alternative to the Hollywood studios. Francis defined the new enterprise as "a utopian film company which would give people an opportunity to do films who might not so easily get that opportunity."

Every aspiring filmmaker in America must have either written to the company or landed on its doorstep on Folsom Street. But the utopian dream quickly turned into a nightmare. Francis later said, "Thousands of people wrote and came or sent their films. At first, to avoid being like a Hollywood studio, we tried to see them. At one point, there were three people whose only job was reading these letters and talking with these people. I kept that up for seven months. But tremendous numbers of people would use or borrow or steal our equipment. The first year of operation, we lost almost $40,000 worth of equipment."

American Zoetrope was started at around the same time as Bert Schneider's BBS Films, in the same kind of countercultural spirit. But it did not come close to matching BBS's record. The reasons for the company's failure were many. Unlike Bert Schneider, Francis did not have a major studio headed by his father and his brother to provide support for American Zoetrope. An even more important problem was Francis's poor head for business. "My enthusiasm and my imagination far outpaced any kind of fiscal logic," he admitted. "And I wasn't associated with anyone who was the businessman of the group." His brother-in-law, Jack Schwartzman, puts it more succinctly: "Francis is the worst businessman in the world."

Francis made an extraordinary blunder when he first set up Zoetrope. Warner Bros. agreed to bankroll the company, but with a loan rather than an outright subsidy; Coppola would be required to pay back money if the scripts and films he developed did not live up to the studio's expectations. In Hollywood, it is virtually unheard-of for someone to enter into such an arrangement. Nonetheless, Coppola was giddy with enthusiasm and simply couldn't conceive of the possibility that his movies might fail. After his company's first production, George Lucas's *THX-1138*, bombed, Warner Bros. dropped its support for American Zoetrope and demanded that Coppola repay the initial loan. Since Warner Bros. would not approve any of the projects Coppola wanted to direct, however, he had no way of paying off the debt. He admits that one reason he agreed to direct *The Godfather* was to raise enough money to satisfy his obligation to Warners, which exacted $600,000 from his profits on *The Godfather*. "I thought they really were rats," he said of the Warner management.

At the time of the American Zoetrope fiasco, Coppola doubted that he would ever direct another movie. He got his chance because Paramount was having trouble finding a director for *The Godfather*. Paramount had optioned a twenty-page treatment from Mario Puzo in 1966. The studio staked Puzo $80,000 to complete his Mafia novel, which they rightly perceived as a hot property. The book did indeed top the best-seller list on its publication in 1969, and Paramount assigned Albert S. Ruddy to produce the film. But most directors offered the chance to film the novel felt it could never be more than a B-picture. Peter Yates (*Bullitt*) and Costa-Gavras (*Z*) both turned thumbs down. Paramount was eager to put the movie into production quickly so as to capitalize on the notoriety of the novel and the controversy developing around the film. Italian-American anti-defamation groups were lobbying to persuade Paramount to drop the project. Even the Mafia got into the act, according to Ruddy. "They did not want that film made," Ruddy said, "and it was made obvious to me in various threats that I should drop the idea. But I persisted."

Eventually, Ruddy and Paramount lowered their sights and looked for a less prestigious director. In Paramount's view, Coppola's Italian background was his strongest credential. The studio's vice president in charge of production, Robert Evans, had met Coppola, and he said at the time, "[Francis] knew the way these men in *The Godfather* ate their food, kissed each other, talked. He knew the grit."

Coppola needed the assignment, but he disliked Puzo's novel when he first read it; he still dreamed of doing small personal films on the order of *The Rain People*. His father claims that *he* helped to talk Francis into doing the film when he met him by chance at the Burbank Airport. Francis had come down to Los Angeles the day before to meet with Paramount, and he was returning to San Francisco, when he saw his father waiting in line for the same plane; Carmine was going to San Francisco to work on the score of a documentary film. "Francis had a book in his hand," Carmine recalls, "and it was *The Godfather*. He told me, 'I was at Paramount all day yesterday, and they want me to direct this hunk of trash. I don't want to do it. I want to do art films.' I hadn't read the book, but I knew about it. I told him to make the film. make some money, and then he could do what he wanted to do. By the end of that airplane trip, I think I had talked him into it."

Carmine had his own reasons for urging Francis to make *The Godfather*; he wanted to contribute to the film's score. Since working on *Finian's Rainbow*, Carmine had had trouble finding other jobs in films. "Hollywood was very slow," Carmine says, "or I was not in the mainstream of things. Things were a little bit lean, so I went to the L.A. School District and told them I had a degree in music and wanted to do some substitute teaching." For a few years, he taught music in San Fernando Valley schools. Although one might expect him to remember the experience as a humiliating comedown, he speaks of it with some affection. "One of the most pleasurable moments of my life," Carmine muses, "was a few years ago when I was at Von's supermarket, and there was a youth filling up my shopping bag. I didn't recognize him, but he said to me, 'Mr. Coppola, I was a student at Taft High School when you came in to teach music. You turned around my thinking about music and made me love good music. I was just a rock-and-roller, and now I buy Beethoven records.'"

When Francis went to work on *The Godfather*, he did hire his father to compose the incidental music that would embellish the main theme by Nino Rota. Carmine wrote all the music for the wedding scene that opens the film, he drew on memories of the Italian weddings he had attended in his youth. With his credit on *The Godfather*, at long last, Carmine says, "I was on my way."

The film played at least as crucial a role for Francis's sister Talia, who was then married to composer David Shire. Talia had studied acting on a scholarship at the Yale Drama School. Like her brother, she had worked in a few Roger Corman movies, but her career was hardly in high gear in 1971 when Francis began preparing *The Godfather*. At the urging of her psychiatrist, Talia asked her brother for a part in the film; her therapist felt it was necessary for her to begin asserting herself within the family. When she requested the job, Francis said no. Talia persisted, and Mario Puzo and Robert Evans finally agreed to let her audition for the part of Connie, the younger Corleone sister whose wedding opens the film. Evans and Puzo selected her for the part, but Francis was livid when he learned of their choice.

"He was real angry that I had accepted without asking him first," Talia says. "You have to understand that at the time he was thirty-two and scared. He was asking for real interesting casting, and people make trades; you don't want a sister there who may suddenly fall on her face. I understand the situation. At the same time, just because you're a genius and very gifted doesn't mean that you're completely developed emotionally. I had the same mother and father, so I understood his secrets and fears. Perhaps he's also subject to that programming that says women shouldn't compete. That may be tucked in there."

After Talia was hired, Francis frequently grew irritable whenever she was on the set. Their mother recalls one occasion when Francis started screaming, "Tallie's too pretty for the part. I'm going to fire her! A guy who's going to marry into a Mafia family has to have a fat little dumpy Italian girl with an ugly face. Tallie is wrong. She's got to go!" Italia begged Francis to keep his sister on. Finally, he yelled at the makeup department, "Put my sister's hair up, make her less beautiful, or else she has to go!"

Francis's testiness was intensified by the pressure he faced from the studio. At first, his casting suggestions provoked reactions of stunned disbelief at Paramount. For the powerful but ailing Don Corleone, Coppola and Ruddy wanted Marlon Brando, still regarded by many as the greatest actor of his generation. But Brando had not appeared in a successful movie for over a decade; he had a reputation for being impossible to work with and was considered well past his prime. At Francis's urging, Brando prepared his own makeup for his screen test, and he so completely transformed himself into the soft-spoken but deadly Mafia chieftain that the studio skeptics were won over. Coppola's choice of Al Pacino to play Michael was equally controversial. Though Pacino had won Obie and Tony awards for his stage work, his movie career was off to a shaky start. He had appeared in one film, a bleak study of heroin addiction called *The Panic in Needle Park*, that had been a box office bomb. Yet Francis felt he had the perfect mixture of vulnerability and quiet strength that the part required; the director refused to consider more established stars for this key role. Eventually, Coppola got his way on casting. The main reason was the studio's desire to complete the movie before the book was forgotten.

The casting conflict was merely the first problem raised during the filming of the epic. Coppola and Ruddy also disagreed about where to shoot the movie. Francis wanted to film on location in New York, but Ruddy felt costs could be controlled more efficiently if they filmed at the studio in Los Angeles. Ruddy won this battle. When Coppola began shooting, things went from bad to worse. "Paramount said the footage looked terrible and couldn't be cut," Coppola reports. "My editor, who wanted to direct it himself, was meeting with the studio people, telling them the film couldn't be cut together. He and the assistant director wanted to get me fired. Finally, I fired them instead. They all hated Brando's first day. Bob Evans started to make inquiries to see if Elia Kazan was available; they figured that Kazan was the only director who could really work with Brando. I couldn't even quit. My agent said, 'Don't quit. Let them fire you.' If they fired me, I would still get the money, whereas if I quit, I would lose it all, and Warners would foreclose on what I owed them. Finally, after the first three weeks, Charlie Bluhdorn [chairman of Gulf and Western] had a nice meeting with me and gave me his support. Then I took control of it."

Even a few weeks before its opening, the industry was buzzing with rumors that *The Godfather* was an unreleasable disaster. Defying the know-nothing pundits, the film opened to some of the best reviews of the decade. "It is a movie that exemplifies what is great in the Hollywood tradition," *Time* magazine declared. The film went on to win the Oscar as best picture of 1972, though Coppola himself lost the best director award to Bob Fosse (for *Cabaret*). Coppola had imbued the fairly routine gangster plot with his own intense feelings about family loyalty and enriched it with his memories of growing up in a close-knit Italian-American household. "I think the fact that my background is Italian helped enormously," he said in 1972. "I made a very conscious decision to get all the Catholic rituals into the film. That's where the idea of the ending came from—the baptism intercut with the murders. It's all very authentic. The wedding was really what those weddings were like. The decorations, the dances were all exactly as I remembered them. They used to throw the sandwiches, and that's why they were called football weddings. Someone would say, 'Send me a prociutto sandwich,' and the other guy would throw it to him."

The film is one of the most unabashed celebrations of family fealty ever to reach the screen. At one point in the movie, Michael admonishes his brother Fredo, "Fredo, you're my older brother, and I love you. But don't ever take sides with anyone against the family again." That is the film's dominant motif, and helps to explain its extraordinary appeal. Even though the Corleones trade in murder and extortion, they have a cohesiveness that was fast disappearing from the lives of most American families. Brutal as it was, the movie stirred nostalgic feelings for that kind of close familial bond.

The film did not evade some of the darker sides of the Italian code; it was especially pointed in dramatizing the Sicilian prejudice against women. At the wedding of Connie Corleone, a Mafia thug offers the ultimate felicitation to his Don: "May their first child be a *masculine* child." The memorable ending of the film—in which Michael closes the door on his wife Kay (Diane Keaton), shutting her out of the business of the family—was a stinging demonstration of the sexual biases of this Old World clan. If Francis has sometimes shared this bias himself, at least he was self-critical enough to realize it.

Despite the dramatic indictment of certain Mafia mores, audiences surrendered to the film's portrait to the Corleones as tarnished but still grand conquistadors clinging to a code of honor in an amoral world. "People love to read about an organization that's really going to take care of us," Coppola admits. "When the courts fail you and the whole American system fails you, you can go to Don Corleone and you get justice. I think there is a tremendous hunger in this country, if not in the world, for that kind of clear authority. Of course, that is a romantic conception of the Mafia. There is a difference between the Mafia as it really is and the Mafia as we depicted it."

The Godfather grossed $300 million worldwide, and Francis personally made almost $7 million on the film. Contemplating his change in fortune at the time, he said, "If you were raised as I was, everything you do is to make your family proud of you. It relates to the immigrant thing. Get an education, have a good reputation, have your picture in the paper in a suit, and have lots of money and security. It's hard for me to decide to do anything that doesn't have that as a possible end. Yet I know that's over. I now am as successful as I ever want to be, and I'm pretty rich, so I've got to change all my motivations. I'm resentful that people all say, 'Do you think you can top *The Godfather*?' I know I could never top it in terms of financial success. But I do want to make a film that tops it as a really moving human document."

From 1972 to 1974, invigorated by his success with *The Godfather*, Francis threw himself into his work and enjoyed a remarkably fertile period. He directed a play for the American Conservatory Theater and an opera for the San Francisco Opera. Paramount hired him to write the screenplay for the Robert Redford-Mia Farrow version of *The Great Gatsby*. Francis detested the finished film, feeling that director Jack Clayton's soft-focus style and sluggish pacing had sabotaged his script. He publicly attacked the movie, and Clayton was understandably furious. During this same period, Francis started *City* magazine in San Francisco, a weekly publication that lasted for a year. He also produced *American Graffiti* for George Lucas, though this collaboration was to mark the beginning of the end of the close friendship between the two. Lucas accused Coppola of reneging on his agreement to give part of his profits from the film to co-producer Gary Kurtz and cinematographer Haskell Wexler. Coppola eventually did pay both men but the squabble over money permanently damaged his relationship with Lucas.

In addition to these sundry activities, Coppola wrote and directed two movies of his own, *The Godfather, Part II* and *The Conversation*. In writing *The Conversation*, he wanted to prove that he could create an original screenplay of substance. The Kafkaesque horror story followed a professional eavesdropper, a coldly detached technician who records a conversation that seems to warn of an impending murder; he agonizes over whether or not to intervene. Brilliantly acted by Gene Hackman, the film is a gripping psychological study and a chilling vision of a completely amoral, chaotic, and sinister universe. While editing *The Conversation*, Coppola was also preparing *The Godfather, Part II*, a monumental undertaking. This time, Francis aimed to produce as well as direct so that he would have complete control of the film. Since Al Ruddy, the producer of the first *Godfather*, was busy on another movie, *The Longest Yard*, Paramount gave Coppola the total authority that he sought. The studio wanted *Godfather II* ready for release by Christmas of 1974, placing tremendous pressure on Francis to complete the film quickly. He complained that he did not have enough time to edit either *Godfather II* or *The Conversation* as carefully as he would have liked. The last-minute rush to finish *Godfather II* led to some confusing and imprecise transitions, particularly during the sequence in which Michael Corleone is subpoenaed to appear before a Senate Committee investigating organized crime. Despite these gaps in continuity, the film was even superior to the original *Godfather* in the artistry and force with which it portrayed the disintegration of the once-vigorous Corleones. Using a bold structural design, the film intercut scenes depicting the rise of young Vito Corleone (Robert De Niro) in the early part of the century with the decline of his son Michael (Al Pacino), who rules the family business in the corporate age. It is one of the most incisive films ever made about the tenacious grip of family and the question of succession, building a powerful determinist vision of the ways in which children's lives are inexorably shaped by parental experiences and expectations. Michael is unable to break free of his father's rigid law, even though the ancient Mafia code has lost its meaning. The movie ends with a flashback scene of Michael as a young man, declaring that he is completely free to be whatever he wants to be. This closing scene strikes a poignant and ironic note because we know by then that Michael is helplessly enslaved to the past; he is impotent to do anything but pursue the path laid out for him by his father.

In addition, Coppola wanted to remove any romantic ideas about the Mafia that might have been fostered by the first film. He did this by undercutting the image of familial love celebrated in *The Godfather*; now he dramatized the decay of the Corleone family. In the course of the movie, Mama Corleone dies, Michael's wife leaves him, and Michael arranges the murder of his brother Fredo. "This time I really set out to destroy the family," Coppola said. "Yet I wanted to destroy it in the way that I think is most profound—from the inside. The movie is meant to be like *The Oresteia*, showing how evil reverberates over a period of generations."

His sister Talia feels that both *Godfather* films can be related to the experience of the Coppola family. "*The Godfather* is really about family structure," she says. "This brother is first, this one is second. The girl, Connie, is screwed up until the mother dies. Then when the queen is dead, long live the new queen. There's some of that in our family and some of that in all Italian families and in all families of the world, which is why they connected with the movie."

The making of *Godfather II* was a happier collaboration for Francis, Talia, and Carmine than *Godfather I* had been. Francis was in a much stronger position—he had the right of final cut, which he had not been granted on the first movie—and so he was less anxious about having his family work with him. He and Talia enjoyed a more rewarding professional relationship; she even supplied a crucial plot suggestion. Originally, Francis imagined that Michael's wife, Kay (Diane Keaton), would take her third baby and leave her husband. It was Talia who suggested that Kay have an abortion instead. "The hardest thing you can do to an Italian man," she notes, "is to get rid of his baby. I thought it was more exciting to give her an active choice to say, 'I'm not going to let this family continue.' It was my idea, and Francis used it. And when I gave him that, he wrote that beautiful speech for me where the sister sits down and speaks to her brother, tells him why she hated him and why she has decided to come home. He gave me an opportunity to do something instead of just being brought in to scream or yell. He gave me an opportunity to *act*. I think it was because we sort of traded."

Godfather II provided Talia with the showcase she needed to prove that she was a serious actress. She made Connie a complex and comprehensible character, illuminating all the stages in her transformation from the defiant, upstart daughter to the steely head of the household. The role won her the New York Film Critics award as best supporting actress of the year, and she was also nominated for an Academy Award. Carmine, too, received an Oscar nomination; he had written much of the music for the film and shared a credit with Nino Rota as composer.

Oscar night in 1975 was a tense occasion for the Coppola family. Francis had the remarkable distinction of being in competition with himself. In fact, for the first time in decades, one director had made two of the nominees for best picture: both *The Conversation* and *The Godfather, Part II* were in contention. (The last time it happened was in 1940, when both John Ford and Alfred Hitchcock had two films nominated. But that year there were ten nominees for best picture, so Francis's achievement was more extraordinary.) Francis was also nominated in the two screenwriting categories—*The Conversation* for best original screenplay and *Godfather II* for best adaptation. Francis himself received five nominations in all, and he took the triple crown for *Godfather II*: best picture, best director, and best screenplay adaptation (shared with Mario Puzo). Carmine also won the Oscar for best score, and Francis delightedly thanked the Academy for honoring his father as well as himself.

Yet there was a hint of friction on that triumphant night, at least among the distaff members of the family. Italia recalls, "Francis was jumping up in the air saying, 'This was the best night in our lives.' Well, Tallie lost that night, and she said, 'I'm a girl, so you forgot about me.' Then Carmine gave his speech: 'If it wasn't for Francis Coppola, I wouldn't be here tonight. However, if it wasn't for me, *he* wouldn't be here.' I said to him afterwards, 'Gee, Carmine, you did a great job. I hope the labor pains weren't too bad.' Francis said to me, 'If I get another Oscar tonight, I'm going to mention you.' He got the third Oscar and went up there and said, 'I had something I was going to say, but I don't remember what it was. But thanks for giving my Dad an Oscar.' So he forgot me, too!" The next day, a friend sent Italia a telegram tweaking her about Carmine's acceptance speech: "Is Carmine Coppola a widower?"

Despite this minor fuss, the Coppola family was riding high. Francis was widely regarded as *the* premier American director, the most original creative talent of his generation. With the millions he made from *American Graffiti* and *Godfather II* added to his fat percentage of *The Godfather*, he was also one of the richest. Carmine's career, too, received a shot in the arm from that Oscar victory; he went on to score a couple of TV movies and also worked on most of his son's subsequent films.

As for Talia, even though she had lost the Oscar to Ingrid Bergman (for her role in *Murder on the Orient Express*), she was in demand for the first time. Other film offers started coming in. The script that was to give her career the biggest boost came not to her, however, but to her husband. United Artists had agreed to film the story of a small-time boxer, written by a little-known actor named Sylvester Stallone. The script was sent to David Shire in hopes that he would agree to compose the score. He turned it down, but Talia read the screenplay called *Rocky* and decided to audition for the film. Her first child, Matthew, had just been born and had barely survived a difficult month in intensive care. "That kind of experience levels the silliness here in Hollywood," Talia says. "I had come out of it with a kind of strength. I read the script and went in to audition. When I met Sylvester, I felt he was like my mother's fourth child. And if there's anything I know how to do, it's to partner like a dancer that kind of guy. We had an immediate rapport. And it was a breakthrough for me; the horror of the audition, of being tested, left me. My kid was at home, and I had things in perspective. If I did good work in an office, that was enough for me."

Talia won the part of Adrian, the shy pet-store clerk living at home with her overprotective brother (Burt Young). No doubt her real-life situation helped to give her an intuitive understanding of the character. "Adrian was me," she says. "That whole syndrome: Please God, don't notice me, but won't somebody notice me? Sylvester wrote very much Rocky's female counterpart in that script. There was a kind of simplicity and purity to it." The truest scenes in the film were the halting, funny courtship scenes between Rocky and Adrian. For the second time, Talia won the New York Film Critics award, and she was nominated for her second Oscar.

Rocky turned out to be a blockbuster, and her role proved once and for all that she was something more than Francis Coppola's kid sister. "When I did *Rocky*," Talia says, "I felt I had finally come into my own. It was a funny kind of feeling of pride and relief. It was going to be okay. I was talented."

IN the wake of *Godfather II*, the Coppolas all seemed productive and confident of their talents. But this sudden prominence proved to be a mixed blessing, at least as far as Italia was concerned. She says, "I feel about this fame that if it didn't happen I would have loved it. We are less happy. I hate fame. All of a sudden, people were writing letters from all over the world, asking if they're related. They've come out of the woodwork. And the relatives have broken my heart. I don't mean the immediate family—but Carmine's relatives and my relatives. They push everybody away to get to Francis. And if there's a bad article about Francis, right away they'll send it to us. I'll ask them, 'Why didn't you send me this nice article that appeared?' And they'll say, 'We already lined our garbage can with it.'"

Nonetheless, the "immediate family" seems to have survived Francis's success rather well. At least no irreparable conflicts have arisen among the parents and their children. Talia feels it is their fierce pride that has kept the Coppolas as close as they are. "Nobody in my immediate family kisses the other one's ass," she says. "What makes my mother angry is that all of a sudden there are a lot of relatives—aunts and uncles and cousins—all too willing to kiss Francis's ass and trade on his status. We won't do it. My mother won't let Francis buy her a house. We're all real proud. And that's why we can get together."

After achieving a remarkable string of successes in the first half of the decade, Francis was looking for new adventures, and he embarked on the greatest challenge of his career—the making of *Apocalypse Now*. He had originally acquired the script by John Milius during his American Zoetrope days. Milius's screenplay transposed Joseph Conrad's *Heart of Darkness* to the jungles of Indochina; an army officer journeys up river in search of a demented Green Beret commander who has reverted to savagery during his years in Vietnam. The premise sounded provocative, offering Francis an opportunity to stretch his talents even further. But as he immersed himself in the arduous undertaking, he seemed not to be rising to new heights but to be sinking into a morass.

Talia points up one of the perils of success, which affected

Francis just as it has beset others in his position. "One person starts to get famous," she notes, "and the very thing that he needs to remain extraordinary starts to fall away, and that is egalitarian relationships. Instead you get an entourage, and they will tell you whatever you want to hear. They will justify what you shouldn't have justified. You're physically cut away from the world. It happened to Sylvester, too. All of a sudden, your only friends are your bodyguards. So I think some of this occurred with Francis. Remember, his success came early. I don't know if he is still able to really know who he should trust. He isn't able to discriminate."

Francis also surrendered to hedonistic excesses, collecting women like a latter-day pasha. This put an added strain on his already troubled marriage. His wife Eleanor was an artist when Francis married her in 1962, but ever since then, her career was always subordinated to his. "Francis will often help a strange woman from the outside," Talia notes. "But if it's a family member, there's a kind of almost violent reaction. You're just not going to get that kind of support from him. He will seek a woman who is his equal in a marriage, and yet he won't be too comfortable with allowing her to do her thing equally." Eleanor has done writing, photography, animated films, collages. Yet her talent has never fully emerged because it fell to her to take care of Francis and their three children, Gian-Carlo, Roman, and Sofia. One sees a parallel between Eleanor Coppola and Irene Selznick—women of talent and intelligence who stifled their own creativity in their relationships with powerful men. Eleanor confessed that "a part of me wants him to fail . . . I guess women have a hard time as the man grows more successful, powerful, and wish for a time when the balance was more equal." Eleanor tolerated Francis's infidelities much as Irene Selznick had tolerated David Selznick's philandering a generation before. In *Notes*, her published diary chronicling their faltering relationship during the making of *Apocalypse Now*, Eleanor wrote, "If I tell the truth, we both strayed from our marriage, probably equally, each in our own way. Francis has gone to the extremes in the physical world, women, food, possessions, in an effort to feel complete. I have looked for that feeling of completeness in the non-physical world. Zen, EST, Esalen, meditation. Neither is better or worse than the other." Yet Eleanor was not always able to sustain such a serene mood of understanding. Later in the book, she wrote more angrily, "It has taken until now for me to accept that the man I love, my husband, the father of my children, the visionary artist, the affectionate family man, the passionate and tender lover, can also lie, betray, and be cruel to people he loves."

As he immersed himself in the making of *Apocalypse Now*, it seemed that Francis was losing control of his life and his work. The megalomania he helped capture in the script of *Patton*—that drew him to larger-than-life characters like Don Corleone and Napoleon—had always been a part of his boisterous personality. But it had previously been held in check. Now, however, he began carrying on like a blowhard general. His movies had never before been financially extravagant. *The Godfather* went $1 million over budget, from $6 million to $7 million, but the overage was insignificant. Even *Godfather II*, with its extensive period scenes, including the reconstruction of Havana on the eve of Castro's takeover, had cost just $13 million—a high budget for 1974 but by no means out of line with the film's size and grandeur. *Apocalypse*, on the other hand, was budgeted originally at $12 million and ended up costing more than $30 million.

In many ways, it seemed that Francis was deliberately sabotaging himself. He had always toyed with danger; it was part of his gambling instinct—the appetite for risk-taking that he shared with the early moguls like Zanuck and Selznick. But now his self-destructive gestures were becoming more extreme. "There's a difference between going out on the limb and cutting the limb off," Talia comments. "You've got to learn that. Francis will cut off the limb. It's like Napoleon going to Russia. Francis is Catholic, or an ex-Catholic, and we deal in punishment. We almost say, 'Please take it away, and we'll show you we can make it again.' But I think he's learning he can't live on the edge any more. He's not twenty-three. The body takes a beating."

His body and spirit took a terrible beating during the making of *Apocalypse Now* in the Philippines. Suffering from dysentery, the bearish, overweight director became shockingly emaciated. He was knee-deep in mud while directing part of the film, aflame with fever much of the time. Shortly after filming commenced in 1976, Typhoon Olga destroyed two major sets, causing $1.3 million worth of damage and forcing a delay of several weeks. When shooting resumed, Marlon Brando—cast in the brief but pivotal role of the sadistic Captain Kurtz—arrived on location ninety pounds overweight; he had to be photographed in murky shadow to conceal his bulk. To compound these problems, the script needed radical surgery. Once again, Francis had begun with an unfinished screenplay, and while on location, he admitted he "realized that the script wasn't really engaging . . . I should have been working more as a writer." In her book, Eleanor described the moment of "ultimate nightmare" for Francis: "He was on this huge set of this huge production with every asset mortgaged against the outcome; hundreds of crew members were waiting. Brando was due on the set, and he was delaying because he didn't like the scene, and Francis hadn't been able to write a scene that Marlon thought was really right." There were further delays when Martin Sheen—who had replaced Harvey Keitel after filming began—was hospitalized with a heart attack. When the company finally left the Philippines after more than a year mired in the jungle, Francis said, "I've never in my life seen so many people so happy to be unemployed." There were 1.1 million feet of film to edit—eight times more than directors usually shoot.

Francis survived the movie, but Talia feels that the production took its toll. "Nobody really understands what happened when movies were taken out of the back lot," she says. "In those days, a man could come back home to his family at the end of the day, and there was an opportunity to do magic and still keep your sanity. When you go out on location, it's different. Francis was two years on *Apocalypse Now*. He brought his family out there to get lice in their hair. It cost him spiritually. He was absolutely exhausted. He brought back something extraordinary, I think, and then he saw *Kramer vs. Kramer* win all the awards. Now that movie was relevant in terms of all of us dealing with divorce and multiple relationships, but it wasn't anything close to this monumental masterwork, *Apocalypse Now*. I think that hurt him."

Francis has persistently argued that *Apocalypse Now* is a cinematic landmark equivalent to *The Birth of a Nation* and that its greatness will be more widely recognized in years to come. He could be wrong on both counts. All of the postponements cost the movie one of its major virtues—novelty. When Francis began preparing *Apocalypse*, it was the first major Hollywood feature to dramatize the Vietnam War since John Wayne's jingoistic *The Green Berets* a decade earlier. But partly because of Francis's example, several other filmmakers began making their own movies on Vietnam in late 1976 and 1977. *Coming Home*, *Go Tell the Spartans*, and *The Deer Hunter* were all released a full year before *Apocalypse Now*, and they stole much of its thunder.

Besides, *Apocalypse* marked a radical change in style from Coppola's previous works. Instead of concentrating on plot, characterization, and acting—his greatest strengths as a director—he experimented with the purely visual and aural properties of the medium. He seemed to be trying cinematically to emulate what Michael Herr (the author of the film's narration) had attempted in writing his highly-acclaimed *Dispatches*—to suggest the hallucinatory way that stoned soldiers perceived the war in Vietnam. The approach produced some striking moments, but the film was short on dramatic momentum, narrative clarity, and psychological depth; ultimately, it had the shallowness and self-importance of a druggie's incoherent ramblings. Writing a harsh but accurate assessment in *Time* magazine, Frank Rich called *Apocalypse* "emotionally obtuse and intellectually empty. It is not so much an epic account of a gruelling war as an incongruous, extravagant monument to artistic self-defeat."

TALIA'S career began to go downhill at around the same time. She appeared in a trio of turkeys: *Old Boyfriends*, an anemic drama about a woman tracking down the men in her past life to learn where she has gone wrong; *Prophecy*, a misbegotten horror movie about an ecological monster that looked about as menacing as Smokey the Bear; and *Windows*, the fatuous tale of a frail young woman pursued by a predatory lesbian (played by Elizabeth Ashley). Talia now feels that her miscalculations on those films derived from her fear of asserting herself, a timidity that had its roots in her childhood conditioning. "Because I was brought up the way I was, I didn't know I was allowed to speak up. On *Windows*, they changed the script I had agreed to do, and I didn't know I could say, 'I'm not going to do that!' For six months, I was a good girl. I became the little sister. I didn't know how to be selfish or aggressive. I felt it was my role to help all these directors. I always want to help some guy. Also, I was frightened to carry a film by myself."

Her dissatisfaction with those films began to infect her personal life as well. "I was playing mousy roles," she says, "and after a while, you become what you play. I saw this happen to De Niro. There was a point when he played a role with chutzpah, and he became that. When Francis made *The Godfather*, he borrowed that strength. I was playing these dreary women that even a dog wouldn't want to be, and you become smaller and smaller, till you're not interested in watching yourself."

At the same time, her marriage to David Shire was breaking up, and the correlation between her depressing film roles and her depressing life at home got to be scary at times. "I remember when I was doing *Prophecy*," she recalls, "David and I were separating, and one day my poor little boy, who was two-and-a-half, came to the set and saw me with all the monsters. I had blood all over me, and he was horrified. At the same time, he was experiencing the violent breakup of a marriage. I realized that what you play, you bring home."

The dissolution of the marriage also had an effect on David Shire's career. He was one of the most successful composers in Hollywood; he had written the score for Francis's *The Conversation*, had done the musical arrangements for *Saturday Night Fever*, and had scored *All the President's Men* and *Farewell, My Lovely*, among many other films. Originally, Shire was to write the score for *Apocalypse Now*, with Carmine helping out on the source music. Shire gave up an assignment on Warren Beatty's *Heaven Can Wait* in order to work on *Apocalypse*. But at the time he and Talia separated, David left *Apocalypse*, and Carmine took over the entire score. Italia claims that Francis was simply displeased with Shire's music. But the Shires' domestic difficulties may well have affected the family's working relationships. Now that some years have elapsed, Shire is once again on good terms with the entire Coppola family, including Talia.

Despite its exorbitant cost, *Apocalypse Now* eventually eked out a profit, and Francis plunged into more ambitious schemes. In 1980, he bought the old Hollywood General Studios for $6.7 million and renamed it Zoetrope; he envisioned it as "a family or a large repertory company engaged in making movies." The other Coppolas lent their support to the new studio. When Francis needed money to close the deal, Talia rushed in to assist him. "I told Francis I would give him my point to *Rocky II*," she reports. "Little did I know that points mean nothing in the way the pie's divided. You never see your share because it's been cut under the table. But when Francis went to the bank, he was able to tell them that and somehow keep the negotiation going. Then I was pregnant and a good friend of ours is the banker Francis was dealing with. I ran up to him and said, 'My brother doesn't have collateral. Take this baby as collateral.' I was always very protective of him."

Zoetrope was a revival of the dream embodied by American Zoetrope a decade earlier; the new studio would be a haven for gifted filmmakers who could not fit into the Hollywood establishment. Francis brought in an old classmate from UCLA film school, Carroll Ballard, a talented documentarian and maker of short films, to direct *The Black Stallion*, based on Walter Farley's classic children's book. Aided immeasurably by Carmine's majestic, richly melodic score, the film won glowing reviews for its evocation of a child's universe, and it was a box office success to boot.

Francis and Carmine embarked on another remarkable venture—presenting a restored version of Abel Gance's 1927 silent epic, *Napoleon*. Carmine had remembered seeing Douglas Fairbanks in *The Thief of Bagdad* as a youngster; the picture played with a live orchestra at a large Broadway movie house, and the thrill of that boyhood experience had always stayed with him. Now he had his chance to revive the tradition. He wrote four hours of music to accompany *Napoleon*, and with typical bravado Francis announced that the film would premiere at Radio City Music Hall with a sixty-piece orchestra led by Carmine. At first, Carmine doubted that anyone would come. "I told my son, 'You might be interested in seeing the film because you're a film buff, and maybe there will be a few others, but you're liable to have fifty people in the theatre. The Music Hall has almost 6000 seats.'" To Carmine's astonishment, the showings of *Napoleon* were completely sold out; it grossed $800,000 in just eight performances at the Music Hall. Carmine recalls, "The opening night was so tempestuous—the applause and the hurrahs and the bravi. I'll never forget it. We had invited Abel Gance, but he was ninety-one years old and very ill. We called him in Paris. His nurse was with him, but we held the phone, and he heard the cheers going on for five minutes. The nurse said later on that tears came out of his eyes. Not long after that, he died." For Carmine, the film represented almost as big a triumph as for Gance. He had finally managed to fulfill his dream of becoming a world-famous conductor. He toured with the film all around the country and then took the road show overseas; a high point came when *Napoleon* was presented at the Colosseum in Rome.

Exhilarated by the success of *Napoleon*, Francis arranged for Zoetrope to distribute other foreign films. In addition, he tried to establish the studio as a gathering place for new and established filmmakers from all over the world. Gene Kelly and director Michael Powell (*The Red Shoes*) came to serve as artists-in-residence. Directors as different as Jean-Luc Godard and Dennis Hopper were invited to develop projects there. Zoetrope represented Francis's attempt to become the cinematic impresario of the 1980s. He missed the vitality of Darryl F. Zanuck's Hollywood. "The great motion picture industry, the great crafts, the great traditions have been systematically dismantled while no one noticed," he declared. "And they were dismantled for the same reason that everything is dismantled: to make something a more *reliable business*." Francis set out to restore a bit of Hollywood's vanished grandeur.

"The dream of having a creative community where people would help each other and stimulate each other was really important at a time when everyone was very, very isolated from their fellow artists," says Talia. "Michael Powell was talking about the sharing that went on at the old studios, where people would go over to the next sound stage and say, 'I'm having trouble with a special effect,' and another director would come over to help. That's what Francis wanted to create." He even brought in his brother August to start an educational program on the Zoetrope lot. August arranged for the students at nearby Bancroft Junior High School to come in and work as apprentices with the studio's various craftspeople.

The first order of business, however, was to initiate a slate of films. Francis hired German director Wim Wenders to film *Hammett*, an adaptation of Joe Gores's psychological novel about Dashiell Hammett, Caleb Deschanel, the talented cinematographer of *The Black Stallion*, was hired to direct his first feature, *The Escape Artist*, starring Ryan O'Neal's son Griffin. And Francis himself began preparations on a movie of his own, *One From the Heart*, which was originally envisioned as a fragile love story—a modest effort meant to be a relief from the rigors of *Apocalypse Now*.

Within a year, everything had fallen apart. After nine-tenths of *Hammett* was completed in 1980, Coppola suddenly shut down production to have the script rewritten. Filming was resumed a year later, and the movie finally opened—to poor reviews and worse business—three years after shooting had originally begun. *The Escape Artist* was so murky and lethargic that it was released in only a few cities and then shelved. And the budget of *One From the Heart*, originally conceived as a "little" picture, leapt to a staggering $27 million. Francis built a huge Las Vegas set on the Zoetrope lot and experimented with new computer techniques that saw him directing most of the movie from inside a giant trailer while the actors worked outside. The movie was beset with financial crises. As Francis told Gay Talese, "Shy of George Lucas, I may be the wealthiest filmmaker. But I'm not liquid." He claimed to be worth $100 million, but since most of it was in real estate, he had to sell property before he could meet his payroll. Only when Jack Singer, a Canadian real estate developer, appeared to bail him out did Coppola manage to complete the film. Even after that rescue, the high drama that always surrounds a Francis Coppola movie continued. Francis arranged two previews at Radio City Music Hall without informing the distributing company, Paramount Pictures. Irritated by Francis's high-handedness, Paramount chairman Barry Diller announced that Paramount would not release the movie. Two weeks before the scheduled release, Francis frantically arranged screenings for the other studios. Columbia picked it up at the eleventh hour.

Before its release, Francis proudly announced that *One From the Heart* "will work on a trillion levels." To most audiences, it seemed to work on none at all. It was a commercial catastrophe and was pulled from release after just a few weeks. As Vincent Canby wrote, "*One From the Heart* has no characters, no performances, no story, no comedy, and no romance, only what Hollywood calls 'production values' . . ." The failure of the film and of the other Zoetrope movies put an end to Francis's dream of a revolutionary new studio. The staff was let go, and the studio was sold to Jack Singer in February 1984. "The financial tragedy of *One From the Heart*," says Jack Schwartzman, "was the impact that it had on the studio. Everybody makes big films that lose money and small films that lose money. But the sad thing was that all the money went into the film that could more properly have gone into maintaining an institution which had a longevity to it that the film didn't have. The money was misdirected. It's sad because the picture sunk the dream, and the dream was right."

After the failure of *One From the Heart* and the collapse of Zoetrope, Francis refused to admit defeat; he tried once again to get back to basics. He went to Tulsa, Oklahoma and filmed *The Outsiders* and *Rumble Fish*, two novels by S. E. Hinton, the bestselling author of "young adult" fiction. A group of California high school students had written Francis, telling him that he was their first choice to make a film of their favorite book, *The Outsiders*. Intrigued by this unusual fan letter, Coppola undertook the project, and also filmed *Rumble Fish* while on location in Oklahoma.

Both *The Outsiders* and *Rumble Fish* were more modestly budgeted than his other recent pictures, and they were both made with young, predominantly unknown actors. "I was a little fed up with the movie business," Francis said of this phase in his career, "and the idea of working with new actors appealed to me. I wanted to work with people who hadn't yet learned to make things difficult.

In a sense, I wanted to leave the adult system of making movies—the Hollywood system. It appealed to the Boy Scout leader in me. I used to be a camp counselor, and I've always tried to work with young people." Hinton was both exhilarated and a bit bewildered by the chaotic way in which Francis worked, but she was swept along by his enthusiasm. Unfortunately, neither movie quite managed to break the box office jinx that has plagued all of Coppola's efforts after *Apocalypse Now*.

During recent years, Francis has grown obsessed with style at the expense of substance; he has struggled to express himself through visual imagery and music rather than through traditional narrative. As he told Gay Talese, "I see myself becoming more of a film composer. All my future films will be musical—with songs and dances and more fluid imagery." One can certainly appreciate that an ambitious artist would want to stretch himself, reach beyond what he has done in the past. Coppola felt that he had pushed conventional storytelling to its limit in the *Godfather* films, and he wanted to make more radical use of the film medium; he wanted to experiment with new forms of technology.

The only problem with this decision is that Coppola has so far been unable to demonstrate the same talents as an experimental visual artist that he once demonstrated as a more traditional dramatic filmmaker. George Lucas once commented on how he and Coppola differed: "I'm more graphic, filmmaking, editing oriented, and Francis is more writing, dramatic, actor oriented. So we complement each other." Since his rupture with Lucas, Coppola seems to have set out to compete with his former protégé, struggling to prove that he could surpass Lucas as a master technician. Even if he succeeded at his goal, one wonders if it would be worth the effort. Coppola's movies have become technically prodigious but increasingly hollow. "Some artists become Jesus freaks," Pauline Kael wrote. "Movie artists are more likely to become technology freaks." Her devastating review of *One From the Heart* sums up Francis's misguided approach:

There are easily recognizable danger signals:
    When a director announces that the movie he is working on is "ahead of its time," you can guess that he's in deep trouble, because what he's saying is that the public won't know enough to appreciate what he has done.
    When a director announces that he is becoming a film "com-

poser," you know he's saying that he doesn't have much in the way of a story or characters.

When a director says that his movie is about "fantasy and reality," you suspect he's carrying on in the ringmaster tradition of Fellini.

When a director starts talking about his "revolutionary" video-film technology, you squirm, because you're not sure you understand what he's saying, and the parts you do understand make you squirm even more.

Put it all together and it spells Francis Ford Coppola's *One From the Heart*.

This movie isn't from the heart, or from the head, either; it's from the lab.

Only a very few filmakers have demonstrated an intuitive grasp of purely visual imagery. George Lucas is one, along with Federico Fellini, Alfred Hitchcock, and Akira Kurosawa. They are masters of *film*, able to create not just pictorial beauty but dramatic tension through their composition and juxtaposition of images. Coppola has tried to match them, but his effects have been mainly arty, self-conscious, and laborious. At the same time, his later movies have lost the narrative sweep and the acuity of characterization and performance that once distinguished his work. His recent films seem bloated and insubstantial—dominated by their cinematographers (Vittorio Storaro, Stephen H. Burum) and their art directors (usually Dean Tavoularis)—but showing no firm directorial hand.

Even more disturbingly, Coppola has lost sight of the theme that animated his best work—the theme of family relationships so crucial to *The Rain People* and both *Godfather* films. This theme played no part in *Apocalypse Now* and *One From the Heart*, and in adapting S. E. Hinton's *The Outsiders*, Coppola eviscerated the core of her story—the tensions among three brothers. Only when he returned to the family theme in *Rumble Fish* did he regain some of his artistic vitality. Although still excessively stylized and insufficiently dramatized, it was his most adventurous and affecting film in some time.

CARMINE composed the score for *The Outsiders*, and since then he has scored an Olympics commercial for Transamerica and has given a number of concerts around the country, a "Film Night with Coppola," in which he performs excerpts from his scores. The latest project that he hopes will come to fruition is a rather bizarre concept brought to him by a couple of independent film-makers who belong to the Jews for Jesus religious sect. They want to do the definitive film about the life of Christ and hope to present the picture with a live orchestra and chorus under the direction of Carmine. So far, the financing has been elusive. Carmine's opportunities apart from Francis remain limited, but even in his seventies, he seems determined to prove that his career is not entirely dependent on his more famous son. "Had nothing happened with Francis," Carmine insists, "I would still have written my opera and symphonic music, still have done the road stuff with Merrick, still have done routines for the Rockettes. Of course, it was an enormous boost to get *The Godfather*." His wife is even more likely to bristle when the charge of son-to-father nepotism is raised, and she is furious when she speaks of the interview Francis gave to *Film Comment* in 1983. Asked if he felt he had helped Carmine professionally, Francis replied, "I made his career." Italia points out that Carmine could have gone to work in the movies in 1955 but chose to return to New York. "If we had stayed here then," Italia snorts, "they would have said Carmine gave his son Francis Ford Coppola a break. As far as I'm concerned, Carmine went to the top when he was with Toscanini. If he never did anything else after that, it wouldn't have mattered; he was on top."

At this point, Carmine and Francis may not be pursuing many more joint ventures. They argued frequently when they worked together, but Francis has always praised the "really terrific melodic imagination" of his father. Francis has indicated that in the future, however, he wants to try writing music of his own; it is a fantasy that obsesses him more and more. His father does not endorse Francis's musical aspirations. "He's not encouraging me at all," Francis said, "but he knew that I wanted to do the music on *Rumble Fish*, and when he heard a little tape—some of it had been recorded—he commented how a section of it sounded just like something he had written. I neglected to tell him that that same section also sounded like something some guy a hundred years ago had written. But my father has never been a very encouraging man."

If Carmine's career is tapering off, Talia's seems to be in full swing again—behind the camera rather than in front of it. After she divorced David Shire, she announced that she was carrying the baby of entertainment attorney Jack Schwartzman, whom she later married. Their son Jason was born in 1980, and they had a second child, Simon, in 1982.

Because of his legal background, Jack was called in to help Francis straighten out the financial predicaments that grew out of *One From the Heart*. In return, Francis helped unofficially to rewrite the script for the movie that Jack hoped would propel his career as an independent producer, *Never Say Never Again*, starring Sean Connery in a return engagement as James Bond.

The original producer, Kevin McClory, owned the rights to a James Bond screenplay he had written with Ian Fleming twenty years earlier. That screenplay had formed the basis for *Thunderball*, made in 1965. A decade later, McClory decided to remake the film. The Ian Fleming estate, along with Albert R. Broccoli, producer of all the recent James Bond movies, tried to stop McClory from making his film. Feeling besieged on all sides, McClory was about to abandon the project when Schwartzman used his lawyerly expertise to surmount all these legal challenges and get the film back on the track. A grateful McClory turned the project over to Schwartzman to produce. Schwartzman set out to entice Connery back into the Bond series one last time. But Connery would not even consider the project unless the producer guaranteed him a $3 million pay-or-play deal. "He had script approval," Schwartzman explains. "What that meant was that he could have read the script and said, 'Thank you very much. I'm not interested. Please send me the check for $3 million.' So before he read the script, we had to go on the hunt for the $3 million. We signed away the house."

"And that's why I did *Rocky III*," Talia adds. "We needed the money for the Bond movie."

Talia worked closely with Jack on the development of the script, the casting, and the final editing of the movie. "Essentially, she co-produced the film," Jack says. "But that was a credit that was impossible to give. The credit she got on the film is one of those things which aptly describes her role and then doesn't begin to do it justice; the credit was consultant to the producer, which was the nicest way to say it without ruffling all the artistic feathers. There were a lot of nervous people on this movie. I once described it as like those old pirate movies where you walk into the captain's cabin and Maureen O'Hara's there. And someone says, 'What's she doing here? You can't take a woman on board a ship. She's a curse.' That was the way some people felt about Talia. She was as vitally involved as anybody. It was unfortunate that she had to do it in the closet."

Part of the problem was Francis Coppola. "Just before the

picture got off the ground," Jack says, "her brother became involved as a consultant to me and was very, very helpful. He gave the picture a creative shot in the arm at a time when it was teetering on the brink. His presence became an enormous threat to certain people. And to those same people, Talia's presence represented Francis's presence. Everybody involved was scared to death. Connery was coming back in the role after his last several pictures didn't work. If this one didn't work either, it could have been all over. The director, Irvin Kershner, was coming off one successful picture—*The Empire Strikes Back*—the only successful picture in his life. And everyone was asking, was that George Lucas or was that him? Well, you can see where he would have been very threatened by Francis and, by extension, by Talia."

As a result, Talia had to make her suggestions indirectly; she would communicate to Jack but was forced to remain invisible most of the time. "I wasn't really allowed to participate as vigorously as I would have liked," Talia admits.

"Maybe the film was too complicated for what it was worth," Jack concludes. "You spend three years making a Bond film, and who wants to leave behind a Bond film as his body of work?" Nonetheless, the film accomplished what it was meant to do. It made a fortune, and it established Jack and Talia as bona fide film producers who are now being courted by other studios. In 1984 Schwartzman announced a slate of four big-budget movies, one of which—*Lionheart*—will be produced by Talia. She says that she still wants to act in "one last lovely part and then finish it off and get behind the camera."

Talia feels that her marriage to Schwartzman has allowed her to fulfill herself professionally as well as personally. "I don't want to just partner a powerful man as Irene Selznick did," Talia asserts. "I didn't want to pick another man like my brothers. This relationship with Jack is very exciting for me because it shows I've achieved something coming from my background. I'm finally allowing a man to give me an egalitarian relationship. I can cherish and partner his talents, and he doesn't forget that. He then gives me my turn. He doesn't ask me to forfeit my power. We practiced a little bit in the Bond film—a real sharing of problems."

Still, one wonders whether Talia has entirely escaped her feminine conditioning. She goes out of her way to emphasize that *Never Say Never Again* was primarily Jack's movie; she is his biggest booster, and she seems willing to retreat so that the spotlight can shine on him. Their professional relationship is still in the process of being defined. "I'm in a strange period," she admits, "like a snake shedding its skin. I really like being a mother. I really like being married. But I want to do everything, not just use that one muscle which creates a terrible distortion in people. I don't want my children to be casualties. It's real clear that if you're a lady who has a certain kind of energy and you're not using it, you're not going to make your kids too happy. I certainly don't think it's the right way to raise boys. I have three boys, so I'm not going to be let off any hooks in my life."

The task of juggling child-rearing and moviemaking is a challenge that excites both Talia and Jack. "Whatever we do has to work compatibly with three young kids," Jack says. "We've both been in the business long enough to know what the pitfalls are. Neither one of us is really that greedy or ambitious that we'll sacrifice everything for a big company. I know that most Hollywood families suffered to a greater or lesser extent in deference to the *business* of the family. I don't want that to happen to us. Now maybe that means we will not be a successful company, but maybe we'll have the most successful *balance* of professional and family life."

THE Coppolas are survivors. Every time Francis seems to have used up the last of his nine lives, he lands on his feet once again. His career had reached its lowest point when he was rescued, at least temporarily, by an offer to direct *The Cotton Club*. He was paid $2.5 million to rewrite the script and direct the film. His rescuers were the very same people who had salvaged his career in 1971, when he was offered the chance to make *The Godfather*. The original author of the *Cotton Club* screenplay is Mario Puzo, and the producer is Robert Evans, who had been running Paramount when Francis made *The Godfather*. Clearly all three men hoped that lightning would strike again.

Filming did not go smoothly. (Jerry Wexler, the music editor who was let go by Francis, called the production "a mammoth train wreck waiting to happen.") Evans and Coppola were at each other's throats. "You may have an ugly marriage, but beautiful kids," Evans said regretfully. "That's the essence of our relationship, unfortunately. We don't spend our weekends together on a cruise." In addition, the financiers—a pair of Las Vegas casino owners, Ed and Fred Doumani—grew increasingly nervous as the budget climbed. In reshaping the screenplay, Coppola returned to a fraternal theme: the story of two pairs of brothers—Richard Gere and Nicolas Cage, Gregory and Maurice Hines.

As usual, Francis hired several of his relatives to work with him on the film. His two sons, Gian-Carlo, age twenty, and Roman, age eighteen, both served as production assistants; Gian-Carlo was also one of the film's editors. The boys have already worked on several other Coppola films, beginning when they were young teenagers. In addition, Francis's nephew—August's twenty-year-old son, Nicholas—has a co-starring role, as he did in *Rumble Fish*. He has changed his name from Coppola to Cage so as to downplay his family connections; his grandmother calls the name change "a stupid, dumb thing." Nicolas himself is quite touchy on the issue. When questioned about his family ties on the set of *Racing With the Moon*, he stormed off in a rage. Perhaps his youth and inexperience make him especially sensitive on the point. He went straight from acting in plays in Beverly Hills High School to a featured role in *Rumble Fish*, and even now, he can hardly be said to have paid his dues as an actor, although he did have the male lead in *Valley Girl*, a low-budget hit in 1983. He also co-starred with Sean Penn and Elizabeth McGovern in *Racing With the Moon*.

At times, all the Coppolas have chafed at suggestions that they benefit unduly from family favoritism. Yet their careers have been inextricably intertwined for the last decade. Although Francis initially resisted hiring his sister on *The Godfather*, he has since become the family's unapologetic benefactor. Whereas many other Hollywood families have gone to great lengths to avoid working together, the Coppolas have eagerly sought this kind of collaborative interplay. Their willingness to do business with one another is tied up with the traditional Italian value of allegiance to family. "Americans are peculiar about nepotism," Talia observes. "You know, we left the British Empire because we don't like royal families. And that's absolutely right; you do it on your own. At the same time, we love it if something tells us a family does have magic, and we can see it passed on. It's a peculiar contradiction about royalty."

It requires a certain self-assurance for someone to hire members of his family to work on a film, especially when the film is a big-budget studio production. "You're taking an enormous risk when you work with family," Jack Schwartzman says. "Let's say I'm producing a film and Talia is directing, and three weeks into the film it's my clear creative decision that I should fire the director. Tell me how I'm going to do that. Given that problem, I'm not sure I can understand why Francis would want to work with anybody in his family. I think it takes an enormous amount of confidence and courage on all their parts to undertake that working relationship, because underneath it is a nuclear bomb."

Talia, however, believes that she understands what draws the family to take those risks. "In circus families," she observes, "the most dangerous acts are done by family members, because if you're risking your life and there's no net, it had better be your brother or your mother who's going to catch you. If I am ever going to do a triple as an actress, it really won't be with a lot of directors. It would be with Francis, because I know that if I go to the limit with my ability, he will structure me and edit me and make me look my best, whereas another director will be jerking off—excuse my language—and the stuff will never get cut together. In one sense, it's damn dangerous to work with family, and in another sense you'll do your best work. Francis will get the most out of Nicolas and the best from my father. He'll take me as far as I can go, and I know it'll be there on the screen. And by the same token, I would do my best for him."

With their intense devotion to the idea of family, the Coppolas stand apart from other Hollywood dynasties. In contrast to the Selznicks or the Douglases, they aren't obsessed with establishing their independence; their best work has been done in collaboration with one another. The Coppolas are rekindling the spirit that animated Hollywood in its earliest days, both in their appetite for audacious gambles and in their reverence for the ties that bind.

11

COMING HOME

WHEN Francis Coppola's *The Godfather* appeared in 1972, it startled viewers with its graphic scenes of mayhem—garrotings, machine-gun massacres, and ritual executions. But the film's most disturbing violence was emotional rather than physical, and its fiercest battles were not those fought in the back alleys of Little Italy but the ones that raged on the home front. *The Godfather* held audiences in thrall because it revived an age-old fascination— not just with bloodbaths, but with blood ties; it was an explosive family drama at a time when such stories had all but vanished from the screen.

Starting in the late 1960s and continuing through the next decade, "buddy movies" had become the fad: *Midnight Cowboy, Easy Rider, Butch Cassidy and the Sundance Kid, M*A*S*H, The French Connection, The Hot Rock, The Sting, Papillon,* and *Scarecrow* exemplified the new vogue. Women were relegated to weak supporting roles or else dropped from sight entirely. Newman and Redford, Sutherland and Gould, Hoffman and Voight—these were the romantic teams of the era. Even more significantly, the male duos who dominated the screen during this period were almost invariably devoid of family connections. Who were the mothers and fathers of Butch Cassidy, Ratso Rizzo, or Captain America? These characters seemed to be free-floating vagabonds of unknown origin, cut off from parents and siblings. The bonds they struck up with one another were an emotional recompense for the family ties missing from their lives.

This impulse to substitute male camaraderie for heterosexual romance and family responsibility is not without precedent in American culture. Critic Leslie Fiedler has identified it as a salient— perhaps *the* salient—phenomenon of our literature, from the *Leatherstocking* series to *Moby Dick* to *Huckleberry Finn* to *The Sun Also Rises*. The tendency had long been evident in American films as well, but it was balanced by an equally profound interest in family relationships. Down through the years, some of the most unforgettable scenes in American cinema have been primal familial encounters: Barbara Stanwyck standing outside the window during the wedding of her estranged daughter at the end of *Stella Dallas* (1937); Tim Holt spiriting his adored mother away from her suitor, Joseph Cotten, in *The Magnificent Ambersons* (1942); war veteran Fredric March reunited with his wife and children at the start of *The Best Years of Our Lives* (1946); young Brandon De Wilde keeping a watchful eye on his mother, Jean Arthur, as she dances with the mysterious gunfighter, Alan Ladd, in *Shane* (1953); the climactic confrontation of two warring brothers, Marlon Brando and Rod Steiger, in *On the Waterfront* (1954); James Dean achiev- ing a deathbed reconciliation with his stern father, Raymond Mas- sey, in *East of Eden* (1955); Gregory Peck struggling to explain Southern justice to his son and daughter in *To Kill a Mockingbird* (1962).

Despite the powerful impact such films traditionally had on audiences, their themes were suddenly and unaccountably neg- lected by Hollywood—or were consigned to television, where they were treated antiseptically. In the late 1960s and for the most of the 1970s, the very awareness of family began to evaporate from our movies.

During this same period a new group of filmmakers emerged. Weaned on the values of the youth culture of the 1960s, most of the newcomers were unattached and uncommitted to parents, spouse, or offspring. Their entrée to the movie studios was not through the family connections that had opened doors for so many of their predecessors, but through a buddy system established in their film-school days. Francis Coppola was the first to prove that a cinema-school graduate could be "bankable" in Hollywood. He became the spiritual godfather to this new coterie, starting when he took George Lucas under his wing during the making of *Finian's*

Rainbow in 1968. "Francis was the great white knight," Lucas has said. "He was the one who had made it. He was the one who made us hope."

Coppola was a UCLA product; Lucas had attended the rival film school at USC during the mid-1960s. The two institutions had different personalities. UCLA was more theoretical in orientation and its students were more iconoclastic in their approach to the Hollywood system. USC, on the other hand, was closely tied to the industry, and it operated along the lines of a trade school. The purpose of USC's curriculum was specifically to train students to work in the movie business.

Arthur Knight, a teacher of Lucas's at USC, once remarked that "a degree in cinema can be your fastest way of landing a job in a shoe store." That all changed in the 1970s. With the aid of Coppola, Lucas managed to get his shoe in the studio door. He then brought in his friends and classmates, who included John Milius (the writer of *Apocalypse Now* and writer-director of *The Wind and the Lion*), Willard Huyck (co-writer of *American Graffiti*), Hal Barwood and Matthew Robbins (writers of *MacArthur*), Walter Murch (editor of *The Conversation* and director of *Oz*), Gary Kurtz (producer of *Star Wars*), Randal Kleiser (director of *Grease*), Basil Poledouros (composer of scores for Kleiser's *The Blue Lagoon* and Milius's *Conan the Barbarian*), and Caleb Deschanel (cinematographer on *The Black Stallion* and *The Right Stuff*).

Lucas has described his days at USC film school and the dream of friendship fostered there: "There was a sort of renaissance at that period at that school. There were about thirty or forty of us, and we all liked each other. We were all very bright and very ambitious; we were friends; we had no competitive drives with each other; we'd help each other on our movies. We all had a lot of fun, and we've grown up together, and of that group, almost all have made it into the film business."

The most successful of the USC group took to calling themselves the Dirty Dozen. Except for Gloria Katz, a UCLA film school graduate who married Willard Huyck and became accepted as one of the boys, the gang was all male. Several of them were unmarried; almost none had children. Miki Herman, who worked as associate producer for Lucas, has evoked the flavor of the group's get-togethers. When Lucas was doing the sound mixing on *Star Wars*, she recalled, "George would sit there for hours and all his friends would drop by. It was like a men's club—he would really confide in them and they had great fun. They're all like a bunch of little boys."

As the Dirty Dozen solidified its standing in the industry, the circle was expanded to include other up-and-coming young filmmakers. Steven Spielberg, whose poor high school grades had prevented his being accepted at USC film school, won a TV contract at Universal after finishing at Cal State Long Beach; there he became friendly with Lucas, Milius, Barwood, and Robbins. Two New York-based directors, Martin Scorsese (*Mean Streets, Taxi Driver*) and Brian De Palma (*Greetings, Phantom of the Paradise*), were initiated into the fraternity when their early films won acclaim. Eventually the network spread to include some two dozen young filmmakers who socialized regularly, talked movies constantly, and collaborated frequently.

For example, Willard Huyck and Gloria Katz contributed to the screenplay of *American Graffiti*; they also helped Lucas unofficially on *Star Wars* and were rewarded with two percentage points of the movie's astronomical profits, and later with the plum assignment of writing *Indiana Jones and the Temple of Doom*, the 1984 sequel to *Raiders of the Lost Ark*. Hal Barwood and Matthew Robbins wrote Steven Spielberg's first feature, *The Sugarland Express*; Spielberg and Lucas subsequently helped Barwood and Robbins to secure financing for two movies of their own, *Corvette Summer* and *Dragonslayer*. Lucas and Spielberg themselves collaborated on *Raiders of the Lost Ark* and *Indiana Jones*. Milius and Spielberg were co-producers of the World War II bomb, *1941*, which was written by Robert Zemeckis and Bob Gale, two more Spielberg protégés; Zemeckis later directed *I Wanna Hold Your Hand* and *Used Cars* under Spielberg's aegis. Lucas helped Willard Huyck win backing for his first directorial effort, *French Postcards*. Lucas was also instrumental in persuading The Ladd Company to allow Lawrence Kasdan, writer of *The Empire Strikes Back* and *Raiders of the Lost Ark*, to direct his first film, *Body Heat*. Some of these young filmmakers even agreed to trade percentage points on their separate films; they did well on *Star Wars* and *Close Encounters of the Third Kind*, not so well on Milius's *Big Wednesday*, Spielberg's *1941*, and De Palma's *Home Movies*. In many ways, the young boys' club formed by the Dirty Dozen and their chums operated almost as incestuously as the family networks of yesteryear. This was the bloodless nepotism of the 1970s.

The movies fashioned by the group of film-school cronies were almost invariably celebrations of callow friendship, reflecting their own rather insulated world and its particular values. It is not surprising that they should have lit on this theme, considering that so many of them owed their careers to the buddy system. *American Graffiti* was the seminal work of this cycle. It affirms the union of four very different teenage boys—macho John Milner (Paul Le Mat), wimpy Terry the Toad (Charles Martin Smith), serious-minded Curt (Richard Dreyfuss), and blandly all-American Steve (Ron Howard). The boys' parents are invisible until Curt's family shows up in the very last scene to bid him goodbye at the airport. The film summons up an adolescent never-never-land in which the most meaningful connections are those between a group of selflessly devoted pals. In the neon-lit dreamscape of *American Graffiti*, differences in background, personality, intelligence, and popularity are all dissolved in the common bond of friendship.

Lucas transposed the formula to outer space in *Star Wars*, which exalts the friendship of another loyal troupe—impetuous Luke Skywalker (Mark Hamill), dashing Han Solo (Harrison Ford), spunky Princess Leia (Carrie Fisher), their cuddly wookie and their pair of robots. Indeed, the very same format re-appeared in almost all the movies made by members of the Lucas-Spielberg axis, though usually without the wistful charm of *American Graffiti* or the mythic charge of *Star Wars*. Barwood and Robbins produced their feeble teen caper in *Corvette Summer*, starring Lucas discovery Mark Hamill as a pixilated car freak. Zemeckis and Gale concocted *I Wanna Hold Your Hand*, about a pack of high schoolers desperate to meet the Beatles. Milius's *Big Wednesday* was a hymn to surfers; it asked us to grow misty-eyed contemplating the undying fellowship among a band of blond beach boys waxing their boards and "hanging ten" together. Huyck and Katz produced a tepid variation on *American Graffiti* in *French Postcards*, about a group of college kids romping through Paris during their junior year abroad.

Just as the rosy valentines to domestic bliss devised by the old guard were often belied by their makers' real-life experience, the odes to faithful friendship composed by the Lucas-Spielberg set rarely reflected the tensions that existed among the putative pals offscreen. These were not movies about complex adult friendships; they were idyllic dreams of adolescent camaraderie, hatched in the days when the boys worked side by side on their student films. The real interactions among these young filmmakers were seldom as benign or placid as the vision of companionship depicted in

their movies. Conflicts, resentments, and jealousies festered—
just as they had within the networks of filmmakers related by
blood. Within this band of spiritual brethren, the less successful
ones sometimes mocked the superstars behind their backs, and
occasionally took a few public jabs as well. In a 1983 interview,
for example, Brian De Palma tweaked Steven Spielberg for his
preoccupation with toys and gadgets. "I've seen Steven working
day in and day out on *E.T.* toys," De Palma remarked. "It's real
bad. I'm a creative person—why would I want to worry about
designing *E.T.* lamps?"

Moreover, just as the sons and daughters of the Hollywood
dynasties often fought to break away from their powerful parents,
the filmmakers within the new non-family webs waged their own
battles for independence. After Francis Coppola and George Lucas
fell out over the question of how to divide up the profits from
American Graffiti, Lucas broke with Coppola. Eventually Lucas
surpassed his mentor in terms of wealth and power. Today Coppola
still takes private digs at Lucas, and Lucas still seems eager to
establish that he does not owe his career to Coppola. As Dale
Pollock has reported in his biography of Lucas, the final rupture
between the two men came as a result of *Apocalypse Now*. Lucas
had originally wanted to direct John Milius's script, but Coppola
acquired rights to the property when forming American Zoetrope
in 1969. Later, after the release of *American Graffiti*, Coppola
offered Lucas a measly $25,000 salary—plus ten percent of the
profits—to direct *Apocalypse* under his sponsorship. Lucas felt
ripped off, declined the offer, and Coppola took over the film
himself. Commenting on Coppola's actions, Milius made a stinging remark: "As Talleyrand said of Napoleon, "He's as great as
a man can be, without virtue.'"

THE professed communal spirit among young filmmakers had a
counterpart in the executive suites of the studios during the 1970s.
Hollywood continued its infatuation with youth that began after
the success of *Easy Rider*. First the industry courted young directors, then young screenwriters—anyone who promised a pipeline
to the increasingly important teenage audience. Finally the corporate chairmen began to believe that the answer to the industry's
woes lay in hiring young executives who could anticipate the tastes
of tots and teens. And so the previous cadre of studio chieftains—
Mike Frankovich, Robert Evans, James Aubrey—was swept out,
and the hunt was on for a newer, younger breed. Enter the "baby

moguls," many of whom reached the upper echelons of power before their thirtieth birthdays.

Some of the new executives, like Paula Weinstein and Jeff Berg, had family connections in the business. Some were friends from college days, like Weinstein and Mark Rosenberg, the man who would later become her husband. Many of them were veterans of leftist campus politics, including Rosenberg, Weinstein, Universal's Thom Mount and Twentieth Century-Fox's Claire Townsend, the daughter of *Up the Organization* author Robert Townsend.

Much like the phalanx of USC film school graduates, these baby moguls hung out together, helped each other get jobs, shared worries and triumphs, and adopted an unostentatious lifestyle quite distinct from that of the older generation of studio brass. They valued comradeship over domesticity, and they resisted starting families of their own. In fact, most of them dissociated themselves from anything that smacked of permanence, aspiring to live as perennial college kids. "None of us cooks," Paula Weinstein said. "I barely know anyone who owns a dining room table." Her husband Mark Rosenberg concurred. "I'm not into possessions much. I live in an apartment with some records and books."

In a 1978 article on this new generation of movie mogul, *New West* reporter Maureen Orth wrote, "Sometimes, they date each other and often, when they sense trouble—trouble is defined as 'pictures and deals going down the tubes'—they call each other, both to lend support and to be critical." Paramount's young vice president Don Simpson told Orth, "I am concerned and care about a lot of people who are in fact my competition. I am convinced people don't talk to each other the way Thom Mount and I do in business or when we meet socially because of our shared background of the sixties."

That "shared background" has been a sensitive point among them and something of a joke to insiders who saw an irony in a clique of militant SDS-ers conniving to land $300,000-a-year jobs producing teen comics. "The sixties will have come to nothing," Paula Weinstein declared in 1978, "if we have come through them and don't know how to apply those cultural experiences—if we become so involved in power and the accoutrements of power, the big bucks and fast money, that we forget the passions we've learned."

Today Weinstein is more contemplative and self-critical as she ponders her journey through Hollywood's executive corridors. Jeff Berg is another young power broker bred in the 1960s who questions the gap between his present position and the ideals of his college years. He describes an informal meeting he attended during which one ex-radical film executive declared, "All of the movie companies are doing well. We're making a lot of money. But what the hell difference does it make if the infrastructure is falling apart and we're going to war in Central America and people don't have enough to eat?" Mulling over that remark, Berg comments, "I think anyone who came out of a campus environment of the 1960s who is a reasonable success fifteen years later has to be asking himself, 'Did we pursue the logical and political destiny that we contemplated fifteen years ago?' The answer to that question is, probably not."

THAT is in fact the very question that haunts the characters in Lawrence Kasdan's *The Big Chill*, the popular 1983 comedy about a group of seven college friends who swore allegiance to the radical values of the 1960s but, a decade-and-a-half later, find that they have surrendered to more conventional versions of the American Dream. When they reassemble for the funeral of their idealistic comrade who committed suicide, they are impelled to take stock of their own lives. One of them is a business tycoon, his wife is a dissatisfied doctor, another friend is a vapid TV star, still another a hack journalist, another a bored suburban housewife, and a once-idealistic female attorney has drifted into the more lucrative field of real estate law. *The Big Chill* sums up the disillusionment of the Hollywood generation that came to power in the 1970s. It also returns to the theme of *American Graffiti*, nostalgically celebrating friendship as an alternative to the traditional nuclear family.

And yet one significant twist lends a completely different coloring to the picture. The ultimate act of friendship in *The Big Chill* is offered by the married couple (Kevin Kline and Glenn Close) who agree to have the husband impregnate their unmarried friend (Mary Kay Place) because she so desperately wants to have a child. A movie that begins by reviving the mellow mood of 1960s-style friendship ends with a rediscovery of family.

This concern for family connections has begun to permeate other American movies; the theme has even shown up in the movies of Lucas and Spielberg, the most resolutely childlike film-makers of their age. Lucas's *Star Wars* trilogy, which began as an unabashed tribute to intergalactic camaraderie, metamorphoses into a family saga. In *The Empire Strikes Back* Luke Skywalker—who thought he was an orphan—learns that the evil Darth Vader is in fact his father. In *Return of the Jedi* he discovers that Princess Leia is his sister, and he achieves a reconciliation with his long-estranged father; it is Vader, his former arch enemy, who saves his son's life at the end of the film.

A similar progression could be observed in Spielberg's work. His 1975 thriller *Jaws* is essentially a high-adventure buddy movie about three men who leave their families behind as they take to the high seas together. *Close Encounters of the Third Kind*, made in 1977, is a Peter Pan fantasy. At the end, the boyish hero (Richard Dreyfuss), who has been shaken by his encounter with a flying saucer, opts to leave his wife and children and accompany the munchkin-like aliens into outer space—an escape to the paradise of eternal youth. Spielberg's *E.T.* reworks many of the same motifs, but at the end of that 1982 film, the alien creature returns to his spaceship, and young Elliott stays behind with his earthbound family. In a rudimentary, halting way *E.T.* tries to say something about the pain of divorce and the pull of family relationships; this theme is subordinated to the more fantastical elements of the story, but the fact that it is included at all suggests a crucial change in Spielberg's orientation.

After a long period of denial, family themes have once again become a staple of American film. *The Turning Point*, *Kramer vs. Kramer*, *Ordinary People*, *On Golden Pond*, and *Terms of Endearment* are all stories about families in conflict, and they have been among the most popular and award-laden movies of recent years. These movies vary widely in quality and sometimes have a cloying, mawkish tone; but at least they address the kinds of urgent human questions that Hollywood moviemakers ignored for over a decade.

By 1983, it was apparent that the public was ready to embrace a range of offbeat, provocative films about family relationships. *Testament*, for example, dramatizes the horror of nuclear war by focusing on one close-knit family devastated by the holocaust. *Tender Mercies* captures the anguish of a down-and-out country singer hoping to do better as a husband and father the second time around. Barbra Streisand's *Yentl*, "dedicated to my father, and all of our fathers," celebrates the loving bond of father and daughter and the tradition of learning that a parent can instill in his child. (*Yentl* gives evidence of a number of changes in the movie industry since the days of Goldwyn, Zukor, and Cohn. Those early Jewish moguls wanted desperately to blot out the memories of the *shtetls*, and they would have been horrified at the idea of making a film that so blatantly acknowledged their roots. Could any of them have imagined that an American audience would stand in line to see a $15 million musical about a female yeshiva student obsessed with learning talmud?)

Far from being idealized portraits, most of these new movies dealing with parents and children have confronted painful truths about the changing state of the American family. *Kramer vs. Kramer* concentrates on a vicious custody battle; *Ordinary People* considers teenage suicide and the aborted communication between husband and wife, as well as between parents and son; *Terms of Endearment* portrays a prickly mother-daughter relationship and ends in a very tough-minded way, when the terminally ill young housewife tells her feckless husband that she does not want him to raise their children after her death. In short, all of these films acknowledge the dissolution of traditional family values, the sometimes savage discord within a household, and the destruction wreaked in the name of family love.

If earlier generations of filmmakers were drawn to the subject of family, it was partly because familial rivalries, battles for succession, and struggles for self-definition were so important in their own lives. For the second-generation moviemakers who have been involved in creating these major new films about family, similar concerns provide the animating emotion. Stanley Jaffe, the producer of *Kramer vs. Kramer*, has indicated that the dissolution of his own marriage contributed to his sensitivity to a story about the plight of a child of divorce. Jane Fonda, the driving force behind *On Golden Pond*, wanted the making of her film to become a vehicle for expiating unresolved feelings about the tortured relationship she had with her father Henry. And Timothy Hutton, whose Oscar-winning performance in *Ordinary People* turned him into a major star, has suggested that his role in the film helped him sort through his own feelings of loss after his father, actor Jim Hutton, died of cancer. There was a correlation to his own life experience when, at the conclusion of the film, his character breaks the grip of the past and recognizes that he has the strength to survive on his own. A few years after *Ordinary People* appeared, Hutton actively sought the leading role in *Daniel*, the film version of E. L. Doctorow's acclaimed *roman à clef* about the children of the Rosenbergs. Hutton responded passionately to the story's emotional climax, in which the young protagonist at last lays to rest the grief engendered by his parents' death, while rediscovering the value of his family heritage.

In effect, such a spiritual liberation is what most second-generation Hollywood personalities have attempted to bring about in their own lives. By and large the descendants of filmmaking dynasties whose accomplishments have been most impressive are those who, at some point, took charge of their own careers and formulated a game plan distinct from that of their parents. That is certainly the common thread that links such second-generation achievers as Jane Fonda, Richard Zanuck, Alan Ladd, Jr., Tom Mankiewicz, Stanley Jaffe, and Jeff Berg. Others—like Junior Laemmle or Mary Jennifer Selznick—who simply pursued the course laid out for them by their famous parents tended to be the washouts and the casualties, the wastrels and the suicides.

As Timothy Hutton comes to realize at the end of *Daniel*, it is the burden of each generation to acknowledge its heritage and then move forward. Despite the instability and pain that so often seemed to accompany their upbringing, a few children of Hollywood have managed this feat of reconciliation and transcendence. To paraphrase the words of one writer whose stay in Hollywood was briefer and less fruitful, they are the ones who have not merely survived, but endured.

BIBLIOGRAPHY

IN doing the research for this book, numerous newspaper articles, short magazine pieces, film reviews and reference texts were consulted, in addition to the books and longer magazine articles cited below.

June Allyson with Frances Spatz Leighton, *June Allyson*, New York: G. P. Putnam's Sons, 1982.

Diana Barrymore and Gerold Frank, *Too Much, Too Soon*, New York: Henry Holt and Company, 1957.

Rudy Behlmer, ed., *Memo From David O. Selznick*, New York: Viking Press, 1972.

Ronald Bowers, *The Selznick Players*, New York: A. S. Barnes and Company, 1976.

Helen Gurley Brown, *Having It All*, New York: The Linden Press, 1982.

Bo Burlingham, "Politics Under the Palms," *Esquire*, February 1977.

Corinne Calvet, *Has Corinne Been a Good Girl?*, New York: St. Martin's Press, 1983.

Gary Carey, *All the Stars in Heaven*, New York: E. P. Dutton, 1981.

Gary Carey, *More about All About Eve*, New York: Random House, 1972.

Peter Collier, "I Remember Fonda," *New West*, September 24, 1979.

August Coppola, *The Intimacy*, New York: Grove Press, 1978.

Eleanor Coppola, *Notes*, New York: Simon and Schuster, 1979.

Christina Crawford, *Mommie Dearest*, New York: William Morrow and Company, 1978.

Gary Crosby and Ross Firestone, *Going My Own Way*, Garden City, New York: Doubleday, 1983.

Bosley Crowther, *Hollywood Rajah; The Life and Times of Louis B. Mayer*, New York: Henry Holt and Company, 1960.

Anne Douglas, "My Awful Wedded Husband," *Saturday Evening Post*, November 24, 1962.

Kirk Douglas, "The Actor in Me," *Saturday Evening Post*, June 22 and 29, 1957.

John Drinkwater, *The Life and Adventures of Carl Laemmle*, New York: G. P. Putnam's Sons, 1931.

John Gregory Dunne, *The Studio*, New York: Farrar, Straus & Giroux, 1969.

Carol Easton, *The Search for Sam Goldwyn*, New York: William Morrow and Company, 1976.

Douglas Fairbanks, Jr., *The Fairbanks Album*, Boston: New York Graphic Society, 1975.

Leslie A. Fiedler, *Love and Death in the American Novel*, New York: Criterion Books, 1960.

Jane Fonda, *Jane Fonda's Workout Book*, New York: Simon and Schuster, 1982.

"Francis Coppola and Gay Talese: The Conversation," *Esquire*, July 1981.

Gerold Frank, *Judy*, New York: Harper & Row, 1975.

Michael Freedland, *The Warner Brothers*, New York: St. Martin's Press, 1983.

Kenneth L. Geist, *Pictures Will Talk: The Life and Films of Joseph L. Mankiewicz*, New York: Scribner's, 1978.

William Goldman, *Adventures in the Screen Trade*, New York: Warner Books, 1983.

Sheilah Graham, *Confessions of a Hollywood Columnist*, New York: William Morrow and Company, 1969.

Fred Lawrence Guiles, *Jane Fonda: The Actress in Her Time*, Garden City, New York: Doubleday, 1982.

Mel Gussow, *Don't Say Yes Until I Finish Talking: A Biography of Darryl F. Zanuck*, Garden City, New York: Doubleday, 1971.

Anthony Haden-Guest, "The Rise, Fall, and Rise of Zanuck-Brown," *New York*, December 1, 1975.

Hutchins Hapgood, "The Earnestness That Wins Wealth," *The World's Work*, May 1903.

Ronald Haver, *David O. Selznick's Hollywood*, New York: Alfred A. Knopf, 1980.

Brooke Hayward, *Haywire*, New York: Alfred A. Knopf, 1977.

Ben Hecht, *Child of the Century*, New York: Simon & Schuster, 1954.

Marilyn Henry and Ron De Sourdis, *The Films of Alan Ladd*, Secaucus, New Jersey: The Citadel Press, 1981.

Charles Higham, *Warner Brothers*, New York: Charles Scribner, 1975.

Irving Howe with Kenneth Libo, *World of Our Fathers*, New York: Harcourt Brace Jovanovich, 1976.

John Huston, *An Open Book*, New York: Alfred A. Knopf, 1980.

"Idols of the King: Francis Coppola Interviewed by David Thomson and Lucy Gray," *Film Comment*, October 1983.

"Interview With Henry Fonda," *Playboy*, December 1981.

Alva Johnston, "The Wahoo Boy," *The New Yorker*, November 10 and 17, 1934.

Pauline Kael, "Raising Kane," *The Citizen Kane Book*, Boston: Atlantic–Little, Brown, 1971.

Thomas Kiernan, *Jane Fonda: Heroine for Our Time*, New York: Delilah Books, 1982.

Bela Kornitzer, *American Fathers and Sons*, New York: Hermitage House, 1952.

Charles Krauthammer, "Stretch Marx," *The New Republic*, August 16 and 23, 1982.

Rochelle Larkin, *Hail Columbia*, New York: Arlington House, 1975.

Jesse L. Lasky with Don Weldon, *I Blow My Own Horn*, Garden City, New York: Doubleday, 1957.

Jesse L. Lasky, Jr., *Whatever Happened to Hollywood?*, New York: Funk & Wagnalls, 1975.

William R. Lasky with James F. Scheer, *Tell It on the Mountain*, Garden City, New York: Doubleday, 1976.

Aaron Latham, "Hollywood vs. Harrisburg," *Esquire*, May 22, 1979.

Helen Lawrenson, "The Beautiful People," *Esquire*, April 1957.

Beverly Linet, *Ladd: The Life, The Legend, The Legacy of Alan Ladd*, New York: Arbor House, 1979.

Frances Marion, *Off With Their Heads*, New York: Macmillan, 1972.

Samuel Marx, *Mayer and Thalberg*, New York: Random House, 1975.

Joseph McBride, *Kirk Douglas*, New York: Pyramid Books, 1976.

David McClintick, *Indecent Exposure: A True Story of Hollywood and Wall Street*, New York: William Morrow and Company, 1982.

Richard Meryman, *Mank: The Wit, World, and Life of Herman Mankiewicz*, New York: William Morrow and Company, 1978.

Diane Disney Miller, *The Story of Walt Disney*, New York: Holt, 1957.

Vincente Minnelli with Hector Arce, *I Remember It Well*, Garden City, New York: Doubleday, 1974.

Russell Nye, *The Unembarrassed Muse: The Popular Arts in America*, New York: The Dial Press, 1970.

Laurence Olivier, *Confessions of an Actor*, New York: Simon and Schuster, 1982.

"One Man Studio," *Time*, June 12, 1950.

Maureen Orth, "Hollywood's New Power Elite: The Baby Moguls," *New West*, June 19, 1978.

"*Playboy Interview: Peter Fonda*," Chicago: Playboy Press, 1971.

Dale Pollock, *Skywalking: The Life and Films of George Lucas*, New York: Harmony Books, 1983.

Mario Puzo, *The Godfather Papers and Other Confessions*, New York: G. P. Putnam's Sons, 1972.

Michael Pye and Lynda Myles, *The Movie Brats*, New York: Holt, Rinehart and Winston, 1979.

Edward G. Robinson, Jr. with William Duffy, *My Father—My Son*, New York: Frederick Fell, Inc., 1958.

Lillian Ross, "Some Figures on a Fantasy," *The New Yorker*, November 8, 1982.

Dore Schary, *Heyday: An Autobiography*, Boston: Little, Brown, 1979.

Richard Schickel, *The Disney Version*, New York: Simon and Schuster, 1968.

Richard Schickel, *His Picture in the Papers*, New York: Charterhouse, 1973.

Budd Schulberg, *Moving Pictures: Memories of a Hollywood Prince*, New York: Stein and Day, 1981.

Budd Schulberg, *What Makes Sammy Run?*, New York: Random House, 1941.

Donald M. Scott and Bernard Wishy, Editors, *America's Families, A Documentary History*, New York: Harper & Row, 1982.

Irene Mayer Selznick, *A Private View*, New York: Alfred A. Knopf, 1983.

Melville Shavelson, *How to Make a Jewish Movie*, Englewood Cliffs, New Jersey: Prentice-Hall, 1971.

James Spada, *Judy and Liza*, Garden City, New York: Doubleday, 1983.

John Springer, *The Fondas*, New York: Citadel Press, 1970.

Karen Stabiner, "Playing Hardball With a Hot Agent," *American Film*, July-August 1981.

Howard Teichmann, *Fonda: My Life*, New York: The New American Library, 1981.

Bob Thomas, *King Cohn: The Life and Times of Harry Cohn*, New York: G. P. Putnam's Sons, 1967.

Bob Thomas, *Selznick*, Garden City, New York: Doubleday, 1970.

Bob Thomas, *Walt Disney*, New York: Simon & Schuster, 1976.

Tony Thomas, *The Films of Henry Fonda*, Secaucus, New Jersey: Citadel Press, 1983.

Tony Thomas, *The Films of Kirk Douglas*, Secaucus, New Jersey: Citadel Press, 1972.

Jean Vallely, "In the Office of Alan Ladd, Jr.," *Esquire*, April 11, 1978.

Jack L. Warner with Dean Jennings, *My First Hundred Years in Hollywood*, New York: Random House, 1964.

Tennessee Williams, *Memoirs*, Garden City, New York: Doubleday, 1975.

Keenan Wynn as told to James Brough, *Ed Wynn's Son*, Garden City, New York: Doubleday, 1959.

Norman Zierold, *The Moguls*, New York: Coward-McCann, 1969.

Jill Schary Zimmer, *With a Cast of Thousands*, New York: Stein and Day, 1963.

ABOUT THE AUTHORS

Neither Stephen Farber nor Marc Green has any relatives in Hollywood. They were born in Cleveland, Ohio and were classmates at Amherst College. After graduating from Amherst, they both received Woodrow Wilson Fellowships to do postgraduate work in English; Farber at U.C. Berkeley and Green at Harvard. Stephen Farber has published articles on film in *The New York Times*, *The Los Angeles Times*, *Saturday Review*, *Film Quarterly*, *The Hudson Review*, *Partisan Review*, *American Film*, and many other publications. He is the author of *The Movie Rating Game* and was film critic for *New West* magazine from 1976 to 1980. Marc Green has taught at Harvard and George Washington University. He was the film reviewer for *Books & Arts*, and he has written for *New West*, *Performance*, *Washingtonian*, *The Chronicle of Higher Education*, and other periodicals. Farber and Green have also collaborated on articles, screenplays, and a play which will be presented in Los Angeles this year.